QUATREMÈRE DE

AND THE INVENTI

MODERN LANGUAGE OF

CW01084945

QUATREMÈRE DE QUINCY
AND THE INVENTION OF A
MODERN LANGUAGE OF ARCHITECTURE

SYLVIA LAVIN

THE MIT PRESS   CAMBRIDGE, MASSACHUSETTS   LONDON, ENGLAND

This book was set in Bodoni by DEKR Corporation and was printed and bound in the United States of America.

Library of Congress Cataloging-in-Publication Data

Lavin, Sylvia.
  Quatremère de Quincy and the invention of a modern language of architecture / Sylvia Lavin.
       p.   cm.
  Revision of the author's dissertation (Columbia University, 1990).
  Includes bibliographical references and index.
  ISBN 978-0-262-12166-8 (hc. : alk. paper)
  ISBN 978-0-262-51986-1 (pb.)
    1. Quatremère de Quincy, M. (Antoine-Chrysostome), 1755–1849—
  Philosophy.   2. Architecture—Language.   3. Aesthetic, French—18th
  century.   I. Title.
  NA2500.L38   1992
  720'.1—dc20   92-7001
                                                            CIP

The MIT Press is pleased to keep this title available in print by manufacturing single copies, on demand, via digital printing technology.

To Max

CONTENTS

ACKNOWLEDGMENTS

This book is largely a revised version of the dissertation I completed at Columbia University in 1990 under the supervision of Robin Middleton. My gratitude to him is matched only by the extent of his generous, comprehensive, and unwavering guidance. Richard Pommer led me to perceive new dimensions of my own work that played a central role in my revisions and was singularly helpful and supportive throughout the publication process. The manuscript has been read in various forms by Kenneth Frampton, Barry Bergdoll, David Van Zanten, and Dora Wiebenson, and I am grateful to them for their comments and suggestions. The text benefited significantly from the extraordinarily thoughtful and thought-provoking criticism of an anonymous reader. My father's help reached so beyond the boundaries of paternal responsibility that I am able to offer my thanks as an aspiring colleague rather than only as an eternally grateful daughter. I am in my mother's debt for the professional model her commitment to her own work has offered me and other women of my generation, and I owe my sister a great deal for urging me to try to keep up with her. I would also like to thank Christian Hubert for the helpful criticism and much-needed encouragement he offered during the final stages of my preparations.

PREFACE

One of the fundamental concepts of modern architectural theory is the idea that architecture is a form of language. Although often taken for a philosophical truth that needed only postmodernism to be discovered, the marriage between language and architecture belongs to a process of creative intellection that began in the eighteenth century. This book explores the intellectual history of the idea and the role it played in the work of Quatremère de Quincy, perhaps the leading theorist of French neoclassical art and architecture. Quatremère used language to provide architecture with a conventional rather than natural model, a conceptual transformation that led him to equate architecture's capacity for progressive development with its sociality. Although he is often cast in the role of conservative academic, Quatremère's underlying emphasis on the social contract of architecture, I will argue, rather than the neoclassical style he explicitly promulgated, is the key to the persistent interest in his writings. He was not the first to consider the relationship between language and architecture, nor was this issue the primary focus of his vast literary production.[1] He did develop the idea with extraordinary concentration and critical energy, however, and used his findings to structure a theory of architecture able to accommodate a wide range of formal expressions and generate dissimilar discourses. His treatment of the subject thus offers a unique opportunity to understand why the idea developed and how it subsequently took root with such astonishing tenacity.

The first three chapters of the book correspond to the three principal features that, in Quatremère's view, linked language and architecture: their origins, their evolution, and their use. Although these components describe a historical progression, their conceptual sequence is more important to an understanding of his work, and hence elucidating the structure and logic of this unfolding of ideas has been my primary objective. At the same time, each component has distinct intellectual ramifications, which I have explored by using each chapter to engage somewhat different disciplines and kinds of material. The first chapter is concerned with what has come to be called origin theory. This hypothetical line of inquiry was the context in which language and architecture were first brought together, in Quatremère's work specifically and more generally in eighteenth-century discourse. In order to redefine the nature of man, writers of that period attempted to identify and describe the most elemental aspects of civilization. On this intentionally comprehensive and universalist ground, language and architecture stood out together as particularly and equally fundamental to society. Because they were distinguishing characteristics of civilization, the study of their origins was critical to establishing the genesis of humankind. Most importantly, the search for origins framed a view of nature in relation to which language and architecture seemed artificial.

Although the agenda was theoretical rather than historical, the exploration of origins led to profound changes in the understanding of history and of evolutionary process. These changes are explored in the second chapter. Ethnographic and etymological studies construed language and architecture not only as articulate reflections of social development but as social developments themselves, active agents in the historical creation of civilization. Indeed, by the end of the century society was no longer seen as naturally or supernaturally determined but as an artificial structure that could be reshaped and transfigured. One of the major consequences of this newly abstract conception of history and its relationship to social development was the relativization of language, both verbal and visual. The possibility that evolution could produce multiple types of historically and socially contingent languages demanded new criteria for the evaluation of both the process and the results.

The third chapter is concerned with how architecture, once understood as language, was to be used. Architecture was not now a necessity preternaturally configured by God nor the embodiment of an ideal aesthetic perfection achieved by the ancients, but an artifice created by social convention. Hence the function of architecture, understood with respect to its enunciatory capacity rather than its practical duties, consisted in instantiating a host of social choices. Imitation was identified as the principle that directed these choices and established connections between architecture, language, and society. Quatremère himself conceived the resultant forms in terms of the classical tradition, yet that tradition was a by-product rather than the starting point of his thinking because his view of imitation concerned process, not form. This view made mimesis a potentially progressive instrument because, according to Quatremère, by conflating the abstraction of architecture with that of language, imitation could lead to abstract and progressive social thought.

To regard it as language means, above all, to see architecture as woven into the fabric of society, and a fourth chapter deals more fully with Quatremère's understanding of the relations between the two. The principal vehicle for this investigation is another locution Quatremère played an important role in inventing, the "Republic of the Arts." This phrase insinuates the arts into the tradition of the Republic of Letters and thereby involves a fundamental redefinition, indeed a reversal of the traditional relationship between art and the public sphere. Coterminous to Quatremère's notion of a socially embedded architecture was the notion of a social body whose political structure might be defined, in his view articulated, by architecture. The Republic of the Arts and the language of architecture were thus interrelated because a Republic of the Arts involved an architecture generated not by iconic value but by the social structure of language.[2]

Quatremère's contribution to the formulation of "the language of architecture" took place largely in the context of his analysis of Egyptian architecture. While other of his writings will be used when necessary for a full exposition of his ideas, his texts on Egypt, particularly his *De l'architecture égyptienne* of 1803, will be my primary sources. In Egyptian buildings the hieroglyph forcibly brought architecture and language together, and from the observation of their physical union came Quatremère's views about their substantive equivalence. That Egypt should have been the locus for this conceptualization was far from coincidental. The study of Egyptian culture and civilization brought together many important strains of eighteenth-century thought. Its great antiquity, the role it had come to play in certain aspects of theology, and its exotic and mysterious associations made Egypt one of the sacred cows the secularizing and rationalizing Enlightenment sought to topple. Several emerging disciplines that contributed to the formulation of the idea that architecture is language—linguistics, architectural theory, and ethnography—had common ground in the subject of Egypt. Historically as well as methodologically, therefore, Egypt provides a coherent as well as relatively comprehensive means of examining this idea.

Quatremère's work on Egypt was relevant to his invention of "the language of architecture" for other, less integral but equally important reasons. Quatremère's first text devoted to architectural theory in any form—a competition essay submitted in 1785 to the Académie des Inscriptions et Belles-Lettres (not the first volume of his *Encyclopédie méthodique*, as is often assumed)—concerned Egypt. This unpublished and previously unknown competition essay was radically emended and published almost 20 years later as *De l'architecture égyptienne*. The differences between these texts have never been noted, much less analyzed, yet they permit the evolution in Quatremère's understanding of architecture to emerge more clearly than do his other writings, most of which are clouded by murky publication histories. Even more significant is the fact that the two versions of the essay are separated by two events of great importance to the subject: the French Revolution and the Napoleonic expedition to Egypt. As to the first, Quatremère seems to have been both an active participant in and later a casualty of the Revolution, but he remained firm in his republican convictions.[3] Moreover, he considered the Revolution to have been the cause of a complete conceptual reformulation of social practices. I have not attempted to explain the emendations to his essay on Egypt in terms specific to contemporary Revolutionary events, but I have explored how the realization that society could suddenly be transformed affected the implications he drew from the social bond between language and architecture.

The Napoleonic expedition to Egypt and the early stages of the preparation of the resulting *Description de l'Egypte* raise historiographical questions that shed light on Quatremère's perception of his own activities. An important reason for his persistent interest in Egypt was his dissatisfaction with most available literature on the subject, which he considered to be insufficiently objective and retardataire. The first version of his essay was designed to serve as a corrective. In contrast, the second version was itself retardataire in relation to what Quatremère and his contemporaries considered (and modern scholars still consider) Napoleon's monumental contribution to the development of scientific archaeological and historical practices. Quatremère's self-conscious preoccupation with these methodological and historiographical shifts, which are most overtly expressed in the context of his study of Egyptian architecture, is interesting in itself. But it also reveals a good deal about how and why intellectual boundaries came to be established separating historical analysis from theoretical speculation, a division that has dogged Quatremère's reputation and that continues to haunt contemporary criticism.

The final reason for focusing on Quatremère's Egyptological texts is that these do not turn exclusively on classicism. Quatremère was an advocate of classicism throughout his life, yet the commonly held view of him as an uncritical ideologue in this respect has not only proved detrimental to his reputation, but has obscured an understanding of why he has an important reputation at all. His embrace of a classical ideal might be regarded as radical—even revolutionary—in the context of the late eighteenth century, if he were less frequently considered a mere follower and summarizer of a preexisting taste, and hence denied both originality and influence even during the early part of his career. The most devastating mark on Quatremère's historical good name, however, is that he remained true to his classical ideal—in the context of the nineteenth century he appears to have done nothing more than grind an academic, antiromantic axe. These generaliza-

tions disregard several essential aspects of his work and its implications. Quatremère was far from a mindless follower of the
prevailing aesthetic currents and the authority of the ancients. On
the contrary, he devoted his most penetrating energies to the analysis and substantiation of the need to coopt the classical tradition
for contemporary use. His classical bias was the result of an
informed and independently considered approach to antiquity. If
this had not been the case, there would have been little reason for
Jacques-Louis David to have credited to Quatremère's influence the
utter transformation in his attitude toward the classical past as
early as the 1770s.[4]

Quatremère's unwavering support not just of classicism
but of ideal classicism has also led to a commonly held view of
him as a static thinker, obstructing an appreciation of the degree
to which his conception of architecture developed. Differences
between his encyclopedia and dictionary of architecture have frequently been noted, for example, but never explored systematically. Quatremère's association with the Academy has certainly
been an important factor, since academicism has become almost
synonymous with intellectual stasis. The Academy was not a monolithic institution—the very essay on Egypt that is the basis for this
study was engendered by the Academy. Most deleterious, however,
is a prevailing misconception of classicism itself, which despite
dynamic differences among its various manifestations is still considered an immobile ideal rather than a historically contingent
idea. To the contrary, one of the things that distinguishes what is
called neoclassicism, even in its idealized form, is precisely the
fact that it began to question the exclusivity of previous classi-
cisms. Neoclassicism fundamentally challenged classicism, narrowly defined as a lexicon of the orders and their accoutrements,
and radically weakened the idea that classicism was unique in its
coherence as an architectural tradition. It was just such infractions
against orthodoxy that made neoclassicism a step toward pure
historicism in general and ultimately toward the abolishment of
historical forms altogether. Quatremère's desire to maintain the
hegemony of classicism did not exclude an interest in Egypt.

Indeed, he embraced the differences between these two traditions, and the contrast played a central role in his understanding of the relationship between language and architecture.

Shifting attention away from Quatremère's interest in classicism is also central to my attempt to shift attention away from his efforts to control building practice in France and focus instead on the nature of his ideas. Control of building practice may have been Quatremère's major concern, but searching for buildings that directly illustrate his theory is an ineffective way to understand his contribution. There is no building that stands in relation to Quatremère's ideas as directly as Soufflot's Ste.-Geneviève is said to stand in relation to Laugier's ideas.[5] My purpose is to explore the possibility that the importance of his theoretical contribution lies not in having provided a specific model for the production of buildings but in having developed a framework for conceptualizing architecture. Because Quatremère's framework does not in itself prescribe architectural form, the degree to which it continues to inflect the discourses of contemporary practice has gone unrecognized. For his part, Quatremère himself realized that his fundamentally speculative way of thinking about architecture may have reduced the capacity of his ideas to exalt one form of practice over another. But he was not convinced that his theoretical constructs were thereby invalidated. He once mused, "I think that beautiful works of art have more often given birth to theories than theories have given birth to beautiful works of art. However, theories do exist that are themselves, in their way, beautiful works of art that have given many great pleasure. Hence, one should no more ask the purpose of a poetic than one should ask the purpose of a piece of poetry."[6]

Quatremère de Quincy
and the Invention of a
Modern Language of Architecture

INTRODUCTION

Quatremère de Quincy and the
Genesis of the Prix Caylus

Antoine Chrysostôme Quatremère de Quincy was born in 1755 to a family of Parisian merchants. As a young man he honored his father's wishes by studying law but soon developed an increasingly exclusive interest in the arts, particularly those of classical antiquity.[1] Hoping to become a sculptor, he entered Guillaume Coustou's atelier in 1772. His artistic efforts received little encouragement from his family, not much more from his *maître*, and none at all from the Académie Royale de Peinture et Sculpture. As a result, only following the death in 1776 of his mother, from whom he acquired a small inheritance, was he able to go to Rome where the objects of his artistic passion could be seen at first hand. With the exception of a brief trip back to Paris in 1780, he remained in Italy until 1784. During these formative years, which have been little studied, Quatremère traveled to Sicily, Paestum, and Naples, made the acquaintance of Giambattista Piranesi and Italian collectors, and established a fast friendship with Antonio Canova.

By the time he returned to France permanently he had given up the dream of becoming an artist. Instead, he began to champion the rights of artists in the political arena and finally to champion the cause of constitutional monarchy in general. His support of the Revolution during its early years brought him several important posts, including a position on the Comité d'Instruction Publique. He was a representative for the Commune of Paris and deputy to the Department of Paris and thus had access to an inner circle of important new political leaders. However, as Revolutionary fervor began to build and as political goals became increasingly radical, Quatremère's hope of reforming the existing monarchy and his association with the Constitutionalists came to be branded counterrevolutionary. Denunciations against him began by September 1793. He went into hiding: only Danton knew of and guarded Quatremère's whereabouts.[2] This refuge proved momentary and he was arrested and incarcerated in the spring of 1794. Ultimately, thanks to Talleyrand who warned him ahead of time and provided him with money and a passport, he escaped to Germany following the coup d'état of 18 Fructidor (September 4, 1797).[3]

Although recalled by the amnesty of 18 Brumaire (November 9, 1799), Quatremère remained relatively out of the public eye until the Restoration in 1814. Thereafter, except during the 100 days, he acquired a growing number of offices and honors. He was a royal censor, a member of the Legion of Honor, Intendant of public arts and monuments, member of the Conseil Honoraire des Musées près de la Maison du Roi, art editor of the *Journal des savants*, Professor of Archaeology at the Bibliothèque du Roi, and again a deputy to the Department of Paris. The range and number of official positions and honors bestowed on him were equaled only by those of his publications on the arts. He wrote about opera and theater, painting and sculpture, numismatics, architecture, contemporary art, and antiquities. He made the first collected edition of Poussin's letters and published monographs on Raphael and Canova as well as a dictionary of architects.[4] He wrote important archaeological texts, notably a reconstruction of the Temple of Jupiter at Olympia that made a significant contribution to the development of polychrome architecture, as well as a host of shorter archaeological essays.[5] He explored biography as well as criticism. Above all, he wrote unceasingly about art and architectural theory until he began to suffer from ill health, failing memory, and perhaps dementia. He died on December 28, 1849.

Quatremère's architectural theory in particular has experienced something of a renaissance in recent years. Despite the extraordinary range of his interests, there is reason to believe that even during his own lifetime he was particularly associated with architecture. The earliest known portrait of Quatremère, disputably attributed to Jacques-Louis David, depicts him with the plans of a classical temple (fig. 1).[6] His first publications, those consid-

1. Jacques-Louis David, attributed, portrait of Quatremère, 1779, private collection

ered to be the basis on which he rose in professional stature, were about architecture. Two of his biographers suggest he took particular pains to pursue his architectural education.[7] The *Etrennes à la vérité ou Almanach des aristocrates* of 1790 describes him as an architect, and in 1791 he was charged with supervising the transformation of Soufflot's Ste.-Geneviève into the Pantheon.[8] Although he never constructed a single building, shortly after his death he was still called an architect. In Napoleon's tomb at the Invalides, for example, he is named along with Visconti and Silvestre de Sacy as an architect at the Imperial university.[9] Finally, the most accessible and thus perhaps influential of his many publications were his encyclopedia and dictionary of architecture.[10]

Quatremère had many interests and a multifaceted career, but he was above all an academician. He received his first professional appointment of any duration in 1804 when he was made a member of the Académie des Inscriptions et Belles-Lettres. He exercised a great deal of control over the Académie de France in Rome, but his most important position, from which much of his power derived and from which he exerted tremendous influence on the arts, was as permanent secretary of the Académie des Beaux-Arts. Elected to this post in 1816, he did not resign until 1839 and even then was retained as an honorary secretary. Although Quatremère failed to receive any encouragement from the Académie Royale de Peinture et Sculpture as a young art student, the Academy would come to be the source of his authority. This paradox was later inverted, for the successes Quatremère accrued within the Academy became rather a liability and he came to seem the "personification of academicism."[11] Even for those most recently engaged in eighteenth- and nineteenth-century architectural studies, Quatremère's academic affiliations remain an embarrassment owing to that institution's image as a bastion of philistinism.[12] His legacy has been distorted by wide fluctuations in attitude toward the Academy, exacerbated by his extraordinary longevity (late in life because of failing memory and mental capacity Quatremère himself remarked, "I have the right to be dead. Act as though I were").[13] Depending on which period of his professional life is emphasized, Quatremère still appears as he did to his contemporaries: a wild-eyed reformer in the early 1790s, a reactionary member of the old guard in the 1830s (figs. 2 and 3). While most recent literature tends to emphasize his youthful and most obviously nonacademic work, a potentially more cohesive picture of this early period and its relationship to his later life emerges if the Academy is recognized as both central to and typical of the conditions of his development.

Quatremère's unusually long academic career began in 1785. At the age of 30, marking the end of his student years, he entered and won an essay competition for the Prix Caylus sponsored by the Académie Royale des Inscriptions et Belles-Lettres. This initial success has been cited as the event that paved the way for his later achievements, such as the commission to write the dictionary of architecture for Panckoucke's *Encyclopédie méthodique*.[14] Despite its undoubted importance for his career, the competition's intellectual significance has been underestimated and the text itself described as "truly a humble effort, unfocused and woefully incomplete."[15] These assessments reveal very little about the essay, reflecting the assumption that it was soon outdated by the Napoleonic expedition to Egypt, which began in 1798, and the publication of the resulting *Description de l'Egypte*.[16] The *Description de l'Egypte* did place the archaeology of ancient Egypt on an entirely new level, yet the perfunctory dismissal of Quatremère's early essay on the grounds that it contains nothing of empirical value has led to a neglect of the essay's fundamental contributions in other respects. Moreover, the few comments that have been made about Quatremère's Egyptology are based not on his competition entry but on the very different version of the essay he published in 1803 as *De l'architecture égyptienne considérée dans son origine, ses principes et son gôut, et comparée sous les mêmes rapports à l'architecture grecque*, from which he deliberately excluded the recent findings.

Quatremère's participation in the Prix Caylus must be seen in a pre-Napoleonic intellectual context. Complex circumstances surrounded the 1785 competition and reveal that the Academy itself was in a period of flux and reevaluation characteristic of the last days of the *ancien régime*. Part of this instability was due to the fact that the Academy was becoming an increasingly loose conglomerate of scholars from an ever wider variety of quickly changing fields. Although the period is thought of as fundamentally interdisciplinary, a more appropriate term might be intradisciplinary. Not yet discretely classified areas of study more often overlapped within the Academy than confronted one another. Moreover, these emerging spheres of knowledge often sought to discover relationships between distinct cultural traditions, which introduced an unprecedented relativism to academic scholarship. This association of interwoven and vaguely defined disciplines was to be the institution's most substantive contribution to Quatremère. His first important theoretical treatise was written in response to a question posed by the Academy and already interlaces a broad range of issues and ideas that were to characterize the core of his intellectual achievement.

During the eighteenth century, administering competitions was one of the primary functions of the Académie Royale des Inscriptions et Belles-Lettres. Because they were one of the few academic activities open to the public, the competitions had traditionally played an important role in attracting new members and disseminating information.[17] Moreover, the competitions were often commemorative, calling attention to and honoring a particular member of the Academy and thereby preserving the elevated status of academicians in general. The Prix Caylus was established by the Comte de Caylus in 1754 as a yearly prize in support of the study of antiquities.[18] The reward was a gold medal worth five hundred livres. Caylus was strongly committed to the competitions, as is suggested by the fact that he also established prizes for the Académie de Peinture et de Sculpture, one for expression in 1759 and one for perspective in 1763.[19]

By the time Quatremère submitted an essay for the Prix Caylus, however, the Academy had begun to debate the value of its competition system. At the very moment deliberations regarding the *concours* of 1785 were taking place, an offer of funds to establish a new prize prompted a revealing resumé of the current status of the *concours*. The minutes of meetings held by the Académie des Inscriptions et Belles-Lettres reflect concern that an additional

QUATREMÈRE

Deputé du Dep.ᵗ de la Seine au Conseil des Cinq-cents.

A Paris rue Sᵗ Jacques, Nᵒ 195.

2. François Bonneville, portrait of Quatremère as deputy to the Département de la Seine, 1797, Bibliothèque Nationale, Paris

3. J. Boilly, portrait of Quatremère after his election to the position of permanent secretary to the Académie des Beaux-Arts, 1820, Bibliothèque Nationale, Paris

prize might only exacerbate an already difficult situation. The numbers of submissions to the *concours* were dwindling dramatically: at times there were no entries at all. Worse, perhaps, in the eyes of the academicians, was the fact that frequently the essays were of unacceptable quality. If no one deserved the prize, the Academy was forced to make a new call for papers, a process that might be repeated up to three times. When even multiple efforts failed, a mediocre entry might be given a prize in order to avoid the embarrassment caused by having to cancel the competition.[20] The distress expressed by the Academy over this state of affairs suggests that whatever advantages might accompany the winning of a competition, such as financial remuneration, permission to publish the essay with academic privilege, or, ideally, entry into the Academy, public interest in and respect for the laureate were no longer guaranteed.

The Prix Caylus of 1785, and thus the reception of Quatremère's essay in particular, exemplifies the general dilemma then confronting the Academy. Access to these prizes was open to the public and virtually unrestricted. Participants, who could be of any profession other than members of the French Academy and of any nationality, were subject to only two conditions: the essays had to be written in either French or Latin and had to be received by the *secrétaire perpétuel* by a given date, in the case of the 1785 Prix Caylus by the feast of St. Martin, July 1.[21] Despite this almost total lack of formal or bureaucratic obstruction, on July 5 Joseph-Bon Dacier, the *secrétaire perpétuel*, was sufficiently concerned to announce at an assembly that he had received only two entries. One was by Quatremère and the other by Giuseppe Del Rosso, a Florentine architect and restorer whose most important work is the Oratory of Sant'Onofrio built at Dicomano, outside Florence, in 1792.[22]

Technically, Del Rosso's essay was ineligible, having complied with neither of the two regulations. His *mémoire* was received in two sections, the first on July 4, 1785, three days late, and the second on September 6, two months late, and although the essay begins in French, over half is in Italian. Despite Del Rosso's apologetic lament that the topic required more time than

had been allowed, the jury must have been dismayed by the ama-
teurish presentation of his essay, quickly scribbled and full of
corrections, in contrast to Quatremère's illustrated and elegantly
penned *mémoire*.[23] Effectively Quatremère had no competition
whatever; rather than a masterful and decisive victory, one might
conclude that he won by default.[24] However, although it did so
reluctantly, the Academy was willing to postpone adjudication
when essays were of poor quality or even reject all entries outright,
as it had done in 1783 and in 1784.[25] Quatremère not only won,
but won on the first round and without any discernible hesitation
on the part of the jury. Furthermore, the importance attached to
this essay by the early biographers is surely not merely fabricated
with the knowledge of hindsight. The significance accorded the
mémoire might more profitably be attributed to an evaluation of
its perceived meaning rather than to the professional reputation
it may or may not have advanced. Hence it is necessary to examine
in some detail the substance of the competition, both the question
posed and the responses elicited.

In this instance, the Academy went to great lengths in
preparing the subject for what was simply one of various yearly
competitions. Three separate sessions were required to determine
the subject's final formulation. On the first day of deliberations,
March 23, 1784, the Academy was unable to reach any conclusion.
On the twenty-sixth of that month it was determined that the
subject would relate in some unspecified way to Egyptian architecture. Four days later the Academy further refined the topic,
specifying a study of the nature of Egyptian architecture in general
and its relation to Greek architecture in particular. The final
formulation was: "What was the state of Egyptian architecture and
what do the Greeks seem to have borrowed from it."[26] The topic
was announced to the public on April 20.[27]

The Academy's concern for the architecture of ancient
Egypt is symptomatic of an often neglected eighteenth-century
interest in nonclassical phenomena.[28] Despite a persistent preference for classical antiquity, Egypt had in fact become an important
component of much art historical inquiry. The Comte de Caylus
himself and Julien-David Le Roy, two of the Academy's most

celebrated members, had both written extensively on the history of Egyptian architecture.[29] Egypt also had a strong presence in the architecture of this period, most clearly seen in the work of architects such as Piranesi, Claude-Nicolas Ledoux, and Etienne-Louis Boullée.[30] This art historical and aesthetic interest in Egypt was itself a manifestation of the much larger role Egypt played in the intellectual developments of the Enlightenment. Egypt had fascinated Western civilizations since antiquity and had traditionally been of central importance in the construction of world histories. Classical authors, for example, presented conflicting accounts of the relationship between Greece and Egypt and argued about the historical priority of each civilization. During the Middle Ages the interest in Egypt came to be characterized by a concern for the theological implications of the historical position of Egyptian culture. Prefigurations of the Christian age were sought in Egypt in efforts to prove the universality of God's plan. The belief that Egypt held the mysterious key to the pre-Christian world culminated in the seventeenth century.[31]

The scrutiny of eighteenth-century empiricism did not diminish the traditional importance accorded to Egypt with respect to human history. Instead, with increasing intensity and from an ever expanding range of viewpoints, the study of Egypt became progressively less mystical and more scientific. This modern research provided unassailable evidence that Egyptian civilization was more ancient than that of the Jews. Hence Egypt was increasingly presented as the cradle of civilization, a view made commonplace by Diderot's *Encyclopédie*. This view, however, contradicted the Bible: if Egypt was indeed the cradle of civilization, then the book of Genesis, the text that traditionally provided explanations for the source of all things in the visible and invisible worlds, was mistaken. Whereas Egypt had previously been used to support the universal and eternal validity of biblical history, by the eighteenth century it began contributing to the downfall of orthodox historiography.

With divine authority thus obscured, the elemental nature of things was sought instead through an analysis of their primeval manifestations. Rationalism gave rise to a quest for empirical knowledge of Egypt, but its historical position of supreme antiquity led to questions beyond the reaches of history and outside the world of tangible phenomena. Because Egypt was thought to be the oldest civilization and therefore most proximate to primitive society, to ask a question about Egypt was ultimately to ask a question about the origins and nature of man. While various theories of origins were tested using evidence from the deepest recesses of man's past, they were only apparently historical in nature. Rather, their goal was to illuminate man's present condition by discerning the degree to which it was dependent on divine intervention. Studies of the book of Genesis were replaced by searches for the genesis of earth, of man, and of civilization, and Egypt became the territory on which this battle between a sacred and a profane view of humanity was fought.

The Academy's move toward empirical enlightenment is reflected by developments in its institutional structure. A reorganization began in 1701 and took more definitive shape in 1716 when the title was changed from Académie des Inscriptions et Médailles to Académie Royale des Inscriptions et Belles-Lettres, a name it was to keep until 1793. The new appellation reveals the Academy's effort to extend its focus beyond the documentation of royal numismatic history and the consideration of inscriptions for public monuments.[32] The Academy thus began to acquire the characteristics of a scholarly research institute concerned with the study of the history and literature of all countries through the ages. The growing number of Egyptological essay competition questions, and that of 1785 in particular, reveal how its new structure enabled the Academy to transform Egypt from a topic of exotic curiosity into a civilization vitally important in human history, subject to modern standards of scientific research.[33]

The Academy's topic for the Prix Caylus of 1785 reflects this new attitude toward Egypt in a variety of ways. Egyptian architecture is the prime focus; Greek architecture is a secondary concern—a disproportionate emphasis suggested not only by the question's phrasing but also by the fact that the inclusion of Greek architecture was indeed an afterthought. The supposition that an actual, measurable relationship existed between these two cultures, while not in itself a devaluation of the classical ideal, transformed this ideal by denying its autonomy and presenting it as a facet of a larger historical framework. By 1785 the magnetism of Egypt was such that it toppled even the independence of classical antiquity. In asking only about what the Greeks had borrowed from the Egyptians, the Academy's question moreover assumed a particular historical relationship between the two cultures. Egypt is implicitly presented as the cradle of architectural civilization; the classical world, however important as the source from which other cultures derived, itself appears derivative. The Academy's question was thus comparative and historicist in structure, a combination of elements that questioned both the biblical and classical sources upon which traditional views of architecture's past were based.

Despite the increasingly empirical goals of the Academy, in 1785 Egypt still remained essentially beyond the reach of modern archaeology. Architectural remains were the single most important source of information available and were discussed in most architectural publications written in the previous decades, but factual knowledge of Egyptian civilization was hypothetical at best and fantastic most often.[34] The topic of 1785 thus posed a question the answer to which was bound to be largely speculative and apparently at odds with the Academy's new emphasis on verifiable knowledge. This discrepancy, however, suggests that hypothetical and ultimately ideological re-creations of primitive man were disguised as historical reconstructions of ancient man in Egypt in order to make them acceptable to Enlightenment rationalism.

The Academy's attitude toward the history of art changed in a fashion parallel to the new attitude toward Egypt. Traditionally, the Academy had posed questions involving generalized histories of monuments. Most often the questions concerned attributes of particular divinities and cults, rather than matters of a comprehensive cultural nature, and could be addressed solely on the basis of literary records.[35] Increasingly, however, painting and sculpture were used as supporting evidence, and although generally the figurative arts alone were mentioned, in 1766, for

example, temples were explicitly included in a list of such corroborative material.[36] Thus the Academy developed a progressively
more inclusive attitude toward the history of the visual arts during
the eighteenth century. Simultaneously, these art forms came to
be regarded less as tools in the search for new royal iconography
and more as historical documents valid in themselves. The Academy's development of a comprehensive approach to the history of
art is best revealed by Caylus's assessment of the benefits he had
derived from his academic affiliation: "Before having been graced
by the honor of admission to the academy, I was able to see the
remains of antiquity that had escaped the barbarities of time only
from the point of view of art. You have taught me to attach an
infinitely superior merit to these relics—the merit of encompassing
a thousand singularities of the history, the cult, the customs and
mores of those famous people, who by the vicissitude of all things
human have disappeared from the earth they once filled with the
sound of their name."[37] Just as the question of Egypt implied
matters of larger import than the details of ancient history, the
question of art implied matters of larger import than the details
of aesthetics and iconography.

The breadth of the question posed by the Academy is
significant, both with respect to its individual elements and to
their combination. The tendency to demystify Egyptian culture,
the search for empirical data and its paradoxical application to
speculative theories of human origins, the comprehensive
approach to the history of architecture—all these facets of the
Academy's question entailed some of the most pressing philosophical issues of the day. Although the competition attracted only two
formal participants, the topical and inclusive nature of the subject
stirred an interest that can be documented in four cases: Quatremère himself, Del Rosso, Jacopo Belgrado, and J. L. Viel de Saint-
Maux.[38] A possible fifth instance is that of the person who seems
to have proposed the topic, Le Roy; he was not only present at all
sessions when it was discussed but was a member of the two-man
jury. Le Roy had, moreover, already defined the problem in the
second edition of *Les ruines des plus beaux monuments de la
Grèce*, where he wrote of the monuments of Egypt and Greece,

4. Jacques-Louis David, *Pyramid in an Imaginary Landscape*, 1770s, The Metropolitan
Museum of Art, New York

"it seems that neither the marked relations that connect them nor
the striking differences that separate them have been sufficiently
observed."[39] Similarly, certain projects by Le Roy's close friend
Boullée patently seek to explore the relationship between primitive Greek and Egyptian architecture. The interest in this particular aspect of the study of Egypt was not limited to architects, as
can be seen in a drawing by David in which the archetypal and
elemental form of the Egyptian pyramid and the equally archetypal and elemental form of the classical pediment are combined
(fig. 4).[40] Thus, although the actual participants in the competition
were few, the substance of the question itself was neither marginal
nor academic but was vital to the concerns of a wide range of
people. Prompted by the Academy's formulation of issues that
were already current, Quatremère began the exploration and crys-
tallization of what became a central thesis in his architectural
theory.

I

ORIGINS

Quatremère's Mémoire *on Egyptian Architecture*

T he Academy posed a question for the Prix Caylus of 1785 that was intended to establish the universal genesis of human-kind. This goal, however, was particularized in two ways. First the problem was restricted to the relationship between Egypt and Greece and second it was required that this relationship be addressed in terms of architecture. These two localizations of a global issue would be conflated by all those responding to the com-petition into the singular question of the relationship between the origins of Greek and Egyptian architecture. Hypothesizing forms taken by primitive architecture was a common yet somewhat nar-row theoretical activity for architects, first attempted by Vitruvius and dominated by the idea of the primitive hut ever since. Qua-tremère's *mémoire* for the Prix Caylus belongs to this tradition, yet even his preliminary discussion indicates that he had begun fundamentally to rethink the traditional views established in the canonical texts on the subject. Quatremère's reformulation of this standard notion became more extreme as he revised his competi-tion essay prior to its publication. The most important innovation was his introduction of the idea that the origins of architecture were related to those of language. This idea began to transform a thesis only implicit and loosely formulated in his *mémoire* into a markedly unconventional theory of architectural origins.

Quatremère submitted his essay in 1785 on his return from Rome where he had been immersed in the study of classical art and architecture, visiting Pompeii and Herculaneum, scouring the collections of the Vatican, the Villa Albani, and private *cabinets d'étude*, and making on-site measured drawings of ancient tem-ples.[1] The fact that he was not in Italy as a winner of the Prix de Rome but as an independent traveler touring at his own expense reveals how the direct observation of ancient monuments had become a sine qua non for anyone seriously interested in the arts at that time.[2] An essential aspect of this new self-proclaimedly rigorous classical revival was the plethora of publications that appeared during the eighteenth century reproducing increasingly accurate images of Greek and Roman art. However, either for lack of interest or lack of funds, specialists in archaeology had not yet begun to explore territories beyond the centers of these classical cultures. There was no equivalent to Stuart and Revett's *The Antiquities of Athens* for Egyptian architecture.[3]

Quatremère bitterly lamented the paucity of available data on the architecture of the Egyptians, complaining that "we know their monuments only imperfectly. No one has traveled to Egypt with means sufficient to establish precise notions of their architecture. Nothing has been measured and travelers have been content to make a few rapid plans, readjusting them according to their own fancy. We are reduced to some superficial drawings made on the sly by men with little instruction in architecture and the arts of design."[4] Quatremère's concern for this deficiency was adamant, yet he made no concerted effort to overcome it. While Del Rosso devoted at least part of his essay to a chronological history of Egyptian architecture, Quatremère organized his *mémoire* thematically, constructing an abstract framework within which a theoretical analysis of the speculative elements central to the Academy's question could be presented. Quatremère's essay contains five sections that begin with the problem of origins, move from construction through form to decoration, and end with the issue of imitation.[5] The first section, "Of Architecture and of Its Origin in Egypt," establishes the general principles on the basis of which architecture is to be approached; the second, third, and fourth sections provide the raw material for this analysis; and the fifth draws theoretical, historical, and prescriptive conclusions. The essay's overall structure moves from the general to the particular, from the speculative to the instrumental, while each section is subdivided in a similarly rational and increasingly specific fashion. Quatremère had no new empirical material: innovation could only come from an analysis of known facts and a reconsideration of traditional ideas. The structure of his essay was designed to underscore this theoretical dimension.

Quatremère began by establishing as prerequisite a principle that might distinguish aspects of the art of building that were inherent and therefore universal from aspects that were historically and geographically specific:

> Before considering the state of architecture in ancient Egypt, it would not be inappropriate to fix, with a few simple principles, the general idea one ought to have of this art in itself and of its origin in Egypt. This will permit one to proceed in this examination with greater order and will enable one to perceive more surely the relationship and points of comparison between Egyptian and Greek architecture. Without these principles one risks being unable to distinguish that which nature teaches men in all times and in all places with respect to the art of building and independent of the exchange of ideas, from points of resemblance that communication alone can have transmitted from one people to another.[6]

According to Quatremère the most essential aspect of architectural evolution was the causal relationship between primitive forms of building and more advanced architectural constructions. He argued that although early, "fetal" structures belonged in the same category as other elemental life support systems and thus did not constitute an art, they contained certain characteristics that determined architecture's development and were never eradicated, even by its most brilliant achievements. All architectures revealed the operations of this mechanism and therefore any subsequent patterns of resemblance between the architectures of different cultures affirmed only the universal validity of the principle and not particular results of its application.

While the notion of the interdependence between primitive and advanced building was drawn from a long-standing tradition, Quatremère placed a novel emphasis on the universality of this connection. The relationship contributed not only to the development of certain architectural cultures, as had often been said of Greek, but constituted the primary directive of all architecture. Quatremère further enriched this tradition by associating it with the nature of primitive societies. The distinction between primitive building and the art of architecture was to be made first on the basis of social structure rather than technical or aesthetic development. The transformation from one to the other was the result of the establishment of nations and states that became possible only after civilizations reached a certain level of sophistication and luxury (*luxe*). As rustic work was abandoned in favor of urban pleasure, the building of shelter was replaced by the erection of monuments.

The precise form assumed by these determinant structures was similarly dictated by the essential nature of primitive societies. Depending on a wide range of primarily environmental conditions, such as climate, the availability of natural materials, and the profile of the local terrain, one of three types of society developed, each identifiable by the way in which it gathered food—hunting or fishing, shepherding, or agriculture. Hunters, according to Quatremère, did not build at all, properly speaking. Owing to their frequent movements, they found it more convenient either to dig or to take advantage of caves formed naturally. While fisherman remained sedentary along the shores of oceans, rivers, and lakes, the laziness (*paresse*) engendered by this lifestyle similarly led them to seek out caves provided by nature. In contrast, societies of shepherds tended to emerge in flatlands where there were no available caves. Their constant search for new pastures obliged them to move frequently and to construct dwellings that were easily transported, a combination of factors that favored the use of tents. Finally, the sedentary life demanded by agriculture suggested shelter that was both fixed and solid, resulting in the erection of wooden huts. According to Quatremère, in the caves, tents, and huts of "these three states of natural life, the origin of every type of construction associated with all people as well as the differences between them" could be found.[7]

Having described the seeds out of which the art of architecture was to flourish, Quatremère discussed to which of these three states Egypt belonged. While he used the Chinese as an example of a shepherd people whose peripatetic lifestyle demanded the use of tents, he argued that the bounties of the Nile

had for centuries provided early Egyptians with sufficient suste-
nance, enabling them to remain sedentary as well as delaying the
need for agriculture. This society of fisherman did, however, need
to escape from oppressive heat, accomplished first by simply
appropriating natural caves for shelter and later by actually digging
new caves. Over time, and encouraged by abundantly available
stone, this primitive and instinctive form of self-preservation was
transformed into an active preference: long after the capacity for
building other types of structures had been developed and even
after palaces were constructed in place of mere shelters, caverns
were still employed. Quatremère cited grottoes that were used for
habitation even in more advanced times to prove that "if this kind
of dwelling was used during the height of Egyptian prosperity,
then there is all the more reason to think that it would have been
used by Egypt's first inhabitants."[8] The primitive experience of
the cave became the essential taste (*goût*) of the sophisticated
Egyptian and molded the architectural form of buildings that had
otherwise relegated the cave to ancient history. Quatremère concluded that "everything in their architecture retraces this first
origin."[9]

In Quatremère's opinion the future of Egyptian architecture was determined by this prehistoric retreat into the underground. He also maintained, however, that at a somewhat later
stage in their development Egyptians had built wooden huts. Egyptian architecture thus had had a double origin in both the cave
and the hut. Such a concurrence was not unique to Egypt; agricultural peoples who originally lived in cabins, such as the Greeks,
had sometimes used the cave for supplementary and limited functions, particularly funereal practices.[10] In Egypt, however, the
impact of this double origin was limited. Although the hut normally produced a richer and more varied architecture than did
the cave because of carpentry's intrinsically more complex and
ordered nature, the Egyptian hut was itself modeled on the earlier
cave and consequently was unable to have much effect. Thus,
while Egyptian buildings reflected a mixed origin in both stone and
wood, the former dominated. As a result, the cave constituted the
seminal basis for all Egyptian building types and technologies.[11]

Following this general introduction, the second section of Quatremère's text consists in a systematic analysis of Egyptian construction and is subdivided into articles on material, stone cutting, mechanical means, the construction of pyramids and temples, roofing, and vaulting. While the section as a whole is more descriptive than the first, its goal is to support Quatremère's original proposition with regard to the cave and its decisive influence on Egyptian architecture. As he had in the previous section, Quatremère began with a general statement, this time asserting the reciprocity between architectural structure and architectural form. The section's individual articles serve to illustrate his hypothesis, and each article in turn follows a similar outline moving from principle to proof. His premise is none other than Vitruvius's "firmness," which he defines as "the principal merit in architecture" and as the equivalent to health in the human body.[12]

Quatremère's admiration for the solidity of Egyptian building was unbounded: "Despite the efforts of time, despite the ravages of centuries past and centuries yet to come, it is possible adamantly to maintain and without fear of hyperbole that these masses, victors over time until now, will continue to watch other cities and nations be annihilated and return to dust. These masses will survive and as the final destruction of the globe arrives they will be the last testaments to the frailty of humanity."[13] He was, however, quick to attribute this unsurpassed talent for permanence not to artistry but to the same environmental conditions that had led to the primitive Egyptian use of caves: "This nation received from nature for the construction of its buildings the best means to render them eternal—in the least destructive environment Egypt was able to use the most indestructible materials."[14] The only trees available, such as the palm and acacia, were not suitable for building, and as a result even during the earliest time construction was primarily in stone.

The constant exposure to and need to build in this material forced the Egyptians to develop their stone-cutting abilities. Quatremère, however, distinguished this "coupe des pierres" from the "art du trait," a modern technique invented to overcome the weakness and other imperfections of local raw materials. There was no need to develop a science aimed at the joining of separate small pieces of stone when single and expansive squared slabs could be used. Rather than explore the geometry and science that according to Quatremère had liberated the French from their imprisonment by poor materials, a subjugation he maintained had produced Gothic architecture, the Egyptians perfected hewing stone in precise though simple shapes. Their talent lay in the scrupulous assemblage, mirrorlike polish, and imperceptible joints of enormous and consistently rectilinear masses.[15]

Quatremère noted that as one receded further and further into history one found man tending to used increasingly large blocks of stone, culminating in the colossi of Egypt. While Quatremère somewhat sarcastically suggested that the uninformed might be led to believe in a race of giants, he himself preferred more logical explanations such as the inherent quality of available materials.[16] Similarly, although the scale of their projects implies an equally extensive mechanical ability not only for the carving of the stone itself but for its transportation and erection, Quatremère asserted that Egyptian mechanical technology remained parallel to Egyptian stereotomy, impressive yet uncomplex.[17] To emphasize that these Egyptian achievements were marked by "an infinity of inventions as ingenious as they were simple," Quatremère compared them to the elaborate devices used by Sixtus V to raise the obelisks in Rome.[18]

Quatremère hoped to deconstruct the myths and "puerile fables" surrounding Egypt, and his attack is at its most strident in his analysis of the construction of pyramids and temples. While pyramids had held the world's attention for centuries, it was principally the ways and means of their erection that had led to their classification as wonders of the world.[19] Quatremère ridiculed the fantastic theories of both ancient and modern writers about how the pyramids had been built and the purposes they served. He categorically rejected all enigmatic and mysterious symbolism associated with the form of the pyramids and, without attempting to mitigate their effect, unequivocally insisted that they were tombs.[20] Moreover, describing a logical, almost simplistic process of construction, he argued that the key to building the pyramids had been nothing more than their geometry, which enabled them to be self-supporting during construction and which dispensed with the need for scaffolding and other apparatus. Moving on to discussions of the structure of temples, their walls and columns, roofing and vaults, Quatremère hoped to demonstrate that Egyptian architecture was not really characterized by wondrous feats of construction but by a spirit of simplicity, grandeur, and solidity.[21] His goal, however, was less to explain Egyptian building techniques precisely than to "diminish the wonder of these monstrous buildings" and to reveal the all-encompassing influence of the primeval cave.[22] The simplicity of this original form led to simple types of permanent structures, and this simplicity was finally mirrored even in the ways the Egyptians had devised for erecting their buildings.

In the essay's third section, "On the Form of Buildings," the notion of simplicity is replaced by the related one of uniformity.[23] Quatremère is here most concerned with temples, the building type in which "the Egyptians displayed all the pomp of their architecture and from the ruins of which one can best formulate ideas about their ability and taste."[24] He begins, once again, with a general observation, now on the intimate relationship between form and function. Because temples are subject to the needs of religion they tend to be of a similar disposition throughout each country. In the case of Egypt, where the population was attached to a single cult, this uniformity was particularly marked. Unlike the Greeks and Romans, who had different kinds of temples as well as words to express this variety, Egyptian temples were always composed of the same essential elements and varied only in terms of scale. Throughout the remainder of the essay, Quatremère elaborates on this theme of uniformity, ultimately relating it, as he had that of simplicity, to the cave.

Egyptian temples, according to Quatremère, were an assemblage of porticoes, courts, vestibules, galleries, and rooms, one linked to the next and the whole enclosed by a wall.[25] This multiplicity of parts, while apparently an exception to the rule of uniformity, was in fact its product. He contends that this internal subdivision was created intentionally to counterbalance the lack of variety offered by the model of the original cave dwelling but that its effect was reduced by the absolute and repetitive regularity with which the separate units were distributed.[26] For Quatremère, the controlling plan was more important than the constituent parts. The same factors that had led primitive Egyptians to take shelter in caves also produced simple, facile plans, scaled according to a quest for enormity rather than proportion, and absolutely uniform.[27]

Elevations, in Quatremère's view, are based on a building's plan, and as a result he found in Egyptian elevations nothing more than identical forms repeated to the point of monotony and no other character than that of solidity pushed to excess.[28] All contributed to a re-creation of the cave. Entablatures, having played a minimal structural role in stone construction, never became a decorative focus as they had in Greece. Egyptians had no need of vaulting and therefore ceilings were left smooth and unarticulated, often made of a single slab of stone. Doors, despite their prodigious number, were only of two types, square or pyramidal, and windows were almost nonexistent.[29]

There was one exception to this echoing of the cave, found in what Quatremère considered to be the primary element of any elevation: the column. According to Quatremère, Egyptians had built two kinds of columns, either round or polygonal. While the former varied only with respect to the presence or absence of hieroglyphics, the latter took many forms. He attributed both the basic shape of the polygonal column and its capacity for diversity to the secondary origin in wooden huts he had allowed Egyptian architecture in his opening section. He maintained that

this column reveals the history of its origin too clearly for it not to be recognized and demonstrates that one must not attribute to Egyptian architecture a unique cause. It is evident that the form of this column derives from early constructions in wood. These were made from trees of such a small size that builders had to assemble several together in order to make up for the absence of large beams. To secure this assemblage and make a single solid entity, it was necessary to tie them together with either cord or circles of iron. These various forms were then transported into the stone columns that architecture substituted for the earlier imperfect supports.[30]

While the round and static columns could be related to caves—Quatremère compared them to supporting pillars in quarries—the richly varied polygonal columns owed their origin as well as their variety to the wooden hut, sharing these characteristics with the hut's finest progeny, the glorious orders of Greek architecture.[31] Quatremère disliked the evident "bizarrerie" of Egyptian capitals, a term he used with biting derision and one he would later reserve for the work of Ledoux.[32] He maintained, however, that the underlying logic and structure of these capitals, like those of the polygonal columns, had escaped the tyranny of the monotonous cave.

Quatremère began the fourth section of his treatise by distinguishing between two types of Egyptian architectural decoration: "The first type arises from diverse objects of embellishment that are foreign to the form of buildings, such as statues and other similar things. . . . The second type adheres to the forms of architecture themselves and is essentially part of them, such as ornament, bas-relief, painting, etc. This very evident distinction defines the natural division of this section."[33] Quatremère is somewhat ambiguous in this passage because he refers to two classes of decoration and defines ornament as a subcategory of one of these, although the text itself maintains a categorical distinction between ornament and decoration. Decoration there consistently refers to forms that are external to structure, such as statues, obelisks, and sphinxes, while ornament always refers to forms that inhere in structure, such as columns, doors, and niches. The earliest and most integral of this latter type of Egyptian ornament consisted, according to Quatremère, in the quality of stone chosen and the great polish it was given. The most prominent decorations, on the other hand, were hieroglyphs, a sacred writing that covered literally every surface of Egyptian buildings. Because their figures were mostly carved in bas-relief and often colored, he held that hieroglyphics were the source of Egyptian style in both sculpture and painting. Most important, however, was the fact that their primary function as "public characters" necessitated the preservation of their original form.

The need for legibility and clarity condemned Egyptian ornament not only to a monotonous and strictly regular distribution but to a lack of historical development. Similarly, decorative objects, as distinguished from ornamental objects, were also subject to the characteristically Egyptian search for solidity and perpetuity. Painting and sculpture were restricted by their hieroglyphic origin in a way parallel to the intransigence of the model of the cave. Statues came, for example, from mummy cases, yet their function was less to commemorate man after death than it was to perpetuate his image amongst the living.[34] Uniformity in plan and construction was recreated, according to Quatremère, both in the style and evolution of decoration, and as a result, Egyptian architectural embellishment was unable to progress beyond a state of essential infancy.

Quatremère saw in certain aspects of architectural ornament origins that had been created by man rather than offered by nature. He criticized those who had "tried too hard to find the origin of ornament in nature. In vain people pretend that plants fortuitously growing around buildings or seeds brought by the wind to the various parts of the huts gave birth to this type of embellishment. It is more reasonable to say on this subject that sacred buildings were decorated with flowers, fruits, and plants on festival days as offerings to the divinity, just as they were with the heads of victims, the instruments of sacrifice, and other similar things. In order to perpetuate these ephemeral ornaments, sculpture rendered all these different objects in stone."[35] Quatremère similarly maintained that capitals were not representations of leafs growing on trees but rather of the plants man himself had applied as adornment, just as he argued that columns were not direct imitations of trees but of logs already treated and transformed by the art of carpentry. Most important is the fact that Quatremère reserved praise only for those elements that were not direct copies of nature but of man-made artifacts: the prime example of such an artifact was the hut itself. Thus his great admiration for the variety and richness of Egyptian capitals approached his unbounded appreciation of Greek architecture as a whole. His preferences were consistent because he perceived them both as resulting from a metamorphosis of similarly unnatural and uncavernous originals.

The final section of Quatremère's essay is devoted to an analysis of this principle of transformation and its role in the determination of the historical relationship between Egyptian and Greek architecture. Despite the ingratitude of a nation characterized by vanity, and the fact that the Greeks "did all they could to deny the enormous debt they hoped not to pay," it was, according to Quatremère, incontestable that there had been direct communication between Greeks and Egyptians from the most distant times.[36] More importantly, as a result of this contact "there had been a great analogy between Greek and Egyptian art for a very long time," and in support of this thesis Quatremère provides an extensive list of Egyptian architectural inventions imitated by the Greeks.[37] For example, the Greeks shared the Egyptian taste for large blocks of stone and solid construction as well as the care they lavished on funerary monuments. Having derived their religion from Egyptian traditions, and despite a new character imposed on this tradition, the Greeks built temples whose plans strongly recall those of their Egyptian predecessors. The squat, primitive Doric column had its origin in Egypt, and Quatremère calls the Corinthian capital a "manifest larceny."[38] The Egyptian caryatid reappeared in Greece as did the labyrinth, and the sphinx, having entered Greek mythology, was represented in a wide range of Hellenic monuments.

Quatremère presented an impressive mass of material supporting the notion that Greek architecture was indebted to and had actively imitated Egyptian traditions. However, because of the essential difference between the cave and the hut, he maintained that radical distinctions could be found even in such points of great apparent resemblance. The different requirements of wood construction gave Greek art the time "to mature more slowly, to make more trials, and to delay the realization in permanent materials of the rough drafts that Egyptians hurried to fix and capture in their buildings."[39] Whereas the Egyptians simply mimicked their caves and never learned to "exchange natural dwellings for ones made by art," the Greeks, transposing wood into stone, trans-

formed their huts into monuments of unsurpassed achievement.[40]
From this difference between the hut and the cave and the consequent production of two architectures fundamentally opposed
in character, Quatremère drew his concluding response to the
Academy's question:

> According to this explanation, it is evident that because the first
> causes of Greek architecture differed in certain points from
> those of Egyptian architecture, Greek building must have devel-
> oped a generally original character, one imprinted by the Greek
> nation. This nation knew how to hide and cover up its larcenies
> from Egypt. Yet from every point of view, Egyptian architecture
> cannot be considered anything but the rough draft of Greek
> architecture. The Greeks, through the superiority they attained
> in the other arts of imitation, developed a reasoned system of
> proportions with which they fixed the rules of this art. The
> justness of their taste, which knew to seize that middle point
> between all opposing qualities, gave us true models of beauty
> and left us despairing ever to equal them. *If therefore the
> Egyptians invented architecture, the Greeks invented "la belle
> architecture."* . . . The Egyptians conceived the first ideas, but
> they did not submit them to reflection and criticism nor did they
> reduce them to principles. As a result, the Greeks may be
> excused for having believed that they were masters of this genre;
> the nation that has always vanquished its rivals in the arena of
> the arts must once again carry off the crown.[41]

For Quatremère, the long list of Greek borrowings only proved
the degree to which they had surpassed the Egyptians by having
created a thinking man's architecture.

Architectural Egyptology of the Eighteenth Century

Quatremère's conclusion, that the Egyptians had invented architecture while the Greeks had invented "la belle architecture," was unexceptional. A comparison with the essay submitted by Del Rosso, his only competitor, reveals in fact that both came to the same conclusion, at least superficially. The means by which Quatremère drew his conclusion, however, were noteworthy and the implication of these means was unprecedented. Whereas underlying Del Rosso's thesis was a polemic regarding the status of Roman architecture, Quatremère's essay was based on a highly tendentious selection of elements from standard accounts of the origins of architecture. His extrication of particular ideas from the arguments they had been designed to support weakened their ability to perpetuate tradition and, once conflated into a new matrix, ultimately disoriented prevailing convictions. The principal object of Quatremère's efforts was the primitive hut and its status as the source of the aesthetic superiority of Greek architecture. While he did not question the latter judgment, he did reconsider the foundations of this truism and in doing so altered its meaning.

In his Prix Caylus essay, Del Rosso also asserted that the fundamental difference between Egyptian and Greek architecture was qualitative. Like Quatremère, Del Rosso began his essay with a discussion of primitive architectural models and their relationship to the forms of more advanced building. He argued that having first been developed in Egypt, architecture was transported to Greece during a subsequent period of colonization. His analysis also distinguishes between construction and ornament and discerns with reference to the latter that the Greeks were "endowed by nature with a more delicate taste."[42] His final point, more aggressively stated but still like Quatremère's, was that the Greeks had "copied every type of building that had been produced by the enterprising spirit of the Egyptians," but that nevertheless "the distinction of Greek architects, one that cannot be sufficiently praised, consisted in the intelligence and good taste with which they designed their buildings, particularly with respect to proportions, ornament, the lightness of the masses and contours, as well as with respect to that grace and elegance with which their felicitous productions are filled."[43]

Quatremère and Del Rosso came to parallel conclusions because each had derived the basic elements of his *mémoire* from standard eighteenth-century architectural texts. The Comte de Caylus, for example, unequivocally posited Egyptian architecture as the source of Greek. With great precision, based on classical accounts, even giving the exact date of 1857 B.C., Caylus maintained that Egyptians had established colonies in Greece and had brought their architecture with them.[44] Primitive Greek architecture was the result of a direct imitation of this imported style, characterized by its heaviness and imposing solidity.[45] Immediately following this period of simulacra, local and natural differences of taste directed the Greeks away from this heavy style and toward the birth of what the eighteenth century defined as the classical ideal. In fact, for Caylus, the question of the source of Greek architecture was ultimately less important than the progress it made away from that source: "I am not astonished by the beginnings of this art . . . they are easy to conceive. Instead I am astonished by its progress, especially when I consider the state in which the Greeks received this art and the state in which it left their hands."[46]

Caylus believed that the Egyptians had applied themselves more to architecture than to the other arts. Despite this effort, Egyptian architecture was "not one that strikes us with its agreeable harmony and that announces at first glance the nature of the thing it adorns, but is rather one of solid and majestic building in which one sees the germ of all that the Greeks could therein discover."[47] While thus acknowledging Greek dependence on Egyptian building, as well as the grand and impressive character of that tradition,

Caylus maintained that only to the Greeks could one attribute "the finesse and proportions that we admire in their architectural works as well as the just and delicate sentiment they brought to bear on all the arts and sciences." Indeed, he argued, Egyptian architecture was led "to the ultimate degree of sublimity by the taste, delicacy, sentiment, and lightness added by the Greeks."[48] The same opinion, similarly emphasizing not historical connection but qualitative difference, was expressed earlier by the Abbé Laugier: "The Egyptians sketched architecture heavily, the Greeks drew it with much grace. . . . The former astonished by the grandeur of their masses . . . and the latter shined . . . by inventing the most beautiful forms."[49]

In his *Cours d'architecture* of 1771–1777, Jacques-François Blondel also used Egyptian architecture as a foil in his presentation of the aesthetic perfection the Greeks had attained:

Unity of composition is one of the principal beauties in architecture, at which the Greeks excelled. If truth be told, however, the Greeks owed a great deal to the Egyptians, although the latter did nothing more than prepare the art's rough draft, so to speak. . . .

Before the Greeks, art had nothing to recommend it other than the enormity of its masses and the immensity of its enterprise. But these more enlightened people believed it preferable to please the spirit than to astonish the eyes. They judged that unity and proportions had to be the basis of all works of art.[50]

Here too Egyptian architecture is allowed to precede and give birth to Greek, yet rather than acquire authority and admiration because of its age, Egyptian architecture is enfeebled by it. Its antiquity was equated with unsophisticated infancy, something to be excused rather than venerated. For Blondel, Greek architecture developed and perfected "le bon goût" in the degree to which it distanced itself from its more primitive ancestor.

The historical continuity between Egyptian and Greek architecture on the one hand, and their aesthetic disparity on the other, were arguments developed and maintained by the Academy. However, the Academy was also the site of the introduction of an important departure from this tradition. Le Roy, the probable author of the 1785 essay competition question and a highly regarded academician, wrote in his *Les ruines des plus beaux monuments de la Grèce:*

> When one considers that the Egyptians had already executed most of the monuments we have been discussing at the time that some of their heroes traveled in Greece and taught its still savage inhabitants their laws and the cult of their divinity, one is tempted to believe that the Greeks owe a large number of the discoveries they attributed to themselves to the Egyptians. But if, on the other hand, one examines how many steps the Greeks took from the simple disposition of huts constructed out of necessity *before they knew the Egyptians,* to the most magnificent temples; if one observes again that they formed a regular system of the orders while it seems that the Egyptians followed no system at all, one is forced to recognize the Greeks as a people who invented, with the exception of a few ideas they may have taken from the Egyptians, the art of constructing buildings. Thus, if we accord to the Egyptians the glory of having signaled themselves as the first by virtue of the grandeur and immensity of the buildings they erected, we cannot refuse the Greeks the honor of having imagined the architecture that carries their names.[51]

Le Roy challenged neither conventional chronology nor the traditional stress on the superior aesthetic achievements of the Greeks. He did, however, credit them with a measure of independent original invention not admitted by others who described Greek architecture as a refinement, however extensive, of Egyptian creations. Le Roy maintained that the Greeks had built huts before having any contact with the Egyptians. Giving a Greek origin for this particular primitive structure is significant because the hut was traditionally regarded as the source not just for columns but for the entire system of the orders and hence for the essence of classical architecture. Isolating the hut as a local invention enabled him to explain how the Greeks had produced orders without having to contradict empirical data that suggested that the Egyptians had used columns first. Le Roy's removal of the hut from Egyptian roots limited and restricted the reach of Egyptian influence, and protected the Greek birthright of this core element of the classical tradition.

The importance attached to the role the origins of architecture could play in legitimizing the hegemony of Greek architecture grew at a dramatic pace during the second half of the eighteenth century. The issue had not much interested Caylus when he presented his paper on ancient architecture to the Academy in 1749. Despite the publication of Laugier's seminal *Essai sur l'architecture* in 1753, Le Roy himself was somewhat skeptical about the study of architectural origins when he published the first edition of *Les ruines* in 1758.[52] By the time of the second edition in 1770, however, the origins of architecture had become crucial for him. This development reflects the degree to which the Enlightenment gave ever more weight and foundational significance to primary causes. A more concrete manifestation of this shift was the growing number of visits to and appreciation for previously scorned sites such as Paestum, considered to epitomize primitive Greek architecture.[53] Le Roy, for example, now discerned aesthetic achievement even in such early Greek architecture: "The first steps taken by Greek architecture were so felicitous that they were never discarded. . . . Greek cabins were designed with such wisdom that their forms were always conserved, even in the most magnificent temples."[54] In this description the first steps of architecture are "heureux," where before they were nothing more than "ébauches." However, as Paestum came to be valued because rather than despite the fact that it was primitive, the possibility arose that Greek architecture would lose value because Egyptian architecture was even more primitive. Thus it became ever more essential to protect Greece from being tainted by Egyptian roots. Le Roy provided this protection precisely by exploiting this new valorization of the primitive, using it to rewrite the history of architecture. Where most histories explained the relationship between Greek and Egyptian architecture developmentally, Le Roy saw them as contradictory: one architecture could not produce another of such a fundamentally different character and quality, differences that were visible from the beginnings of each civilization.

Le Roy's thesis gave an independent origin to Greek architecture but only at the cost of relativizing the concept of origin, since it inferred more than one. Others, however, most notably Johann Joachim Winckelmann, attempted to preserve classical hegemony by universalizing the matter of origins. For Winckelmann, the antiquity of Paestum made possible a relationship with Egypt, just as considerations of Paestum's style—proportions almost unrecognizable to eyes trained by Palladio, baseless Doric columns, and massive scale—gave formal and visible credence to the Egyptian derivation of Greek architecture. The mounting evidence Paestum offered in favor of an Egyptian-Greek continuum, however, led him to take a different and perhaps more radical step toward disassociating Greek from Egyptian architecture. Winckelmann universalized the primitive as the foundation for his effort to replace a history of art based on narrative chronologies with what he called a system of art.[55] He attempted to make the question of Egyptian influence on the development of Greek architecture moot by arguing that the primitive was an essential and atemporal principle that carried with it no intrinsic historical or chronological information: "The origins of the arts of design were more or less the same in people separated one from the other. This is so not because these people had communicated their means of working or the ends they had in working, but because nature always teaches the simplest and easiest things first."[56] Winckelmann's *Histoire de l'art chez les anciens* adheres to the traditional chronologies, but not because early Greek architecture resembled Egyptian.[57] This similarity, which to many of his contemporaries proved the connection between Greek and Egyptian architecture, proved nothing at all for Winckelmann except the universality of the primitive.

By 1785 Le Roy and Winckelmann had begun to face the threat to the supremacy of classicism posed by the relativizing influence of architecture from other traditions and the increasing importance and appreciation of first causes, both factors epitomized by the success of architects such as Ledoux whose work increasingly included ferociously elemental and exotic forms. The Prix Caylus hoped to complete the disarmament of this threat.

Since Quatremère and Del Rosso reaffirmed the superiority of classicism, to understand the outcome of the competition it is instructive to consider in greater detail how they defended their assertions.

In his 1785 essay, Del Rosso directly attacked Le Roy's notion that the hut had produced two independent developments, one resulting in Greek architecture, the other in Egyptian. Del Rosso had written:

> Mr. Le Roy seems to have been mistaken when he suggested that a rustic cabin had served as a model for the biggest Egyptian buildings, a prejudice perhaps derived from Vitruvius who said the same of Greek buildings. It seems a reasonable conjecture that the first Egyptians, before national unification, lived like troglodytes in the caves and rocks of Ethiopia. Given that fact, a cave would have served as model for their first architectural efforts and not a hut. . . . It seems then that Mr. Le Roy only imagined huts as architecture's model because he did not perceive that huts had themselves been modeled after caves, the first artificial retreat of human kind.[58]

At first glance, Del Rosso's solution, which recalls a schema proposed by Laugier in the first chapter of his *Essai*, should have more than satisfied the Academy's goals. By introducing the cave as an architectural model, Del Rosso is able to account for the massive, simple, and heavy style of Egyptian architecture, and by maintaining the primitive use of the hut in Greece he is also able to explain the origin of the orders. Moreover, because he makes the cave itself the model of the hut, the traditional chronological and developmental thread between Egypt and Greece is extended to an earlier stage and remains unbroken. On the other hand, Del Rosso's adoption of an apparently conventional formula was neither conventional nor even acceptable from a French point of view since his purpose was not to assert the primacy of Greek architecture. He emphasized the importance of the cave in the development of the hut, and hence the dependence of Greek architecture on Egyptian, in an overwhelming spirit of nationalism inspired by Piranesi. His militantly pro-Italic polemic was to demonstrate that in its derivativeness Roman architecture was in no way different from Greek. Del Rosso's essay thus doubled the threat to Greek architecture by defining it as fundamentally dependent on Egyptian architecture on the one hand, as well as no more independent than Roman on the other.[59]

Quatremère's success in the 1785 competition was no doubt assisted by the fact that he made no such overtly radical assertions. In fact, the skeleton of Quatremère's essay is quite traditional: the importance of primitive building to the art of architecture, the chronology, the basic organization of the text, which seeks a principled method of analysis and does so to a significant degree by separating the discussions of construction and ornament, as well as the Hellenic bias, all typify the French eighteenth-century academic point of view. Above all, Quatremère reveals his most important debt to this tradition by his use of the term "belle" to encapsulate the crucial distinction between Egyptian and Greek architecture.

Quatremère's use of the word "belle," however, also reveals his most important departure from this tradition. Unlike his predecessors, Quatremère did not define the concept in terms of direct aesthetic evaluation and canonical standards of ideal perfection alone. Indeed, instead of using the unerring "goût" of the Greeks as a point of departure and measuring stick, as Del Rosso did when he described them as "endowed by nature with a more delicate taste," Quatremère's entire essay may be seen as an effort to explore how this "goût" came into existence. He began by attempting to dismantle "in a triumphant manner that wooden hut that has always been hailed as the source of all architecture of all people."[60] Like Del Rosso, Quatremère considered that the cave was a primitive model for architecture, just as was the hut, but he denied that there was a necessary and universal developmental link between them: in Quatremère's view, the cave had been the model only of the Egyptian hut, not of the hut as a basic form. He went further still by introducing the tent as yet a third, equally elemental architectural model. Each of these independent seminal forms had an intrinsically distinct character and each was the generator of a correspondingly distinct architecture. In the case of the relationship between Egyptian and Greek architecture, only because there had been some overlap of these models was a condition created in which influence was possible. Quatremère thus asserted that the specifically and empirically historical aspects of the question posed by the Academy could not be answered until the origins of architecture had been determined.

In his essay of 1785 Quatremère's triumph over the primitive hut was not yet complete, insofar as he allowed the possibility of some original congruity, but he had significantly weakened the claim that the structure was architecture's universal source. He did so by conflating Le Roy's relativization with Winckelmann's universalization of the primitive. Quatremère multiplied Le Roy's thesis that there had been more than one original hut into the idea that architecture could be traced back to either the cave, the tent, or the hut. Although Quatremère preserved Winckelmann's belief in the atemporality of the primitive, he used his pluralistic view of Le Roy's thesis to controvert Winckelmann's suggestion that the primitive was monolithic. For Winckelmann, the primitive in art and architecture was everywhere the same and limited to precise formal characteristics. By combining the apparently antithetical views of Le Roy and Winckelmann, Quatremère transformed the significance of both positions. Because his system of multiple architectural origins was relativistic, it implied no formal specificity, and because it was ultimately joined to a conception of the primitive as a universal principle, it also implied no historical specificity.[61]

In Quatremère's scheme, the origins of architecture were no longer able to connote a particular location in a temporal continuum and were no longer assumed to have taken a specific and singular form. The result of this double loss of specificity was that the primitive hut could no longer explain the perfection achieved by Greek architecture or attest to its uniqueness. Quatremère had to develop new criteria with which to define and judge the previously unmeasurable beauty of "la belle architecture." The origins of architecture now constituted an entirely hypothetical structure that rested on a still more fundamental principle. More elemental even than the primitive architectural forms themselves was the nature of the society each was created to protect. Although he did not neglect other factors that were often used to explain national and regional differences, such as physical and environmental conditions, the cornerstone of his new analysis of primitive architecture was its relationship to society. Various means for maintaining society produced different social structures which then demanded distinct architectural structures. The development of both forms of construction progressed in unison and never ceased to be mutually reflective. The building of society, in Quatremère's view, determined the building of architecture.

Quatremère maintained that the origins of architecture also had an original cause, and it was the relationship between these primordial forces that transformed the meaning of the word "belle" in his description of the difference between Egyptian and Greek architecture. For most other writers on the subject, the hut was a natural or God-given condition, a simple fact that sufficiently explained its evolution into the unassailable beauty of Greek architecture.[62] For Quatremère, on the other hand, the ability to construct "la belle architecture" was not a talent inspired by a natural model but a skill acquired through the act of constructing an artificial one.[63] The Greeks were not endowed naturally with taste or with the hut, but had actually created both. Finally, because the hut as well as the cave and tent had social models, architecture now had to be explained in social terms. As a result, in order to define the "state" of Egyptian architecture Quatremère did not judge it against an uncontested and predetermined aesthetic ideal but sought its origins in "the moral institutions" as well as "the political and religious causes" that influenced it.[64] Over the course of the next 20 years, the crown Quatremère unfailingly bestowed on Greek architecture came to rest less on the taste and beauty it embodied than on the society it served.

De l'Architecture Egyptienne

Eighteen years after receiving his prize from the Academy, Quatremère published his *mémoire* on Egyptian architecture. This delay has been noted, but its potential significance has never been seriously considered.[65] The circumstances under which Quatremère brought his essay to the public differed significantly from those under which it had first been written, most dramatically because of the Napoleonic expedition to Egypt. This enterprise initiated an empirical revolution that transformed eighteenth-century conjectures about the murky and mysterious artifacts of ancient humankind into the beginnings of a modern archaeology. The revisions Quatremère made to his essay during this interval, on the other hand, are almost entirely hypothetical in character and focus primarily on the thesis that social and architectural origins were interconnected. Quatremère himself perceived that his essay was caught in the discrepancy between the positivist nature of the Napoleonic expedition and his own theoretical interests. Indeed, he began to develop the idea that architecture was language in response to the challenge posed by this conflict.

The simplest explanation for the fact that Quatremère did not publish his prize-winning essay as soon as possible is that he was unable to do so. He was greatly occupied during the intervening years, first by the preparation of the *Encyclopédie méthodique* as well as by the responsibilities of public office, then by his administration of the Pantheon works, and later still by prison and exile. On the other hand, Del Rosso had published his *mémoire* without significant revisions as early as 1787. Winning an academic prize may, by 1785, have lost some of its prestige, but it would certainly have been to Quatremère's advantage—still a young, unknown and unpublished *amateur des arts*—to see his newly premiated *mémoire* in print. There is, however, no evidence to suggest that Quatremère attempted to do so before the Revolution.[66]

If it is difficult to determine precisely why Quatremère did not publish his essay in the 1780s, it is even more challenging to understand why he did publish it in 1803. The obsolescence of the essay was practically guaranteed by the Napoleonic expedition to Egypt and imminent publication of the *Description de l'Egypte*.[67] There is no doubt that Quatremère was aware of these developments.[68] Moreover, Vivant Denon, an old acquaintance of Quatremère's, had already published his *Voyage dans la Basse et la Haute Egypte* and must have told Quatremère of the great mass of material to be included in the official publication.[69] Nevertheless, Quatremère chose to publish a supposedly scholarly and archaeologically accurate work on Egyptian architecture at the very time when everything previously known about the subject was being rapidly superseded.

His decision to publish it when he did sheds light on the essay itself as well as on the role it played in Quatremère's career. By these first years of the nineteenth century, the reputation he had established during the early years of the Revolution may well have been tarnished by his troublesome political past or it may simply have faded during his long imprisonment and exile.[70] In any case, Quatremère had no position that generated a proper income and, more importantly, that could give official sanction and power to his interest in shaping the art and architecture produced by his contemporaries. Quatremère's former success within the Academy made that institution the logical place to seek a position.[71] In fact, the publication of his essay, a new copy of which he immediately offered to the Academy, was the first step in this effort.[72]

A letter Quatremère sent to the Academy along with the copy of his new book reveals that he was well aware of the objections that might be made about the relevance of his work and that he consequently felt the need to defend both the publication and his position in the eyes of the Academy. Quite ingeniously, however, he inverted the situation and put the Academy itself on trial, implicitly challenging the Academy to recognize that, since it had both posed the question and premiated Quatremère's answer, any shortcomings of the essay were ultimately its own responsibility. From Passy, on 10 Germinal of the year 11, Quatremère wrote:

> The learned society that lives once again through you and that the government has just returned to its former task, previously and graciously deigned to receive the work I am honored to offer you.
>
> In proposing research on Egyptian architecture and in calling the attention of learned Europe to this subject, the Académie des Belles-Lettres encouraged the literary conquest of Egypt, insofar as it was then possible. The discoveries owed to the memorable expedition that has since taken place, to the labor of learned men, and to the munificence of the government that supported them will no doubt shed a new light on all the arts of that country and will clarify a great number of questions. Perhaps you will find that these circumstances do not favor the publication of a work written twenty years ago on one of the principal arts of Egypt. However . . . I was emboldened by the guarantee of the celebrated society that had deemed the knowledge acquired up to that time sufficient to the program the society itself had established. . . .
>
> To present this work again today, while recalling that it previously obtained your approbation, is to place it again under a protection as useful as it is honorable. I hope I may take advantage of this opportunity to solicit once again the same benevolence that encouraged my first effort, benevolence that I will always consider the most precious reward my work has received.[73]

The Academy agreed with Quatremère, realizing that to impugn his essay as a futile and ungrounded effort would have been a form of self-condemnation. Sticking by its earlier estimation of the essay's worth, the Académie des Inscriptions et Belles-Lettres elected Quatremère a member in 1804.[74]

Assistance in fulfilling his academic aspirations was not the only benefit Quatremère received by publishing his *mémoire* in 1803. He realized, somewhat ironically, that he actually stood to benefit from the impending *Description de l'Egypte*. Indeed, any work on Egypt could only gain by the tremendous public attention focused on that civilization as a result of the expedition. Capitalizing on the new Egyptian craze, Quatremère asserted that a summary of the state of pre-Napoleonic Egyptology would enhance the new work by highlighting how far it had progressed. In the *avertissement* of the 1803 publication Quatremère wrote:

> This text, graciously received in the past by the Academy, has not yet been published. . . . I thought that at a moment when all minds were turning toward ancient Egypt—toward its arts, its genius, and its taste—it might be relevant to publish the information that had been amassed in the old reference works, even if only to shed light on all we shall owe to the new ones. I thought that a parallel between what we knew and what we will know might better establish the level of knowledge recently acquired. I also imagined that anything that might give rise to discussion of such a curious subject could only be useful to the arts.[75]

Deftly transforming potential adversity into an asset, Quatremère suggested that the importance of his work lay in its very obsolescence.

This notion of obsolescence, however, is key to another and more substantive reason for Quatremère's resurrection of his eighteenth-century text. Although he wrote, with respect to his publication, "perhaps people will think it appears too late or too early. I will respond to neither objection," he did in fact offer an explanation.[76] Both in his letter to the Academy and in his book's *avertissement*, Quatremère reveals that he feared being empirically outmoded less than he did the possibility that his particular approach to the study of architecture would be superseded. He asserted that his work had been "conceived from a point of view and within a system of research and criticism that is in large measure independent of the positive observations the results of which the public is now awaiting," and thus that the new material was irrelevant to what he had hoped to accomplish in 1785.[77] He reiterated this distinction between the nature of his work and that of the Napoleonic corpus in his 1803 *avertissement:* "I repeat, I did not describe monuments and thus had no need to discuss such details. My only goal was to form for myself and to give an idea of the origin, the principles, and the taste of Egyptian architecture and to compare it in the same terms with Greek architecture."[78]

Between 1785 and 1803 Quatremère introduced significant alterations and additions: the published text is in fact almost twice as long as his original essay.[79] Despite Quatremère's sensitivity to the possible impact on his own work created by the new Egyptological survey, none of the added material is archaeological in nature.[80] Even the plates of the new publication are based on the old and now antiquated sources (figs. 5–13). On the other hand, the changes he made to his dissertation reveal that he took advantage of the years following 1785 to reinforce and refine the essay's theoretical content. In fact, these emendations suggest that his decision to publish in 1803 was not merely opportunistic but stemmed from his explicitly stated sense that his "system of research and criticism" was imperiled by the overwhelming influx of Egyptological facts and the emphasis they placed on a positive rather than a speculative understanding of the history of architecture.

Whether Quatremère published his essay in 1803 in spite of or because of Napoleon's archaeological revolution, he believed that a profound shift in the goals of those studying architecture's past was taking place, a shift based on the difference between analyses seeking ahistorical principles and those seeking historical facts. The structure of his publication reflects and reinforces this distinction. The published version is divided into three parts, which Quatremère describes as follows: "The first section will contain research on some of the causes that shaped the state of the arts in Egypt, especially its architecture. The second will analyze and trace the development of Egyptian architecture, under the triple headings of construction, disposition, and decoration. The third part will offer a resumé of the principles, character, and taste of this architecture, of the essential differences separating it from Greek architecture, and of the correspondences that can be perceived between them."[81] Only the second part of the new version is devoted to a positive description of Egyptian architecture, and while it is therefore the part one would expect to have been most altered in light of the expedition, it in fact reproduces almost verbatim the corresponding sections of the original essay.[82] Moreover, this part is the only one that does so. In contrast, Quatremère expanded the manuscript's 22-page last section, "On Greek Imitation," into a 60-page critical evaluation of Egyptian and Greek architecture, and roughly tripled the 17 pages of the manuscript's first section, "Of Architecture and Its Origins in Egypt," into a lengthy essay entitled "Research on Some of the Causes That Influenced the State of Architecture in Egypt." The theoretical development contained within these additions almost requires conceiving the essay published in 1803 as an independent work written in response to an entirely new context, rather than as a reformulated version of the 1785 text.

Quatremère's own understanding of this distinction is succinctly reflected by the title he gave the essay for its publication: "On Egyptian architecture, considered with respect to its origin, its principles and its taste and compared in the same terms with Greek architecture." In contrast to the original Academic formulation, "What was the state of Egyptian architecture and what do the Greeks seem to have borrowed from it," Quatremère's new title reveals an interest in three elements—origins, principles, and taste—that are ahistorical and for which archaeological precision, and thus by implication the Napoleonic campaign, are largely irrelevant. In fact the theoretical and speculative nature of Quatremère's title contrasts dramatically with the objective science implied by the title *Description de l'Egypte*.[83] Moreover, Quatremère's title, in and of itself, eliminated two crucial aspects of the Academy's original question: its request for a positive description of Egyptian architecture at a time when empirical data were scarce and unreliable, and its imposition of a historical or chronological relationship between Egypt and Greece. The 1803 title does not announce a comprehensive study of Egyptian architecture nor does its reference to origins, principles, and taste presuppose a particular temporal or developmental relationship between Egypt and Greece.

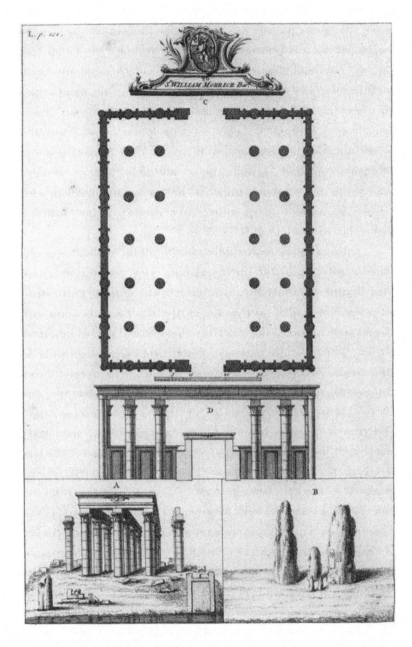

5. Richard Pococke, *A Description of the East, and Some Other Countries* **(London, 1743), plate L, Temples at Ombus and Phylae**

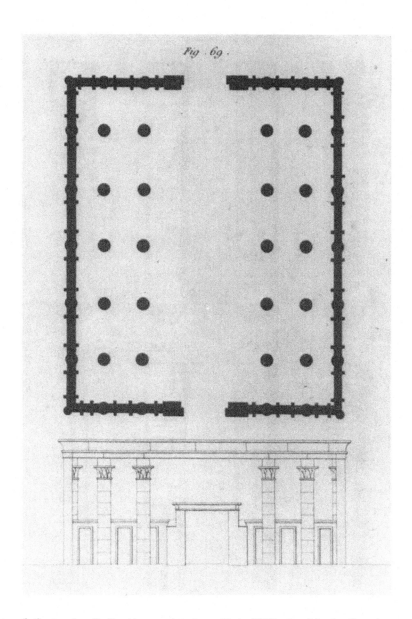

6. Quatremère, *De l'architecture égyptienne* (Paris, 1803), plate 18, after Pococke

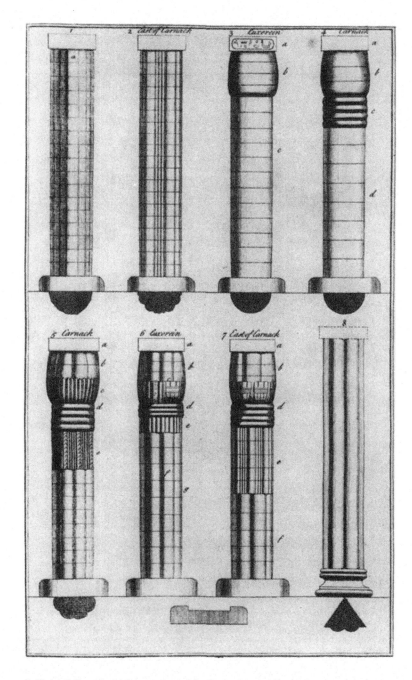

7. Richard Pococke, *A Description of the East*, **plate LXVI, Egyptian pillars**

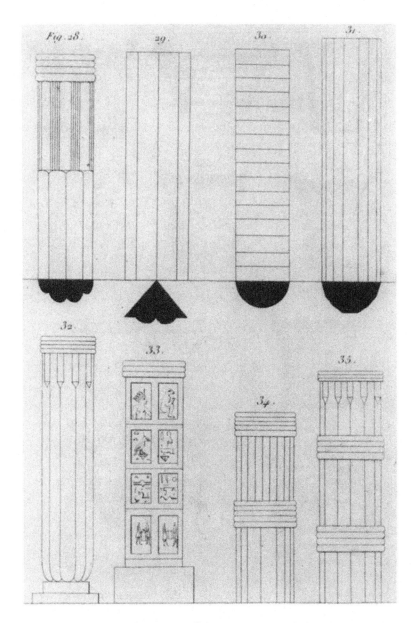

8. Quatremère, *De l'architecture égyptienne*, **plate 5, Egyptian column shafts, after Pococke**

EGYPTIAN CAPITALS.

To William Windham Esq.

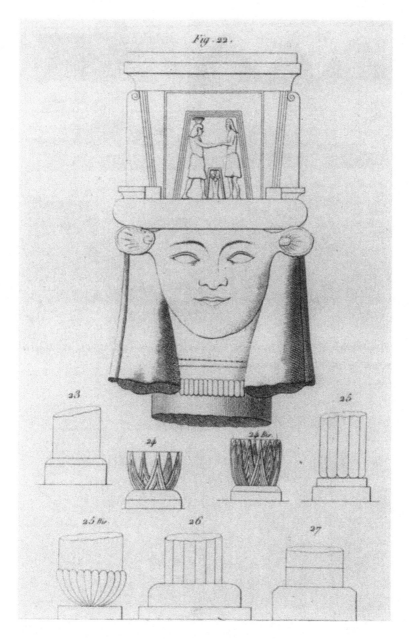

9. Richard Pococke, *A Description of the East*, plate LXVIII, Egyptian capitals
10. Quatremère, *De l'architecture égyptienne*, plate 4, capital with the head of Isis and column bases, after Pococke

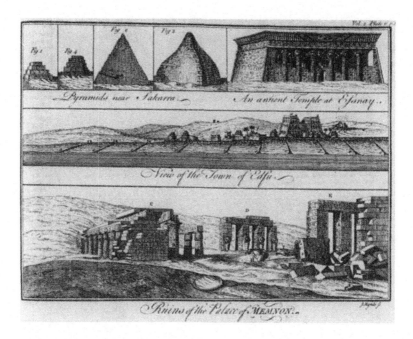

11. Frederick L. Norden, *Travels in Egypt and Nubia* (London, 1757), vol. 2, plate 6, ruins of the Palace of Memnon

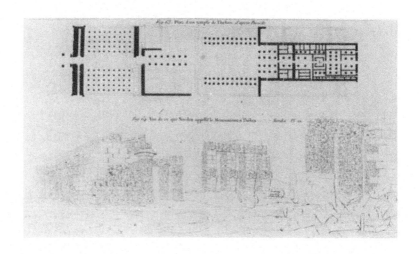

12. Quatremère, *De l'architecture égyptienne*, plate 14, views of Thebes, after Norden and Pococke

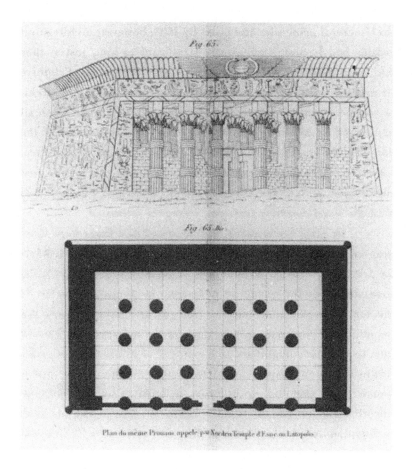

13. Quatremère, *De l'architecture égyptienne*, plate 15, view and plan of Egyptian pronaos, after Norden

For Quatremère, the most important of these three elements was the question of origins. The centrality of origins was
already clear in the 1785 essay where he explored their seminal
and universal role for architecture, and by implication also for
architectural principles and taste. By 1803, however, architectural
origins had become increasingly significant to him, just as they
had been more important for Le Roy than for Caylus. Primitive
or original building had become the single most important architectural element to Quatremère, the *unguis leonis* from which all
else could be inferred. This new emphasis is demonstrated by the
fact that the question of origins is the focus of the most radical
alterations Quatremère made to his essay. The title of the first
subdivision is "On the Diversity of Architectural Origins," and
with the word *diversity* profound change is intimated.

In 1785, Quatremère had suggested that there were three
original architectural forms, the cave, the hut, and the tent. While
he felt that Egyptian architecture originated primarily with the
cave, he attributed certain of its features to the hut. He wrote: "I
do not think that one must exclusively and uniquely seek the
principles of Egyptian architecture in the subterranean caverns
dug by the first inhabitants of Egypt. . . . I think that the architecture of some peoples may have had a double origin, and it
seems to me that this was the case in Egypt. I do not reject the
idea that the hut had an origin in Egypt. . . . This is why one finds
in Egyptian building a mixture of these two principles."[84] Although
the cave, tent, and hut were sufficiently distinct to generate each
an original architecture, Quatremère did not see them as mutually
exclusive. A seminal overlap, or double origin, had in fact been
the basis on which he had responded to the historical dimension
of the Academy's question. The parallel dependence, albeit in
different degrees, of Egyptian and Greek architecture on the
model of the hut had permitted direct influence to take place.
However, while his allowance of a double origin for Egyptian
architecture had enabled him to address the Academy's question,
it had also obstructed his goal to discredit "that wooden hut that
has always been hailed as the source of all architecture of all
people."

What had been, in 1785, a latent and indecisive suggestion now developed into a patent and clearly expressed revolution in Quatremère's understanding of architecture. By 1803, his dismantling of the uniquely original hut was indeed triumphant, for he now presented the cave, hut, and tent as three radically distinct, indigenous, and equally controlling original forms. Greek architecture remained rooted in the hut, while Egyptian architecture now derived only from the cave. As a result of this essential difference he concluded: "One should consider these architectures as lacking any generic connection, as two species distinct in their essential structure. The anteriority of one or the other, particularly because this is so difficult to determine, is an argument of little value in this matter. The date of their birth is, in effect, not important if each was born of a different germ."[85] The singular origin of architecture that he had previously sought in Egypt was now multiple and to be sought both in Egypt and in Greece.[86] Given architecture's multiple or diverse origins, the Academy's historical view of Greek and Egyptian architecture had ceased to be germaine. Quatremère retained the comparative structure of the Academy's original formulation, since more than one architecture was necessary to demonstrate his principle of diverse origins, but he rejected the question's historical objective.

In order to accomplish his own objective Quatremère needed a method of analysis that was as ahistorical as were the ideas he intended to address. Introducing a fundamentally new principle of architectural investigation, he replaced history as a framework for comparative study with ahistorical principles borrowed from eighteenth-century language theory. If the opposing natures of the hut and the cave had, in 1785, explained the differences between Greek and Egyptian architecture, universal grammar could now explain their interconnection. He wrote:

If language belongs to humanity, do the languages that are local modifications of this general faculty belong to specific societies or nations? . . . In studying this matter one would be gravely mistaken to confuse the general principles of universal grammar that belong to language with the rules of syntax proper to individual languages. This error might lead one to establish a filiation between two languages based uniquely on the fact that they both have declensions and conjugations. No one, as far as I know, has fallen into this trap in the context of language.

One can say, on the contrary, that almost no one has escaped this trap with regard to architecture. The general principles of the art of building common to all architecture have almost always been confused with the particular principles and original conditions of individual architectures. The result has been that filiations and genealogies have been imagined between the most foreign of species.[87]

The principle of universal grammar to which Quatremère referred was a manifestation of the acceptance of the doctrine of the uniformity of human nature. Predicated on a Cartesian understanding of language as reflective of man's reason, this notion maintained that the workings of all men's minds are similar, and so also are the languages they develop. Universal grammar thus indicated that the structural identity found among various languages revealed the commonness of man and not the existence of any tangible or historical connection between men.[88]

The concept of universal grammar enabled Quatremère to combat what he now called, borrowing another linguistic term, the "filiation" typically drawn connecting Egyptian and Greek architecture. He proclaimed that "to infer from general similarities shared by two architectures that one is the product of the other is as indefensible an abuse as it would be to define one language as the derivative of another because they share features of universal grammar."[89] Quatremère went on to use universal grammar as a way of discounting the very piece of evidence that in the past suggested a historical relationship between the two cultures and on which most such discussions had focused: the presence of the column both in Greece and Egypt. He argued: "How many authors have claimed that the origins of Greek architecture are to be found in Egypt because the Egyptians used columns, capitals, and cornices in their buildings before the Greeks did. . . . Neither very profound ideas nor a great force of reason are necessary to understand that many parallels between different architectures do not indicate a common origin or a communication of taste."[90] According to Quatremère the post and lintel system (though not the orders, as he makes clear) was to building what universal grammar was to language, a phenomenon without national allegiance or historical specificity. The coincidence of columns in Egypt and Greece proved the inherent logic of the structural potential of the column, not a direct chain of influence. The column now belonged to a universal grammar of building.

The notion of universal grammar also enabled Quatremère to discern a structural similarity between architecture and language, a relationship he felt was relevant to his theory of multiple origins. With respect to the origins of architecture he wrote:

An opinion has been generally established by authors who have spoken of architecture—an opinion that no one, it seems to me, has undertaken to discuss—that tends to place the origin of this art in one primitive nation. Thus, a first people of *inventors* are honored with this discovery that they then transmitted to neighbors and step by step to all other nations.

Egyptians, having been from many points of view the first people historically known to us and having actually been in more ways than one the school of people that historical documents show appearing later on the scene of the world, Egypt has naturally been regarded as the inventor of many arts and sciences; the cradle of architecture has been placed in Egypt, its invention has been attributed to that country.[91]

In order to refute what Quatremère felt was a mistaken commonplace, he once again borrowed from theories of language, arguing that "the invention of architecture must be seen as parallel to the invention of language. That is to say that neither one nor the other invention can be attributed to any man because both are attributes of men."[92] Without a unique inventor, language may in fact have had multiple origins. Moreover, according to Quatremère, linguists recognized the difference between such mother tongues, the origins of which were unknown, and composite ones that had been derived from preexisting languages.

Quatremère maintained that the same difference could be found in architecture. As proof, he compared the multiple piers of Egyptian and Gothic buildings. The former, according to Quatremère, derived directly from a bundle of trees, the strings used to tie them together still visible in stone examples. Because the only possible model for these columns was nature itself, however transformed, Egyptian architecture was to be classified as a "mother tongue." Gothic pillars, on the other hand, were made of a series of shafts that each had its own capital. He strongly attacked the traditional idea that Gothic architecture, like Egyptian, had a natural origin in trees and forests: the presence of multiple capitals convinced him that Gothic piers were a composite of classical columns rather than trees. Moreover, he felt the assemblage itself had a constructed rather than natural model since there existed pre-Gothic buildings that were supported by collections of antique pillars.[93] Unlike the Gothic, therefore, which constituted a dialect, Egyptian and Greek architecture were original or "mother" architectures. Models for the latter type could only be hypothetically reconstructed out of natural elements, while models for the former could be found by tracing in reverse the historical development of artifacts.

Quatremère associated language and architecture on the basis of similarities in the principles of their structure and of their origins. Yet we have seen that he also associated architectural origins with social origins, and hence he ultimately made a triadic connection between the beginnings of architecture, society, and language. The coincidence of these three elements had already been intimated by Vitruvius in his celebrated discussion of the origin of the dwelling. Before describing the origins of the house itself, Vitruvius reconstructed those of society and language:

The men of old were born like the wild beasts, in woods, caves, and groves, and lived on savage fare. As time went on, the thickly crowded trees in a certain place . . . caught fire. . . . After it subsided, they drew near . . . [and] brought up other people to it, showing them by signs how much comfort they got from it. In that gathering of men, at a time when utterance of sound was purely individual, from daily habits they fixed upon articulate words just as these had happened to come; then, from indicating by name things in common use, the result was that

in this chance way they began to talk, and thus originate con-
versation with one another.[94]

Vitruvius's anecdote loosely connects the births of society, language, and architecture. By the eighteenth century, however, when
the definitions of language, architecture, and society had changed,
the two former elements were not only seen as born coincidentally
with society, but were deemed its most important constituent
and preserving constructs. Quatremère went further still by integrating these elements into a coherent theory, claiming that the
invention of architecture and the invention of language were part
and parcel of the invention of society. Reflecting this tripartite
relationship, he saw the nature of nascent societies written on their
monuments.[95]

The Academy's essay question of 1785 had explicitly
sought only a demonstration of the historical relationship between
Greek and Egyptian architecture. Quatremère's original essay
offered evidence in support of the Egyptian roots of Greek architecture, but his publication of 1803 fundamentally denied any such
connection. His final response to the stated question was: "I feel
that I fully address the aims of the Academy's program when I
demonstrate that the two architectures here under discussion
could not have and did not have a connection nor could one have
derived from the other."[96] Quatremère was led to make such an
apparently antiacademic claim precisely because he responded to
the problem of origins that was implicit in the Academy's question.
Having begun by considering whether Egypt was the cradle of
civilization, he developed a theory of the diverse origins of the
three constituent elements of civilization: architecture, language,
and society. His perception of what he felt was the identical structure shared by these elements was no doubt aided by the intradisciplinary model provided by the Academy as an institution. The
perception itself, however, led Quatremère to conceive of architecture as a social language, a notion that ultimately transformed
the academic tradition into the foundations of a modern theory
of architecture.

II

ARCHITECTURAL ETYMOLOGY

The History of Ethnography

The Académie des Inscriptions et Belles-Lettres allied itself to the generalized contemporary search for origins by combining specific references to Egypt and to architecture for the Prix Caylus of 1785. Although this quest for origins was generally not concerned with positive historical accuracy, it had profound historical implications. In architectural terms, for example, however mythical and hypothetical the reconstructions of the primitive hut since Vitruvius had been, these efforts were characterized by a search for the first building.[1] The idea of a single prehistoric building type allowed for a comprehensive and unbroken chain of development linking architectures throughout the world and enabled the construction of a monolithic history of human progress that could be measured in a linear, chronological fashion. The formulation of the academy's question, "What was the state of Egyptian architecture and what do the Greeks seem to have borrowed from it," with its emphasis on the continuity between two apparently different civilizations, thus implied a faith in the monogenesis of man. The notion was indeed a matter of faith, for only a monogenetic theory of human origins could be made to accord with sacred history.

In the essay of 1785, by allowing Egyptian and Greek architecture a parallel origin in the hut, Quatremère preserved the integrity of monogenesis. By simultaneously introducing the cave as an additional model for Egyptian architecture, however, he deflected attention away from the omnipresent hut, calling into question the universal reach of a divine and singular origin. Finally, in the emended essay of 1803, he presented the cave, tent, and hut as three equally primitive forms of architecture and conceived of them as distinct, historically unrelated categories. His unconventional tripartite division and fragmentation of the principle of the "original" precluded the notion of a single, universal history of mankind and constituted an epigenetic theory of human origins.

Quatremère's speculations on architectural origins depended on a long history of similar reconstructions by writers on architecture. Especially in France, with the widespread influence of Cordemoy and Laugier, architectural theory had been dominated by a search for origins. Precedents existed for Quatremère's emphasis on the universal importance of the primitive as well as for his inclusion of the cave as an early form of building. While these efforts brought greater refinement and complexity to reflections on the origins of architecture, Quatremère was the first architectural theorist to make a radical break with the tradition of monogenesis. In part, his innovation consisted in borrowing the concept of epigenesis from other fields of inquiry and applying it to the discussion of architectural models. In its turn, epigenesis was but a final stage in the development of an increasingly secular and abstract approach to the study and meaning of history.

The concern for architectural origins was itself a facet of a larger interest in the origins of all aspects of man and his world. Comparisons between the different known cultures sought to discern common elements, or to distinguish between what was natural to man and what were his own creations. Also of primary concern during the eighteenth century were discrepancies in the levels of social development attained by different cultures. The suggestion of an imbalance in the progress made by man was corroborated by the influx of evidence provided by contemporary explorations of the New World as well as exotic parts of the Old.[2] In fact, the same territorial broadening of Europe's cultural horizons that was weakening the hegemony of the classical ideal also increasingly seemed to contradict the possibility of a single beginning for mankind: accounts of modern primitives cast doubt on no less an orthodoxy than the equilibrium of God's plan.[3] Substitutions for this lost belief were developed by replacing the scriptural account of the history of man with parallel secularized concepts. For example, the biblical flood, which traditionalists such as Jacques Benigne

Bossuet used to explain the dispersal of humanity throughout the globe, came to stand for the more general concept of natural disasters that catastrophists such as Nicolas-Antoine Boulanger defined as the generators of historical change.[4] Still others seized upon the flood as a device that, irrespective of when and whether it actually took place, permitted a hypothetical reconstruction of the development of man as if he was of natural rather than divine origin.[5] The continuing search for ways to reconcile the facts of natural development with the biblical accounts thus ultimately contributed to the secularization and increasing abstraction of history itself.

The task of maintaining faith in monogenesis despite regional, cultural, and developmental difference was a burden confronted by most early ethnographers and anthropologists.[6] As they attempted to preserve the integrity of the theory of the divine provenance of all mankind, they sought increasingly flexible ways with which to construct the march of human progress. The Christian doctrine of the uniformity of man was transformed into attempts to define less theologically determined and less literal aspects of human commonality. New emphasis was placed on variable although universal factors such as the influence of climate and the very existence of culture and social institutions, including architecture. Comparative structures, such as that implicit in the 1785 Prix Caylus topic, were fundamental to the efforts to account for such differences. Motivated initially by the will to prove human monogenesis, the relativism and anachronism often embedded in this structure proved to be of great importance to the divorce of sacred time from secular history.[7]

Despite the potentially heretical results of this line of inquiry, or perhaps out of a desire to forestall such results, the Académie des Inscriptions et Belles-Lettres became an active contributor to this debate. In 1758 Joseph de Guignes, a celebrated orientalist who had been made a member of the Academy in 1753, took the lead when he read his *Mémoire dans lequel on prouve que les Chinois sont une colonie égyptienne*. De Guignes's *mémoire* attempted to support the traditional monogeneticist view of

Egypt as the cradle of civilization by drawing a parallel between Egyptian hieroglyphs and Chinese ideograms. Because China was both ancient and exotic, determining its historical position in relation to Egypt was almost as imperative as determining that of Greece.[8] De Guignes's proposal was much supported within the Academy, particularly by Le Roy.[9] Moreover, because de Guignes was present at all the meetings relevant to the Prix Caylus of 1785, one might conclude that he helped formulate the question in the hope that an essay on this topic would assert the value of his own thesis.

Although Quatremère went so far as to address the question of the relationship between Egypt and China in his *mémoire* as well as the more general issue of origins that was embedded in de Guignes's thesis, Quatremère's essay did not support de Guignes. In fact, it supported de Guignes's most vociferous opponent, another comparativist scholar, Cornelius de Pauw. Born in Amsterdam in 1739, de Pauw established his reputation on the basis of his *Recherches philosophiques sur les américains* (1768–1769).[10] He attracted much critical attention and was particularly well received by Diderot and d'Alembert. His radicalism, however, was severely criticized by the Jesuits, sending him into a melancholy, deepened by the Revolution, from which he did not emerge before his death in 1799. Although de Pauw already found himself in the midst of controversy in the 1760s, his dispute with the Academy began in 1773 when he wrote *Recherches philosophiques sur les Chinois et les Egyptiens* as a heated refutation of de Guignes's *mémoire*. Rather than illustrate the degree to which Egypt was the ancestor of other cultures, de Pauw was determined "to show that no two nations ever resembled each other less than the Egyptians and the Chinese."[11]

De Pauw's work—its thesis and more significantly its principles of analysis—was one of Quatremère's most important sources. Despite the risk of censure by the Academy, Quatremère made his knowledge of and allegiance to de Pauw in the controversy with de Guignes quite apparent: direct references to de Pauw appear in both Quatremère's competition essay and its published version.[12] Although it is impossible to know precisely which texts Quatremère used other than those specifically cited, it is both possible and necessary to address the intellectual contexts of works he mentions in particular.[13] De Pauw's book very much belongs to a series of texts that explored a set of interconnected issues, and one can assume Quatremère had some familiarity with these studies, even if only indirectly through de Pauw.

One of the more influential of the secularized and conceptualized efforts to sustain monogeneticism was made by Joseph-François Lafitau, who, like de Pauw, studied native Americans. Born in 1681, Lafitau went to Canada as a Jesuit missionary, where he investigated Indian tribes between 1712 and 1719. On the basis of his direct observations, Lafitau wrote *Moeurs des sauvages ameriquains, comparées aux moeurs des premiers temps* (1724).[14] The basic structure of this paradigmatic ethnographic work makes modern primitives and ancient man equivalent, so that information gathered about one group sheds light on the other, irrespective of temporal disparity. He wrote: "I have not limited myself to learning the characteristics of the Indian and informing myself about their customs and practices, I have sought in these practices and customs, vestiges of the most remote antiquity. . . . I confess that, if the ancient authors have given me information on which to base happy conjectures about the Indians, the customs of the Indians have given me information on the basis of which I can understand more easily and explain more readily many things in the ancient authors."[15] In this passage, aspects of contemporary and ancient man are presented as interchangeable and thus as common throughout time. Ultimately, the comparison brings to light a universal basis of society in religion that serves Lafitau in his effort to prove both the divinity and the singular nature of man's origin. Despite his certainty in this traditional goal, Lafitau acknowledges the hypothetical nature of the inquiry into the origins of humanity. He describes the early times of man as "centuries of obscurity in which periods cannot be fixed and which are regarded as mythical, of which consequently, [one] can report no known fact nor can [one] say anything with certainty."[16] On the other hand, the very unknowable and atemporal nature of the origin gave this concept a flexibility that enabled him to make origin theory the methodological basis of his religious polemic rather than its factual basis. Lafitau preserved the essence of the Bible's historical tableau only through a process of abstraction that denied it weight as literal history. Thus unburdened, he transformed Catholic dogma into cultural anthropology.[17]

Certain comparative studies went beyond Lafitau in their secularization of the study of humanity. For example, Antoine-Yves Goguet's *De l'origine des loix, des arts et des sciences, et de leurs progrès chez les anciens peuples* of 1758 concentrates on demonstrating the progressive sophistication of social and cultural institutions rather than on discovering elements of a universal religion.[18] Although Goguet (1712–1758) was not a man of the cloth but rather a lawyer to the Parlement of Paris, like Lafitau he was a traditional monogeneticist. *De l'origine des loix* is organized in three volumes around three eras of biblical history: from the deluge to the death of Jacob, from his death to the establishment of a Hebrew kingdom, and finally from the kingdom to the return of the Jews from Babylon. Moreover, Goguet's premise is also inherently anachronistic, since the evidence he uses to construct this history of ancient man is in large part derived from the accounts of the New World provided by modern travel writers, including Lafitau.[19]

Goguet attempted to demonstrate the global and historical uniformity of man, yet he transformed this traditional goal by emphasizing the products rather than the source of civilization. Thus while he defined three historical epochs on the basis of events described in the Bible, he analyzed each on the basis of six secular categories of social constructs: government, arts and crafts, sciences, commerce and navigation, military arts, and mores and customs. Moreover, as had the Académie des Inscriptions et Belles-Lettres, Goguet determined that architecture in particular offered an extraordinarily fertile ground for exploring both the nature and history of society, especially with respect to its form in ancient Egypt. Goguet's *De l'origine des loix* contains a chapter entitled "On the State of Egyptian Architecture," which may well have inspired the Academy in its formulation of the Prix Caylus

14. Antoine-Yves Goguet, *De l'origine des loix, des arts, et des sciences* (Paris, 1758), vol. 3, plate VI, view of ruins of Thebes, after Norden

of 1785. Furthermore, although he discusses the architecture of other nations, only his analysis of Egyptian architecture is enriched by plates, engraved by Pierre Patte (fig. 14).[20]

Goguet traces the development of architecture throughout the three stages of history outlined in *De l'origine des loix*. Using the flood as a device for establishing an evolutionary tabula rasa, Goguet describes the nature of men during this first epoch as "of such a cruel and ferocious character that they shared neither society nor commerce. . . . Little different from brutal beasts, they dwelt in nothing more than lairs and caves. . . . Lacking even the simplest and most ordinary ideas, these people had only the appearance of man."[21] Far from admiring such men, he almost denies them distinction from animals and, with the support of travel accounts describing modern more often than ancient people, maintains that these primitives lived in nothing but caves.[22]

Goguet then introduces the hut as part of man's progress away from this state of ignorance. Although the hut is thus descredited as the absolute origin of architecture, it maintains its position as the first man-made architecture. Goguet includes the capacity to build in brick and stone as the final stage of development during the world's first antediluvian era, but concludes that "the first monuments of architecture properly speaking must have been quite crude and quite ill-formed."[23]

In the second and third volumes, devoted to the eras between the death of Jacob and the return of the Jews from Babylon, Goguet offers extensive descriptions of architecture in ancient Egypt, Asia Minor, and Greece. Once again, he cites ancient and modern writers indiscriminately and his conclusions strongly echo the opinion of the contemporary architectural establishment.[24] For example, his aesthetic judgment is based on traditional elements such as grace and proportion as defined by the classical ideal. Accordingly, he argues that "all civilized people began with more or less the same degree of understanding of the arts" but concludes that Greek and Egyptian architecture ultimately took very different forms: Egyptian architecture remained unprincipled and inelegant, whereas the orders of Greek architecture produced the best that was possible, "whether measured in terms of majesty, beauty, delicacy, or solidity."[25]

Goguet's interest in the light shed by architecture on theories of origins led him to anticipate the essence of the 1785 Prix Caylus. He too recognized the urgency and breadth of the dilemma encapsulated by the relationship between Greek and Egyptian building, and much of the third chapter of his second volume enumerates the architectural benefits Greece derived from the influx of Egyptian colonies. *De l'origine des loix* thus addresses the same material as the Academy's question, and it also contains a parallel to Quatremère's response. Goguet wrote:

> The Greeks did not in fact invent architecture, if by this word one simply means the art of combining different materials and from them composing commodious buildings that satisfy various functions. . . . But architecture does not consist uniquely in hand craft and simple mechanical labor. . . .

Architecture received the regularity, the disposition, and
the unity that are able to charm our eyes from the Greeks. In
this sense, one can say that the Greeks invented architecture.
They borrowed nothing in this regard from other nations.
Architecture is an art entirely of Greek creation.[26]

In this passage, Goguet considers Greek and Egyptian architecture
in terms of what the former did or did not "borrow" from the
latter, just as the Academy did in its 1785 competition topic. Similarly, both he and Quatremère analyzed the question in the context of "invention."[27] In particular, by distinguishing qualitatively
between building and architecture, Goguet anticipated Quatremère's first *mémoire* by presenting Egyptian and Greek architecture as developmentally connected but fundamentally disparate.[28]

A most important aspect of Goguet's presentation of architecture is its reduced emphasis on aesthetic evaluation, an attitude
Quatremère did not express with great clarity until 1803. Goguet
systematically included architecture in his categorical and comparative analysis of civilization's elemental products, irrespective
of its level of aesthetic achievement. He clearly expressed his
preference for Greek architecture; nevertheless, he argued that it
was not the beauty of Greek building that rendered it capable of
cultural expression but rather its essential nature as architecture.
He considered any and all architecture, whether of high or of poor
quality, to be inherently and consistently revelatory of human
civilization and a profoundly social phenomenon. Quatremère
therefore followed Goguet in conceiving of architecture as part of
an interconnected network of cultural and social institutions, each
of equivalent importance.

Henry Home, Lord Kames, although less directly concerned with architecture, also developed secularized means with
which to analyze the theological dimension of origin theory and
its relationship to historical method. Born in 1696, Home was a
lawyer and a leading figure in the Scottish Enlightenment. Some
of his more important publications include the *Law Tracts* of
1758, translated into French in 1766, and *Elements of Criticism* of
1762, which quickly dampened the popularity of Rollin's *Traité
des études* in England.[29] Motivated by the same issue as most

eighteenth-century students of origins, Home published *Sketches of the History of Man* in 1774, beginning his schematic history with an attempt to explain the diversity of men and of languages. He immediately focused on the core of the dilemma by underlining the contradiction between the variety of races suggested by what he called "natural history" and the single pair of the human species created by God according to revelation.[30] In order to solve this inconsistency, he turned to the book of Genesis and its story of the tower of Babel: "That this is real history," he wrote, "must necessarily be admitted, as the confusion of Babel is the only known fact that can reconcile sacred and profane history."[31]

According to Home, the building of the tower of Babel scattered and reduced society to a state of degeneracy and savageness that paralleled the conditions humankind would have confronted had there been no initial Divine intervention. Having thus found a way to return humanity to a hypothetical state of origin that did not contradict the Bible, Home was free to trace society's independent "progress towards maturity." He divided this subsequent "real" history of man into three states defined on the basis of techniques for collecting food: those of hunters (which included secondarily fishermen and the gatherers of wild plants), shepherds, and farmers. The three states, or more precisely stages, were sequential, and the progression from one state to the next brought with it important social transformations, such as the development of government, nations, arts, and sciences.[32] Although Quatremère did not recreate this linear relationship between the three states, he did retain the nature of their distinction and even reinforced it by assigning to each an explicit architectural form. Thus, Quatremère linked together Home's three states of fishing, shepherding, and farming with the cave, the tent, and the hut.

Home used the tower of Babel to posit a form of pseudo-epigenesis because like Goguet he was ultimately less concerned with the nature of man's beginning than with exploring the achievements of postlapsarian society. Waiving "the question, whether the human race be the offspring of one pair or of many," Home focused on the source and evolution of human accomplishments: "Some useful arts must be nearly coeval with the human race; for food, cloathing, and habitation, even in their original simplicity, require some art. Many other arts are of such antiquity as to place the inventors beyond reach of tradition. Several have gradually crept into existence, without an inventor. The busy mind however, accustomed to a beginning in things, cannot rest till it find or imagine a beginning to every art."[33] Home discerned, again in the context of invention, the impact of this secularized origin theory on the historical imagination. By replacing the literal account of the Bible with a history of man based on a theoretical notion of social progress, he established a connection between cultural achievements and social organization. Quatremère extended the tradition exemplified by Home's three states of man by defining them as ultimately independent phenomena, not inter-connected stages in a linear sequence. More importantly, however, he incorporated the relationship of these states to the achievements of society as a constituent element of his architectural theory.

With varying degrees of immediacy, the efforts of these ethnographers constitute the background to the question posed by the Academy in 1785. In order to formulate his response, there-fore, Quatremère had to insert himself into this process of the rewriting of human history in the light of changes in theories of origins. The point of entry he chose was the work of de Pauw, who began the preliminary discourse to his *Recherches philosophiques sur les Chinois et les Egyptiens* as follows: "In this work we pro-pose to examine how far the ancient Egyptians resembled the modern Chinese, and in what points they differed from them. It is necessary on all such matters to enter into very considerable discussions; for those, who trust entirely to appearances, are in danger of experiencing continual illusions. The analogy sometimes supposed to exist between distant races of men, may readily prove fallacious, when more pains are taken to form systems than to make researches."[34] De Pauw did for the relationship between Chinese and Egyptian culture what Quatremère later did for Egyp-tian and Greek architecture: he discredited the notion of historical dependence by revealing differences in points of origin. In order to do so, he maintained that "when two nations are supposed to have a common origin, it is necessary to examine in what degree they cultivated the fine arts."[35] Thus, like many of his ethnographic predecessors, de Pauw turned to the artifacts of civilization for hard data in his analysis of the hypothetical question of origins. He emphasized the particular importance of architecture in this context, as had Goguet, devoting an entire chapter to "Considerations on the State of Egyptian and Chinese Architecture" and even including a discussion of the relationship between Egyptian and Greek building.[36]

The difference between Chinese and Egyptian primitive forms of building played a central role in de Pauw's effort to disassociate historically the two civilizations. De Pauw maintained that "many mistakes seem to have been propagated with regard to the model adopted for the first Egyptian houses." Criticizing Le Roy, he wrote: "Mr. Le Roy must be deceived when he pretends that the rustic shed had been adopted by the Egyptians, in the same manner that Vitruvius says it served among the Greeks, as a model for the most superb edifices on earth. Everything tends to prove that the Egyptians, prior to their being united as a nation, lived like Troglodytes in the caverns of Ethiopia. Thus a grotto, rather than a cottage, must have afforded the first notions of their architecture. The savages of Greece, on the contrary, from the diversity of soil and climate, which in such cases has a great influence, were under the necessity of erecting huts."[37] Although de Pauw was determined that Egyptian architecture derived from a cave while Greek architecture derived from a hut, he also maintained that

the Chinese evidently imitated the form of their tents. From all that we can learn of their primitive state, they were originally Nomades, or Scenites, like all the Tartars; and consequently encamped with their flocks, previous to their settlement in towns. This, without doubt gave rise to the singular construction of their present dwellings, where the roofs remain after the walls are thrown down, because they have no connexion with the timber-work. An inclosure of masonry had been made in this manner round the tents, to contain the cattle; and such was certainly the first step, leading from a pastoral and wandering life towards fixed habitations.[38]

Thus de Pauw isolated the origins of Egyptian, Chinese, and Greek architecture, ascribing to them respectively the form of caves, tents, and huts.[39] Moreover, he saw the source of the character of each civilization's developed architecture in these original forms. While from the tent de Pauw derived the principle of modern Chinese houses, from the Egyptian cave he "derived likewise all the characteristics of their architecture."[40]

De Pauw felt that because "the principal works erected by the Egyptians and Chinese [display] the essential difference of genius in the two nations," he could demonstrate that the two architectures were "diametrically opposed."[41] This radical view was based on a simple fragmentation of the traditional unity of the original dwelling, a disintegration that became of critical importance to Quatremère's theory of architecture. In fact, 35 years after having written his first *mémoire* on Egypt, Quatremère continued to be indebted to de Pauw's ideas. He wrote:

> The need to construct a systematic thesis of the origins of peoples and their arts has always led men to search for a fixed point of departure from which all knowledge derived. The desire is for nations to have succeeded one another (and this is inherent to the nature of analogy) like generations. Hence, just as they posit a first man, they want also to posit a primitive people to whom one can turn to find the origin of all other people and the source of all inventions.
>
> For a long time the Egyptians have been construed as this primitive people and it has been in Egypt that the roots of all knowledge, of all beliefs, of all the opinions that ever reigned in the world have been placed. Some have gone so far as to imagine connections even between Egypt and China.[42]

In de Pauw, Quatremère found a theory of primitive building that enabled him to detach Greek and Egyptian architecture at their very roots. This separation led Quatremère to discover an epigenetic view of mankind. Perhaps most importantly, the entire ethnographic tradition revealed to him a new and thoroughly flexible way of looking at history. Ultimately, Quatremère was to connect these ideas and to use ancient architecture as a way of describing a larger picture of the nature of man and his social institutions.

Etymological Science

Eighteenth-century ethnographic studies were often comparative analyses that were neither synchronic nor diachronic but related to essentially achronological speculations on origins. Data culled from the ancient world were the tools predominantly used by those seeking to reconstruct the beginnings of man. Although these materials were in fact old, they were intended to shed light less on the past than on the contemporary world, because the hypothetical nature of the search for origins had transformed the original into a conceptual rather than a chronological category.[43] One important consequence of this divorce of theoretical from actual origins was the beginning of a progressive disassociation of the passage of time from the notion of historical development. As primitive peoples came to mean those who lived in a state of nature rather than those who were temporally remote, the grip of chronology on the conception of history was loosened.[44]

While the Academy's question of 1785 was informed by this tradition, as well as by the emphasis it often placed on architecture and on Egyptian architecture in particular, Quatremère's essay delved into the tradition directly, finding corroborative evidence in it for his expanding concept of architecture and its relationship to society and social development. Moreover, he not only appropriated ethnography's secularizing approach to origin theory but, by 1803, had accepted its ultimately epigenetic conclusion. Integrating the speculative and ahistorical methods of writers such as Lafitau and Goguet with structural concepts like Home's three stages of man and de Pauw's association of the cave, tent, and hut with Egypt, China, and Greece, Quatremère arrived at a revolutionary theory of architectural origins.

The formulation of this theory in the published version

of his competition essay is a striking example of the development
and refinement of Quatremère's ideas between 1785 and 1803.
More important, however, is the fact that when he came to articulate his novel view of the origins of architecture he did so by
introducing elements of origin theory as they had been explored
with respect to language. Many ethnographers included language
in their analyses of culture, but eighteenth-century studies of language were themselves predominantly concerned with issues of
origins and, perhaps even more overtly than ethnography, with
the modification or rejection of scriptural history.[45] For example,
the ethnographer's secularized version of the Christian doctrine
of human uniformity was regarded by linguists as the purely theoretical and nontheological structure of universal grammar.[46]
Moreover, language studies generally played a central role in much
eighteenth-century philosophical inquiry and were the context
within which many of the most important developments in origin
theory took place.[47] It might even be said that the origin of language epitomized and encapsulated all other forms of genetic
inquiry.[48] By discussing architecture explicitly in relation to language theory, Quatremère participated in this increasingly urgent
and comprehensive search for origins.

The topicality of language studies encouraged Quatremère
to associate language with architecture, yet his recognition of an
essential social and functional parity between these two forms of
human expression was an even more important factor. Just as his
ability to speak distinguished man from beast, so did his ability
to construct his environment. Language and architecture played
similarly crucial roles in defining the character of man. Quatremère therefore considered theories regarding their origins to be
equally capable of shedding light on whether the genesis of man
had been sacred or profane. None of the works cited by Quatremère in *De l'architecture égyptienne* has language as its primary
subject, in part because such a focus was rare in the eighteenth
century. The centrality of issues concerning language is indicated
less by the number of texts devoted exclusively to the nascent
discipline of linguistics than by the number of widely disparate
books in which language was an aspect of critical inquiry. Quatre-

mère was able to use terminology typical of these studies, such as "universal grammar," "filiation," and "etymology," without feeling that his architectural audience needed to have the vocabulary defined. His appropriation of these terms reflects contemporary developments in the understanding of language that help to explain why the subject suddenly became useful to the study of architecture.

The first important transgression of the orthodox account of language as an act and gift of God came with the publication in 1660 of the *Grammaire générale et raisonnée*, commonly known as the Port-Royal Grammar.[49] While this work maintained ties with orthodoxy insofar as studies of grammar were still considered to be an aspect of theology, it applied to this tradition new rationalist means of analysis.[50] The Port-Royal Grammar tempered revelation theory with the notion that language reflected man's ability to reason: the result was a novel assertion that language was an invention of man.[51] Despite the fact that this mental capacity, which both preceded and permitted language, was itself considered of divine origin, the introduction of the model of man's mind meant that language could be approached as a rational creation. Informed by the Cartesian faith in the existence of general principles governing the operations of the universe, this rational or conventional theory broke with scriptural tradition in its belief that language was a wholly explicable phenomenon, created and thus penetrable by the human mind.[52]

Once language had become, to some degree, a philosophical problem rather than a matter of faith, the proponents of a sensationalist or organic theory began to explore and refine the Port-Royal suggestion that language was of human origin.[53] Condillac in particular argued that language was not "an inevitable and mechanical expression of man's mind," but the product of man's experience.[54] The empiricism of this approach suggested that language was not a static phenomenon but rather had an evolutionary and thus historical dimension. Attention then shifted to the development and thus to the origin of language. Finally, thorough, albeit conjectural, reconstructions of language in its original state became necessary. The ensuing speculations about the actual forms and functions of primitive language brought to the fore what had hitherto been a latent aspect of linguistic theory. Without relinquishing the importance of the relationship between language and reason emphasized by the rationalists, a new urgency was given to the problem of the relationship between language and society.[55]

The rare ancient discussions of the origins of language took place in the context of the origins of society.[56] The rationalists had expanded upon this tradition insofar as they attempted to achieve an understanding of the significance of language to contemporary man.[57] Cartesians, such as Géraud de Cordemoy, considered language to be an institution essential to society because it permitted rational discourse.[58] Rousseau gave an ironic twist to the rationalist tradition when he wrote that "if Men needed speech in order to learn how to think, they needed even more to know how to think in order to find the art of speech."[59] Thus he too maintained that language, in its reciprocal relationship with human thought and in its contribution to the development of human ideas, separated man from beast.

For Rousseau, language "belongs to man alone" and was "the first social institution."[60] Despite his typically provocative manner, questions he posed such as "which was the more necessary, an already united Society for the institution of Languages, or already invented Languages for the establishment of society," made an important contribution toward thinking of language in social terms.[61] His *Essay on the Origin of Languages* in particular, which contains a chapter called "The Relationship of Languages to Governments," has been called a parallel to his *Social Contract*.[62] Rousseau's perception of an interrelationship between language and society was a view shared by his contemporaries. For example, Antoine Court de Gébelin (1719–1784), author of the massive *Monde primitif*, wrote: "The effects of speech are inestimable; speech is the base of society and is the source of the benefits we derive from society. Through speech we manifest our needs, our fears, our pleasures, our knowledge, and through language we receive from others help, the counsel, the advice, and the information we need. It is by this means of communication that the

human species attains the degree of perfection to which it is susceptible. Without . . . [it], man, isolated, plunged in stupid lan-
guor, would be scarcely superior to animals."[63] Like Rousseau,
Court de Gébelin was interested in the way language actually functions to maintain human society and not only in the way language
reveals man's mastery of God-given reason. Similarly, the sensationalists sought an understanding of language that went beyond
the rationality of grammar to the role of language in man's social-
ization. No longer considered a mere aspect of society, language
was now seen as one of society's constituent elements.

While the simultaneous births of language and society had
been recognized since antiquity, their substantively parallel and
interdependent nature became of particular concern during the
eighteenth century.[64] Hypothetically reconstructing primitive language was often tantamount to envisioning the conditions of early
society. According to Rousseau, for example, primitive language
was fundamentally parallel to human organization in a state of
nature: it was "passionate" and directly expressed the emotional
needs of man without necessarily rational intervention.[65] The
social counterpart of this form of language was the biologically
determined nuclear family. Through an innate instinct toward
sociability and a desire for personal gain, this simple unit developed into a more complex state of social union. Simultaneously,
a language of arbitrary and social convention gradually replaced
one of action and gesture.

The difference between primitive and modern society
referred to by Rousseau had long been assumed but had not previously been coherently applied to language. During the seventeenth century, for example, the essential sociality and artificiality
of contemporary language was recognized, but not in relation to a
nonartificial or a chronologically distant form of language.[66] Since
its "natural" model was the innate rationality of man, language
was both artificial and atemporal. By the mid-eighteenth century
a profound change had taken place in the conception of human
rationality: it was now seen as a shift away from rather than a
defining characteristic of a natural state, and this change made it
possible to distinguish between primitive and modern society in

other than chronological terms. Finally, following the development of the notion of sociolinguistic evolution, this distinction was applied to the difference between natural and artificial language. According to this view, "natural" language was, in effect, onomatopoetic, presocial, and prehistoric, in opposition to "artificial" language, which was rational, conventional, and both socially and historically evolved.[67]

The increasing acceptance of a historical distinction between primitive language of gesture and involuntary sounds and the highly articulate speech of modern man encouraged the development of the modern science of etymology.[68] The *Encyclopédie*'s article on the subject defined etymology as that art that attempts "to go back to the source of words, to untangle the derivation, alteration, and disguises of these same words . . . and by this means to return them to their original simplicity." Etymology was predicated on the assumption that modern languages, while they consist in words that "have no necessary relation to what they express," developed from early languages of natural simplicity. This developmental model made it possible to scrutinize otherwise inexplicable aspects of language by a rational science or art that had clear principles and rules of operation. Because etymology continued to embrace the speculative theological as well as historical issues posed by theories of origins, the notion of linguistic naturalism became associated with divinity while linguistic artificiality was associated with man. Hence, rather than neutralizing the hypothetical questions of origins by subsuming them in a historically verifiable framework, the sacred or profane genesis of language remained an essential concern of etymology.

In the case of Court de Gébelin, an avid etymologist, his unshakable belief in the divine origin of language led him to reject the notion that it was fundamentally arbitrary. He conceded a distinction between primitive and postprimitive language, but the pervasiveness of his divnity precluded any possibility of an unnatural language, a point succinctly illustrated in the frontispiece to his *Histoire naturelle de la parole* (fig. 15).[69] With respect to the development of language he wrote:

Men understand each other according to the same principle

15. Antoine Court de Gébelin, *Histoire naturelle de la parole* (Paris, 1776), frontispiece, "Mercure conduit par l'Amour ou Invention du langage et de l'écriture"

used by animals when they cry to make known their needs, their sensations, and their desires.

The moment when words were used for the first time has been confused with later times when previously known words were used; a man beginning a society [differs from] a man existing in an already formed society, already in possession of a language to which he is obliged to conform. It is certain that in the latter example one can never discern a model found in nature; such a model is nowhere visible and one perceives only usage. This usage, which undergoes continuous variations, seems to be absolutely arbitrary. But one would nevertheless be mistaken if one concluded that this model did not exist and that words were arbitrary.[70]

Court de Gébelin thus used etymology to confront the apparent difference between natural and arbitrary language in order to prove the superficiality of this difference and to discredit any notion of a fundamental linguistic artificiality. The effort required greater specificity with respect to the analysis of language itself, however, and in this way etymological studies, even if they were theologically tendentious, contributed to the increasingly objective understanding of natural and artificial languages.[71]

Changes in attitudes toward language in general and the sensationalist conception of its structure in particular ultimately had a strong impact on the methods and implications of etymology. Condillac, for example, felt that the essential difference between arbitrary and natural language was related to the slow development of man's ideational capacity.[72] Like Court de Gébelin, Condillac described the gradual transformation of natural into arbitrary language, which he regarded as real progress. His emphasis on fundamental linguistic change brought about by sequential trans-formations in the operation of the mind introduced a temporal dimension to language.[73] In his view, modern language was the product of a structural evolution rather than of static natural principles. Unlike speculative theories on origins, which led to a form of etymology that could explain the systemic difference between natural and artificial language, with Condillac's emphasis on the development of language etymology became a tool for exploring the historical difference between primitive and modern language.[74]

Etymology's concern for the link between arbitrary and natural language made explicit the historical implications embedded in the controversy over theories of origins. Nevertheless, this new historicism remained influenced by the way in which the search for origins had separated history from factual and chronological specificity. Historical etymology might link a modern word to its primitive antecedent or construct what was called a filiation by tracing the connection between an entire modern language and its original source. Etymology might even describe the change from inarticulate to articulate speech in terms of either the lifetime of a child or the lifetime of a civilization. Historical analysis, once freed from chronology through its association with origin theory, could be applied to an infinitely collapsible and expandable time frame, and thus became thoroughly abstract.[75]

Because of the relationship between language and society, the evolution of language became a principal tool for establishing the historical development of civilization.[76] Court de Gébelin believed that "from the language of a people one can, in a word, paint [them] much more exactly than one can from their historical monuments; in language one can effortlessly trace the progress of the sciences and arts and the path of their development."[77] Similarly, the Président de Brosse, whose *Traité de la formation méchanique des langues et des principes physiques de l'étymologie* was one of the most important texts available on etymology, wrote: "The history of colonies and their movement across the surface of the earth is closely related to the history of languages. The best way to discover the origin of a nation is to follow, searching backward, the traces of its language and to compare these traces with the languages of other people with whom it is traditionally thought they had some contact."[78] Having established a fundamental connection between language and society, as well as an abstract and flexible view of history, etymology embraced the development of civilization as a whole and became the key to a comprehensive genealogy of human culture.

An important result of the inclusiveness of etymological

science was the linking of language theory to that of art.[79] Condillac, in the context of his studies of primitive man, conjoined aesthetic and linguistic theory when he described language and art in terms of social function: "The object of the first poetry is clear. When societies were first established men could not yet afford to concern themselves with pure embellishment, and the needs which had obliged them to come together limited their vision to those things that were useful or necessary to them. Poetry and music, therefore, were only cultivated to make known religion and laws. . . . This was the only means available since writing was not yet known. Moreover, all the monuments of antiquity prove that these arts, at their birth, were intended for the instruction of the people."[80] The recognition of their original unity and simultaneity made evident the role of language and art in the establishment and preservation of society. The study of art, understood as a social function, was no longer restricted to the identification of beauty with truth as established by canonical aesthetics.[81] Owing to this erosion of the traditional confines of artistic evaluation, the association of language and architecture took on special meaning. Architecture had often been distinguished and excluded from the fine arts because it was functional.[82] However, through their identification with language all the arts came to be considered essentially functional. In this context, the social and public utility that had hitherto obscured the artistic potential of architecture now served to clarify its linguistic potential. In fact, because language and architecture could be credited with making identical contributions to the definition, structure, and maintenance of society, Quatremère implicitly favored architecture as the most structurally articulate of all artistic phenomena.

The Transformation of Type

Quatremère's exploration of primitive building convinced him that architecture had a coherent system, which he defined as "the theory of the originating principle from which this art is born." He asserted, moreover, that "this idea of system is applicable to more than one kind of architecture and that each architecture can have its own."[83] For Quatremère, this concept was essential as well as universal and could therefore serve as the basis for what he called an architectural metaphysic, a notion he claimed to have invented and which has proven to be an enduring aspect of his influence. Part and parcel with this metaphysic was Quatremère's notion of architectural type, an idea that brought together much of his work on origins and consolidated many of his views on the fundamental interrelatedness of architecture, language, and society. The notion of type has long been associated with Jean-Nicolas-Louis Durand—who in fact never used the word—and with a functionalist notion of programmatic systems in design.[84] It was Quatremère, however, who introduced type into architectural theory, and his aim in doing so was to transform theoretical speculations about systems inherent in architecture into operative means for making architecture in the modern world.

Between 1785 and 1803, Quatremère pursued the original building until it dissolved into an abstract principle that operated in all places and directed the development of architecture in all times. As his belief in the universality of primitive architecture strengthened, his faith in the original building weakened. Contradicting a long and powerful tradition, Quatremère had held in his Prix Caylus essay that the primitive hut was not the single "source of all architecture of all people." Having challenged the theoretical tyranny of the primitive hut by positing it as only one of three primary architectural forms, he went on to challenge the historical tyranny of Egypt. By 1803, he was in fact no longer writing a historical account of Greek and Egyptian architecture because the lack of a single first building proved the fallaciousness of supposing "that there exists an architecture common to all people, an architecture that would have had an original location and that requires therefore nothing more than a genealogical unraveling."[85] Determining the chronological relationship between Greek and Egyptian building was of secondary importance in light of the fact that the two architectures were born of different seeds.[86]

These all-important germs Quatremère came to call types.[87] There were thus, he held, "three principal types . . . the tent, underground [caverns], and the hut or carpentry."[88] His description of the third type, the hut or carpentry, demonstrates that each type was itself multivalent and involved distinct sorts of material, form, and construction. Equally integral to Quatremère's definition of type was social organization, for it, along with physical conditions, determined which type was to take root. He wrote:

During their first stages, societies were necessarily divided between three ways of life. Nature, depending on the diversity of the countries in which these societies were located, presented each with one of these three states that today still distinguish different regions of the globe. Men were, depending on their various locations, either hunters, gatherers, or farmers. . . .

Hunters or fishermen would have had no need to build any habitation for a long period of time. They would have found it simpler to dig dwellings out of the earth or to take advantage of excavations already prepared by nature. . . . Gatherers, who moved constantly . . . would have been unable to use these dwellings hollowed by the hand of nature. A fixed habitation would have been useless; they needed mobile dwellings that could follow them: from this fact came, in all times, the use of tents.

Agriculture, by contrast, demands a life both active and sedentary. Agriculture must have suggested to men that they build more solid and fixed shelters. The farmer, moreover, living on his field and on what it produces, has provisions to store. The farmer needs a sure, commodious, healthy, and extensive dwelling. The wooden hut, with its roof, must have arisen quite soon.[89]

Type was thus the fruition of Quatremère's exploration of origin theory. Type was entirely speculative—he offers no historical or archaeological proof for his assertions—and was universal. According to Quatremère every architecture could be traced to one of three typological conditions. Type established a primary connection between architecture and society and, because of its triple form, adhered to an epigenetic view of man.

For Quatremère, type was not only a static architectural element, it was also an operative principle of creation. In his view, type was the single most important factor in the development of mature architecture. The hut, tent, and cave were "the three principal types from which all the different architectures known to us emanated."[90] Thus he wrote that "the essential type of carpentry, with all its constitutive parts, is found imprinted in the ensemble and in each detail of Greek architecture." Conversely he wrote of Egypt that "the particular character of its architecture reveals none of the forms or combinations of carpentry; in the end, Egyptian architecture was modeled on a type completely different from that of the Greeks, and that type was underground caves."[91] Finally he attributed the quality of "legerté" that distinguished Chinese architecture to the nature of the tent.[92]

Quatremère's notion of architectural type reflects a dramatic evolution in his thinking. Just as the concept's constituent elements were not clearly defined when he wrote his first text on architecture for the Prix Caylus in 1785, the word itself is used only once in that early work. In his *mémoire* Quatremère most commonly speaks of primitive building in descriptive terms such as architecture's "first origin," "first form," or "first models."[93] As part of his attempt to demonstrate that there was an evolutionary rather than only sequential relationship between architecture's "first" and later manifestations, he also referred to these same early forms as fetuses. This word certainly suggests the notion of development, yet at the same time its evocation of the anthropomorphic tradition in architecture restricts the growth to a linear and biologically or naturally determined development.[94] By contrast, Quatremère discusses the origins of sculpture in quite different terms: "It is reasonable to search in mummy cases for the first type of Egyptian figures. The desire to conserve and perpetuate the image of a man after his death inspired the idea of assimilating the body's envelope with the form it contained."[95] "Type" is here used to indicate that the development between primitive and mature form is the result not of nature but of an inspired idea and is an act of self-conscious creation.[96] Moreover, the creative act itself is presented as part of a process wherein social phenomena, in this case funerary rituals, are given permanent artistic expression.

Quatremère's most succinct definition of architectural type was not published until 1825, when he devoted an article to the idea in the final volume of the *Encyclopédie méthodique*.[97] The chronology of Quatremère's work on the *Encyclopédie* is difficult to determine and is therefore not a reliable gauge for tracing the refinement of his ideas. Nevertheless, using the *Encyclopédie méthodique* in concert with other publications that can be more precisely dated, it becomes clear that although the complete insertion of type into his metaphysics of architecture was a slow process, certain basic aspects of the concept were present even in his early work.[98] In the celebrated article on "Architecture" published in the first volume of the *Encyclopédie méthodique* in 1788, Quatremère is still very close to the ideas presented in his academic *mémoire*: he refers to Egyptian architecture as having had a double rather than singular origin, and in describing these origins he uses words such as *model* or *principle*.[99] Elsewhere in the same volume, however, he describes the tree as "the primitive type of the column, not the tree as it exists in nature, but the tree already cut and fashioined by carpentry."[100] Even at this early stage, Quatremère was already using *type* to describe the transformative power of man in the act of creation.

As Quatremère's use of the word *type* became more frequent and systematic it came to refer more exactly to the hut, the tent, and the cave, to the social configuration that accompanied

them, and most importantly to the character and mode of production of the architecture that resulted from this combination of
elements. Certain of the more sociological components of Quatremère's notion of type can be traced to thinkers such as Rousseau,
de Pauw, Home, and Vico. These authors, and many others, had
divided man into the three states of fishing, shepherding, and
farming and had also attempted to characterize the relevant kinds
of buildings. Aspects of the form and content of Quatremère's
theory of type can also be found in other eighteenth-century architectural texts. Laugier, for example, believed firmly in the determining role played by the primitive hut in the development of
classical architecture. In keeping with his naturalistic view of this
development, however, he referred to the hut not as a type but as
a model.[101] Rondelet, on the other hand, did use the word *type* in
the article on the art of building that Quatremère asked him to
write for the *Encyclopédie méthodique*. Their professional relationship suggests a correspondence of ideas, but their uses of the
word *type* subtly differ. Rondelet argued that "the different forms
of construction were architecture's first types."[102] He thus retained
the sense in which multiple types constitute the connecting thread
between primitive and mature architectures as well as the role that
construction played in establishing the connection. Because he
refers only to construction, however, he suggests, unlike Quatremère, that type was a purely structural and material phenomenon.
Taking the notion in the opposite direction, Viel de Saint-Maux
was concerned with the way in which architecture embodied the
mysterious types and symbols of divine attributes.[103] Francesco
Algarotti came closest to Quatremère's notion of type when he
asked, "Finally, where in the world can one find houses made by
the hand of nature that architects should use as an archetype?"[104]
Both Viel and Algarotti thus emphasized the need for human
intervention over and above the force of nature in the establishment and use of architectural types.

The word *type* had highly specific meaning for the eighteenth century. Diderot's *Encyclopédie* defines *type* first by giving
its Greek root: "the copy, image, or resemblance of some models."
Type and *model* are not simply interchangeable, however. Most of

the *Encyclopédie*'s article on type is devoted to an analysis of the signification of the term in theological, particularly scholastic, discourse. In this context, type is defined as "a symbol, a sign, or a figure of something yet to come. . . . Types are not simple conformities or analogies that nature makes between two otherwise different things, nor are they arbitrary images that are founded only on a casual resemblance between one thing and another. It is additionally necessary that God particularly intended to make a type and expressly declared that this type is in fact a type."[105] Thus type is not an arbitrary result of the force of nature but a correspondence created exclusively by divine intervention. More specifically, types were elements found in the Old Testament that prefigured the New Testament: the sacrifice of Abraham is, for example, the type of Christian redemption just as the brazen serpent is the type of the cross of the crucifixion.[106] The recurrence of these images proved the continuity between the Old and New Testaments and united them under one God. Types were prime evidence in favor of monogenesis and the universality of God's plan; the more types emerged, the more His plan was strengthened.[107]

Quatremère's use of the word *type* constitutes a radical secularization of this tradition.[108] In his case the plurality of types identified his epigenetic position, a notion completely at odds with Scholastic typology. Similarly, while types were traditionally used to reveal the divine source of creation—amongst Platonists, for example, the ideas of God were in fact the types of all created things—Quatremère's architectural types functioned by virtue of human invention. He also eliminated the theological implications of the historical component of the Scholastic definition of types. Critical to their religious meaning was that they come again and again throughout time: the recurrence of the original type, in whatever form, proved the steady control of God in historical continuity. Quatremère similarly applied this notion to explain the mechanisms of architectural continuity and to illuminate the relationship between past and present building: type revealed how the primitive hut developed into a stone temple. For Quatremère, however, that historical relationship was not determined by God or nature alone. Rather, applying the increasingly secular and atemporal interpretation of the history of man he had derived from ethnography, Quatremère used type to express an abstract notion of historical continuity in architecture produced by man.

By the next century, the divine resonance of type had been stilled to such a degree that the first definitions offered in dictionaries often referred to typographical character, a usage also derived from the Greek word for image or model but in the sense of an actual physical mark or sign.[109] This somewhat pedantic definition, however, was in fact related to the theological definition of type, and it was in the context of the hieroglyph that these two facets of type joined. The hieroglyph was at once a tangible sign and an expression of eternal divine principles. Hieroglyphics had been used as types in the Scholastic sense as images that were revelatory not of the continuity between the Old and New Testaments but between the entire pagan world and the Christian faith.[110] Kircher's studies of Egypt contain perhaps the best-known attempts to use hieroglyphs as proof of the omnipresence of God's plan. Central to his beliefs was the Neoplatonist notion of a correspondence of spiritual and earthly forces. This concept, however, now called attention not only to the meaning of the hieroglyph but to its physical form. Neoplatonic correspondences were manifest in the hieroglyph because it was an imitation of nature.[111]

By the eighteenth century the hieroglyph had become a subject of critical importance because it embraced the contemporary interest both in Egypt and in language. When Quatremère wrote his Prix Caylus essay almost every source available to him on Egypt contained discussions of the hieroglyph. As a result of this feverish, increasingly scientific interest, and long before they were finally deciphered, an antimystical and antihermetic interpretation of hieroglyphs had developed that explored their mimetic and linguistic qualities rather than their supposed revelatory nature.[112] Quatremère was deeply indebted to this development, and his descriptions of hieroglyphs reveal that his knowledge of them was not superficial. He was familiar with one of the most important texts on the subject, the *Divine Legation of*

Moses by the bishop of Gloucester, William Warburton. Quatremère was also undoubtedly aware of the central role hieroglyphs played in the work of Condillac, Court de Gébelin, and others.[113] Some of his expertise may have come from his cousin Etienne Quatremère, one of the most important contemporary orientalists whose work played a critical role in Champollion's eventual decipherment of hieroglyphs.[114] Quatremère's use of the antimystical method developed to analyze the hieroglyph in relation to Egyptian architecture produced a wealth of ideas that reinforced the connection he had discerned between architecture and language. Ultimately the hieroglyph would become for him a crystallized image of the relationship between the typological origins and linguistic essence of architecture.

Quatremère's view of the hieroglyph is in part revealed by his astonishing interpretation of Egyptian buildings covered in hieroglyphs: "With all their surfaces destined to receive inscriptions in symbolic characters, they must be regarded as enormous books always open for the education of the public. . . . All [Egyptian] monuments were a form of public library; their ornaments were legends. . . . These monuments were—utterly unmetaphorically—the depositories of the rites, dogmas, exploits, glory, in the end, of the philosophical or political history of the nation."[115] This passage is one of Quatremère's richest and most concisely formulated statements on the way in which architecture functions as a form of social expression, for in it buildings are conceived as legible books written for public consumption. Quatremère's architectural books of social history came into being when he exploited the contemporary understanding of hieroglyphs to alter and usurp the traditional metaphor of the book of nature. One of the metaphor's prime functions had been to convey the notion that the external characteristics of nature were revelatory of divine intent. In this sense, the natural world was a book written by God in symbolic or hieroglyphical characters.[116] The new, more profane view displaced the notion that nature and God were revealed through the hieroglyph. Despite the fact that he was a theologian, Warburton himself stressed the role of man in the development of hieroglyphs and recognized that they were, at least in part, institutional.[117] Although a natural language, hieroglyphs were nevertheless a human invention and therefore through them man was revealed. Integrating this understanding of the hieroglyph with his own view of architecture—a social artifact of neither natural nor divine origin—Quatremère presented architecture as a book written by man about mankind.[118]

The new metaphor deconsecrated architecture in the same way that hieroglyphs had been deconsecrated, while reemphasizing the fundamental likeness of language and architecture. Quatremère's description of these social institutions as established by man for his own preservation and advancement, and his suggestion that the architectural books were "open for the education of the public," were also dependent on a recently developed view that challenged the traditional theory that hieroglyphs were legible only to a few initiates. Warburton believed that although hieroglyphs were ultimately used for secrecy and the concealment of knowledge, they were not invented for that purpose. He argued that the Egyptians employed hieroglyphs "to record, openly and plainly, their laws, policies, public morals, and history; and in a word, all kinds of civil matters."[119] Warburton's idea is clearly echoed in Quatremère's description of hieroglyphs as expressions of "the philosophical or political history of the nation." For Quatremère, then, Egyptian hieroglyphs were directly linked not with God but with social institutions. Once the divinity of its origins and content were discredited, the hieroglyph and the architectural pages upon which it was written became public languages.

As the traditional emphasis on the sacred meaning of hieroglyphs waned, a new interest developed in the way in which they pictured objects in the natural world. Warburton explained that "what truly denotes a writing to be hieroglyphical is, that its marks are signs for things." He based his complex classification of different kinds of hieroglyphs on the various ways in which these signs represented nature.[120] Because of its figurative as distinct from its symbolic nature, the hieroglyph was often compared to Egyptian sculpture and was considered to be the principal form of Egyptian architectural ornament. Quatremère himself saw hieroglyphs as a form of bas-relief: "On the walls of the great Egyptian

temples one sees sculpted hieroglyphs . . . , a phenomenon that
represents fairly well what one means by bas-reliefs as a form of
architectural ornament."[121] Quatremère was also well aware, however, that *hieroglyph* technically meant "sacred character," and
that this definition had theological implications. His reading of
the hieroglyph as architectural decoration is another rejection of
the divine in art. Secularized in form, content, and function, the
hieroglyph became a linguistic and artistic mode of human expression that spoke above all of human concerns.

The notion of the book of architecture and the use of
hieroglyphic inscriptions as architectural ornament permitted a
metaphorical association of language with architecture. The relationship Quatremère perceived between hieroglyphs and architectural type, however, encouraged him to link language and
architecture in a way that was at once substantive and ametaphor-
ical. He believed that hieroglyphs were a frozen expression of the
moment during which art and language had had simultaneous and
identical births in drawing or, one might say, writing an image.
According to Quatremère, "it must be said that the arts of design
veritably owe and owed their origin to the needs of writing."[122]
Thus, because hieroglyphs, or "speaking pictures" as they were
called, embodied the first and purest act of translating ideas into
permanent form, they constitued images of the very birth of art.[123]
Moreover, rather than manifest a link between God and man, they
were essential signs of human creation and invention. In this sense,
the hieroglyph was the type of every work of art and the types of
architecture were themselves a form of hieroglyph. As a result,
Quatremère described Greek architecture as "imprinted" with the
types of carpentry and claimed that the constituent parts of the
primitive hut were "written" on Greek architecture in "the most
evident and least equivocal characters." Type and its meaning were
impressed on the book of architecture in a language "of form and
of line."

Quatremère's notion of type expressed his belief in the
epigenesis of architecture, its primary nature as a social institution, and reinforced his belief in the essential similarity of art and
language. His systematic negation of the divine provenance of these

various phenomena produced a man-made picture of intertwined social, intellectual, and artistic creation wherein the contractual basis of society is echoed by the abstract basis of language, art, and, most particulary, architecture. The most important aspect of Quatremère's theory of architectural type, however, and its most secular and abstract component, is the conception of history upon which it is predicated. Having relinquished the two normal modes of understanding historical continuity provided by the orthodox view of architecture as inspired by God and the theory of architecture universally modeled on the natural hut, he found an alternative historical framework for architectural typology in studies of language.

Hidden within speculative theories of the origin of language and of the relationship between its natural and artificial form was the question of how language developed historically. To confront this issue, linguists explored the growth of single languages within the framework of etymology and the relationship between different languages in terms of filiation. These two strategems established ways of describing the evolution of modern language that were divorced both from the typological history of the Bible and from the strictly linear march of chronological time. In his analysis of the relationship and relevance of original or historic architecture to that of his own time, Quatremère referred to the linguist's new approach to history. Exploiting the connection he had made between architecture and language, he constructed architectural etymologies and redefined the historical "filiation" of architecture.

Type was the framework within which Quatremère articulated his understanding of the history of architecture. In defining three types he invalidated chronology as a criterion for determining the relationship between Greek and Egyptian architecture. Rather, the hut, tent, and cave became themselves the criteria for constructing architectural filiations. On the basis of typological identity, Quatremère could define distinct "mother tongues" of architecture and could trace the etymology of their components.[124] Thus, Greek and Egyptian architecture were independent architectural languages, which made the borrowing of particular

"words" irrelevent. On the other hand, classical and Gothic architecture, their differences notwithstanding, sprang from the same
type and should therefore be seen as variant dialects of a single
language.[125] The distinction between a "mother tongue" such as
classical architecture and a derivative such as Gothic could be
made on the basis of type, for it demonstrated what was basic to
architecture and what was variable.[126]

Quatremère's use of type to distinguish what was innate to
architecture from its historical filiations was dependent on his
translation of universal grammar into a concept applicable to
architecture. According to him, language and architecture each
had innate operating systems such that "columns, cross beams,
capitals, and other things that are the natural elements of the art
of building are, consequently, and to all architectures throughout
the world, the same as the elements of universal grammar are to
diverse languages."[127] Thus, because there was a universal system
or grammar of architecture, a false impression of continuity
between architectures, notably Greek and Egyptian, was often
created. The true key to the identification of mother languages of
architecture and subsequent architectural variations or dialects
was the determination of typological origins.

Parallel to the way in which one could determine the
filiation of architectural languages and thereby correct prevalent
misconceptions, the "etymology" of individual elements of architecture and its decoration could be traced through reference to
type. For example, the traditional etymology of entasis that traced
the diminution of the column to its type in the tree was mistaken,
according to Quatremère. Rather, a correct etymological analysis
of the column revealed that its true type was the tree transformed
by man. Therefore, Quatremère argued that architecture's only
"natural etymology" was to be found in an artificially generated
typology "born from the fantasy of man alone."[128]

Quatremère's radical epigenetic typology assisted in toppling a
deeply entrenched historical view of the chronological relationship between Egyptian and Greek architecture and enabled other

abstract notions to control the construction of history. Quatremère pursued type, rather than chronology, as a means of relating Greek architecture to Egyptian, and more importantly modern building to that of the past. If type was one of the most important elements of the metaphysical dimension of his theory of architecture, embracing "the art's essence in particular," it resulted in what he hoped would be a practical dimension of theory that could "guide the artist in making and the public in judging works of art."[129] For Quatremère, the problem of the relationship between primitive and modern architecture was none other than the process of the transformation of type, a conceptual metamorphosis required each and every time a building was designed. As a result, architecture's past type became the key to its future and most importantly to its public legibility.

Quatremère's theory of type claimed an operative dimension because it determined not just the genesis of the world's first buildings but the geneses of every building: types became architecture in the same way that gestures became words. The development from natural to abstract speech could be traced from primitive to modern man but was also repeated and retraced during the lifetime of every child learning to speak. Similarly, type regulated the transformation of hut to temple that took place during the age between prehistory and the Parthenon, as well as the momentary transformation of the hut that produced, for example, the Ecole de Chirurgie.[130] Thus the growth of artificial language out of natural language had no temporal character, whether the language was verbal or architectural, and a modern reference to type, such as those embodied by most hutlike buildings of the eighteenth century with freestanding columns, did not imply a pessimistic enslavement to the past.[131]

The understanding of history implicit in Quatremère's notion of architectural type is fundamentally abstract and atemporal: time is collapsible and chronology is telescopic. Thus, while type revealed the historical dimension of all architecture, it did not, in Quatremère's view, produce architecture that was inherently historicist. Although he is often considered a mere imitator of Winckelmann, it was precisely in his conception of history and therefore of historicism in architecture that he differed most from the German theorist. Despite immense and heartily acknowledged respect for Winckelmann, Quatremère wrote: "However praise-worthy [Winckelmann's] *Histoire de l'art* may be, it still resembles a chronology more than it does a history."[132] Many years later Quatremère was making the same distinction between chronology and history when he expressed a longing for an architectural text that would be "simultaneously chronological, historical, theoreti-cal, and didactic; a work that could become the universal treatise of this art."[133]

Quatremère was not alone in his belief that every modern building is anticipated by and reflects back to its ancestral origin and in his belief that this interrelationship was fundamental to contemporary architecture. The immediate and practical impli-cations of eighteenth-century theories of origins were widespread but were particularly clear in architecture: the suggestion that hypothetical reconstructions of man's primitive dwellings were to be the basic generating element for modern design was a common-place of that period.[134] What distinguishes Quatremère's position is that he did not consider this process limited to the primitive hut and the classical tradition but inherent to architecture uni-versally. Such a determination was only possible after a new rela-tivism, based on the comparative model of ethnography and other social and historical sciences, had permitted the consideration of nonclassical architecture. This enlarged sphere of interest encour-aged Quatremère to search for a universal system of architecture, but more importantly it also encouraged an enlarged view of archi-tecture itself and, in particular, a wider appreciation of its social function.

The variety of sources Quatremère considered pertinent to his work manifests in itself an expansive view of architecture as one of many interdependent facets of culture. Moreover, the sources he chose consistently present an integrated view of culture and its artifacts, reinforcing his belief in the particularly social nature of architecture. Ethnographers had used architecture in their comparative analyses of man and his culture, and thinkers such as Condillac suggested a connection between architecture and

language. Benefiting from the interaction of all these ideas, Quatremère was able to assert not only that architecture had an important role in society but also that architecture, like language, was
itself a profoundly social institution.

With Quatremère's integration of new attitudes toward
history, language, and architecture, traditional theories about the
origins of building became an operative theory of architectural
typology. His view of the development of architecture differed
significantly from that of many of his contemporaries because it
implied a profane rather than divine origin of mankind, and
because it was defined in social terms. Most importantly, Quatremère maintained that those social terms were expressed mainly
through society's invention of a universal system that made of every
architecture a language. Quatremère believed even more urgently,
however, in the need to choose a particular architectural language
that articulated social concerns most precisely. The book of architecture and its typological hieroglyphs had to be legible to society
at large. Every distinct architectural tradition was equally conditioned by the universal system of architecture, but "it does not
necessarily follow that all . . . are equally beautiful and that none
are to be considered preferable."[135] As a result, after having transgressed the traditional boundaries of classicism in his search for
universals, Quatremère went on to search for the architecture that
spoke most accurately and eloquently of the nature of modern
society. This quest led him to reaffirm the classical tradition.

III

THE LANGUAGE OF
IMITATION

Architectural Imitation

Quatremère reformulated and enlarged the traditional definition of type by relating it to ideas developed by contemporary ethnographers and linguists. His semantic transposition described a new conception of the history of architecture in which the temporal and linear dimension of its evolution was suppressed. The fundamental connection between language and society inherent in his notion of type enabled him to stress the responsibility of man, rather than of divine intervention, in the creation of architecture. Quatremère's system of typology, however, effected a further and final change when it became the central element in the generation of a new theory of architectural imitation. This development began with his competition essay, yet imitation remained at the center of his interests even after *De l'architecture égyptienne* was published.[1] Quatremère's various analyses of mimesis reveal a progression of ideas that are parallel to and rooted in his evolving understanding of architecture as an articulate social phenomenon. The progression involved apparent paradox: the general focus of his thought went from the imitation of style to that of nature, but the end result was an unprecedented emphasis on abstraction.

Quatremère's first discussion of imitation focused on the Ciceronian notion of the transmission of style. In the fifth section of his *mémoire*, to which he gave the title "Of Greek Imitation," he discussed specific elements that the Greeks had stolen from Egyptian architecture and defined them as elements of "positive imitation."[2] Other writers such as Del Rosso and Belgrado had seized upon this stylistic continuity as evidence for a universal and singular development of architecture. At the same time, by distancing Greek architecture from nature and diminishing the

Greek role in the invention of the arts, Del Rosso and Belgrado hoped to call attention to Italianate traditions that were losing their absolute authority as stylistic models.[3] Quatremère, in contrast, excused the Greeks their detachment from nature and their consequent "larcenies" because they had submitted these stolen elements to reflection and criticism, and had thereby reduced them to principles. In the hands of the Greeks, the inelegant columnar colossi the Egyptians had copied directly from nature became the proportioned system of the orders, while the monotonous regularity of Egyptian temples became the rich forms of classical building indirectly parallel to nature in their variety. Thus, despite the fact that Greek architecture was somewhat further removed from nature than Egyptian architecture, in Quatremère's view a process of stylistic imitation characterized by rational reflection had enabled the Greeks to make clumsy Egyptian examples become "true models of beauty."

When Quatremère first articulated his admiration for Greek architecture in his academic *mémoire* of 1785, he despaired that contemporary building would ever be its equal.[4] Shortly thereafter, however, as he moved away from a strictly scholarly context in an effort to influence aesthetic standards, he became more optimistic. Speaking now directly to matters of design and to architects themselves, he started to emphasize evaluative and didactic aspects of this theory concerned with the imitation of style in the tradition of Winckelmann. In 1801 in the *Journal des batimens civils*, Quatremère published a venomous diatribe against those architects he felt were creating nothing but "reliquaries filled with the debris of antique monuments."[5] He proposed instead that they imitate "good Greek architecture." This directive had two stages: the determination of what constituted "good Greek architecture" and the definition of what constituted "good" imitation. First, he condemned the use of Roman architecture as a model for imitation because "Rome, poor but free, knew only the Rustic order of the Etruscans. Rome, opulent and enslaved, found insufficient riches even in the Corinthian order, the richest order of all. [Rome] demanded luxury as exaggerated as its power and the Composite, which vainly wants to be an order, became a monument to Rome's impotent pride." Denigrating the Roman heritage that had been the inspiration of architects since the Renaissance, he claimed that only Greek monuments of the Doric and Ionic orders were proper models.

Quatremère went on to argue that there were two ways to imitate Greek architecture: "one consists in imitating its style, the other in grasping *its principles and spirit*." He described the first form of imitation as "a mimicry able to do nothing but discredit the taste of those who do not know to unmask the imposture." Although he honored this method with the word *imitation*—later he would prefer the word *copy*—he gave his approval only to the second type. According to Quatremère this latter and uniquely valid means of imitation consisted in "penetrating the spirit [of Greek architecture], divining its reasons, deepening its principles, developing its means, discovering the secret routes through which it affects our soul, and in researching the causes of the grand impressions, simple and varied, that one experiences at the sight of its monuments." Thus, while at first glance it seemed that Quatremère was concerned with the imitation of styles generally, his opposition of "style" and "principles" reveals this not to be the case. Rather, he claimed that the rational principles that rendered Greek architecture exclusively worthy of admiration and imitation were features not of a stylistic but of a natural model: "In point of fact, to imitate Greek architecture is nothing other than to know and to imitate nature."[6] Exhorting contemporaries to stop being "slaves of the ancients," Quatremère proclaimed that the correct manner of imitating the correct model left by the Greeks would not leave the architect in despair but would render him "worthy of being associated and compared" with his antique counterpart.[7]

Quatremère's identification of the intrinsic nature of Greek architecture with nature itself played an important role in the development of his theory of imitation. On one level it reflects a move away from stylistic tradition and its symbolic or iconographic value in design to a new stress on the importance of nature. On a deeper level, however, it indicates a conceptual shift in the opposite direction, away from nature. A fully composed and highly articulated Greek temple can be considered natural only given a particularly abstract view of nature, one based on ideas of order and principle rather than physical matter. For Quatremère, Greek architecture was parallel to nature not because it was naturalistic but because it was rational.

Quatremère focused on style in his first discussions of architectural imitation partly in order to supply the clarification of the relationship between Greek and Egyptian architecture demanded by the Prix Caylus. He also gave some attention to an independent form of imitation that had produced the individual identities of Egyptian and Greek architecture, namely the imitation of nature. He argued that every architecture had a natural model in one of three possible forms of primitive dwelling. Although he devoted most of his attention to the stylistic relationship between Egyptian and Greek architecture, the imitation of nature actually played the dominant role in his analysis; the stylistic imitation of Egyptian architecture that had taken place in Greece had itself been made possible only by the degree to which both nations shared the natural model of the hut. Quatremère left the processes of mimesis relatively unexplored in his *mémoire* of 1785, and his analysis of the cave, tent, and hut was similarly undeveloped. Even at this early date, however, the relationship he sketched between primitive natural dwellings and their built counterparts was, at least implicitly, the real key to architecture's status as an art of imitation.

By the time *De l'architecture égyptienne* was published, Quatremère's understanding of the importance of the hut, tent, and cave had developed into a theory of type, and demonstrating the implicit role of those models in architectural imitation had become the explicit goal of his efforts. Most of the new material added to *De l'architecture égyptienne* is devoted to an analysis of imitation, a word he now used almost exclusively in the context of the imitation of nature and in discussing what he called the essential principles of architecture, rarely in describing formal or stylistic borrowings.[8] Although the imitation of nature was a principle that had differentiated and bound together the fine arts since antiquity, the role given to this form of mimesis in theories of architecture was often ambiguous. Architecture was frequently excluded from the ranks of the imitative arts, both because it was not representational and because it was functional. When architecture was considered to be imitative, the path to its natural model was almost always described as indirect: thus the human figure became the model of the orders through its reduction to a system of proportion, or a central plan imitated the divinity by reproducing its perfection through geometry. Although at times a more direct form of imitation was suggested, as with the phrase "the arms of the church," most architectural imitation was defined not by references to the physical presence or character of the natural world, but rather by analogy with the processes of nature itself.[9]

Attitudes toward imitation in the fine arts as a whole often fluctuated between a preference for direct mimesis, *natura naturata*, and for indirect mimesis, *natura naturans*. The inherent abstraction of architecture, however, lent itself most readily to the more abstract, indirect definition of imitation. The principle of *natura naturans* was of particular relevance to architecture since it was the only way nonfigurative building might attain the status of a fine art. In this context of idealized imitation, moreover, architecture's analogic relationship to nature not only raised building to the level of painting and sculpture, but actually elevated it beyond them. For example, in his *Histoire de l'art chez les anciens*, Winckelmann had given the following explanation of the peculiarities of architectural imitation:

> Sculpture and painting attained a level of perfection earlier than architecture did. The reason is that architecture is much more ideal than the other two. Architecture has no determinant object in nature that it must imitate: it is based on the general rules and laws of proportion. Sculpture and painting, having begun by simple imitation, found all their rules in the contemplation of man. This model encompassed all possible rules. Painting and sculpture thus had nothing to do, so to speak, but look and execute. Architecture was obliged to seek out its rules in the combination of countless proportions: an infinite number of operations was necessary for their discovery.[10]

If the goal of imitation was the abstract perfection of the "idéal," architecture achieved it more readily if perhaps more slowly than the other arts.[11] Algarotti, too, found an ironic advantage in the fact that architecture lacked a natural model. He argued that the figurative arts find examples on which to base a system of imitation in their physical surroundings quite easily. Architecture, in contrast, "must raise itself up with intellect and must derive a system of imitation from ideas about things that are the most universal and farthest from what can be seen by man. It is hence reasonable to say that architecture is to the arts what metaphysics is to the sciences."[12] Although at the time of the publication of the first edition of Diderot's *Encyclopédie* the inclusion of architecture amongst the imitative arts was still contested, the notion that the distinction of architectural mimesis lay in its ideal nature was part of a long-standing tradition.[13]

Heir to these ideas, Quatremère wrote that architecture, "apparently more enslaved by matter than the other two arts, is in fact more ideal, more intellectual, and more metaphysical than they are."[14] When Quatremère maintained that architecture only imitated nature "by transposing the qualities of its models into its own works," and that it was an art that "imitated no single form but rather imitated the spirit of those forms that surround it," he was repeating earlier declarations of the necessarily analogic nature of architectural imitation.[15] In fact, his classification of architecture according to the notion of *natura naturans*, his emphasis on the "idéal," and the distinction he made between architectural imitation and that of painting and sculpture were all dependent on earlier analyses of the subject. Yet Quatremère did not feel his ideas were conventional; on the contrary, he claimed that "this theory is, as I well know, utterly new."[16]

The novelty of Quatremère's theory of architectural imitation is due, in part, to its relationship to his theory of type, for he presented his trio of primitive dwellings not just as generic classes of original buildings but specifically as models for architectural mimesis. He wrote, "we have indeed seen that primitive dwellings, suggested by need, became everywhere a kind of model offered to the imitation of art."[17] His deconsecration of type, however, negated the traditional view of architectural imitation as

a terrestrial representation of divine ideas. Similarly, while related
to natural phenomena, types themselves were not intrinsically
naturalistic as he defined them—"but this model is not nature . . .
and one can only call an art that imitates nature an art of imitation."[18] Thus the principle of analogy as traditionally defined did
not suffice in a typological context, for although it explained the
detachment between an architectural model and its copy, the principle was predicated on nature as the referent, no matter how
removed or divinely inspired. The typological referents in Quatremère's theory of imitation, in contrast, were conceived of as
predominantly social constructs and were evaluated in terms of
their artificiality. Having been removed from the book of nature,
types now suggested a form of denatured imitation wherein both
model and copy were the products of rational invention.

Quatremère had already interpreted abstraction as a manifestation of reason when determining criteria for evaluating the
imitation of style. In the context of his understanding of the architectural imitation of nature, however, abstraction evolved from a
corollary and passive characteristic of architectural imitation to
its prerequisite and generating ideal. This shift was the key to
Quatremère's denigration of Egyptian architecture. He argued that
the caves from which Egyptian architecture derived were not like
nature, but were indeed natural, "hollowed out by the hand of
nature."[19] Even when constructed rather than found, the cave
remained a work of nature rather than of man: "Caves must have
presented such a finite and complete kind of model that imitation
had nothing to add and nowhere further to go. . . . Caves offered,
everywhere and in every sense, nothing but cold and smooth surfaces. Nothing [about caves] . . . presented either the reality or
even the idea of parts, relationships, divisions, and proportions.
The very objects that art thought up in order to correct this monotony—being fundamentally alien to the principle that created
them—reveal that no aspect even of the decoration of this architecture is necessary or based on reason."[20] Because of the complete
architectural replication made possible by the nature of the cave,
Egyptian architecture, normally considered closest to nature, was
in effect not mimetic at all. In a startling reversal of traditional

views of mimesis, having a model that could be found in nature became a congenital obstacle in the development of "true architectural imitation."

Chinese architecture, according to Quatremère, had also been unable to attain a veritably mimetic status, although its model, the tent, was manifestly unnatural. He condemned the model itself because it had "too many little things to imitate" and lacked the appearance of solidity necessary to full architectural expression.[21] However, the real basis of his criticism of Chinese architecture was its process of imitation. Quatremère maintained that there were two different ways for architecture to imitate, "one tangible, the other abstract. One is based on the first models of the original dwelling of each country, the other is based on a knowledge of the laws of nature and of the impressions our soul receives from perceiving relationships between objects."[22] Chinese architecture was born of the former process, wherein the primitive tent was simply duplicated. Almost total conformity, particularly with respect to materials and multiplicity of tiny details, characterized the relationship between the tent and its double.[23] Hence, a Chinese building was not an imitation but a copy made through a process of what might be called natural and therefore nonrational replication.

According to Quatremère, "veritable imitation" required an unnatural model constructed in adherence to the principles rather than the forms of nature and demanded a similarly abstract process through which the model became architecture. While the cave was disqualified on the former grounds and the tent was eliminated on the latter, the primitive hut met both criteria. Quatremère maintained that the hut was not a product of nature but of man's following the process of nature, which moved "slowly, by a series of almost imperceptible trials and repetitions."[24] He argued that "before the hut could become the type of Greek architecture, it was necessary for the hut to attain its own perfection. . . . The hut, without losing the simplicity of its first form, would have seen its supports, roof, porches, ceilings, and proportions successively combined, modified, embellished, and arranged with increasing refinement and elegance." Following this almost indis-

cernible progression that unfolded in analogical adherence to the
principles of nature, the "model attained the force and authority
of nature relative to the imitating art."[25] Invented not by nature
but like nature, the primitive hut was the first prerequisite to
architectural imitation.

The strongest argument for replacing the imitation of
ancient styles with the imitation of the primitive hut was made by
the Abbé Laugier in his *Essai sur l'architecture*. Laugier's resurrection of this ancient structure from the mythical past and his
presentation of it as the normative model for contemporary architecture was widely influential and affected Quatremère's theories
in particular.[26] By the time Quatremère wrote about architecture,
Laugier's reputation was such that Quatremère cited him again
and again in the context of architectural origins and imitation,
invoking him as a great authority. Yet although both Laugier and
Quatremère believed in the hut's potential to revitalize contemporary architecture, they differed fundamentally in their conceptions of the hut and its implications for architectural imitation.
For Laugier, the hut was a vehicle for the return to nature because
it was itself a model of natural simplicity: "All the splendors of
architecture ever conceived have been modeled on the little rustic
hut. . . . It is by approaching the simplicity of this first model that
fundamental mistakes are avoided and true perfection is achieved.
. . . Let us never lose sight of our little rustic hut."[27] Only by
adhering strictly to its forms, which dictated that "in an architectural order only the column, the entablature, and the pediment
may form an essential part of its composition," could the contemporary designer rid himself of the erroneous conventions and
distortions of nature that had come to misdirect the true path of
architecture.[28]

Quatremère, in contrast, went to great pains to refute the
notion that the hut was a natural model and argued instead that
"this model, however real or fictitious it may be, was itself already
a work of art."[29] Similarly, while in Laugier's opinion the great
virtue of the hut was its reproducibility, Quatremère felt its virtue
was its irreproducibility. The architect inspired by the hut was
forced to distance himself from his model because it eventually

became necessary to transpose wood into stone and tree trunks into orders. Quatremère maintained therefore that the Greeks "only considered this imitation of carpentry to be the skeleton of the art, a skeleton suited to being clothed with forms rationalized by proportions. . . . Carpentry was more the rough draft and less the model of this art. . . . [The Greeks] understood that pleasure, enemy of servitude, shook off the chains that might be imposed by an overly rigorous imitation of . . . form. From this understanding an ingenious metamorphosis was born that in this imitative system disguises the object imitated under a veil of invention and masks the truth with the appearance of fiction."[30] Just as the hut was an appropriate model for imitation because it was removed from a state of nature, the act of its duplication was mimetic because it necessitated the transposition of wooden forms into stone. This distinguishing and denaturalizing change indicated the presence of reason, and without it—as in the case of Egyptian architecture, where stone simply copied stone—there was no true imitation.

The dialogue between reality and illusion created by the relationship between wood and stone in Greek architecture fulfilled what Quatremère saw as the function of imitation because it gave the viewer the intellectual pleasure of being "fooled without being led into error."[31] This falsification of the model was not only the constituent element of imitation, but was an untruth through which imitation became a vehicle for honest architectural expression:

> In general the true aim of imitation is not to make a substitute so close to its model that the resemblance produces an identity capable of deception and of subterfuge. To the contrary, for us to enjoy imitation we must perceive that the imitating object is only the image of the imitated object. In effect, where either by an excess of factitious illusion or natural conformity one thinks one sees the imitated thing itself in the thing that imitates it, one no longer sees the image of this thing. And where one thinks one does not see the image of a thing, one thinks one does not see imitation. In fact, one does not see any [imitation].[32]

Mimetic architecture, in Quatremère's view, was not a natural phenomenon but rather an artificial invention, and this truth was articulated only when a tangible difference between model and counterfeit called attention to the absence of nature and therefore called attention to the presence of art.

The visible metamorphosis of wood into stone was the cornerstone of Quatremère's theory of imitation. His emphasis on this point, however, had the additional function of focusing attention on his refutation of Carlo Lodoli.[33] Lodoli had formulated a theory of architecture that celebrated a different conception of the medium's intrinsic nature and, more importantly, a different notion of truthful expression. By eliminating the role of imitation altogether, Lodoli aimed to exploit the distinguishing structural and material identity of architecture. He described an architecture that was naturalistic and therefore honest not by virtue of a representation of the human form, or by an imitation of the primitive hut, or even by any system of analogy, but by virtue of an unadulterated expression of its physical form.[34] Implicitly speaking of Lodoli, Quatremère wrote:

> There are many people who reproach architecture for having reduced itself to imitating the first constructions in wood. They find it wrong for stone to represent another material. They pity marble for being degraded by an inferior role, subjected as marble is to rendering the poor and miserable forms of the first huts. These people would prefer that each material drew from itself and from within its own nature the diversity of its forms. We have already demonstrated that stone, in copying itself or rather in not copying anything, offered to architecture neither form, visual variety, nor any relation to the spirit. This fact is proven by Egyptian architecture and by the cold, monotonous, and insipid nature of its elevations.[35]

For every measure of adherence to nature suggested by Lodoli, Quatremère countered with demands for detachment. Both sought the moral advantage of articulating truth in architecture, but only Quatremère believed that falsehood was integral to the process.

Quatremère maintained that Greek buildings were "friendly and truthful liars," and that they were mimetic works of art because they revealed themselves to be unnatural.[36] The didactic dimension of his theory of imitation was aimed at explaining how that revelation was made manifest, but what he called its moral dimension was aimed at demonstrating the meaning of this revelation. In each of its many guises, his conception of architectural imitation included an emphasis on the importance of abstraction, whether the imitation was of style or of nature. Abstraction was, in Quatremère's view, the physical manifestation of reason and the metaphysical manifestation of man. Human intelligence was necessary for the leap from trees to hut, for example, and from hut to temple. Thus, the invention of the hut, the development of carpentry, and their ideal representation in stone could alone make of architecture "a reasoned art."[37] While Quatremère's celebration of Greek rationalism was consistent with traditional theories of imitation, no one before him had moved so far from nature in order to celebrate the inherent abstraction of architecture and to use this abstraction as proof of the rational presence of man.

Speaking Pictures

The notion that imitation was the key to the way in which the fine arts conveyed meaning stemmed from antiquity. Classical literary and rhetorical theory had established a metaphorical connection between art and language by exploring the mimetic aspects of painting and poetry, a connection greatly developed during the Renaissance. As an even more consistent system of the arts was established during the eighteenth century, the ancient connection between painting and poetry was expanded to include a wider range of the visual arts. In general, however, the link between language and the fine arts remained, as it had been in antiquity, a metaphorical way of describing the expressive mechanisms of different media. Although informed by this traditional interest in the ways in which the arts of language and the visual arts had used imitation in order to create effect, Quatremère was equally interested in their structural identity. In his view, architecture was not merely like language but was itself a language.

Simonides is said to have been one of the first to associate verbal and visual forms of art. To him is attributed the notion that painting is mute poetry and poetry a speaking picture, a notion that indicates a common capacity for mimesis and expression.[38] This early association was reformulated in Horace's famous simile, *ut pictura poesis*. The creative misinterpretations this simile underwent in the Renaissance attempt to give to painting the status of a liberal art, long enjoyed by poetry, have been well documented.[39] Notwithstanding the polemical function of the reference to Horace, the principles of imitation thought to underlie his adage became an increasingly strong link between painting and poetry. As the transformations of the original meaning of *ut pictura poesis* continued, parallels came to be drawn between imitation in poetical language and even nongraphic media, such as music and dance.

Architecture was for the most part excluded from this tradition because its particular form of imitation did not accommodate the issues inferred from the conventions of *ut pictura poesis*, such as narrative and action. Nevertheless, architecture did come to be included in similes illuminating the relationship between various media. Although it was thought that architecture could not imitate the nature of man and his actions directly, it could imitate his form indirectly when translated into a system of proportion.[40] As architecture was increasingly seen to be equally though less directly mimetic as the other arts, it was more frequently included in metaphorical equations linking the visual arts to the arts of language. Eventually *ut pictura poesis* became *ut architectura poesis* and buildings, too, became speaking pictures.[41] The most patent example of the migration of literary theory first to painting and then to architecture is the chapter from Germain Boffrand's 1745 *Livre d'architecture* entitled "Architectural Principles Drawn from Horace's *Art of Poetry*." Boullée's discussions of the poetry of architecture, the celebrated epigram borrowed from Correggio with which he introduced his *Architecture: Essai sur l'art*—"And I too am a painter"—as well as the later classification of his work as "architecture parlante" belong, at least in part, in this context. Participant in this explosion of the originally more limited implications of *ut pictura poesis*, Quatremère claimed that imitation gave to architecture the "vivacity of poetry or of ocular music."[42]

The expressive conventions of rhetoric were another aspect of classical theories of the use of language that reinforced the connection between language and the fine arts and encouraged the extension of this association beyond the confines of painting and poetry.[43] Where the major concerns associated with *ut pictura poesis* tended to exclude architecture, rhetorical theory seemed to suggest architectural metaphors. For example, the rhetorician's concern for the most effective balance between structure and ornament was readily elucidated by architecture. Bernard Lamy wrote in his *Rhétorique ou l'art de parler* that the construction of discourse began with things that were like the "foundations of an edifice" and finished with the "ornaments of eloquence."[44] Although rhetoricians preceded architects in establishing this analogy between the use of ornament in language and in architecture, architects themselves quickly adopted the metaphor and it appears in writers as diverse as Perrault, Blondel, Boffrand, Algarotti, and Viel de Saint-Maux.[45] When Del Rosso in his competition for the Prix Caylus discussed the appropriate use of ornament, he too claimed that "variety is the source of pleasure: in discourse as in architecture, variety serves to divert the spirit as well as the sight."[46] In 1825, Quatremère himself was still arguing that "the forms, types, and details of Greek architecture . . . are nothing other than what words are, so to speak, to the art of writing."[47]

The notion became common that a well-ordered sentence was parallel to a well-ordered building because both were principled structures that supported applied ornament. As a result, parallels were made in the way architecture and language used their grammars and ornaments to produce different styles of eloquent discourse. Lamy wrote, "Vitruvius . . . remarked that temples were constructed with the order that expressed the character of the divinity to whom the temple was dedicated. . . . It is the same in discourse; the flowers and gentilities of eloquence would be inappropriate to a serious and majestic subject."[48] Similarly discussing the appropriate use of the orders, Algarotti maintains that their variety produces different styles parallel to those of rhetoric and suggests that "a minute and precise analysis of the basic rudiments of architectural grammar, so to speak, might well be able to unravel the arguments of the most subtle philosophy."[49] When Quatremère characterized the distinction between Egyptian and Greek architecture as parallel to the distinction between "the free language of prose and the language of poetry," he participated in this long rhetorical tradition.[50]

Through the conventions of literary and rhetorical theory, the reach of imitation expanded, and Simonides' speaking pictures ultimately included all of the various art media. This development was codified in an extraordinary fashion in a chart that categorized the arts in terms of the structure of their respective languages, included in the first volume of the *Encyclopédie méthodique*'s *Dictionnaire des Beaux-Arts:*

Arts or languages whose productions are transitory or instantaneous

The art of pantomine	Language of action
The art of speech	Language of articulated sounds
The art of music	Language of modulated sounds

Arts or languages whose productions are fixed and durable

The art of sculpture	Language of the imitation of forms and of all visible and palpable objects
The art of architecture	Language by means of the ingenious and signifying dispositions to which constructions are susceptible
The art of painting	Language by means of colors, disposed and applied with intelligence and intention on unified surfaces.[51]

This schematic classification of the languages of art according to medium is undoubtedly related to the tradition of *ut pictura poesis*. On the other hand, the analysis of the media here implies a concern that extends beyond the expressive possibilities of language in the *ut pictura poesis* tradition to include an interest in language itself. In fact, the ideation of the arts revealed in this chart, in Quatremère's work, and in the work of many of his contemporaries announces the intrusion into art theory of a different tradition in which imitation was used to explain the structure and expressiveness of language as such rather than its literary manifestations.[52]

Imitation was an important principle in eighteenth-century studies of language, for it was the key to distinguishing between artificial and natural language.[53] Natural language was mimetic in the most comprehensive sense and was composed of signs that reproduced nature, recreated its processes, or were natural phenomena themselves, and could be vocal, gestural, or visual. These "speaking pictures" expressed man's reflexive tendency to imitate the world around him and suggested that if language was a fundamental component of society, the instinct to imitate was its prerequisite and basic to man himself. Artificial language, likewise regardless of media but in sharp contrast to natural language, was defined by its arbitrary character, that is, by the fact that it did not reflect nature whether directly or indirectly. Instead, its operative principle was conventional agreement and its form was purely abstract. The Port-Royal Grammar had taken man's peculiar form of arbitrary communication out of the natural world by suggesting that artificial language was the product of reason, and was thus a rational invention, but this and subsequent theories of language did not eliminate the role of imitation in man's invention of language. In fact, because it imitated the operations of the mind, artificial language was considered to be no less mimetic than natural language.

The recognition of the invented and artificial quality of arbitrary language produced a new model for the mimetic process, human intellect itself, and imitation converted into a wholly unnatural and artificial phenomenon. The inclusion of intellect among the elements of imitation became the conceptual basis of the metaphor that "speech is a painting of our thoughts." Although popularized by the *Encyclopédie*, the metaphor was fully developed first by Lamy in his *Rhétorique ou l'art de parler*, the same work that we have seen contains many parallels between rhetoric and architecture.[54] The mimetic tradition with nature as its object, associated with painting, is in Lamy's metaphor transferred to the word, with thought as its object. Because words have an abstract model in reason, they themselves are similarly abstract and arbitrary in form. In this sense, every word, no matter how nonrepresentational and unhieroglyphic, imitates the mind and is therefore a speaking picture.

Quatremère believed that architecture was also a speaking picture, and his theory of imitation reveals that he felt it could speak in a language of either natural or artificial signs. While this notion was indebted to canonical literature on the fine arts, a more substantive debt to theories of language is suggested by the fact that Quatremère's concern was not for differences between verbal and visual media but for the structure underlying all languages: "In nature . . . there is a model common to all the arts. Consequently, there ought to be rules of imitation that are also common to all the arts. Such is the case with regard to the art of manifesting thought by sounds and by signs: universal grammar encompasses the laws of language as language—the property of the human species—and is based on a few principles derived from the laws of intelligence and of sensations. [Universal grammar] also encompasses the varieties and modifications that local and particular causes imprint on each country."[55] He maintained that both Egyptian and Greek architectures were languages governed by the laws of universal grammar, but that one was natural and the other artificial, owing to their distinct grammars of imitation. The particular structure of Egyptian architecture was that of a natural language: its buildings were the products of a mimetic retention of the natural form of the cave. Greek architecture obeyed the rules of artificial language: its model was a rational creation deliberately made manifest through an equally abstract process of imitation. Thus, while the differences between Egyptian and Greek architecture could be likened to differences between rhetorical styles, their structural differences were the same as those differentiating natural and artificial language.

Quatremère saw in the artificiality of Greek architecture not only a language of reason but also a language of convention.

The primary manifestation of the rational mimetic basis of Greek architecture was the fact that the image of its original wooden structure was never eradicated from later stone buildings. While reason dictated that the basic constitution of the primitive hut required a change in material when the type was made into permanent architecture, Quatremère maintained that convention suggested leaving this transformation visible:

> By attentively examining the principles of imitation of each art, one may perceive that certain pacts or contracts, which we call conventions, are made between the imitating art and the imitated nature, and between the art and the viewer. It is by means of these conventions that art produces the pleasures we have the right to expect from it.
>
> The art of architecture, which is an abstraction made of the intellectual or metaphysical imitation of nature in relation to which it can establish a system of principles and rules subject to reason, is, in its positive imitation, in truth nothing more than a composite of conventions.[56]

Not only was the visibility of the vestigial forms of the primitive hut conventional, in his view it was this conventionality that enabled the artificial processes of Greek imitation to carry meaning. Totally reversing the traditional naturalistic visions of the "little rustic cabin," Quatremère now used it as the starting point for a series of agreements among nature, the work of art, and its viewer that created an architecture of abstract convention, what Quatremère considered "intelligible" architecture.

Equally related to the principles of mimesis was Quatremère's perception of a social dimension in the progressive formal abstraction of conventional language. If imitation explained how the abstract operations of the mind were reflected by arbitrary sounds and signs, it also explained how the two were brought together in order to convey meaning. The rational model that underlay articulate speech also corresponded to the social agreement that related word and thought.[57] Thus, language was dependent on three forms of abstraction: its rational model, its artificial formal expression, and the conventional relationship between them. The collusion of these creative inventions had two types of meaning in social terms. First, the social agreement that joined them and enabled them to work in concert was thought to be the first and most essential of all social bonds. Second, their union also gave artificial language a semantic social function of greater import than the obvious exchange of simple facts: the artifices of language empowered words to penetrate higher levels of meaning and to convey the abstract conceptions necessary to civilized society.[58] While language was common to all societies, conventional language was necessary to developed societies. Permitted only by man's reason, the purely intellectual nature of the imitation inherent to artificial language gave to abstraction both a social function and a moral imperative.

Quatremère identified Egyptian and Greek architecture as natural and artificial languages respectively by using abstraction as a means of unifying theories of imitation in art and in language. In order further to substantiate this bond, he conflated the idea of architecture as language with another notion that had been widely explored by language theorists, the idea of progress.[59] While imitation was the element that distinguished natural from artificial language, for some, evolution was the thread that connected them. Court de Gébelin, for example, maintained that arbitrary language is a form of onomatopoetic speech no longer recognizable: "All objects are thus named by imitation or comparison. However, almost all names seem arbitrary . . . , and they unceasingly vary from one language to another. But this fact does not negate the truths we have just developed. Most names, originally imitative, have been imperceptibly altered such that one can no longer perceive their relation to the objects they designate, except with extreme attention."[60] Court de Gébelin's view that arbitrary language was genetically derived from natural language was deeply rooted in the contemporary debates concerning the origins of man and his institutions. In the context of imitation, however, this insistence on etymological continuity had a different impact: however defined, the connection between natural and arbitrary language created an association between linguistic naturalism and the primitive on the one hand and linguistic artificiality and the modern on the other.

It was generally accepted that primitive natural language and modern artificial language were opposites, but there was considerable debate about the value of the linguistic progress thereby implied. The controversy was summed up by Rousseau, who claimed: "Conventional language belongs to man alone. That is why man makes progress in good as well as in evil, and why animals do not."[61] For some, however, such as Condillac, the progress away from the natural language associated with man in a presocial state of nature was a distinctly negative phenomenon, for it weakened man's ability to express, and more significantly have access to, the purity of his first instincts.[62] Conversely, for others, including Quatremère himself, the artificiality of modern language was proof of the positive progress that had been achieved by man. He maintained that "during their infancy societies have ideas that are simple, and consequently language and writing, which are but paintings of ideas, are also simple. . . . As [societies] become increasingly complex, ideas, however simple they might have been, become compound. Languages of figures and writing in signs cease to be feasible because there are no longer a sufficient number of whole figures or complete signs to express all the combinations of thought. At this moment a reign of abstraction begins that has all the subtleties of metaphysics."[63] Because artificial language was the product of reason rather than of instinct, its development reflected an advance in man's ideational capacity. Moreover, rather than hinder social intercourse, artificial language was a principal unifying agent of society and an important contributor to human moral development. This view suggested that artificial language was not merely natural language transformed by social institutions but was itself a social institution.

Quatremère stated that the nature of the mimetic system of Greek architecture is written on its buildings "in such legible characters that nothing in the world can take away from or add to its moral evidentiality."[64] This artificiality alone constituted true imitation and gave to building the capacity for articulate speech. The naturalness of Egyptian architecture deprived its elements of specific meaning. When describing the possible origin of the Corinthian capital in Egypt, Quatremère wrote:

It would be hard to say that it had a particular significance in its country of origin. The intellectual language of architecture was never known to the Egyptians. How can one suppose that men who would indistinctly and promiscuously employ all kinds of capitals in the same building could have had the intention of expressing this or that quality by the use of this or that form, or this or that ornament? How can one suppose that they had finally conceived the idea of an order, which is to say of an assemblage of parts that are interrelated and in such harmony that they necessarily awaken an analogous and corresponding sensation in the soul of the spectator?[65]

The natural language of Egyptian architecture was limited to generalized emotive expressions of primordial instinct and involuntary impressions of solidity and grandeur.[66] The conventional and abstractly mimetic forms of ancient Greek architecture, on the other hand, could be structurally identified with artificial language—they could be deliberately written and they could be precisely read—and could thus enable architecture to fulfill its social function. The conventionality of Greek architecture gave it the moral content and social purpose of all intellectual and intelligible languages.[67]

The debate over the relative value of natural and artificial languages is also pertinent to the development of an interest in universal language. The recognition that languages had a social function and that some language was purely artificial led to many attempts to create totally new languages. Certain of these efforts aimed to reproduce the expressive directness of natural language, while others attempted to improve upon the artificial structure of conventional language.[68] Regardless of their particular form and theoretical basis, the phenomenon of these invented languages has two implications of great significance for Quatremère. They testify to the belief that man has the capacity to choose, even to create the language best adapted to his need for expression, and that if selected properly, this language would be universally meaningful. One could thus choose a picture rationally and make it speak of reason and of reason's universal social and moral consequence.

Translating these ideas into a theory of built form, Quatremère hoped to assist artists in perfecting "this kind of universal language and writing."[69] All architectural languages constituted expressive systems, which varied in character and in efficacy according to their intrinsic mimetic structures. Quatremère's combination of linguistic and architectural traditions thus reveals that his attempt to make classicism the architecture of the modern world was not based on authority of the ancients, the perfected beauty of the classical model, or its symbolic content. Instead, he saw classicism as a universal language of architecture because of its unique ability to express and encourage what he thought was superior moral and intellectual social development.

The Characters of Classicism

Quatremère was not the only theorist to connect architecture's development away from a state of nature with the development of architecture as a social institution, or to maintain that this shift was revealed by the development of architectural abstraction. In his *De l'usage et de l'abus de l'esprit philosophique*, Portalis had written: "Architecture might originally have been a purely imitative art. Two trees that formed an arbor gave the savage the idea of a hut, and this idea gave birth to the idea of a house. Grottoes constructed by nature furnished the first plan for vaults constructed by art. Beautiful trees placed one beside the other could have suggested the idea of our beautiful colonnades. But soon enough, as architecture grew along with our needs and our institutions, it came to belong more to society than it did to nature herself."[70] Quatremère, however, not only disagreed with specific elements of Portalis's description of the transformation of architecture into a social institution but also was dissatisfied by his superficial analysis of how that transformation took place.[71] Rather than simply observing a nexus between architecture and society, Quatremère hoped to penetrate its mechanisms.

The degree to which Quatremère developed a fundamentally social theory of architecture is revealed by the alterations he made to his essay on Egyptian architecture. He added a great deal of new material devoted to the theory of imitation, but added an almost equally large amount devoted to an analysis of Egyptian society. Preceding his preliminary discussion of mimesis in Egyptian architecture, Quatremère included the following new chapters: "Monarchical Government," "The Population of Egypt," "Devotion to Sepulture," and "Cult of the Divinity." Quatremère's analyses of all these aspects of Egyptian civilization parallel his understanding of the means of expression in Egyptian architecture. Indeed, the new chapters, far from being merely illustrative or introductory, provide the foundation upon which he based his theory of imitation.

Quatremère explained the essential formal characteristics of all Egyptian art in relation to some aspect of Egyptian society. The sacerdotal religion, with its invariable rites and constant quest for eternal authority, had its counterpart in the static form of Egyptian temples and the power-oriented nature of their decoration. Its government, also seeking eternal commemoration, demanded an architecture that was colossal and imposing, a demand that undermined the state's own wish for grandeur and created a resistance to progress and change. Great work forces and unlimited availability of stone led to construction techniques that were unimaginatively static and exhibited nothing more than what Quatremère called an "excess of solidity."[72] Not only did these social and political forces combine to condemn Egyptian architecture to a state of uniformity and perpetual monotony, but the architecture in turn functioned to reinforce the paralysis of its social context: "such is, in effect, the irresistible power of this principle of the preservation of society, the principle of immutability, once the principle is born and has fortified itself with the very elements of society."[73]

Quatremère increasingly focused on the hieroglyph as a way of demonstrating how religious, political, and other social structures could become obstacles in the realization of what he believed was the ideal form of imitative expression.[74] He maintained that all mimetic arts had been born of "primitive writing," which had to "lend its signs to the religious cult." In Egypt, however, this primitive writing had been used to consolidate and perpetuate authority, which resulted in the consecration not of meaning but of the signs themselves: "One can see, without even speaking of this or that religious belief that might have a spirit particularly opposed to the perfecting of the signs it adopts, that such signs receive an authority capable of impeding any kind of modification in their forms from the very sanctity of their use. . . . The force of use and the sanction of public respect attach sensations, memories, and relations to these signs that are of such a nature, that they cause an alteration of the sign to produce an alteration of the thing it signifies."[75] Compelled to conserve their original form because "these characters would have ceased to be legible as soon as they started to become imitative," the unchanging hieroglyph forced all Egyptian art to remain "in a kind of savage state."[76]

Quatremère drew a direct and specific correlation between Egyptian religion and the fossilization of Egyptian art through the concept of imitation as embodied by the hieroglyph, yet he was ultimately concerned with a more comprehensive view of Egyptian society and the way it had been opposed "to the emancipation of the imitative faculty in civilized man."[77] Although certain traditional aspects of mimetic theory depended on the retention of a model and therefore accommodated a certain degree of stasis, Quatremère's substitution of nature with an intellectual model had suggested in his mind the importance of change and of transformation. He developed a general theorem that equated, on the one hand, free intellectual development with social progress and true or "ideal" imitation in art and language and, on the other, intellectual immobility with social stagnation and "natural" imitation in art and language. Transferring the word *type* from its meaning as the social germ of architecture to a more comprehensive social germ, he wrote:

> When the type of society rests on a constant and inviolable respect for all that has been; when all institutions tend with all their energies toward the conservation of the social order and privilege the perpetuation of all practices while discrediting the spirit of innovation; when the germ of such a system is developed within a nation, or to say it better, when a nation has developed within such a system, the duration of its way of being seems necessarily eternal.
>
> With a people whose customs are thus constituted, works of art experience a kind of perfecting that differs radically from the perfection that is produced elsewhere by a taste and facility for change. Most noticeable is that the habit of following the forms used by predecessors acquires as much force in things of

little importance as it does in things that seem of great importance. It is for this reason that objects that served as primitive signs to the diverse languages of society stay continually the same. They subsist without alteration and are transmitted from age to age as faithfully as laws, mores, and institutions.[78]

An essentially conservative social type condemned every form of social language to a permanently savage and primitive state. Although frozen and infantilized, however, these natural languages were nevertheless languages and thus expressed the nature of their social context: indeed they were condemned directly and faithfully to mirror their stagnant context. More importantly, active as well as reactive, the arts ossified by society became themselves another factor contributing to the ossification of society.

Because part of Quatremère's goal in writing *De l'architecture égyptienne* was to discredit the growing tendency to give not only historical priority but even aesthetic approbation to Egyptian art, his analysis of the relationship between architecture and society concentrated on a negative demonstration: Egyptian art and architecture did not develop because they were inhibited by a restrictive social context. Quatremère explored the positive half of his argument, however, when his polemical thrust shifted to the situation of the arts in modern France. He did so with particular vehemence in his *Considérations sur les arts du dessin* of 1791, a controversial work that contributed significantly to the Revolutionary overhaul of French art academies. Using the same method of analysis he had first developed for the Prix Caylus, Quatremère began his *Considérations* by demonstrating the inevitable correspondence between the arts and their social context in general terms before moving on to a specific discussion of contemporary art.[79] Quatremère's goal was to reveal the implications, both artistic and social, of the "counterrevolution" he said was constituted by the replacement of enslaved hieroglyphical writing with an alphabet. While the invention of primitive language was part of the revolution that produced society, the invention of artificial language was counterrevolutionary because it was symptomatic of the creation of yet a "new order of things."

Artificial language was created when complete social

emancipation—counterrevolution—had enabled abstract concepts such as that of moral freedom to develop.[80] Because of its unique capacity to convey such abstractions, artificial language became a vehicle for the dissemination of ideas that were the foundation of what Quatremère considered morally civilized society, and so became a truly hieroglyphical or sacred means of expression. The arts, equal participants in this transformation, now free to discover the "beau idéal" and become "depositories of the glory of peoples, became their historians; in fact the arts served society in all the ways that the most eloquent and energetic language serves society."[81] As the final result of this counterrevolution, monuments, statues, and paintings became veritable forms of speaking and writing and the arts, "joined to all civil, political, and religious acts," were incorporated with "all the needs of the social order."[82]

Quatremère maintained that the relation between the fine arts and the essential needs of society was "the first and the strongest productive moral cause of the arts." Not stopping with the influence of society on the arts, Quatremère also demonstrated the way in which the arts "favor society just as strongly."[83] With respect to religion, for example, posthieroglyphical arts no longer lowered God to the level of man by reducing Him to an image of the human form but were able to "elevate man to the level of God" by articulating His moral essence. On the relationship between art and political structure, Quatremère wrote: "I do not wish to speak here of the moral action of government on the spirit of men, an incontestable action that is visible to everyone and can be placed in the realm of the primary influences on the arts. The government that provides all human faculties with the greatest resources is one that rests on the true principles of liberty. But a free government can develop forms that are more or less favorable to the arts of design. The form most propitious for their success is doubtless the popular or democratic form."[84] Finally, having revealed the freedom to develop that the arts acquired "when the people are king," Quatremère suggests how the arts return the favor, fulfilling social functions by presenting tangible signs of equality, moral virtue, and metaphysical truth.

Before concluding his general discussion of the potential benefits of an "intimate connection between the arts of design and all the needs of society, religion, and politics," Quatremère wrote: "I just noticed that without thinking I have almost traced the image of Greece."[85] He thus understood the aesthetic perfection attained by Greek architecture as a function of its relation to an ideal social and political system, one based on moral freedom and popular democracy. By the end of the eighteenth century the connection between architecture and society was frequently made, and not only by partisans of Quatremère's pro-Hellenic point of view.[86] The pared-down classicism of late-eighteenth-century France, for example, has been linked to efforts to coopt for contemporary social purposes references to the *virtù* associated with Republican Rome.[87] Quatremère was far from drawing relatively casual comparisons between art and society or supporting a modern classical revival merely in terms of its appropriate political iconography. Just as he had deepened the link between language and architecture from metaphor to structure, he deepened the relationship between architecture and society from passive mutual reflection to active mutual influence.

Long before the Prix Caylus competition of 1785, the longevity, stability, and vast realm of the Egyptian government was frequently associated with what was perceived as a relative lack of change in Egyptian styles of art and the consistently large scale of their monuments. These factors were seen in a negative light, as crutches that in the end obstructed the development of refined art practice. In 1749 the Comte de Caylus maintained that the Greeks were unable to imitate the Egyptians with regard to "grandeur and solidity":

> The separation of a large number of republics and small states did not allow them to execute enterprises as large as [those in Egypt] and the Greeks wisely remained within their means. I attribute the difference between their operations to this need. Had [the Greeks] been opulent, I think they would have done what the Persians did, which is to say that they would have imitated their models without restriction. A large building mass is always impressive; it is like a colossal figure from which one

does not demand finesse. Great expense or force is sufficient to make it commendable in the eyes of men. . . .

The buildings of the first Greeks were proportioned to their opulence. Their smallness demanded efforts that in the end became a means to perfection and did so all the more because so many things combined to arrive at this goal: religion, exercises, spectacles, and most importantly, the honor of each city that prided itself on and devoted itself to prevailing over other Greek cities by urging its citizens to distinguish themselves by some aspect of the arts or by some virtue. In fact [art and virtue] went hand in hand in the spirit of these people.[88]

Echoing Caylus, Quatremère contrasted the Egyptian government's quest for domineering scale with the Greek republics' quest for "beauty rather than immensity in their buildings; [they sought] that moral grandeur that comes from art and belongs to proportions rather than [a grandeur] that is merely linear and that dispenses with taste and results in a mass."[89] More important to Quatremère than Caylus's descriptive parallel between government and architecture, however, was the degree to which Caylus determined a cause-and-effect relationship between them. Caylus states quite clearly that had the Greek republics not existed, the development of Greek architecture would have taken a quite different path. This conclusion differs dramatically from the more common belief, expressed by Del Rosso for example, that Greek art developed the way it did because the Greeks had been somehow preternaturally endowed with perfect taste. Caylus had begun to see a social dimension in Greek architecture—not in the buildings as mirrors of society, but in the buildings as elements of society.

Quatremère's interest in the structural relationship between architecture and society was also encouraged by the development of an unprecedented emphasis on the role of originality and creative imagination in the fine arts. Ironically, while Claude Perrault was the first to explore the social contingency of architecture when he differentiated between positive and arbitrary beauty in the preface to his *Ordonnance* of 1683, he used the distinction to emphasize the need for strict controls over individual expression.[90] Yet as a belief in the general benefit to art of enlightened social mores grew, artistic freedom was increasingly associated with political and civil liberties. Winckelmann, for example, wrote that "the Greek constitution and government were very favorable for art; [art] arose and was perfected under the shadow of liberty that always flourished in Greece."[91] In Egypt, on the other hand, where religion and government were consolidated and together dictated and controlled the arts, only specifically sanctioned modes and subjects of representation were permitted. As a result, according to Winckelmann, innovation and development were impossible.[92]

Piranesi's work constitutes the most influential demand for artistic freedom of invention made during the eighteenth century.[93] Although Piranesi was a determined anti-Hellene, Quatremère regularly cited this "illustrious draftsman" as an authority on classical architecture in the *Encyclopédie méthodique,* and turned to him specifically when attempting to demonstrate the "fertility" displayed by the ancients in designing capitals.[94] It has been suggested that some of Piranesi's engravings, notably those of the *Carceri,* were pointedly political in content, and it seems logical to assume that Piranesi noted some correlation between civil law and liberty on the one hand and artistic law and liberty on the other.[95] These various traditions come together in Belgrado's essay on Egyptian architecture, a work clearly indebted to Piranesi's pro-Italic campaign. Combining Piranesi's emphasis on unfettered imagination with his own interpretation of Egyptian political structure, Belgrado proclaimed that the fecundity of Egyptian architects was due to their freedom from strict principle and overly numerous laws.[96]

Perhaps the greatest impetus given to the development of a social theory of architecture came from the growing belief in the interdependence of all aspects of culture. Viel de Saint-Maux succinctly articulated this thought when he wrote that "among ancient people everything was inseparably interconnected; the cult, culture, legislation, commerce, arts and sciences, objects presented by nature; all these causes . . . came to be arranged and came into correspondence on their monuments."[97] This comprehensive view of culture was itself part of an increasing concern for distinguishing between the natural conditions of civilization and civilization itself. Of crucial importance to this debate was the precise delineation of the influence of climate, a natural and universal yet variable condition. Montesquieu's *De l'esprit des lois*, published in 1748, was the first systematic exploration of the fundamental link between climate and social, political, and cultural structure and was of great importance for Quatremère. In fact, immediately preceding the brief but important chapters manifestly concerned with social structure that Quatremère added to *De l'architecture égyptienne*, he introduced a new section on what he considered to be an even more basic subject, "On the Egyptian Climate."

Quatremère's interest in the relationship between natural conditions such as climate and art was no doubt equally inspired by Winckelmann's lengthy analysis in his *Histoire de l'art chez les anciens*. Quatremère frequently recalled statements by Winckelmann such as "Greek soil was the best suited to planting the seeds of art and Greek sky the best suited to helping it germinate."[98] Winckelmann was less hyperbolic, however, when he considered climate in terms of Condillac's emphasis on the relationship between sensory perception and intellection. After a discussion of the general importance of climate and its influence on the body's physiognomy—he was particularly concerned for the effect of climate on the organs of speech, in which he saw the causes of the world's different languages—Winckelmann turned to the impact of climate on man's "way of thinking." While the correspondence he saw between nature and man's processes of intellection might suggest that he gave natural forces an absolute and comprehensive control over the human condition, he in fact wrote: "One can easily enough conceive how climate can greatly influence the organic temperament and constitution of men. It is no more difficult to understand how it influences their way of thinking, always modified by external circumstances, notably the education, constitution, and government particular to each people."[99] According to Winckelmann, nature's direct influence on the internal operations of man is conditioned by distinct and external social forces. Although Winckelmann thus observed that physical circumstances and social institutions interact, it was Quatremère who integrated this observation with a theory of art. The result was the difference between Winckelmann's opinion that Egyptian figurative art was deficient because Egyptian people were physically unappealing and Quatremère's belief that a conservative social type had blocked the development of all Egyptian art.[100]

Equally important for Quatremère was the eminent German aesthetician Johann Georg Sulzer, who published selected excerpts of his *Allgemeine Theorie der schönen Künste* in supplements to the *Encyclopédie*, notably entries on "beaux-arts" and "architecture."[101] Although Quatremère never turned to pure aesthetics from a prescriptive art theory rooted in a practical and didactic tradition, he did share certain precepts with Sulzer.[102] For example, Sulzer presented a universalizing and epigenetic view of the origins of architecture: "The origins of architecture reaches back into the most distant times and must not be sought in a single country. It would be agreeable as well as instructive to be able to see before one's eyes the principal kinds of architectural taste, [which could be done] by collecting the designs of important buildings from various nations that cultivated this art without having communicated with one another. This would certainly shed light on the national character of these people. One would no doubt find the same principles everywhere, while the manner of their application would vary significantly."[103] Although Sulzer did not use the vocabulary of universal grammar Quatremère employed, both adhered to its principles in distinguishing between the innate operations of architecture and the peculiarities of individual architectural traditions.

An important aspect of Sulzer's aesthetics involved the relationship between art and society. While he often devoted more attention than Quatremère did to the social role and status of the artist, both believed that the arts themselves had a social function. First, like Quatremère, Sulzer conceived of society as based on contractual union: "What could be more essential in conducting man to happiness and to the principal object of his destination than social ties? Now it happens that these ties are due to the mutual amenities that men procure for themselves." One product of this social framework, according to Sulzer, was the work of art, which did not constitute simply an "extra amenity" but rather a vehicle for "a more noble figure, a character raised closer to our spirit and our heart."[104] Second, although for the most part Sulzer used a biological metaphor to elucidate his views, he also turned to language: "But that which merits more particular attention on the part of those in whose care is confided the happiness of citizens is language, that most important and universal instrument of our principal operations. Nothing is more prejudicial to a nation than a barbaric language, a [language] that is hard and incapable of well rendering the delicacy of sentiment and finesse of thought. Reason and taste are formed and develop in proportion to the perfecting of language, because language is ultimately nothing more than reason and taste transformed into palpable signs."[105] Both Sulzer and Quatremère established a connection among language, art, and society in terms of their mutual moral influence, and assessed their perfection in relation to their rational structure.

Finally Sulzer also argued that the capacity of the fine arts to provide moral edification required a certain political structure in order to flourish: "Because the fine arts should, according to their essence and their nature, serve as a means of increasing and assuring the happiness of men, it is . . . necessary that they penetrate all the way to the humble cabin of the lowliest citizens. The care of directing their use and of determining their purpose must enter the political system and be one of the state administration's essential goals."[106] Works of art, if properly protected and encouraged by a state that left them free to penetrate every social class, could articulate "certain fundamental maxims, certain directive notions that are like the base of the national character."[107] Yet, insofar as Sulzer maintained that the arts needed the artificial assistance and protection of political systems, he implied that the arts were not themselves a social institution and were less fundamental than, indeed were dependent on, social institutions. Quatremère, in contrast, despite the fact that he held clearly defined ideals with respect to both architecture and society, sought to reveal their inner connection and thereby to demonstrate their complete interdependence.

Quatremère presented his view of the relationship between natural and artificial conditions, between society and art, and between art and expression most systematically in his article on character published in the first volume of the architectural dictionary in the *Encyclopédie méthodique.* By the late eighteenth century, character was a subject commonly addressed by architectural theory.[108] Quatremère, however, considered architectural character as the capstone on a pyramid of related and mutually supportive types of character each created by a complex interaction between nature and society. This rich matrix, moreover, was not only the origin of character in theoretical terms but also provided the key to its production in practical terms. Character in architecture was achieved when society succeeded in diminishing its subjugation to natural conditions, both moral and physical. For Quatremère, therefore, character in its highest form was parallel to and only expressible by an artificial language of architecture. This language consisted in a socially coordinated system of conventions, and its characters enabled the architect to endow his buildings with intelligible meaning.

Quatremère prefaced his article on character, the most dense and complex of all his writings on architecture, by a preliminary definition of terms, beginning with the etymology of the word itself.[109] He traced a shift in meaning from literal character, an incised mark reproducing a skeletal image of a physical object, to figurative character, something that indicates "the nature of beings in a manner distinctive and proper to each one."[110] Within the scope of this figurative definition, Quatremère distinguished between physical or visible character and moral or intellectual character. Both are general categories and each encompasses three more specific subcategories of character: the essential, the distinctive or accidental, and the relative. Essential physical character refers to the elemental divisions of nature, such as vegetable, animal, or mineral. Distinctive or accidental character refers to physical differences between members of the same species. Relative physical character refers to a more specific indication of the natural ability inherent to a particular order of being. Similarly, essential moral character refers to the basic behavior patterns of any given species. Distinctive moral character refers to local modifications of those behavior patterns and relative moral character refers to a direct correlation between what something is and what it ought or appears to be. In conclusion, Quatremère maintained that the essential, distinctive, and relative characters of either moral or physical aspects of being are synonymous to force and grandeur, physiognomy or originality, and propriety or "convenance" respectively.

Quatremère devoted the first analytic section of his article to the physical characters of nature. This was by no means an unprecedented field of inquiry but had long since been of interest to garden theorists, such as Claude Henri Watelet, who had catalogued all the characters of nature from the sublime to the "cheerful."[111] Like Watelet, Quatremère believed that the essential character of nature, its force and grandeur, is revealed only by the rare landscape that is full of variety and offers a succession of unexpected vistas of marked contrast—only by a picturesque landscape, in effect.[112] Quatremère, however, was not really interested in nature as such nor in its potential range of expression; in fact, he maintained that nature has no character at all, for the most part. His concern, rather, was to underscore the infrequency with which nature produced the three types of character he had defined. Nature is inexplicably reluctant to combine its tools, such as material, temperature, time, etc., and create the essential character visible in a picturesque landscape. Only on rare occasions does it use those tools to modify itself and produce distinctive character. Although nature is uniformly varied, it must make a particular and concerted effort to impress upon an object or substance a distinctive physiognomy and to endow it with "a particular and remarkable variety." Neither essential nor distinctive character is commonly present in natural phenomena because nature itself seems to impede their development. Relative character is even more infrequent and more dependent on nature's coordination of its own elements. Rarely does nature, in Quatremère's opinion, provide a thing or being of its own creation with a perfect correspondence between exterior form and intrinsic properties and hence provide it with a relative character.

Quatremère began his article with an analysis of the characters of nature because they are decisive for the creation of characters in the unnatural phenomena on which the rest of the essay focuses—society, art, and architecture. The analysis itself, however, suggests that nature does not necessarily constitute a guaranteed starting point for the creation of character, since only when nature harnesses all of its elements does it produce essential, distinctive, or relative character. Instead, Quatremère used his discussion of nature to establish as axiomatic that the three characters are interdependent. Moreover, having emphasized the various ways nature works with or against itself to create and then modify its own production, he revealed that the true point of departure in his exploration of character, like most other fundamental elements in his theory of architecture, is the notion of artifice: character in nature is in fact nature's work of art.

Quatremère explored how combative yet interdependent natural and artificial forces produce moral as well as physical character, in society, in individuals, and finally in all arts of design, "regardless of the language of the different arts, whether it consists in words or in sounds, in colors or in forms."[113] The battle for dominance between nature and society is in fact characteristic of the language of art in general and of architecture in particular. He maintained that

> whatever subaltern and incidental causes may contribute to the formation of the general character of each architecture, I can give no other definition than to refer to the cause of the primordial action of nature. [I must] add, nevertheless, an indirect action of this same nature and a direct action of society, albeit always subordinate to the former. I would say that the architectural character of different people consists *in a way of being, in a conformation necessitated by physical needs and moral*

habits. In this conformation are painted the climate, the ideas, the mores, the tastes, the pleasure, and the very character of each people.[114]

The character of architecture is thus apparently most dependent on nature. Nature, however, according to Quatremère himself, generally has no character. Rather, the "direct action of society" must first lead to the discovery of a character in nature on the basis of which society can then create character in architecture.

The two steps society takes in order to establish the character of its architecture are synonymous with type and imitation. In building his first habitation, primitive man is dependent on natural providence, yet the structure and needs of his society determine how he will manipulate his environment. Similarly, the early developmental steps taken by all architecture consist in imitations and largely faithful reproductions of nature. Society, however, controls the processes of imitation and may ultimately allow architecture to depart from its natural model. Combining the indirect influences of type and imitation, society is able to overcome the lack of character in nature. Once having done so, society is able to create character in architecture. Thus, just as Quatremère considered character in nature to be nature's work of art, he considered character in architecture to be society's work of art.

Quatremère believed that the character of architecture and the language of architecture were related. Both were products of universal social phenomena and were inherent to any form built by man: every architecture constituted a language and every architecture had character. Quatremère maintained that the intelligence of man, rather than only the capriciousness of nature, could always be discerned in the "multiplicity of forms imagined by the different families of men that populate the globe for the construction or embellishment of their dwellings."[115] On the other hand, the degree of intelligence manifested by a language of architecture was determined specifically by its relative character.[116] According to Quatremère, the "art of relative characterization" demands rendering "perceptible by material forms the intellectual qualities and the moral ideas that can be expressed in buildings. Or, by the accord and propriety of all the constituent parts of a building, to make its nature, its suitability, its use, and its function known."[117] Because relative character is a "sign that indicates what a building is or ought to be," it is that which impresses intelligible meaning, in terms both of ideas and of use, onto architectural form; relative character manifests the language of architecture by transforming its universal grammar into articulate speech.[118]

Quatremère distinguished between two kinds of relative character, ideal and imitative. "Relative character of the ideal type" is superior and consists in "the expression of the qualities or ideas that are the resource of the art considered metaphysically." Just as ideal or abstract imitation was the singular domain of Greek architecture, ideal character was also a Greek invention. Greek temples, according to Quatremère, best exemplify ideal relative character because they express only "intellectual affinities by means of architectonic forms."[119] This achievement, however, was not an aesthetic phenomenon but a social one. The ideal character of Greek temples was the result of what Quatremère considered to have been the priority Greek society gave to architecture's intellectual function instead of its pedestrian one. Temples were exempt from subjugation to use and released from mundane servitude because Greek religion demanded of its architecture only the sensible rendering of a divinity that itself was nothing more than an emblem of a particular moral quality. Thus freed from physical constraints, in fact forced to abandon the material world, temples became elemental models of harmony and proportion: "fugitive results of thought," Greek temples were nothing less than pure architectural realizations of abstract ideas.[120]

Quatremère admitted that architecture is normally more subject to social and physical constraints than Greek temples, just as it is in comparison to the other arts. He exhorted, however, "that one must judge in accordance with the nature of the language used."[121] In escaping its material conditions, Greek architecture developed a uniquely abstract language of proportion, analogous imitation, and metaphysical expression that enabled its distinctive signs or characters to be legible down to the smallest detail.[122] The abstraction of this language necessitated a particular reciprocity

of thought between an architect and his public: "if no correlation
of intelligence exists between it and the people to whom it speaks,
this language will quickly die for want of being understood."[123]
Conversely, this same abstraction could guarantee mutual understanding and hence architectural legibility if used to articulate the
very functions from which the Greek temple was exempt.

"Relative character of the imitative type" is the key to this
kind of articulation and consists in "as true, faithful, and varied
an indication as this art allows of the uses and purpose of buildings." In its dependence on program and function, imitative character is conceptually inferior to ideal character, yet this very
dependency yields a practical advantage. "Every building, whatever it may be, is destined to have a use, no matter what or which."
A system of character based on use is therefore "applicable to
every building, is to be found in all places more or less, and can
be amenable to uniform observations and consistent rules." In
order to transform function into a conventional system of universally applicable character, the actual use of a building must be
transformed into an idea of use and into "the visible expression
of this use."[124] Only by distinguishing between real and apparent
use, between fulfilling and articulating a function, does architecture become expressive.

Quatremère says to his reader, "do not fear that the artist
lacks the means to characterize his work or is in want of judges
who can appreciate and understand the language of his art."[125] In
order to locate comprehensible signs that indicate the "moral qualities inherent to each building," the architect need only turn to
the language of the Greek temple. Although invented in a unique
context, the abstraction and hence intelligence of its characters
renders this language capable of expressing any idea. According
to Quatremère, classicism established six modes of conventionalized expression in architecture: relative scale and richness of
buildings, what we now call building type, general architectural
forms, construction, decoration, and attributes.[126] These elements
carry meaning only when their particular conventions are
respected, and Quatremère stresses the loss of comprehensibility
that occurs when convention is ignored. For example, decoration

is "a language whose signs and expressions must be endowed with a precise signification and made capable of rendering ideas. Without this, one would only see an unintelligible jargon composed of puerile and insignificant formulas or of characters that are mute to the spirit. . . . It would thus be in vain for this language to present to the artist the most energetic means of rendering his ideas and of giving to all buildings a kind of visible and, so to speak, ocular eloquence, if the artist did not succeed in acquiring the intelligence of these means or in managing his resources well."[127] By adhering to the conventional language of "significant" characters created in the Greek temple, whether with respect to decoration or to any of its six elements, the contemporary architect gains access to the meaningful speech of a universal language.

Quatremère's last section is devoted to a precise type of decoration, that of attributes, under which heading he includes the use of allegory.[128] With diabolical consistency, and apparently contradicting all his exhortations for plain-speaking architecture, Quatremère demands the replacement of inscriptions with "allegorical writing," exclaiming "what a poor resource is the inscription without which I would have no idea of the kind and purpose of the building that is before my eyes!"[129] Although he did warn that allegory must be used appropriately and conventionally in order to avoid offering "enigmas to people instead of inscriptions," a warning that is consistent with his general emphasis on clarity in architectural expression, the demand for allegory seems in itself inconsistent.

In fact Quatremère's theory of architectural expression is entirely dependent on allegory, for example, on the distinction he makes between solidity and the appearance of solidity, between use and the idea of use, between wood and wood recollected.[130] Adhering to the conventions of allegory makes architectural decoration into "a very intelligible kind of language." This language not only expresses "the general and particular subject it treats" and the "moral goal and physical use of the building," but is itself "the simple and natural expression of those arts of imitation that speak only in signs or in figures."[131] Hence, in his search for total intelligibility, Quatremère reasoned that because allegorical decoration calls attention to the fictive nature of architectural expression itself, because "allegorical decoration . . . says more and speaks better than all the inscriptions that can cover facades and walls," such ornament is most appropriate to buildings that are themselves "friendly and truthful liars."[132]

Quatremère concluded his article on architectural character with what can only be called an allegory of architectural mistaken identity. Supposedly told by the Hellenistic grammarian and archetypal critic Aristarchus—clearly a figure for Quatremère himself—the story is modeled after the old quarrel between the ancients and the moderns.[133] Three ancients, a Greek, a Roman, and an Egyptian, are conducted through a modern city where they are pleased to find architecture modeled after the traditions of their various cultures. Without exception, however, these recognizable forms are used in unrecognizable ways—temples have become stock exchanges, amphitheaters have become granaries, and pyramids have been set upon the roofs of theaters. The ancients do not suffer from a lack of beauty in this modern environment, but from utter and complete confusion. Fleeing this city of unintelligible architecture, the ancient deputies resolve to allow Greece to retain its preeminence and refuse to reconsider the question for another hundred years. Quatremère leaves unclear whether the century is over or not and therefore leaves undecided the contemporary winner in the battle between the ancients and the moderns. The meaning of his fable, however, and of the consequences of transgressions against the characters and conventions of architecture is unmistakable.

Quatremère's theory of character belongs in a larger history of the notion of character in general. Following its migration from Aristotle's *Poetics* through Renaissance theories of art to Charles Le Brun's concept of physiognomical expression, the wide use of the term in French eighteenth-century theories of architecture can be divided into two categories.[134] One reflects the attempt to reconcile the proliferation of building types with the limited number of classical orders. Boffrand, for example, claimed that the three orders provided architecture with a means of conveying "the character that is appropriate to each type of building."[135] Charles Batteux expanded the notion that the orders could articulate the uses of specific buildings into a general concept of architectural expression. He insisted that in architecture "all amenities must *seem* to have a character of utility in order to attain perfection."[136] Blondel combined these ideas by suggesting that the orders could adapt architecture's overall character of utility into specific modes of expression appropriate to "each type of building."[137] He sought thus to accommodate an unprecedented variety of architectural uses by translating the traditional theory of decorum into a flexible system of consistently proper and expressive characters.

The second general direction taken by discussions of character tended to emphasize sensationalist experience and the expression of the passions. With English origins in the philosophic traditions of Hume and Burke, a new, emotive attitude toward design was brought to France by Watelet. Integrated with theories of architecture by Le Camus de Mézières, whose *Le génie d'architecture* is dedicated to Watelet, character was now used to describe a sensual poetry of architecture. Le Camus maintained that variety and proportion are "the origin of the different characters or genres that distinguish the orders of architecture" and that the character of proportion was what made architecture pleasurable. Proportion created character, which in turn produced analogous harmonies in human sensation. Thus, where Blondel attempted to enumerate all possible types of architectural character, Le Camus hoped to define its effect: "Just as when a single action fills the scene in a dramatic play, the unity of character in a building must equally be observed and this truth must immediately fix the imagination by striking the eyes."[138]

Both Blondel and Le Camus regarded character as a means of expression, whose purpose might be utility or emotion. Perhaps more important, however, is that both views share an emphasis on abstraction. The notion of character as first established by Aristotle and Theophrastus was related to the expression of moral and social values. Progressively stylized and conventionalized over many centuries, character remained associated with the expression of human behavior, whether individual or collective, and thus remained anthropomorphic at least to some degree. This aspect of character was of great importance to architecture because of its parallel with the anthropomorphism of the orders. By virtue of this underlying anthropomorphism character became relevant to architecture, and someone like Blondel could speak of male, female, and even dwarflike character in architecture.

By the eighteenth century, however, the expressive range of architecture was increasingly perceived as too limited by its dependence on orders directly representing human types. Blondel based only a few of his categories of architectural character on anthropomorphic representation; to make his list comprehensive, he extrapolated from human characteristics abstract qualities such as lightness, vagueness, grandeur, and hardiness. The dehumanization of this tradition, in the literal sense, was only complete when the orders were transformed into a totally abstract system of proportion.[139] This final rejection of orders conceived in figurative terms constitutes the connecting link between the different camps hoping to make architecture express either a character of utility or a character of sensation. More fundamental than what the participants hoped to convey through character is their common search for infinite architectural expression through the mechanisms of abstraction.

Quatremère's view of character grew out of the bond uniting these traditions. His theory is almost entirely independent of the orders and addresses the articulation of both sensation and utility. His real interest, however, lay in the structure of character as a means of social expression, whatever its object. This concern led him to add to all the traditional definitions of character in architecture the idea of an alphabet composed of abstract units that can be endlessly combined to create specific meaning. The Greek temple, throughout which "the idea of God is written by the art of building in characters indelible even now," had given birth to this alphabet by transforming its type into characters.[140] From these characters, moreover, "the Greeks formed architectural writing, and used [these characters] to express a large number of ideas and diverse sensations."[141] Finally, through abstraction, or what Quatremère called counterrevolution, these characters had stepped out of the confines of the Greek temple: "It is thus not a facsimile of a Greek temple that an intelligent imitator of the antique must strive for in making a church. Rather, by using the forms, types, and details of Greek architecture, which are none other than what words, if one may say so, and the formulas of discourse are to the art of writing, the [intelligent imitator] must endeavor to do not what was done by the great architects of antiquity, but to do what they would have done if other uses, other proprieties, other political, civil, and religious needs had prescribed other obligations."[142] The Greek alphabet of architecture was necessary to the contemporary architect not because it was Greek but because it was an alphabet that enabled articulate discourse rather than constituted a system for iconic representation.

Quatremère's ideas about character in architecture are the final result of his exploration of the relationship between language and architecture. Both are means of expression that society produces to articulate and solidify its emancipation from a state of nature. Every architecture is subject to the conflict between society and nature and every language of architecture makes this conflict manifest. Only one architecture, however, encourages man and society to make continual progress in overcoming the material constraints of the natural world and does so by developing a social language of artificial convention. According to Quatremère, the Greeks had invented this language of architecture and had defined its character of intelligibility. The notion of character in architecture was not new nor was its association with abstraction and expression. Through language, however, Quatremère merged the idea of architectural character with a social theory of architecture, and with this transmutation he hoped to take his vision of classicism out of the ancient and into the modern world.

IV

THE REPUBLIC OF
THE ARTS

The Context of Art

J'appelle République tout Etat régie par les
lois, sous quelque forme d'administration que ce
puisse être; car alors l'intérêt publique domine,
et la chose publique est quelque chose.

Rousseau, *Le contrat social*, II, 6

Quatremère maintained that the language of architecture was a fundamentally social phenomenon. The rationally invented agreements and conventions that enable language to convey meaning and that render the arts intelligible are also the defining elements of the social contract. The same structure or type that establishes liens between a word and its object, between the artist and his public, also establishes the relationship between citizen and state and hence characterizes the political order.[1] Thus, the parallel between society, conceived as a human construct, and the artificial nature of its verbal and visual languages was perceived as a prototypically political relationship.

Quatremère devoted much thought to how the language of architecture might best exploit its enunciatory capacity and determined that the supreme abstraction of classicism was the form best suited to this task. Relegating aesthetic judgment to a conceptually minor role, Quatremère instead supported the use of classicism on the basis of its social utility. This radical shift in attitude toward architecture is evident in the changes he made to his essay on Egypt. He introduced the changes over the course of the French Revolution, in which he actively participated. The question inevitably arises, especially since he adamantly maintained that society and architecture were inseparable, of how the domains of architectural theory and political action may have intersected in his own case. While some scholarly attention has been devoted to documenting how Quatremère put his ideas into practice, notably in the period of the Revolution, very little has been devoted to his conception of society and its institutions, which came to play a central role in his definition of architecture.

Quatremère's political career is difficult to characterize: no comprehensive study of his political writings or actions has been undertaken.[2] We know that he believed in constitutional monarchy of the English kind but not how he regarded the processes of the Revolution, or where his primary allegiance lay. He was both a member of and expelled from the radical Société des Arts. He directed the principal architectural project commissioned by the Revolutionary government but was imprisoned and exiled before its completion. Despite close associations with leaders of early Revolutionary events, he participated in the counter-revolutionary uprising of 13 Vendémiaire and was a member of the royalist Club de Clichy. The commitment to social change he pronounced early in the Revolution by supporting constitutionalism may have been weakened by the violence of later events—a common phenomenon—or it may only appear weakened in comparison with the decade's progressive radicalism.

In the midst of many discrepancies and uncertainties, one thing emerges clearly: Quatremère felt party politics were irrelevant to architecture. While virtually all his writings discuss the importance of political and social structure to the arts, none espouses a rigid political agenda and some even denounce the idea of using the arts as political illustrations or visual aids for propaganda. Nevertheless, Quatremère did incorporate the Revolutionary experience into his theory of architecture and did so in a way that is utterly consistent with the theory itself, namely through abstraction. Uninterested in the Revolution as a historically contained event, he rejected the possibility that it might contribute to architecture a specific political model. Instead, the Revolution was important because it confirmed the idea that the structure of society was no more determined by nature than was that of the arts. No less synthetic and artificial than language, social structure was an invented phenomenon that could be manipulated, rationalized, or destroyed by revolution. Having decided that architecture was a social work of art, Quatremère came to see society itself as a work of art.

Quatremère's development of a social theory of architecture, expressed in the idea that architecture is language, coincided directly and significantly with his participation in the Revolution. As he developed iconographic programs for new Republican monuments, contributed to the reform of art education, dealt with censorship, public patronage, and funding for the arts, Quatremère's socially grounded ideas about art came face to face with a society in the process of recreating itself. Precisely because he viewed this as a process of re-creation, he was determined to demonstrate the leading role that the arts—the epitome of social creations—could play in this transformation. If society was building a republic, and if its languages of art were to assume their proper instructional function in the process of creative change, then a republican structure for art and architecture had to be envisioned.

Quatremère expressed his new conception of the relationship between art and society partly by coining the phrase "Republic of the Arts," one of his most significant and revealing inventions. The parent notion, the famous Republic of Letters, well established and widespread by the seventeenth century, was essentially a state of the mind.[3] The Republic of Letters lacked physical identity of any kind, embracing only the transcendental communion shared by intellectuals.[4] Originally, their use of the term *republic* was wholly metaphorical, suggesting the liberal nature of their art, liberated from all material constraints, and the free nature of their alliance, freed from national and political fetters. The Republic of Letters was also professionally disengaged: as distinct from confraternities or guilds, its currency was not money but the intellect. Defined in opposition to working associations, the Republic of Letters escaped class conflicts because it was at the apex of a social as well as a cultural elite.

By the time groups such as the Commune des Arts and the Société Populaire et Républicaine des Arts, to which Quatremère belonged temporarily, were established, he had reformed the traditional Republic of Letters into a radical Republic of the Arts.[5] Two new meanings were inherent in the change. First, the word *republic*, inescapably after 1789, carried a new political charge. Second, the qualifications for citizenship were fundamentally revised. The principal exiles from the transcendental and conceptual Republic of Letters had been artists, those condemned to dealing with physical matter; in this sense the idea of a Republic of the Arts was an important conquest in the long struggle for political, social, and intellectual emancipation fought by artists since the Renaissance. To transpose the Republic of Letters to the arts, however, and to do so during the Revolution, was also to challenge the traditional view that the arts merely served the state by suggesting that they might be instrumental in defining the state.

Quatremère repeatedly used the phrase "Republic of the Arts" in his works of the Revolutionary period. Significantly, he invoked the notion most frequently in his letters on the Napoleonic spoliation of Italian works of art written to General Miranda, the celebrated South American revolutionary.[6] The publication history of this epistolary manifesto is complex: composed sometime during the summer of 1796 while Quatremère was in hiding after having been sentenced to death by default for participating in 13 Vendémiaire, its first known appearance is as a book of the same year entitled *Lettres sur la préjudice qu'occasionneroient aux arts et à la science, le déplacement des monumens de l'art de l'Italie, le démembrement de ses écoles et la spoliation de ses collections, galeries, musées, etc.*[7] There are good reasons to suppose, however, that the letters, or at least their contents, were known in some form before the *Lettres sur la préjudice* was finally published.[8] Moreover, their meaning has been somewhat obscured by a later publication in which Quatremère joined the seven letters to Miranda condemning the removal of works of art from Italy with seven letters written to Canova applauding Lord Elgin's transferral of the Parthenon sculptures from the Acropolis to London.[9]

Quatremère saw no inconsistency in his views. A contradiction emerged, in his opinion, only when the fact was neglected that the two sets of letters were written in response to fundamentally different situations. The two cases were "materially similar" but differed with respect to "moral interests above all, to the political circumstances that motivated and authorized the spoilage, to matters of science and taste, as well as to the conservation of the works of art themselves."[10] Quatremère raised many issues in his introduction to the collected set of letters, but he stressed the fact that his own work could only be understood in the context in which it had been produced. This self-contextualization, however, had a more important function than simply to explain apparent contradictions: it emphasized his belief in the necessary connection between all works of art and their contexts.

The Revolutionary wars were the context in which Quatremère's letters to Miranda were written. On May 18, 1796, Napoleon announced a truce with the Duke of Parma that provided for the requisitioning of 20 paintings. On June 5, a long list of "objects of art and sciences that were taken to be transported to Paris" was made public.[11] The inventory includes works by Raphael, Rubens, Petrarch, Titian, Correggio, Veronese, the Carracci, and many others. Napoleon's ultimate plan was to establish a definitive national museum in Paris by filling it with admired works of art. Not only would these objects bring honor to France and make Paris the undisputed center of the art world, they would double as tangible and glorifying evidence of Napoleonic victory. Over the next several weeks, however, the press became the arena of a violent battle of letters between supporters and opponents of Napoleon. Indeed, the issue concerning these works of art became a vehicle for voicing fundamental differences in how the new Republic was conceived and defined. The dispute also reflected widely divergent opinions on whether the Revolution ought to be exported beyond French borders in pursuit of a universal republic. The theoretical interest in the relationship between society and art explored over the previous decades now became focused on a real issue: works of art were catapulted directly into the political arena and became weapons in the Revolutionary struggle.[12]

Severing these objects from their context and stripping them of some of their historical value was critical to their politicization. Both sides cited antique precedent, although for the most part the works of art were modern. But supporters of Napoleon went even farther, giving these objects new and invented histories in order to make their physical importation to France signify the exportation and universalization of the Revolution. They argued that because the modern arts in question had been inspired by classical antiquity, the free ages of Greece and republican Rome, it was only just that they be given a permanent resting place in a free state. In this light, rather than appear as willful seizure, Napoleon's removal of works of art became an act of salvation that protected and liberated them on republican soil and engaged the objects themselves as political envoys in the extension of the French Revolution beyond its limits of time and space.[13]

If removing art from its context required some historical sophistry for contemporary purposes, Quatremère could argue similarly for preserving the contextuality of art. He too considered the universality of the new republican ideals to be at stake, yet his goal was not to impose this principle in political terms but to demonstrate its fundamental parallel with the universality of art. Napoleon's defenders invoked antique precedent in order to present the military campaign as one of liberation. Quatremère invoked antique precedent in order to present the military campaign as one of enslavement:

> I would feel it . . . injurious to the eighteenth century to suspect it capable of resurrecting the Roman right of conquest that made men and things the property of the strongest. Who is unaware that this absurd and monstrous right was included in the legal code of Rome on the same basis as slavery? If an old civilization based in a general culture of arts and sciences and a true theory of the sacred rights of humanity and political relations of nations had not long since banished from the public code of Europe the last traces of this so-called right of conquest, the experience and example of the Roman people itself and the memorable castigation that the universe inflicted on this tyrant of peoples would suffice, I think, to disabuse whoever might attempt to reestablish such odious maxims.[14]

In Quatremère's opinion Napoleon's military tactics were incompatible with the goals of the Revolution: "the spirit of conquest in a republic utterly subverts the spirit of liberty."[15] Aggression was

not Napoleon's only travesty of the founding principles of the
Revolution, since it was an aggression born of nationalism, that
"false and partial interest" typical only of "ignorants or knaves."[16]
Quatremère's notion of an ideal republican universe had no need
to guard national boundaries and in fact would by definition serve
to reinforce cultural integration. Quatremère thus argued that the
goal of universal liberty his opponents professed was belied and
undermined by the martial and divisively nationalistic aspects of
its implementation.

If Napoleon's action was seen by some as having republicanized Italian works of art by bringing to light their classical
ancestry, Quatremère invoked the membership of these objects in
the Republic of the Arts to demonstrate the reverse, indeed to
suggest the antirepublican nature of Napoleon's actions.

> In effect, as you know, the arts and sciences in Europe have
> long since formed a republic. Its members, tied together by the
> love of and search for the beauty and truth that constitute their
> social pact, tend much less to isolate themselves in their respec-
> tive homelands than they tend to bring their interests together
> from the very precious point of view of a universal fraternity.
> This felicitous sentiment, as you also know, cannot be stifled
> even by the bloody dissensions that push nations to tear each
> other to pieces. Woe to the senseless and cruel man who would
> wish to extinguish the spark of the sacred fire of humanity and
> of philanthropy that the culture of the arts and sciences still
> keeps alive in the hearts of some. . . . By a happy revolution
> the arts and sciences belong to all of Europe and are no longer
> the exclusive property of any one nation. All thoughts and all
> the efforts of sound politics and philosophy should be devoted
> to maintaining, promoting, and augmenting this community.[17]

Quatremère's language is provocative and coopts for his purpose
the highly charged verbiage of the Revolution. In his view, the
social pacts, fraternity, humanity, and philosophy of the Revolution had already been achieved by the Republic of the Arts. Culture, he argued, constituted an alliance that had long since
exploded the limits of time and space by rising above political and
national allegiance.

An important buttress for Quatremère's argument was the transcendence historically associated with the Republic of Letters. He exploited this tradition explicitly, using, for example, the man of letters' professional disinterestedness as a metaphor for national disinterestedness. He claimed that "philosophy, history, the science of language, the intelligence of poets, the chronology of the world, scientific astronomy, criticism, are different parts of what one calls the Republic of the Arts and are all interested in its integrality."[18] The nonaligned unity associated with the Republic of Letters was thus useful to Quatremère's political and antimilitaristic aim. Moreover, by merely extending its reach and adding the arts to a long list of citizens in this Republic, the metaphor also served in his attempt to elevate the social status of artists. The association with transcendence, however, had been born of the ideal nature of the Republic of Letters, disencumbered of tangible reality in any form. Quatremère's application of this disembodied ideal to a body of politicized works of art was doubly polemical: it underscored the potential of the work of art itself to constitute and convey "l'idéal," and it illustrated the possibility of realizing the ideal republicanism of the Republic of Letters in concrete political terms. By giving the apolitical and metaphorical republicanism of letters tangible form in works of art, Quatremère gave substance to a transcendent concept and the Republic of the Arts became an ideal model for real political action.

Quatremère's attack on Napoleon linked the moral virtue of the Republic of the Arts to the real political significance of the expropriated objects. This conflation illuminates another dual aspect of his argument. He objected to transporting works of art because their transcendent value was degraded by the base notion of national ownership, and he argued that Italian objects must remain in situ because of specific qualities unique to their region of origin. He maintained that much of the significance of these works of art derived from the interlocking web constituted by their physical, social, political, historical, and aesthetic contexts. Hence, while the supporters of Napoleon used a physical dislocation of the work of art as proof of the transcendent republican ideals they had inherited from antiquity, Quatremère argued that the work of art, precisely because of its transcendent value, should remain in context.

The letters to Miranda vehemently attack the act of Napoleonic spoilage itself, but even more strenuously condemn the notion of creating a central museum in France to house the stolen works of art. Quatremère's objection did not extend to museums generally: he strongly encouraged France to restore and preserve the monuments of Nîmes, Arles, Orange, and other Roman sites in order to provide exhibition space for local archaeological discoveries. The idea of a national French museum filled with Italian works of art, however, was anathema to him. Instead, he sought the preservation of an existing museum, "the veritable museum" of Rome itself. This institution, according to Quatremère, "is composed, it is true, of statues, colossi, temples, obelisks, triumphal columns, baths, circuses, amphitheaters, triumphal arches, tombs, stucco works, frescoes, bas-reliefs, inscriptions, fragments of ornaments, construction materials, marbles, utensils, etc., etc. But it is no less composed of places, sites, mountains, quarries, ancient roads, the relative positions of towns now in ruins, geographical correspondences, relationships between all objects, memories, local traditions, still extant customs, and of parallels and connections that can only be made in the country itself."[19] The components of this only true museum are none other than the elements that create ideal character. Quatremère had used this notion to describe how the arts may attain both autonomy and meaning when specific aspects of their terrestrial and historical contexts free them to rise above earthly constraints. The characters of art, he argued, are thus created when a combination of countless local conditions are transformed into a language of abstraction. The letters to General Miranda describe an inverted version of this relationship, analyzing not the process of constructing character but the dangers of deconstructing character. Having achieved their characteristic universality, works of art are imperiled by loss of contact with the context in which they were created.

While Quatremère's theory of character concerned the importance of context in general, in the letters to Miranda he was writing about Rome in particular, which he thought of as "the capital of the Republic of the Arts."[20] This was an idea no doubt shared by those who supported Napoleon's aim of redefining Paris as the capital of this republic and who sought to give a new, French context to appropriated Italian works of art. Quatremère derided this plan by underscoring the immobility of the context to which art belonged. Rome uniquely possessed every element necessary to the creation and maintenance of ideal character, encompassing the geographic and tangible as well as the cultural and ephemeral.[21] To isolate fragment from totality would be to dismember the museum of Rome and would constitute "an outrage against science and a crime of treason against public education."[22] The feature he defined as the most immobile of all, and the most important, was the Roman history Napoleon hoped to rewrite. The politically charged image of historical continuity associated with the Roman context was significant in contemporary terms because it was a modern fiction in the process of being created.

According to Quatremère, in Rome—and only in Rome— the past was being resurrected in the service of the future. "What is antiquity in Rome," he asked, "if not a great book whose pages have been dispersed or destroyed by time and whose voids are filled and whose lacunas are repaired every day by modern research?"[23] Modern studies of this great book were "reconnecting our knowledge to that of the past, . . . bringing back to life a plethora of lost ideas, and shedding new light on philosophy and on the arts": the study of history was in fact inventing the idea of historical unity.[24] Relocating this museum's collection and disrupting Rome's integrity would, in Quatremère's opinion, destroy modern man's capacity to reconstruct the fragile artifice of the city's symbolic historical and physical transcendence. If the universality and eternal virtues of a republic were to be made manifest, they could only be inscribed in the Roman context.[25] Quatremère, who believed "that the discovery, or better said, the recovery of antiquity is a veritable resurrection," wanted neither to write the history of Rome nor to provide the story with a final chapter set in Paris.[26] To do so would make history into a nostalgic symbol for an unreachable past. Instead, he hoped that the revivification of the antique Republic of the Arts would enable Rome to step out of history and realize the universal aspirations of the new Republic.

The Institutions of Art

The letters to General Miranda posit the Republic of the Arts as more republican than the new French Republic and reveal Quatremère's confidence in the positive action the arts might take in assisting society to bridge this gap. One of the principal means by which he thought the arts might exert this influence was didactic: transferring the arts from an aristocratic and privileged realm to one that was open and devoted to the edification of everyone. He asserted that to dismantle the Republic of the Arts was to commit treason not against the crown but against public education. Quatremère spoke at greatest length about the Republic of the Arts in the context of art education and its relation to the public sphere. Although his concern for the way in which society creates itself and its languages of art by means of education was integral to his theory of art before 1789, his participation in the Revolutionary Comité d'Instruction Publique was a platform uniquely suited to his effort to develop a pedagogical system that would befit the new structure of French society.

Quatremère presented a series of three *Considérations sur les arts du dessin* to the Assemblé Nationale in 1791. These texts were important contributions to the long and complex movement toward the reform of the royal academies that culminated during the French Revolution.[27] The *Considérations* also shed light on Quatremère's conception of the public that constituted the social matrix of the Republic of the Arts. In writing these particular tracts, Quatremère's immediate goal was to respond to the following questions: "Does France need to support financially a public school or academy of the arts of design? What would be the most advantageous means of organizing such an institution?"[28] The principal essay is divided into two sections that address these questions

individually. In order to answer the first, Quatremère sketched
the main elements of his theory of art, starting with the principle
of origins and moving to the relationship between art and society;
these basic precepts were prerequisite to all discussions concerning art. Having established this conceptual framework, he then
analyzed the role of education in the production of art and studied
the history of this process in France. Writing with great political
acumen, Quatremère strove to appeal to a wide audience by stress-
ing the importance of the arts in both ideal and real terms. He
demonstrated the positive influence on society and public morality
that the arts exert when properly supported and protected. At the
same time, he devoted a great deal of attention to emphasizing the
strong role that the fine as well as the mechanical arts played in
French economy, both on a national and an international scale.
By presenting the arts as integral to the spiritual as well as financial
health of the new Republic, Quatremère accomplished his principal objective: establishing as essential France's need for a school
of the arts that was public both in its funding and in its open,
unrestricted admission policy.

The second section of the essay is devoted to outlining the
administrative and pedagogical structure of the new school. The
key to Quatremère's institution was to be the free exhibition, a
basic right of every artist that Quatremère likened to freedom of
the press.[29] In addition to organizing what were in effect reformed
salons, the school was to administer courses of instruction and
competitions of several kinds. The faculty was to be comprised of
both permanent and temporary members just as the jurors of the
various *concours* were to be an elected body, some with and some
without positions on the school staff. A system of checks and
balances was central to Quatremère's attempt to ensure the quality
of the individuals in the school as well as the impartiality of the
institutional framework itself. Quatremère eliminated from his
ideal school any primarily titular or honorific function, an idea
that was characteristic of previous attempts to reform the academies. However, his emphasis on the absolutely public, egalitarian,
and especially functional nature of this ideal institution was part
of a new movement to democratize the once largely aristocratic

role of art in society and, more fundamentally, to republicanize all institutions.

If the fundamental internal characteristic Quatremère built into this *école du dessin* was equal access and fair treatment for all students, he used a parallel principle to organize the school's relationship to an external social context. He argued not only that every competition be open to the public but also that the results be realized in the public sphere: the competitions were to be held only for bona fide public monuments and commissions. Moreover, although the school was to be located in Paris because of its accessibility, Quatremère called for lists of commemorable local persons and events to be submitted by provincial delegates. These subjects were to be honored through works of art sponsored by the school's competition system; the commissioned works would not, of course, be incarcerated in museums, but would be exhibited in public places so as to fulfill their task of social edification.[30] Quatremère thus intended his school to contribute to the education of students, who in turn were to produce objects that would educate all of France. At the same time, this ideal school was to generate real activity that would maintain the standards of French art and thus help exploit one of France's most marketable resources. The only exception Quatremère made to this system was the Prix de Rome, for although it did not result in a public commission it did provide the student with an essential part of every artist's education.

In his *Considérations*, Quatremère used the notion of a "republic of the arts" in two apparently paradoxical ways. The first invokes this republic as a metaphor for the democratic structure inherent to the arts of design with a common basis in mimesis. His ideas about the unity of the arts were fairly conventional by the late eighteenth century, but translating them into a call for a unified school of the arts was not.[31] Quatremère was highly critical of the fragmentation of the arts being encouraged, if not caused, by the establishment of distinct educational institutions for each of the various media and for particular aspects of individual media. With respect to architectural education Quatremère complained: "Who would believe that there exist in Paris two architectural schools distinct in terms of locale, faculty, and curriculum? [Who would believe] that one [school] presents architecture as an art of taste and the other presents architecture as an art of need; . . . that there is a school that teaches how to make a temple and another that teaches how to make a bridge? . . . This dismemberment of education has mortally wounded both sides by decomposing the art's essence. It has habituated one group to believe that taste dispenses with solidity and the other to believe that calculations can replace spirit."[32] His opposition to fracturing the unity of design was not limited to architecture: "It never ceases to amaze one that painters and sculptors, constantly obliged to use architecture in their works, do not even know the distinctive characters of the orders or that an architect must ask a strange hand to design the figures with which he ornaments his projects. This is an inconvenience that is obvious to everyone. But more important and less perceived is the consequent real impoverishment of each art. Denied analogy with the others, [each art] watches its patrimony diminish more and more, its ideas contract, and sees the germ of its conceptions wither away."[33] In place of this "division that, instead of a republic in which all artists might be citizens, has made each art into an empire actually separated by the regime of its institution, by the barriers of prejudice, by habit and by rivalry," Quatremère envisioned a school that would make the arts into a "federal republic."[34] His call for architecture—normally the most mundane and illiberal of the arts—to join in an uprising that would elevate the arts to the same conceptual plane as the Republic of Letters was relatively uncommon, although not unprecedented, in the eighteenth century. What was radical was that Quatremère now explicitly and literally paralleled the community of the arts, both in their mimetic nature and in their institutional realization, to a united citizenry. Quatremère asserted that to dismember the integrity of the arts was tantamount to an antirepublican act against the new social order.

Although Quatremère used the concept of the Republic of the Arts to explain and defend his *école central du dessin*, he emphatically rejected the idea of modeling a school on the structure of a republic. When discussing the internal organization and constituency of this school rather than its relation to the general public of France, he claimed instead that "there is no such thing as a republic of the arts . . . a people of artists is a chimera."[35] Hence, although he argued that art itself might have prototypically political mechanisms and might in fact be republican in nature, he refuted for two principal reasons both the politicization and the republicanization of artists and their institutions. First, in his opinion the royal academies had been ruined by the way they made art education an instrument of government. He maintained that art schools should be explicitly apolitical and asserted that an ideal institution would be simply "beyond the reach of political powers."[36] The second and more important reason for his claim that a "people of artists is a chimera" derives from what Quatre-mère felt was the most fundamental aspect of republicanism: the principle of absolute equality shared by the citizenry. This principle was incompatible with the lack of equality he felt inherent, indeed necessary, to a community of artists.

Suffrage, in Quatremère's view, produced an inexorable contradiction between an egalitarian political republic and an "imaginary" republic of artists in which "the right to citizenship could only belong to those most able and knowledgeable."[37] Analyzing the difficulty at great length, he wrote:

The moral principle of every election is that it must be done by those who can do it best and by those who have the greatest interest in it being well done. As a result, it is in the nature of things to want the people itself to choose its magistrates because, always interested in choosing well, one assumes that the people's interest itself contains the wisdom necessary for [the people] to discern those who merit its confidence. . . .

I do not think that other principles should exist for those who are to teach art; but there is the difference that while the political order departs from a definite basis, which is the people, this basis is lacking in the order of the things in question. . . .

It is thus evident that the political principle of elections, or the principle that is based on natural rights, is inapplicable to a corporation of artists because such a corporation is not a republic; it is evident that the moral principle of elections or that which tends toward their perfection would, in the fantastic supposition of a republic of the arts, preclude the possibility of denying the ignorant multitude of the right to elections, unless one were to suppose a republic of equally able artists.[38] Although charged by his own frustration with the stagnating academies as well as by the Comité d'Instruction Publique to republicanize art education in France, Quatremère would adulterate neither the absolute nature of his republican ideals nor his belief that artistic talent was not an absolute natural right. Yet instead of simply allowing the paradox to persist, Quatremère sought to define a principle that might allow a political republic and a Republic of the Arts to coalesce.

Quatremère resolved his dilemma by radically abstracting the notion of a republic. Although political equality was at once synonymous with republicanism and at odds with a Republic of the Arts, moral parity between them could nevertheless be created. He believed that a new system of elections had been the Revolution's primary accomplishment: "With the institution of the new government, which will be the good fortune of France, nothing has been more shocking to the legislature and to the people than the vice of the old elections, all of which stemmed from an arbitrary power."[39] Quatremère intended to reenact the Revolution's accomplishment by basing his school on this new principle that had replaced arbitrary power. Inherent to this effort, however, was the realization that in the context of a Republic of the Arts it was necessary to adhere "more to the moral principle that aspires to the perfection of election than to the political principle that guarantees the rights of the electorate."[40] Thus, inequality in a society of artists could be republicanized by rejecting arbitrary power as a means of differentiation in favor of a system of rational representation. Quatremère was concerned that this exchange of strict political justice with the flexibility of moral virtue was open to misinterpretation: "I sense that this apparent defect in conformity is the point that will have the most difficulty in receiving sanction from those who, sensitive to a symmetrical regularity in all public institutions, tend to evaluate [these institutions] more in terms of the rigor of their principles than in terms of the positive nature of their effects."[41] He was confident, however, of the positive effects of his program. His school, independent of the republic and hence of political constraints, could nevertheless "itself be submitted, by the nature of the new institutions, to all the parallels of equality, to all the censures of liberty, and to all the shocks of public combat."[42] Quatremère concluded that free elections were the only link possible between the fictional Republic of the Arts and the veritable political republic: the public that the school served but with which it was not symmetrical was to be the instrument of the moral republicanization of his ideal institution.

Quatremère resolved the conflict between egalitarian principle and hierarchical practice in education by defining any true republic as a moral sphere parallel to and embodied in the concept of the public itself. This conflation of real and ideal political states through a third realm of moral abstraction was, according to Quatremère, sanctioned by none other than Plato, who had been the first to evaluate the relationship between art and republicanism. He felt Plato had been "falsely accused of having wanted to banish the arts from his republic." To support this assertion, Quatremère pointed to the long history of the cultivation of the arts in Sparta, "the model of Plato's imaginary republic."[43] There were limits, however, with respect to the right of entry to this state accorded the arts. Plato wanted "to make the arts serve, as much by the choice of subject matter as by the perfection of their execution, . . . in forming the heart and in cultivating the understanding of the people."[44] Only arts of "depraved imitation" that offered society "false judgments of physical and moral beauty" were to be rejected. Plato described the arts in terms of mimesis and criticized the principle of imitation, but he defined art's right of access to the Republic in terms of social function. Indeed, Quatremère argued that the misinterpretation of Plato derived from a misunderstanding of the social function of the arts. The notion that the arts were a source of moral corruption because they served tyrants and despots and reinforced "greed, vanity, debauchery, and the passions" neglected the true "reciprocity of action between mores and the arts."[45] In a despotic social context the arts are as corrupted as they are corrupting and by implication in an ideal republic they are as virtuous as they are inspirers of virtue.

Quatremère attempted to overturn the traditional view of Plato's denigration of the arts by demonstrating that an ideal state and the ideal nature of the arts were equivalent in their public function. Many years after he had first explored these ideas and after the initial topicality of the phrase Republic of the Arts had subsided, Quatremère returned to Plato and his republic. Not surprisingly, he did so in a book devoted exclusively to a consideration of the ideal in art. A republic for Plato, according to Quatremère, was a purely ideal concept: "Any complete reading of Plato's *Republic* demonstrates that instead of being a political work, it is in fact a work on morality, in which a metaphorical system of government becomes a point of parallel abstraction for a treatise no less abstract on justice and virtue, both of which are taken to a point far beyond the ordinary capacity of man."[46] This redefinition of Plato's text, in which a political republic became not the ideal but a metaphor for a higher level of moral virtue, paralleled Quatremère's view of the relationship between the languages of art and their social institutions. By virtue of their inherent abstraction, the arts ideally embody the republican principles that political systems can only hope to mirror. In effect, Quatremère politicized and republicanized the arts by inverting the normal relationship that described artistic order as the ape of social order. Instead, the political reality of the republic was a reflection of the Republic of the Arts.

The Art of a New Institution

The implications of Quatremère's notions of a "republic of the arts" may be further explored in the context of his work at the Pantheon. On July 19, 1791, he was named "Commissaire à l'administration et direction générale des travaux de l'édifice ci-devant Sainte-Geneviève." Entrusted to him was the task of transforming this church designed by J.-G. Soufflot, hitherto dedicated to the patron saint of Paris, into a national monument, a Pantheon in honor of the great men of France. Little of Quatremère's work survives: much of the Revolutionary scheme was left incomplete or was destroyed by later building campaigns and political transformations. Moreover, neither the reconsecration of the building, the new commemorative name, or the patriotic dedication were Quatremère's decisions; nor, despite his attempts to do so, did he actually build or sculpt a single work of art for the Pantheon. Quatremère's contribution to the Pantheon was important, however; since he had control over the administration of the transformation, he was virtually unimpeded in the development of a new iconographic program, and he wielded great power in the selection of artists to be employed.[47] His work on the Pantheon, correspondingly, contributed to the development of his architectural theory, and instantiated his effort to reveal the capacity of the arts to enunciate and enact their role in the new Republic.

Quatremère's ideas about the Pantheon survive primarily in the form of three lengthy and official reports written during his tenure as Commissaire.[48] The statements differ, reflecting Quatremère's responses to changes in political climate, his efforts to retaliate against much outspoken criticism, and refinements of his scheme. At their core, however, they contain a coherent system of

ideas that he attempted to realize, with decreasing success, until
he was imprisoned on March 2, 1794. An important thread linking
the *rapports* is Quatremère's idea that his administrative and
artistic responsibilities were intimately connected. He considered
public edification the building's primary function and public
accountability his primary goal with respect to administration.
Hence, the public realm was the common ground between his two
areas of intervention and would be the center of his ideas not only
about the Pantheon but about the Republic of the Arts.

Quatremère's administration of the Pantheon enterprise
was acrimoniously criticized at the time and still contributes to
his image as a conservative if not reactionary figure. He was and
is thought of as having been unenlightened with respect to working
conditions, absolutist in the imposition of his iconographic program, and, most particularly, imperial in his exercise of total
control over the selection of artists who were to realize his design.[49]
Despite his stringent demands for open competitions in the *Considérations*, Quatremère did not organize a single competition for
the Pantheon. Accused of proceeding undemocratically in this
building born from the principles of democracy, he made the
asymmetry between the processes of republicanism and the
Republic of the Arts the basis of his response. He did not doubt
the egalitarianism of the electoral body, but he questioned the
applicability of the principle in this case.

Quatremère argued that while many people might be necessary to the realization of the Pantheon, it was a single work of
art of which he was the creator:

Is it possible to imagine, in all good faith, how one might
establish a grand system of ideas and of decoration for a monument while [individual] artists think it their right to divide all
subjects into equal portions and to distribute the execution of
these subjects as though it were public property?

A perfect monument would be one that received its existence from the hand only of the man that had conceived the
project. . . . This possibility is a chimera. . . . It is in proportion
to the more or less immediate action of the architect on his

cooperators and to the more or less direct influence of the author
on the execution of the [monument's] parts that a building
achieves an appropriate perfection. . . .

How, therefore, can one think of subjecting the inventor
of a project to receive those who collaborate on his inventions,
those who translate his ideas, indeed his coinventors, from a
competition that he did not judge himself?[50]

Rather than contradict the thesis expounded in the *Considérations*, Quatremère's administration of the Pantheon works embod-
ies it. His egalitarianism was qualified and he clearly considered
himself a Guardian-Philosopher in the tradition of Plato. He had
been appointed by a body of elected officials and would be judged
in the arena of public opinion.[51] Any parallel between politics and
art other than dedication to the public good would result in mere
caricature, "the inevitable effect of the absurd system established
by workers who, in an absurd parody of government, regard their
work as their property, the building as a republic in which they
are citizens, and believe consequently that it is their right to name
their directors and inspectors and to distribute the work arbitrar-
ily. It is clear that in such a hierarchy any form of control would
be dangerous, any inspection a vain formality, and that it would
be necessary to form a coalition of reciprocal complacency
between all agents, destructive of any form of subordination."[52]
This aspect of Quatremère's involvement at the Pantheon may not
have survived "the shocks of public combat" unscathed, yet he
maintained until the end of his administrative tenure that he had
done "everything possible to ensure the equitable distribution of
work at the Pantheon."[53]

Quatremère conceded that his organizational duties at the
Pantheon had political aspects, but he was more concerned with
the meaning to be inscribed in the design itself. Three principal
objectives emerge from his texts on the Pantheon: dechristianiza-
tion, dehistoricization, and republicanization. The first objective
arose out of changes in the building's program. Quatremère
believed it necessary to articulate clearly and indelibly that the
function of the building had changed from Christian worship to
civic and patriotic allegiance. He accomplished this secularization

in the first place by architectural means.[54] He called for suppression of the church towers and the lantern and, most significantly, for blocking up the entire lower order of windows that perforated Soufflot's structure.[55] Quatremère explained his treatment of the windows primarily in terms of the need to modify the building's character. Ste.-Geneviève was flooded with "gaiété," a character achieved by means of the lightness of the structure and of light itself—the light of God as well as the light of ecclesiastical architectural convention. By reducing the brilliance of its original illumination, he gave to the Pantheon the character of severity and sobriety appropriate to its new commemorative function.[56]

In this sense, filling in the windows transformed only the imitative aspect of the building's character, since imitative character varied according to use. Ideal character, on the other hand, transcended function. In fact, Quatremère intentionally retained Ste.-Geneviève's ideal character, for it expressed the idea of devotion, an idea also appropriate to his own project: his goal was not to desacralize Ste.-Geneviève but to sacralize the Pantheon, with the Republic as the new divinity.[57] He achieved this reformation because blocking the lower range of windows had an effect distinct from that of making the building appear less like a traditional Christian church. The change in fenestration also created broad expanses of cella walls and concentrated the illumination at the building's upper center. Distancing Ste.-Geneviève from Christian architecture in this way brought it closer to the form of a different kind of religious building, the classical hypaethral temple.[58] By substituting the focused and controlled light of the Republic for the diffuse light of Christian religiosity, Quatremère hoped to articulate the presence of the "truly universal religion" of moral philosophy. He redefined the sanctity of the site in honor of "a new divinity for a free people," the nation itself.[59]

Quatremère referred to the Greek temple in order to dechristianize the church of Ste.-Geneviève because he felt that the inherent abstraction of the classical language of architecture made it possible to articulate sacred ideas, not just illustrate religious icons. He was not, however, imposing a classical costume on a nonclassical form. Soufflot's building had long since been cele-

brated for the degree to which it had appropriated classical tradition and Quatremère himself described this aspect of the church
as possessing "a kind of revolutionary merit."[60] He expressed the
shift in the building's sacral function from Christianity to civic
duty by purifying the revolutionary classicism already implicit in
Soufflot's design. What had been a stylistic revolution, however,
now became an allusion to the French Revolution. Quatremère's
classicization of Ste.-Geneviève served not just to characterize the
secular and philosophical nature of the new order but to convey
its triumph over the Christian and superstitious nature of the old.
Because it was necessary to preserve the memory of the original,
if only vestigially, in order to articulate its submission, Quatremère
hoped to "conquer rather than destroy this monument." Although
he claimed that his "first goal had been to make everything that
might recall the character of a church disappear," his design was
predicated on the fact that "any building destined to be a church
will always retrace this idea in its forms and in its details."[61]
Because Ste.-Geneviève remained intrinsically ecclesiastical, the
appropriation and conquest of the church became manifest and
the secular order of the Revolution was made visible.

Ste.-Geneviève had begun the "recovery" of antiquity Quatremère himself strove for, but he believed Soufflot had had a false
purpose in initiating this process. Soufflot's interest in classicism
derived from his aim of creating an image of historical continuity
as part of a visual scholastic typology that could claim the perpetuity of Christianity. Soufflot had accomplished this goal by conflating the classical tradition not just with a generically ecclesiastical
disposition but with an explicitly Gothic form. Of all the traditions
of church architecture Soufflot could have and did marry to the
Greek temple—the central dome, the lantern, and the Greek cross
plan—only the Gothic was considered fundamentally independent
of ancient architectural form.[62] By exploiting this apparent opposition between the Gothic and the classical, Soufflot created an
architectural typology that revealed how the church could encom-
pass even the pagan past within its eternal embrace.

Quatremère sought instead to create not an image of divine
succession but a legible text articulating the eternal new age of the

Republic. Accordingly, he asserted that Gothic architecture was a dialect derived from the classical language. Negating Ste.-Geneviève's Gothic aspect and intensifying its classical aspect, he exposed the true etymological past of the Gothic tradition. His design subsumed the transience of the medieval variant within the constant and ahistorical presence of the classical type. Quatremère compared his own design to other architectural transformations in which "each generation seems to have wanted to ascribe itself in order formally to record variations in its own style and opinions."[63] Instead, he emphasized the atemporality of Ste.-Geneviève's inherent temple form. Removing the Gothic linchpin of Soufflot's typology of Christianity's history, the windows, Quatremère intended to protect the Pantheon, and through it the ideals of the Revolution, from history itself. In fact, one of his main objectives was to make sure that the Pantheon would not be about the Revolution: "this monument may be the product of the Revolution but it has not been specially dedicated to the Revolution."[64] Quatremère did not want to limit the reach of the Pantheon's historical significance by requiring it to celebrate and illustrate a frozen, single moment in time. Nor was the building intended to reflect a golden past or project a utopian age of the future. The Pantheon's revolutionary function was to speak of an ahistorical time as abstract and eternal as the moral sphere of the Republic itself.

Through a process of historical abstraction, Quatremère used the timelessness of classical architectural convention to reconsecrate Ste.-Geneviève, articulate the Revolutionary nature of the Pantheon, and eternalize the reign of the Republic. He reiterated these goals in his new program of decoration in sculpture, the resources of which he felt gave to architecture "what it lacks: they explain what was indecisive, they develop what was hidden."[65] The elaborate scheme included a new ensemble for the pediment, a series of bas-reliefs for the porch beneath the pediment as well as for the surfaces of the pendentives within the building, and freestanding commemorative sculpture.[66] Responding to Soufflot's sculptural program image by image, Quatremère's new iconography systematically replaced Christian icons with

Republican ideas. Finally, where Soufflot had made his typological expression of the succession of Christianity most explicit, Quatremère made his transformation of this notion into the timelessness of the Republic most complete.[67] Soufflot had placed images of the mysterious and sacrosanct history of Christianity taken from the Old Testament and the Greek, Latin, and Gallic churches on the pendentives of the central crossing. When Quatremère replaced them with signs of the perpetual presence of Philosophy, Patriotic Virtue, Science, and Art, he stripped the physical heart of Ste.-Geneviève and the spiritual core of the Church—its continuity, universality, and even its miraculousness—of divine authority and vested these same attributes in the reasoned realm of the Republic.[68]

Quatremère made Soufflot's image of divine succession into an image of rational eternity by suspending his Gothic church in the ageless dimension of the classical tradition. The most striking example of this process of historical transfiguration, however, concerns Soufflot's plan to place inscriptions of the Ten Commandments of God and the Laws of the Church in panels flanking the central door.[69] Quatremère borrowed this idea but replaced Soufflot's texts with the Constitution and the Declaration of the Rights of Man, intending to suggest "on the one hand, what the nation does for man and, on the other, what man owes the nation."[70] The substitution replaced Soufflot's view of the social order based on divine law with a secular political structure based on contract. Quatremère's design also fundamentally abstracted Soufflot's revelation of perpetuity.[71] Divine law was diachronic, revealing history through the continuity between Old and New Testaments, whereas the new political structure was synchronic, revealing parity across the social order.

Quatremère explicitly connected the ahistorical and abstract nature of the social contract with his ahistorical and abstract treatment of the Pantheon as a work of art: "I thought that the code of our laws, contained on the one hand in a declaration of rights and on the other in a constitution, would be well placed in the portico of this philosophical Pantheon. This idea led me . . . to express by analogy less the traits of the Revolution

than its accomplishments, and less its history than its morality."[72]
In order to express the nature of the relationship between the
Revolution and Revolutionary arts, Quatremère turned to the language of allegory. In his opinion, historical subjects could not
function in the context of the Pantheon whether taken from the
past or the present:

> With respect to events, they would have to be selected either
> from ancient history or from French history, but only [French
> history] after the Revolution.
>
> I thought that in this first national monument one ought
> finally to renounce merely paying tribute to the ancients. It is
> finally time to belong to oneself. Effigies of Greeks and Romans
> must cease to figure at the point when those of the French,
> having become free, begin to shine.
>
> [Yet] it could also be hazardous to assign to sculpture [the
> representation of] Revolutionary events that history has not yet
> disengaged from the personages who were but their instruments.
> [Sculpture] must be able to give these events completely to the
> people that was their motor.
>
> Features of history copied from so near resemble objects
> seen through a magnifying glass. It was thus necessary to sacri-
> fice local and accidental truths for the sake of general truth. It
> was necessary either to erase figures or to resolve to watch them
> be erased by time. . . . The history of the Revolution must find
> its place in the temples that liberty will everywhere erect. Here,
> it was necessary to sing of its effects rather than its actions and
> to celebrate its reign rather than its conquest.[73]

To use the ancient past would be to eliminate the modernity of
the structure and to use the present would be to eliminate its
historical value altogether. Only allegory was sufficiently abstract
to accommodate this crisis of historical identity.

Quatremère conceived of allegory as a formal language
derived from history and rationalized over time to such a degree
that it transcended history. Through this process of abstraction,
allegory had acquired an infinite capacity for expression.[74] The
metahistorical nature of the language of allegory had another,
immeasurable advantage over other languages of art, with partic-

ular respect to the historical demands made of the Pantheon. In its original form, this "language of figures or . . . writing by signs" was the means of expression used during "the infancy of societies."[75] Quatremère was well aware of the fact that many would find this language illegible. He argued, however, that because the nascent structure of allegory was parallel to and thus uniquely expressive of the revolutionary birth of a new society, the public would learn to read this text as part of its own process of self-transformation.[76] Just as Quatremère's revolutionary use of classicism alluded to the Revolution itself, his use of the language of allegory alluded to the Pantheon's role in defining the new Republic.

In his design for the Pantheon Quatremère called on the Republic of the Arts to articulate the processes of secularization, rationalization, and revolution that had led to the creation of the French Republic and the re-creation of the building itself. While the Pantheon honored the Republic, however, it was to serve the whole public of France. Quatremère hoped to make the Republic's "first national monument" play this larger role by adding to its "passive" commemorative function "a more active function, a course of habitual uses."[77] So that the Pantheon might fulfill its moral and physical obligation to the public, Quatremère transformed Ste.-Geneviève into a page literally inscribed by the Republic of the Arts.[78] This text publicly declaring the reign of the Revolution and enunciating its ideals gave active voice and moral priority to the arts in modern society. Finally, by using allegory and by using classical conventions allegorically, he demonstrated the linguistic structure and hence the social consequence of art. In this way, Quatremère constructed a universal language of civic building in which a republican alliance of all the social languages of art proclaimed that the Republic itself was society's most creative triumph.[79]

CONCLUSION

The Sociality of Modern Languages of Architecture

The idea that architecture is language had the effect of assigning to society the task nature had traditionally fulfilled as the progenitor of architectural meaning. This substitution was intimately related to the development of self-conscious modernity. In one way or another, all theories of architecture subsequent to this shift have claimed to be vehicles for the production of socially meaningful buildings and have tended, moreover, to associate their modernity with the degree to which they lead to the integration of architecture with society. Although modernity and historicism are thought of as antithetical, Quatremère's conception of classicism as a product of convention rather than historical necessity, and his association of convention with society, vested the function of architecture in its sociality and thus initiated one of the dominant themes in modern architectural theory.

The importance of the idea that architecture is a form of language derives from the role it played in Quatremère's view of the shift from prototypical nature to social artifice. Encouraged in part by the confrontation with nonclassical civilizations, he no longer saw classicism as simply innate to architecture but as the vehicle by which architecture defined the social structure of the modern world. The principal medium through which Quatremère achieved this new integration of society and architecture was abstraction, and particularly the abstraction of language. By virtue of its abstraction, the classical language of architecture could infiltrate the public sphere and urge the development of concepts such as morality, justice, and equality. He identified these concepts with social abstraction, the key generating force for modern progress. His beliefs that reason can erase difference to produce equality, and that abstraction can embed buildings in a social matrix

and render architecture a progressive and useful public institution, became a credo of modern architectural thought.

What does the language of architecture look like? There
is no single answer to this question, which is at once why Quatremère is important to the conceptual development of modern architecture and why his importance has been underestimated.
Although he privileged the classical language of architecture, he
argued just as strongly that all architecture was a form of language.
The latter assertion was grounded in what he called the metaphysics of architecture, its essential and universal nature, while the
former was based on his theory of architecture, which concerned
particular and practical production. Since the principle that
architecture is language was universal, it could not entail a specific
form. On the other hand, one could prescribe the form of a
particular architecture if one accepted that its value would be
relative and socially contingent.

Quatremère's distinction between universal and particular
architectural principles helps to explain the breadth and depth of
his legacy. Clear evidence for this is the fact that his ideas survived
in two seemingly contradictory contexts: the demise of classicism
and the rise of historical positivism. In the first of these, his notion
that architecture is language, intended to serve in the creation of
a new classicism, contributed instead to the collapse of the classical hegemony and to the genesis of a modern idiom. Sir John
Soane is an architect whose unorthodox use of classicism has long
been included in the canonical march toward abstraction in modern architecture. Although his disregard of convention would have
been abhorrent to Quatremère, Quatremère's ideas played a significant role in encouraging Soane's deviance. A key factor in
Soane's transgression of strict classical convention was his use of
"primitive" architectural form, long considered to have been
inspired by Laugier.[1] It seems, however, that Quatremère was
equally influential on this point. Soane owned three copies of *De
l'architecture égyptienne,* and the notebooks in which he collected
material for the lectures he gave at the Royal Academy between
1809 and 1836 indicate that he read and reread the book over the
course of many years.[2] He purchased his first copy on August 15,

1806, and his annotations, sketches from its plates, and even the beginning of a translation reveal an interest that persisted at least until 1821 (figs. 16 and 10).[3] Soane studied Quatremère's theory of imitation, particularly with respect to the hut and the processes by which it is reproduced, as well as his views on cluster columns in Egyptian and in Gothic architecture. What seems most to have intrigued Soane, however, was Quatremère's theory of origins.

Soane's notes explore in detail Quatremère's ideas on the multiple and contextual origins of architecture. In the lectures as finally given, Soane repeats precisely Quatremère's theory of typology, rooting architecture in the cave, tent, and hut, associating these forms with three classes of primitive social structure (hunters, shepherds, and husbandmen), and locating them in Egypt, China, and Greece respectively.[4] Most important, however, is the stress Soane gives to the fact that "Architecture does not owe its origin to any particular people."[5] He reminds himself to tell his students that "every nation has a separate architecture," but "Before we say any particular nation has been the inventor of Architecture we should recollect it is first a necessary consequence from the wants of man."[6] For Soane, Quatremère's epigenetic view of architecture, the most innovative and controversial thesis of *De l'architecture égyptienne*, was entirely convincing.

In addition to accepting Quatremère's principle of multiple architectural types, Soane reiterated the parallel Quatremère established between the origins of architecture and those of language. Translating directly from *De l'architecture égyptienne*, Soane noted (the oddities of punctuation and grammar are Soane's):

> Architecture, like language is not an invention that any man can ascribe/attribute to himself, they are both attributes of man. . . . Among Languages we must distinguish those whose origin is unknown from those composed or derived from pre-existing languages—we must not confound the *general principles of universal Grammar*, which belongs to language with *the rules of syntax proper to each tongue*, & pretend to establish between two languages a filiation founded on this, namely that they both have *declension & conjugation*, on this hand I believe no man

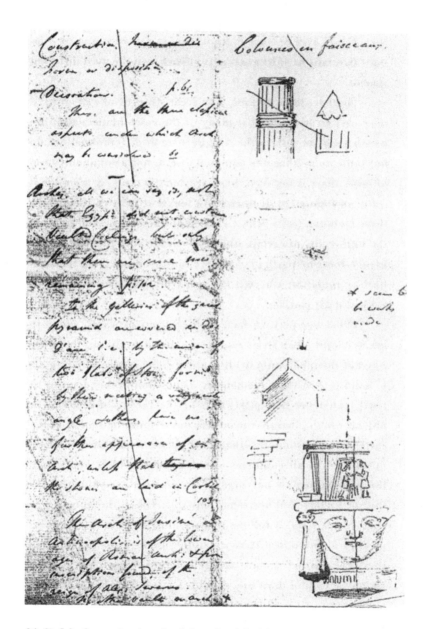

16. Sir John Soane, sketch made of plates 4 and 5 of Quatremère's *De l'architecture égyptienne*, The Sir John Soane Museum, London

has erred: in Architecture it is the reverse, few have escaped error:—they have confounded those *general maxims of the art of building,* common to every species of Architecture, with *particular principles and original given things* of each distinct species [of] Architecture & from them imagined/supposed filiations & relations of likeness/parenté between the most different species.

Neither deep notions, nor great strength of reasoning is necessary to perceive that many of the resemblances/affinities which we meet with in the Architecture of different nations do not indicate neither one common origin, nor a communication of taste, there is between the characteristic traits, & the general traits an important distinction to make: it is by distinguishing these common traits—these elemental likenesses resulting from the uniformity of certain universal causes, with the true resemblance local or particular productions/produite from the filiation or imitation wherein the spirit of true criticism on this subject must consist.

Whatever may, in fact, be the variety of wants, which in every country has given rise to the art of building, there are some of them common to all people, such as those which relate to solidity & certain elementary dispositions dependent on its laws[.] whatever may afterwards be the variety of relations or objects which pleasure introduces in the combinations or accessories of construction:—there are pleasures & tastes common to all men of all countries,—such as those which result from the constitution of our organs, the instinct of symmetry, the love of variety & other sensations inherent in the human species. If this is so, it follows that we must meet in the architectural production of different nations, strangers to each other— the most distinct & most separate certain resemblances from which we cannot draw any conclusion & establish among them a communication of taste, style & principle.[7]

In Laugier, Cordemoy, and others, Soane was able to learn of the primitive hut and of its importance to the development of Greek architecture. The meaning of Soane's architecture, however, is not fully invested in conventional ideas about the primitive hut, since his buildings fail consistently to disengage the orders, as Laugier had prescribed, and often eliminate the orders altogether. Instead, his designs combine and alternate between various primitive forms, incorporating the universal as well as local grammars of architecture. While Laugier's simple focus on the hut was clearly significant, Quatremère's complex theory of origins enabled Soane to develop a principle of design that addressed both the general and the particular architectural needs of man, and encompassed both the historical roots and the contemporary forms of building. The breadth of this principle was due to the abstraction of Quatremère's ideas, which were not confined to the details of classical form and which through Soane contributed to the creation of what has long been considered one of the first veritably modern languages of architecture.

The second context in which Quatremère's distinction between universal and particular principles contributed to the durability of his ideas, the rise of historicism, involves his belief in the independence of theory from historical fact (precisely the reason he gave for publishing his treatise on Egyptian architecture without incorporating the results of the Napoleonic expedition). Already in 1803 a review of *De l'architecture égyptienne* published in the *Moniteur universel* addressed this point:

> It is possible that among men of art [the author] will encounter severe minds that are unable to content themselves with anything other than positive observations. . . . They will find that the author has occasionally tended too much toward conjecture, toward hypothesis. [They will find] that caressing with too much complaisance these children of his imagination, he sought and saw . . . less that which really was than that which might or ought to have been. But [they] will also find . . . that the work . . . contains . . . a dialectic of abundant consequences . . . , [consequences] that might at first seem more specious than solid.[8]

By the mid-nineteenth century this speculative quality of his work caused widespread concern over Quatremère's inescapable presence in the art world. César-Denis Daly in 1847 accused those teaching the theory of art and architecture at the Ecole des Beaux-

Arts of excessively "cultivating" the works of Quatremère de Quincy. He wrote:

> This author is, in effect, one of the most ingenious writers who have ever concerned themselves with architecture: but the philosophical doctrines of Mr. Quatremère faithfully recall the tendencies of the century of his birth, and his theories of art derive very logically from his philosophical ideas. Neither the former nor the latter are therefore complete. They sin by insufficiency and sometimes out of ignorance. They alone cannot respond to the needs of these times. We are now deep in the middle of the nineteenth century and Quatremère's works have their roots for the most part in the eighteenth century. Other times, other doctrines.[9]

Daly's particular emphasis on the eighteenth-century character of Quatremère's work, however, is ironic and perhaps unwittingly perspicacious. Quatremère's "ingenuity" as an architectural theorist derived from precisely those aspects of Enlightenment thinking that freed him to approach ancient Egyptian architecture with what would later be condemned as insufficient knowledge and downright ignorance.[10] Unburdened by positivist empiricism, Quatremère could use Egypt as a vehicle for a speculative analysis of the origins of architecture. From this hypothetical vantage point came some of his most concrete contributions to the history of architectural ideas.

The resilience of Quatremère's basic ideas in the face of detailed criticism is evident from the remarkable tribute paid by Barthélemy Saint-Hilaire, academician, politician, and philosopher. On Christmas Eve of 1855, while camping by a fire in the Egyptian desert, Barthélemy turned to Quatremère's *De l'architecture égyptienne* in order to prepare himself for the visits to ancient ruins he was about to make. That same evening he wrote the tenth of his *Lettres sur l'Egypte*—entirely devoted to architecture—which he began by discussing Quatremère's theory of architectural origins: "I do not deny the value of this theory. . . . But origins are always so obscure that it is better not to try and reach for them. And while I find this explanation very ingenious, I do not stop there. I take it for what it is without attaching too much importance to it. Egyptian architecture is that which is there and sits before us. I think it would be better to study what we see than to try to discover, in the midst of darkness, what concepts presided over its birth."[11] Condemning the ingenious framework within which Quatremère had analyzed Egyptian architecture, Barthélemy nevertheless adopted the analysis itself. He found Egyptian architecture lacking order other than that imposed "in the name of certain religious and political principles that have nothing to do with the principles of art and of beauty." He felt it was monotonous and immutable and ascribed these shortcomings to a lack of liberty and other social strictures that were "written in irrecusable characters on the very stones that formed their buildings." Barthélemy described Egypt's hieroglyph-laden buildings as "the annals of these people, their archives, and their libraries."[12]

Quatremère's study of the radical equivalence between language and architecture had enabled Barthélemy to define Egyptian buildings as documents in which the history and character of society could be read. While he rejected the means by which Quatremère had arrived at this notion, the idea itself constitutes the intellectual foundation of the following question Barthélemy asked of Egyptian architecture: "When we walk through these colossal ruins and when we admire their portals, colonnades, obelisks, palaces, and temples, a painful thought comes to us unceasingly. Here certainly are the homes of priests and kings. But the people, where did they live? Here are the splendid dwellings of the rich and powerful. But the masses, where are their shelters and their homes?"[13] Barthélemy's interest in the masses is a nineteenth- rather than an eighteenth-century concern, yet his ability literally to read in the buildings of ancient Egypt the annals of their social context is in part a debt he owed to Quatremère. Ultimately Barthélemy excused Quatremère's lack of scientific understanding of Egyptian architecture, observing that for "a mind on the order of Quatremère's" the little information available had sufficed for a still unmatched book on Egyptian architecture:

His *mémoire*, which is today 71 years old, has never been surpassed, and I doubt it ever will be. Hieroglyphs, better understood and more studied, certainly will teach us many essential details of the history of the potentates who erected these gigantic edifices. They will teach us nothing of the value of Egyptian art. That is simply a question of aesthetics, which archaeology has no business considering. . . .

It is true that one can be quite inferior to the Greeks and still be great. Quatremère de Quincy's study proves it, even though it ends in a critique. I think that although he placed Egyptian architecture well below its rival, he nevertheless contributed more than anyone else to placing it quite high. For myself, it was [Quatremère] who taught me to . . . penetrate somewhat its mysteries, of which it may not have been conscious itself.[14]

The substance of Quatremère's ideas persisted into the mid-nineteenth century even as specific elements of their framework fell into disfavor.[15] Details of his theory of type, for example, were rejected already in the nineteenth century, but the concept of type remained a viable basis for systematizing the vagaries of design. Alternately located in formal morphology by Durand, in function by Pevsner, in modes of production by Le Corbusier and the Werkbund, the types of architecture are still in operation. Moreover, as architectural typology began once again to include aspects of the history and origins of architecture, as in Aldo Rossi's use of type, its specific lineage from Quatremère was reidentified.[16]

The most transformed yet still most legible trace left by Quatremère's work is the idea that architecture is language. Before his death and the demise of classicism, the metaphor had become explicit, as in the title of an essay published in 1820, "On the Analogy between Language and Architecture."[17] Yet Quatremère's interest in defining a building as a legible text and constructing monuments that are conceived as books open for the edification of the public remained of fundamental importance despite waning interest in ideal classicism. No clearer testimony can be imagined than the works of Victor Hugo and Henri Labrouste. The celebrated chapters on architecture in Hugo's *Notre-Dame de Paris*, which describe architecture as having begun as writing and as having evolved into the "great book of the human race," are inconceivable without Quatremère's earlier explorations. Similarly, and however combative their direct relationship, Labrouste would scarcely have envisioned the embrace of legibility and sociality that is the most renowned achievement of his Bibliothèque Sainte-Geneviève, begun in 1838, without the intellectual model provided by Quatremère.[18] Labrouste certainly did not speak the language of classical allegory, nor did Hugo value the enunciatory capacity of classicism, but in thinking of architecture as a means of articulate speech both depended on the basic structure of Quatremère's theory.

The structure has survived to this day as a stable architectural principle in the context of changing needs. From Quatremère's eighteenth-century point of view, revolutionary society demanded the classical language of architecture. But in its abstractness, the idea that architecture is language, which framed Quatremère's view, encompassed other social and architectural forms. When Quatremère posed the question "If language belongs to humanity, do the languages that are particular modifications of this general faculty belong to specific societies or nations?" he acknowledged the difference between a universal postulate and a relative practice, and in this respect provided a framework for multiple discourses. Quatremère, however, maintained that simply to speak of the "language of architecture" is not necessarily to speak of a socially significant built environment. Since, in his view, all architectures are languages and individual languages only have value relative to their particular contexts, he insisted that the selection of one architectural language over another is a profoundly meaningful social act: "It is extremely important, and I will not stop repeating this point, that if the language of architecture is to have value, if its signs are to be understood and are to have the effect of which they are capable, . . . if these signs are to say something, they must not be used to say nothing."[19]

APPENDIX A

Archives de l'Institut de France, Minutes des procès-verbaux, Académie des Inscriptions et Belles-Lettres, 1778–1789, Cote A84

The material noted in the minutes was transcribed into the official registry and thus can also be found in Archives de l'Academie des Inscriptions et Belles-Lettres, Registre des Procès-verbaux, Registre journal des déliberations et des assemblés de l'Academie Royale des Inscriptions, vol. 1783–1784, A68

du Mardi 23 Mars, 1784

[Members present:] De Sigrais, De Guignes, De Burigny, Dupuy, Garnier, Béjot, Dacier, Arnaud, Anquetil, Ameilhon, Bouchard, De Sibert, De Rochefort, Le Roy, Du Theil, De Villoison, Le Blond, Dussaulx, Larcher, De Kéralio, Brotier, Auger, Vauvilliers.

On a ensuite travaillé au sujet du prix qu'on doit donner à la St. Martin de l'année 1785; mais on n'a rien decidé.

26 Mars, 1784

[Members present:] De Sigrais, De Guignes, De Burigny, Dupuy, Chabanon, Gaillard, Garnier, Béjot, Dacier, Anquetil, Ameilhon, Bouchard, De Sibert, De Rochefort, Le Roy, Du Theil, Désormeaux, De Villoison, Le Blond, Dussaulx, Larcher, De Kéralio, Brotier, Auger, Vauvilliers.

On s'est encore occupé des differents sujets du prix proposés par divers Membres de la Compagnie, et enfin l'on s'est decidé pour celui qui regarde l'architecture Egyptienne; mais sans arrêter la maniere de presenter la question au public.

Mars 30, 1784

[Members present:] De Sigrais, De Guignes, De Burigny, Dupuy, De Bréquigny, Chabanon, Gaillard, Garnier, Béjot, Dacier, Arnaud, Anquetil,

Ameilhon, Bouchard, De Sibert, De Rochefort, Le Roy, Du Theil, Désormeaux, De Villoison, Le Blond, Dussaulx, Larcher, De Kéralio, Brotier, Auger, Vauvilliers.

On a commencer par arrêter le sujet du prix qui doit être distribué à la St. Martin de l'année prochaine. L'academie propose de rechercher: Quel fut l'etat de l'Architecture chez les Egyptiens, & ce que les Grecs paroissent en avoir emprunté?

Du Mardi 20 Avril, 1784 (assemblée publique)

Après cette distribution M. le Secrétaire lut le programme qui contenoit le sujet du prix proposé pour le St. Martin [. . .] 1785, et qui consiste à rechercher: *Quel fut l'etat de l'architecture des Egyptiens, et ce que les Grecs paroissent en avoir emprunté.*

23 Juin, 1785

L'Academie, convoquée par billets pour deliberer si l'on devoit accepter ou refuser le leg[ation] que lui a fait M. Saunier, Conseiller d'Etat, par son testament dont on trouve la copie ci dessus, dans le compte rendu de la séance du 17 de ce mois, a consacré celle d'aujourdhui à la discussion de cette affaire. Aprés l'avoir longtemps examinée et debat[u], et s'être fais lire tout ce qui s'etoit passé lors de la fondation des deux anciens prix par M. Le P[ère] de Noinville, et M. Le Cte de Caylus, on est convenue de diviser la question en trois points.

On a proposé de decider 1. Si la fondation d'une 3e prix est avantageuse aux Lettres et à L'Academie, en supposant que les conditions imposées par M. Saunier convinsent à la Compagnie. Cette proposition a donné lieu à plusiers observations. On a renouvellé toutes les objections qu'on avoit faites lors que M. Le. P[ère] de Noinville proposa l'institution de son prix, et dont une partie est imprimée dans le tome IX de nos Memoires. On a de plus ajouté que le peu d'utilité de ces prix est demontré par l'experience; puis que le nombre des Memoires envoyé à chaque concours, diminue sensiblement; qu'il arrive même quelque fois que le Secretaire n'en recoit aucun; que parmi ceux qui lui sont remis, il est rare qu'il s'en trouve un, au premier Concours, qui sois jugé digne du prix; de sorte qu'on est obligé de proposer le même sujet jusqu'à trois fois, et qu'en fin on se determine assez souvent à donner le prix, soit qu'il soit simple, lorsqu'il soit double ou triple, à un Memoire Mediocre, et qui n'en est pas veritablement digne, par la crainte bien fondée de n'en pas reçevoir de meilleur, et pour s'epargner le desagrement de retirer le Sujet proposé. Cependant les voix ayant été prises par voie de Scrutin, la pluralité a été pour l'affirmative, et il a été arrêté qu'on devoise accepter le fondation de ce troisieme prix si les Conditions imposées par le testateur, et qui font l'objet du second point de la deliberation, paroisoient pouvoir être admises.

5 Juillet, 1785

Aprés la lecture de cette Lettre, M. Dacier a annoncé qu'il n'avais reçu que deux Memoires pour le prix de la St. Martin qui consiste à examiner: *Quel fut l'etat de l'architecture chez les Egyptiens et ce que les Grecs en ont emprunté.* Il a demandé en même temps qu'on nômmes des Commissaires pour l'examen de ces Memoires. La pluralité des voix, prises par Scrutin, ont été pour Mrs. Le Roy et Brotier.

Du Mardi 23 Aoust, 1785

Mrs. les Commissaires, nommés pour examiner les pieces qui concourent au prix, se sont assemblés dans un des cabinets du logement de l'Academie. Le prix a été adjugé au Memoire de M. Quatremère de Quincy. Le sujet étoit *l'architecture des Egyptiens &c.*

Members of the Académie des Inscriptions et Belles-Lettres and dates of their election to the Academy.

Claude-Guillaume Bourdon de Sigrais	1752
Joseph de Guignes	1753
Jean, l'evêque de Burigny	1756
Louis Dupuy	1756
Louis-Georges Oudard Freudrix de Bréquigny	1759
Michel-Paul-Gui de Chabanon	1759
Gabriel-Henri Gaillard	1760
L'abbé Jean-Jacques Garnier	1761
François Béjot	1762
Joseph-Bon Dacier	1762
L'abbé François Arnaud	1762
Abraham-Hyacinthe Anquetil dit Anquetil-Duperron	1763

L'abbé Hubert-Pascal Ameilhon	1766
Mathieu-Antoine Bouchard	1766
Paul-Edme Gautier-de-Sibert	1767
Guillaume Dubois de Rochefort	1767
Jean-David Le Roy	1770
François-Jean-Gabriel de La Porte du Theil	1770
Charles-Louis Ripault Désormeaux	1772
Jean-Baptiste-Gaspard d'Ansse de Villoison	1772
L'abbé Gaspard Michel dit Leblond	1772
Jean Dussaulx	1773
Pierre-Henri Larcher	1778
Louis-Félix Guinement de Kéralio	1780
L'abbé Gabriel Brotier	1780
L'abbé Athanase Auger	1781
Jean-François Vauvilliers	1781

APPENDIX B

Comparative table of Quatremère's Prix Caylus manuscript and De l'architecture égyptienne

Prix Caylus

The manuscript (Archives de l'Académie des Inscriptions et Belles-Lettres, Prix Caylus, 1785, MS D74) is numbered only on the upper right-hand side. Thus, each folio number encompasses two pages of text.

APPENDIX C

Memorandum on payment to Quatremère de Quincy for the Encyclopédie méthodique

Undated manuscript in the Archives of the History of Art, The Getty Center for the History of Art and the Humanities.

Précis pour Mr Quatremere de Quincy

En 1786 Mr Quatremere de Quincy souscrivit entre les mains de Mr Ch. Panckoucke *entrepreneur de l'Encyclopedie par ordre de Matière*, l'obligation de rediger et de composer en 2 vol. in 4o de 100 feuilles à 16 colonnes chacune, un *Dictionnaire d'architecture*, au prix de 48 la feuille.

La 1er tome de ce Dictionnaire, que depuis Mr Panckoucke voulut porter *à 4 tomes*, fut composé par M. Quatremere de Quincy, qui en fut payé vers 1791, autant que sa mémoire le lui rappelle.

Depuis cette epoque jusqu'à la fin du siècle quelque nouveaux arrangements eurents lieu, dont Mr Quatremere n'a conservé aucun titre, ayant, par l'effet des évenemens revolutionnaire de cette époque, perdu ses meubles, ses livres et tous ses papiers.

Au commencement du nouveau siècle et revenu de la *déportation du 18 fructidor* Mr Panckoucke était mort; quelque arrangements nouveaux eurent lieu avec Mr Agasse son gendre, et il fu convenu de réduire l'ouvrage à 3 tomes au lieu de 4. M Quatremere croit se souvenir que vers la 2e ou 3e année du siècle il termina la 1e partie du 2e tome (les livraisons de l'Encyclopedie étoient publiée par demi volume). Il croit se souvenir encore qu'il fut payé de cette 1ere moitié de 2e tome, par Mr. Agasse, qui mourut peu de tems après.

Nouvelle interruption de 8 a 10 ans, après laquelle Mme Agasse sollicite de Mr. Quatremere de Quincy la continuation de 2e tome, qui doit avoir été achevé vers l'an 1820. Mr Quatremere n'a point été payé des 48 feuilles formante ce demi tome.

Mr. Quatremere de Quincy était alors extraordinairement occupé et sur-chargé d'un grand nombre de travaux. Il ne croyait pas pouvoir repondre à l'empressement de Mme Agasse.

Dans cette circonstance il lui fut proposé deux collaborateurs. Ceux ci exigeraient par feuille un augmentation notable de prix et ils la portaient à 100 francs au lieu de 60. Il fut convenue par Mme Agasse, qu'elle payerait la feuille 80 f.

Espérant ainsi être déchargé des deux tiers au moins de la besogne, Mr Quatremere s'engagea par écrit à rient reclamer *pour sa part du travail dans* ce troisième tome.

Cependant les deux collaborateurs ignorant quelle était l'étendue de ce travail, n'y eurent pas plutôt mis la mains qu'ils y renoncèrent. L'un quitta Paris et l'autre se désista de fait.

Dans ces circonstantes Mr Quatremere de Quincy se mis *seul* à la besogne et de 1820 à 1826 ou 1827 il fournis toute la matière de 3e tome.

Mr Quatremere produit l'entier désistement de chacune des deux colla-borateurs qui n'ayant à proprement parlé rien fait [*in margin:* n'exigerent rien] (comme ils le témoignent aujourd'hui par écrit) et Mme Agasse ne leur a rien payé.

Mr. Quatremere ayant tout fait et n'ayant consenti [*in margin:* à renoncer] qu'*à sa part dans le travail* qui devait se faire avec les deux collaborateurs d'ailleurs aujourd'hui par d'autre circonstance, dont il ne parlera point ici, les reclamer ce qui lui est dû. Il demande le payement,

1. de la 2e partie du 2e Volume du Dictionnaire d'architecture pour laquelle il n'a rien reçu

2. des deux tiers au moins de 3e tome qu'il a terminé seul et pour lequel Mme agasse n'a rien payé.

APPENDIX D

"Sur la manière d'imiter la bonne Architecture grecque," Journal des batimens civils, *no. 29 (6 nivose, an 9 [December 27, 1800]), 3–7*

Les français en adoptant l'architecture grecque, ne manquèrent pas de lui communiquer le caractère national, d'y imprimer un goût local. Cette nuance, qui se fit sentir dès le commencement de l'introduction de la bonne architecture, parmi nous, n'a cessé de varier jusqu'à ce jour, avec nos modes et nos habitudes. Ainsi, on finira peut-être par ne plus la reconnaître, parce qu'elle s'éloigne tout-à-fait de sa véritable source.

L'architecture grecque avait reçu de ses inventeurs toute la perfection qu'elle pouvait espérer. Simple dans le dorique, mais pleine de force, de caractère, et de cette energie qui dut accompagner les siècles de la vraie liberté; faite enfin pour des républiques dont la *sobriété*, *l'austerité*, et la *vertu* doivent faire la base, elle acquiert bientôt, sous le climat le plus voluptueux de l'Ionie, cette grace et cette mollesse dont l'ordre, qui en a conservé le nom, nous retrace le caractère. Tant il est vrai que l'architecture porte toujours l'empreinte du génie des peuples qui l'employent!

Mais quels changemens son style et son goût n'éprouvent-ils point dans un même pays, selon la différence des causes politiques qui transforment et dénaturent les états?

Rome pauvre, mais libre, ne connaît que l'ordre rustique des étrusques. Rome opulente et esclave, ne trouve plus assez de richesse dans le corinthien, le plus riche de tous les ordres. Il lui faut un luxe exagéré comme sa puissance, et le *composite*, dont sa vanité veut faire un ordre, va devenir un monument de son impuissant orgueil . . .

C'est donc aux monumens seuls de la Grèce, et à ceux du plus bel âge, qu'on doit une admiration aveugle, et qu'on peut avouer une vénération sans bornes.

Il y a deux manières d'imiter l'architecture grecque; l'une consiste à en imiter le style; l'autre à en saisir les principes et le génie.

La première manière, qui est aujourd'hui en usage, est appelée faussement imitation par nos jeunes architectes: ce n'est qu'une singerie propre uniquement à en discréditer le goût auprès de ceux qui ne savent pas en démasquer l'imposture. Elle suppose aussi peu de génie, que l'autre en exige du véritable imitateur.

En effet, rien de plus simple et de plus facile, que cette imitation illusoire de l'Architecture grecque. Cet art, quant à son essence, étant fixé et déterminé depuis long-tems, il est démontré qu'on ne saurait inventer de nouvelles formes, ne produire de nouveaux genres. L'architecte ne doit donc, en général, que disposer et mettre en oeuvre un certain nombre de formes, de parties et de membres qu'il trouve tous créés et perfectionnés avant lui. Mais, dès que toutes les parties constitutives d'un édifice peuvent entrer dans la composition d'un autre, que fait le stérile imitateur dont nous parlons? Il copie ce qu'il paraît imiter; il croit changer la proportion, lorsqu'il ne change que l'échelle. Et si cette prétendue imitation ne se réduit encore de sa part qu'*à une pratique linéaire,* qui n'exige qu'un talent des plus borné, quelle idée faudra t-il s'en former, et à quoi sera-t-il bon? à être renvoyé à l'école de la bonne antiquité . . .[1]

C'est pourtant par de tels moyens que les projets de tant d'architects, parés comme des reliquaires avec tous les débris des monumens antiques, en imposent au vulgaire ignorant. Mais l'oeil clairvoyant qui sais en découvrir la fraude n'apperçoit dans toutes ces transpositions factices, que les ressources malheureuses d'une pauvreté mal déguisée.

Rien de plus prodigue, de plus abondant dans l'étalage de leurs prétendues richesses, que ces génies parasites qui entassent tous les temples de l'antiquité, et ne savent projeter ou même construire une maison saine et commode . . . Ils sont capables, à la vérité, de vous faire les plans de Thèbes, de Memphis et d'Olympie; mais ne leur demandez, ni le dessin d'une porte, ne la proportion d'une colonne. Sous leur crayon faussement poétique, tout devient temple, et les séjours des plus humbles mortels, n'ont rien qui les distinguent des demeures divines. Mais aussi, réalisez ces projets si beaux, si riches en apparence; plus d'accord, plus de proportion, plus d'harmonie, pas même d'ensemble. L'illusion a disparu; toute cette vaine enflure s'est évanouie dans l'exécution.

Que sera-ce, si de tels imitateurs sont forcés d'exécuter un édifice dont ils ne trouvent point de modèles dans l'antiquité, ou qui ne puisse être de nature à se transformer en temple? C'est alors que se découvre, dans toute son étendue, l'indigence de leur génie. Comme ils n'ont pas su

---

1. C'est ce que la partie instruite du public remarque constamment, dans la grande majorité des projets (exposés au *Muséum*), des colonnes nationale et départementale, et encore plus dans ceux du monument à élever sur le terrain du château Trompette à Bordeaux . . . *O tempus!*

se rendre propres les trésors que nous ont laissés les Grecs, c'est-à-dire surprendre le secret des richesses de leur sublime Architecture, vous n'appercevrez plus alors en eux que le besoin toujours renaissant de dérober, et l'impuissance de le faire avec discernement. Nul caractère propre à leur édifice. La routine devient leur génie, *l'intéret leur seule divinité.* Bientôt ridiculement dépouillés, vous les verrez trahis enfin par tous leurs larcins, retomber honteusement dans la classe qui leur convient, et qu'ils n'auraient jamais dû quitter. (la suite)

"Fin de la manière d'imiter la bonne Architecture grecque," *Journal des batimens civils,* no. 30 (9 nivose, an 9 [December 30, 1800]), 3–5.

La véritable manière d'imiter la bonne *Architecture grecque* consiste à en pénétrer l'esprit, à en deviner les raisons, à en approfondir les principes, à développer ses moyens, à découvrir les routes secrètes par lesquelles il affecte notre ame, à rechercher les causes de ces impressions grandes, simples et variées qu'on éprouve à la vue des monumens. A bien dire, imiter l'*architecture antique,* n'est autre chose que connaître et imiter la nature. Mais ce don d'imitation n'a jamais été le partage que d'un très-petit nombre d'aristes. Il exige une ame à-la-fois sensible et forte, assez flexible et assez molle pour recevoir des émotions qui la pénètrent, assez fière pour résister à *la facilité vulgaire de l'imitation banale*

. . .

. . . A quoi servent tous ces dessins des monumens antiques, minutés et copiés sans art, qui grossissent les recueils de l'architecte? Qu'importe que ses porte-feuilles s'emplissent, si son ame reste vide? De quoi lui serviront ces copies serviles de la main, si l'invisible copie imprimée dans son esprit, ne lui en retrace au besoin le génie qui les anime? L'architecte doit, sans doute, par l'étude des mesures, par l'imitation exacte des plus beaux monumens, se rendre un compte fidèle des moindres détails, et des proportions de l'antique, de ces nuances légères, de ces variétés insensibles qui en modifient les formes et le caractère, et qui échappent à la vue ordinaire et superficielle. Ses premiers pas, sans doute, doivent ainsi se calquer sur ceux de l'antique; mais il faut aussi que, s'identifiant avec lui par la pensée, laissant errer, si on peut le dire, en liberté le génie de l'imitation, se rassasiant de la vue des grands modèles, il quitte en tems la règle et le compas, et laisse germer par la méditation les grands principes dont il s'est *imité.* Cette étude invisible est celle du sentiment. C'est elle qui gravera dans le fond de son ame ces empreintes libres et durables, qui sauront donner à ses ouvrages le caractère inappréciable d'une facile originalité. Alors, cessant d'être l'esclave des Anciens, mais vraiment familiarisé avec eux, il se rendra digne de leur être associé et comparé. Ses ouvrages, pleins d'une richesse qu'il aura in [sic] s'approprier et convertir en *sa propre substance*, s'éloigneront, et de cette profusion indigente, qui prodigue ce qui ne lui appartient pas, et de cette timide parcimonie qui ne saurait donner ce qu'elle n'a point.

Q . . . Architecte

APPENDIX E

Section headings of "Caractère," Encyclopédie
méthodique, *2:477–518*

Etymologie du mot caractère

Définition du mot caractère pris au figuré

Définition plus particulière du mot caractère

Significations et acceptions du mot caractère

Caractère considéré dans la nature prise en général

Caractère considéré dans les Peuples

Caractère considéré dans les Arts du Dessin

Caractère considéré dans l'art de bâtir des différens peuples

Caractère considéré dans l'architecture proprement dite; et moyens par
lesquels l'architecte pourra imprimer aux édifices les diverses qualités
que renferme ce mot.

Caractère distinctif ou d'originalité

Caractère essentiel, ou de force et de grandeur

Caractère relatif ou synonyme de propriété et de convenance

Caractère relatif du genre idéal

Caractère relatif du genre imitatif

Gradation de richesse et de grandeur entre les édifices

Indication des qualités propre à chaque édifice

Formes générales et partielles de l'architecture

Genre de construction

Ressources de la décoration

Attributs

NOTES

Full citations of all sources can be found in the bibliography.

Preface

1. The importance and pervasive presence of this relationship in eighteenth-century architectural theory is generally acknowledged, although little scholarly attention has been given to it. The few studies that have it as their primary focus are the chapter on the linguistic analogy in Collins, *Changing Ideals in Modern Architecture*; Saisselin, "Architecture and Language"; Guillerme, "The Idea of Architectural Language"; Stafford, *Symbols and Myth*; and Guiheux and Rouillard, "Echanges entre les mots et l'architecture dans la seconde moitié du XVIIe siècle."

2. Many of the issues addressed in my fourth chapter are related to concerns explored in Chartier, *The Cultural Origins of the French Revolution*; Habermas, *The Structural Transformation of the Public Sphere*; Landes, *Women and the Public Sphere in the Age of the French Revolution*; Baker, *Inventing the French Revolution*; and Hunt, *Politics, Culture, and Class in the French Revolution*.

3. The tradition of seeing in Quatremère's work the essence of a reactionary mind was cemented in Schneider's still invaluable text, *Quatremère de Quincy et son intervention dans les arts* (1910), which describes Quatremère as hostile to both the radical neoclassicists of the late eighteenth century, such as Ledoux and Boullée, and the radical romantics of the nineteenth century. Schneider, following the lead taken by Benoit's *L'art français sous la Révolution et l'Empire* (1897), established the basic terms of discussion concerning Quatremère, the legacy of which can be traced through Greenhalgh, "Quatremère de Quincy as a Popular Archaeologist"; Krufft, *Geschichte der Architekturtheorie*; and Potts, "Political Attitudes and the Rise of Historicism in Art Theory." Since the 1970s Quatremère's architectural theory in particular has been the subject of a great resurgence of scholarly attention, but this literature for the most part continues to cast his work in a conservative light. Without denying

his historical significance, this recent work still suggests that Quatremère's significance rests on the vociferousness with which he criticized progressive developments. The most important exception is Vidler's *The Writing of the Walls*, which sees in Quatremère an intellectual coherence and rigor hitherto denied.

4. David claimed that a trip to see ancient monuments in Italy with Quatremère had removed cataracts from his eyes and enabled him to see antiquity for the first time. Reported in Guigniaut, "Notice sur la vie et les travaux de M. Quatremère de Quincy," read in 1864 and published in a revised version as *Notice sur la vie et les travaux de M. Quatremère de Quincy* (1866), 367.

5. Soufflot's Ste.-Geneviève is described as an "illustration" of Laugier's ideal by Middleton and Watkin in *Neoclassical and Nineteenth Century Architecture*, 22. Laugier himself was the first to establish the connection between his ideas and Soufflot's building. See Herrmann, *Laugier and Eighteenth Century French Theory*.

6. "Je pense que les beaux ouvrages des arts ont plûtot donné naissance aux théories, que les théories aux beaux ouvrages. Mais il y a de belles théories qui sont aussi en leur genre de beaux ouvrages, et auxquelles bien des personnes prennent plaisir. Ainsi on ne doit pas plus demander à quoi sert une poétique, que demander à quoi sert un morceau de poésie." Quatremère de Quincy, *De l'imitation*, reprint of *Essai sur la nature, le but et les moyens de l'imitation dans les beaux-arts*, xi. All translations in this book are my own, unless otherwise indicated. The original texts are provided in the notes.

Introduction

1. In addition to Schneider's basic biography, other standard sources on Quatremère's life are Rochette, *Discours prononcés aux funérailles de Quatremère de Quincy* (1850); Etienne Quatremère, "Notice historique sur la vie de M. Quatremère de Quincy" (1853; E. Quatremère never completed the second article he had intended to write); Guigniaut, *Notice*; Jouin, A.-C. *Quatremère de Quincy* (1892); Wallon, "Centenaire de l'élection de Quatremère de Quincy à l'Institut" (1903), also published separately as *Notice supplémentaire sur la vie et les travaux de Quatremère de Quincy*; Maury, "Quatremère de Quincy"; Boschot, "Le centenaire d'un esthéticien"; and Boschot, *Maîtres d'hier et de jadis*.

2. Schneider, *Quatremère de Quincy*, 10.

3. Schneider, *Quatremère de Quincy*, 13. This complex period of Quatremère's life has been best recounted by Rowlands, "Quatremère de Quincy," especially 600ff.

4. See Quatremère's *Collection des lettres de Nicolas Poussin* (1824); *Histoire de la vie et des ouvrages de Raphaël* (1824); *Canova et ses ouvrages* (1834); and *Histoire de la vie et des ouvrages des plus célèbres architectes* (1830). Quatremère also published a *Recueil de notices historiques lues dans les séances publiques de l'Académie Royale des Beaux-Arts* (1834) and a *Suite du Recueil de notices historiques* (1837). See in addition his *Notice historique sur la vie et les ouvrages de M. Dufourny* (1834). On Quatremère in relation to Canova, see Messina, "L'arte di Canova nella critica di Quatremère de Quincy," and Howard, "The Antiquarian Market in Rome and the Rise of Neo-classicism."

5. See Quatremère's *Le Jupiter Olympien ou l'Art de la sculpture antique considéré sous un nouveau point de vue* (1814); "Mémoire sur la restitution du Temple de Jupiter Olympien à Agrigent" (1815); *Sur la statue antique de Vénus découverte dans l'île de Milo en 1820* (1821); *Monumens et ouvrages d'art antiques restitués d'après les descriptions des écrivains grecs et latins* (1829); and *Recueil de dissertations archéologiques* (1836). On the importance of the *Jupiter Olympien* to polychromy in architecture, see Van Zanten, *The Architectural Polychromy of the 1830s*, and Middleton, "Hittorff's Polychrome Campaign."

6. On this portrait, inscribed "A mon ami A. Quatremère de Quincy," see Körner and Piel, "'A mon ami A. Quatremère de Quincy,' Ein unbekanntes Werk Jacques-Louis Davids aus dem Jahre 1779." The attribution is based in part on probably accurate but unsubstantiated assertions made by Quatremère's biographers that he and David traveled together to southern Italy during the 1770s.

7. Both Maury, "Quatremère de Quincy," 609, and Wallon, "Centenaire de l'élection," 541, state that Quatremère spent his time in Paris in 1780 studying architecture. There is no external evidence to support this assertion. To the contrary, Quatremère displayed little concern for the structural aspects of architecture. Nevertheless, this discrepancy may reveal more about changing definitions of the professional architect than about Quatremère's interest in architectural practice.

8. The complete entry in the *Almanach* under Quatremère's name is: "Architecte, il n'est ni avocat ni procureur ni académicien et n'a, par conséquent, aucun intérêt à être aristocrate." Cited in "L'état civile des citoyens nobles de Paris en 1789."

9. I am indebted to Philippe Prost for this fact.

10. Quatremère, *Dictionnaire d'architecture*, 3 vols., part of the *Encyclopédie méthodique*, ed. C.-J. Panckoucke (1788–1825); and Quatremère, *Dictionnaire historique d'architecture*, 2 vols. (1832). In order to avoid the common confusion between these publications, the former will hereafter be cited as Quatremère, *Encyclopédie méthodique;* it constitutes one of a series of dictionaries each devoted to a separate subject and collectively called the *Encyclopédie méthodique, ou par ordre de matières.* This vast enterprise was orchestrated by Charles-Joseph Panckoucke in his effort to make a new version of Diderot's *Encyclopédie.* The three-volume work Quatremère produced in response to Panckoucke's commission, which will be further discussed below, is unrelated to the two-volume *Dictionnaire historique d'architecture* that Quatremère wrote independently and at a much later date.

11. Schneider, *Quatremère de Quincy*, 441.

12. An important exception to this tendency is James Henry Rubin's "Allegory versus Narrative in Quatremère de Quincy."

13. "J'ai le droit d'être mort, faites comme si je l'étais." Reported by Jouin, *A. C. Quatremère de Quincy*, 76, and Guigniaut, "Notice," 411.

14. According to Jouin, "le succès de l'archéologue fixa sur lui l'attention. Panckoucke avait conçu l'idée de l'Encyclopédie méthodique. Ami des écrivains les plus éminents de son époque, . . . Panckoucke allait volontiers au-devant des littérateurs d'avenir. Il devina Quatremère de Quincy. C'est à lui qu'il voulut confier le Dictionnaire d'architecture qui rentrait dans le plan de l'Encyclopédie méthodique" (*A. C. Quatremère de Quincy*, 13). Guigniaut also saw the competition as the beginning of Quatremère's academic career: "Survint une circonstance qui l'engagea dans la carrière semée bientôt, comme toutes les autres, de tant d'orageuses et terribles destractions, et qui devait, après vingt ans, le conduire parmi nous comme dans un port" ("Notice," 369). Schneider, Rowlands, and others similarly point to the prize as an explanation for the Panckoucke commission and other accomplishments. However, it is also often

suggested that Quatremère first came to the public's attemtion in 1787 because of a letter regarding the Fontaine des Innocents written to the editor of the *Journal de Paris,* "[Arts:] Aux auteurs du Journal," and because of his political activities.

15. Rowlands, "Quatremère de Quincy," 19.

16. See, in particular, Jouin, *A. C. Quatremère de Quincy,* 12.

17. On the history of the Academy, see Maury, *L'ancienne Académie des Inscriptions et Belles-Lettres,* and Dussaud, *La nouvelle Académie des Inscriptions et Belles-Lettres.*

18. After Caylus's death in 1765 the prize was to be financed by his estate, but lack of funds forced the Academy to distribute it only every other year, beginning in 1773. Royal intervention later returned the competition to a yearly event. See *Histoire de l'Académie Royale des Inscriptions et Belles-Lettres,* vol. 40 (1780), and Maury, *L'ancienne Académie des Inscriptions et Belles-Lettres,* 197. See also the description of the prize in Le Beau's 1766 eulogy of Caylus included in volume 7 of Caylus's *Recueil d'antiquités:* "Ne perdant jamais de vue les Artists, pour leur épargner les fautes dans lesquelles l'ignorance du costume a quelque fois fait tomber les plus habiles, il fonda un prix de 500 liv. dont l'objet est d'expliquer par les auteurs & par les monumens les usages des anciens peuples" (p. xvii).

19. See the entry on the Comte de Caylus in Prevost and d'Amat, eds., *Dictionnaire de biographie française.*

20. The relevant entries from the Academy's *procès verbaux* are reproduced in Appendix A.

21. Essay competitions were often distinguished by the date of the award. In 1785 the Prix Caylus was to be announced on the feast day of St. Martin. The terms Prix Caylus and Prix St. Martin were thus used interchangeably in that year.

22. See Appendix A. The authors remained anonymous until after the prizes had been awarded, thus ensuring impartiality, when their manuscripts were identified by accompanying *papiers cacheteés.* Del Rosso's *mémoire* for the Prix Caylus was published as *Richerche sul'architettura egiziana,* Florence, 1787. A second edition was published in Siena in 1800. The original copies of Quatremère and Del Rosso's

mémoires are located in the Archives de l'Académie des Inscriptions et Belles-Lettres and indexed as Prix Caylus, 1785, MS D 74. For the sake of brevity, the manuscripts will hereafter be cited as Quatremère, Prix Caylus MS, and Del Rosso, Prix Caylus MS, followed by the folio number of the original document. On Del Rosso, see Stoppini, ed., *Dalla 'Libreriola' dell'architetto fiorentino, Giuseppe Del Rosso.*

23. Unfortunately, the original illustrations to Quatremère's essay referred to by figure numbers in the manuscript have been lost.

24. Guigniaut, perhaps defending the reputation of the Academy, described the event at a public *séance* of the Academy on August 5, 1864, as follows: "il concourut, il obtint le prix sur plusieurs compétiteurs dignes d'estime." See his "Notice," 370. Quatremère's cousin made the same mistake when he wrote of the competition, "la lutte fut très honorable; car plusieurs mémoires importants avaient été envoyés au concours." See E. Quatremère, "Notice," 666.

25. Recorded in *Histoire de l'Académie Royale des Inscriptions et Belles-Lettres*, vol. 45 (1793), 9–10.

26. "Quel fut l'état de l'Architecture chez les Egyptiens, & ce que les Grecs paroissent en avoir emprunté."

27. See the *procès verbaux* in Appendix A, which also includes a list of members present during these *séances.*

28. An extremely important discussion of the historiography of ancient Egypt, including many aspects addressed during the eighteenth century and fundamentally relevant to matters raised in this study, is Bernal's *Black Athena*, volume 1, *The Fabrication of Ancient Greece 1785–1985*. Bernal's text focuses on how the relationship between Egypt and Greece was imagined in the context of theories of origins; he persuasively demonstrates the role that religious and racial intolerances played in European attitudes toward ancient Egypt. Although I have emphasized a different and more positive role that these fabrications played, namely that of assisting in the separation of sacred from secular history, Bernal's account offers an instructive counterview of my argument.

29. See Caylus's *Recueil d'antiquités*. He was elected a member of the Académie des Inscriptions et Belles-Lettres in 1742 and had been a member of the Académie de Peinture et de Sculpture since 1731. For Le

Roy on Egypt, see his *Observations sur les edifices des anciens peuples* (1767) and *Les ruines des plus beaux monuments de la Grèce* (1758 as well as the second edition of 1770). Le Roy's nomination to the Académie des Inscriptions et Belles-Lettres took place in 1770.

30. Although Nikolaus Pevsner suggested that the Egyptian elements in the work of Boullée at least were inspired by Quatremère's essay, they were in fact present long before the *concours* of 1785. See Pevsner's "The Egyptian Revival," 231. In any case, an interest in Egypt was pervasive during this period; the *concours*, Quatremère's essay, and the contemporary architectural designs are all responses to the same intellectual climate. Studies of the Egyptian revival during this period include Hautecoeur, "L'Expédition du premier Empire"; Hautecoeur, *Histoire de l'architecture classique en France*, 4:23–26; "Le retour d'égypte"; Greener, *The Discovery of Egypt*; Sauneron, *L'égyptologie*; Wortham, *The Genesis of British Egyptology*; Oechslin, "Pyramide et sphère"; Fagan, *The Rape of the Nile*; Carrott, *The Egyptian Revival*; Clayton, *The Rediscovery of Ancient Egypt*; Curl, *The Egyptian Revival*; Vercoutter, *A la recherche de l'Egypte oubliée*; Anderson and Fawzy, eds., *Egypt Revealed*; and Wittkower, *Selected Lectures*.

31. For example, the Jesuit scholar Athanasius Kircher used Neoplatonic interpretations of Egyptian hieroglyphics as the linchpin of his attempt to harmonize pagan history with that of mankind as revealed in scripture. See Kircher's *Oedipus Aegyptiacus* (1652). On Kircher, see Rivosecchi, *Esotismo in Roma Barocca*. Aspects of this tradition survived through the use of Egyptian motifs in Masonic ritual. Although Quatremère was a Mason (he was a member of the lodge of Thalie from 1782 to 1786) and although his professional interest in Egypt was no doubt influenced by Masonic interest in Egypt, there is no evidence to suggest that his interpretation of Egyptian architecture was specifically determined by his association with Freemasonry. See Le Bihan, *Francs-Maçons Parisiens*, 409, and, on Freemasonry in architecture, see Vidler, *The Writing of the Walls*, 83–102.

32. These activities were associated with the earliest learned societies. See Pevsner, *Academies of Art*.

33. The most obvious result of these efforts was the explosive growth of French orientalism in the late eighteenth and nineteenth cen-

turies, much of which was supported by the Academy. On the professionalization of the Academy, see Dussaud, *La nouvelle Académie.*

34. During the eighteenth century, the most frequently cited works on Egypt were James Bruce, *Voyage aux sources du Nil* (1790–1792); Corneille Le Bruyn, also known as Cornelis de Bruyn and Cornelis Le Brun, *Voyage au Levant* (1725); Caylus, *Recueil d'antiquités;* Paul Lucas, *Troisième voyage* (1719); G. Macartney, *Voyage dans l'intérieur de la Chine et en Tartarie* (1798); Benoit de Maillet, *Description de l'Egypte* (1735); Bernard de Montfaucon, *L'antiquité expliquée et représentée en figures* (1719–1722); Carsten Niebuhr, *Description de l'Arabie* (1779); F. L. Norden, *Voyage d'Egypte et de Nubie* (1755), published also as *Travels in Egypt and Nubia* (1757); Pierre-Adam D'Origny, *Dissertations ou on examine quelques questions appartenantes à l'histoire des anciens Egyptiens* (1752) and *L'Egypte ancienne* (1762); Charles Perry, *A View of the Levant* (1743); Richard Pococke, *A Description of the East,* vol. 1, "Observations on Egypt" (1743), published also in France as *Voyages de Richard Pococke* (1772); and Jacob Spon and George Wheler, *Voyage d'Italie, de Dalmatie, de Grèce, et du Levant* (1724). An excellent reference book on the many eighteenth-century publications dealing with Egypt is Carré, *Voyageurs et écrivains français en Égypte.* Quatremère was also familiar with the Egyptian antiquities located in the Borgia collection in Veletri as well as in his own *cabinet d'étude.* On these collections, see *Catalogue d'objets d'arts . . . de M. Quatremère de Quincy* (1850); Adler, *Museum Cuficum Borgianum Velitris* (1782); and Zoega, *Numi Aegyptii imperatorii prostantes in Museo Borgiano Velitris* (1787).

35. A question typical of this aspect of academic tradition is that posed in 1773: "Quels furent les noms et les attributs divers de Minerve chez les différens Peuples de la Grèce et de l'Italie; quelles furent l'origine et les raisons de ces attributs; quel a été son Culte; Quels ont été les Statues, les Tableaux cèlébres de cette Divinité, et les Artistes qui se sont illustrés par ces Ouvrages." See *Histoire de l'Académie Royale des Inscriptions et Belles-Lettres,* vol. 40 (1780).

36. The question posed in 1766 was "Quels étaient en Egypte, avant les règnes des Ptolémées, les habillements des deux sexes? Y avait-il quelques marques extérieures pour distinguer les magistrats des autres citoyens? Quelle était la forme des temples et des autres édifices? De quels bateaux se servait-on sur le Nil? Quelles étaient les cérémonies usités dans

les fêtes publiques et dans les funérailles? Quels sont les animaux, les plantes et les autres objets que les artistes peuvent employer pour caractériser l'Egypte?"

37. "Avant que vous m'eussiez fait la grace de m'admettre parmi vous, je ne regardois que du côté de l'art, ces restes d'antiquité sçavante échappés à la barbare des temps; vous m'avez appris à y attacher un mérite infiniment supérieur, je veux dire celui de renfermer mille singularités de l'Histoire, du culte, des usages & des moeurs de ces Peuples fameux, qui par la vicissitude des choses humaines, ont disparu de dessus la Terre qu'ils avoient remplie du bruit de leur nom." See his letter to the members of the Académie Royale des Inscriptions et Belles-Lettres included at the beginning of the first volume of his *Recueil d'antiquités*.

38. Jacopo Belgrado in 1786 published a book entitled *Dell'architettura egiziana, Dissertazione d'un corrispondente dell'Accademia delle scienze di Parigi*. While this title reveals Belgrado's interest in the Prix Caylus of 1785, no evidence supports his assertion that he actually participated in the competition. Born in 1704, Belgrado became a Jesuit in 1723 and found himself arrested during the suppression of the order later in the century. A prolific author whose interest in archaeology developed rather late in his career, his other publications include *Delle sensazioni del calore, e del freddo* (1764) and *Dell'esistenza di Dio da' teoremi geometrici dimostrata* (1777). In his *Lettres sur l'architecture des anciens et des modernes* (1787), J. L. Viel de Saint-Maux indicated his intention to compete for the Prix Caylus. On page 37 of his seventh letter, Viel wrote "une question de l'Académie des Belles-Lettres, 'Quel fut l'état de l'Architecture parmi les Egyptiens, & ce que les Grecs paroissent en avoir emprunté,' nous y engage." No evidence of Viel's effort has yet come to light.

39. "Il semble qu'on n'a pas assez observé les rapports marqués qui les lient, ou les différences frappantes qui les séparent." Le Roy, *Les ruines*, viii.

40. David made this drawing while in Rome probably during the late 1770s, the same years he is said to have traveled with Quatremère. More importantly, its subject matter parallels but anticipates that of the Prix Caylus. On Boullée, see Pérouse de Montclos, *Etienne-Louis Boullée*, and Rosenau, *Boullée and Visionary Architecture*.

I
Origins

1. The library of the Institut de France contains a copy of Del Rosso's *Richerche sul'architettura egiziana* on page vii of which the following note was added in what appears to be an eighteenth-century hand, perhaps even Quatremère's: "quatremere de quincy dont l'ouvrage a été couronné n'a jamais été en Egypte, il écrivit sa dissertation a Rome et n'eut d'autres ressources que les galleries et museums que renferme cette ville et particulierement celui de Mr. Borgia a Velletri qu'il visita souvent pour y etudier les monumens Egyptienne qu'il renferme en assez grand nombre." This note refutes Del Rosso's claim that the only reason he lost was that his competitor had had the opportunity to visit Egypt. However, the fact that Quatremère included a *papier cacheté* giving a Parisian address with his manuscript, along with the other available biographical data, suggests that Quatremère did not compose the essay in Rome but in Paris after he returned from Italy.

2. See Momigliano's classic study "Ancient History and the Antiquarian."

3. Although Caylus's *Recueil d'antiquités* includes Egyptian works of art, there are only limited discussions and no plates of architecture. For the material that was available, see above, note 34 of the introduction.

4. "Nous ne connoissons leurs monumens que d'une manière très imparfaite, on n'a jamais voyagé en Egypte avec les moyens suffisante pour avoir des Notions précise de leur architecture, on n'a jamais rien mesuré, les voyageurs se sont contenté de lever rapidement quelques plans qu'ils ont rajustés après à leur fantaisie, et nous somme réduits à des desseins très superficiels, faits à la dérobée par des hommes peu instruits dans l'Architecture et dans les arts du dessin." Quatremère, Prix Caylus MS, 64v.

5. For a list of the essay's section titles, as well as a table that compares the competition essay with the 1803 published version, see Appendix B.

6. "Avant de considérer quel fût l'état de l'Architecture chez les Egyptiens il ne sera hors de propos de fixer, par quelques principes simples, l'idée générale qu'on doit avoir de cet art en lui même et de son

origine en Egypte, a fin de pouvoir procéder avec plus d'ordre dans cet examen, et apercevoir plus sûrement les rapports et les objets de comparaison qui existent entre l'Architecture Egyptienne et celle des Grecs. Sans ces principes on courroit risque de ne pouvoir dicerner dans l'art de bâtir ce que la nature, en tout tems et en tout Pays enseigne aux hommes sans qu'ils se soient communiqués leurs idées, d'avec les points de ressemblance que la communication seule peut avoir transmis d'un peuple à l'autre." Quatremère, Prix Caylus MS, 1r.

7. "On peut, il me semble, rapporter à ces trois états de la vie naturelle l'origine de toutes les constructions et des différences qu'on y remarque ches tous les Peuples." Quatremère, Prix Caylus MS, 2v.

8. "Si ce genre d'habitations fût pratiqué dans les plus beaux tems de l'Egypte, à plus forte raison l'aurat-il été par ses premiers habitans." Quatremère, Prix Caylus MS, 4v.

9. "Tous dans leurs Architecture nous retrace ce première origine." Quatremère, Prix Caylus MS, 4v.

10. Quatremère, Prix Caylus MS, 5r.

11. Quatremère, Prix Caylus MS, 5r–6r.

12. "Le premier mérite de l'Architecture," Quatremère, Prix Caylus MS, 9r. The anthropomorphic metaphor is of course also to be found in Vitruvius. Quatremère discusses the second element of Vitruvius's equation, "commodity," in the next section. His analysis of the relationship between Egyptian architecture and "delight" constitutes the main focus of his essay and recurs throughout. Quatremère's understanding of the notion of "delight" is, however, most pointedly discussed in the essay's final section. The *mémoire* thus follows the sequence of the equation as prescribed by Vitruvius, and my analysis of Quatremère on this point will follow the same sequence.

13. "Malgré les éforts du tems, en dépit des ravages des siècles passés et à venir, l'on peut, sans craindre l'hyperbole, conjecturer hardiment que ces [masses], jusqu'à présent victorieuses des tems, verront encore s'aneantir autour d'elles et rentrer dans la poussiéres bien des Villes et des Nations aux quelles elles survivront, et seroient dans la ruine totale du Globe les dernieres à avoüer la foiblesse humaine." Quatremère, Prix Caylus MS, 9r–9v.

14. "Il est vrai que cette Nation reçut de la Nature pour la construction de ses Edifices les moyens les plus propres à les rendre éternels, et que sous le Ciel le moins destructeur elle pût employer les materiaux les plus indestructibles." Quatremère, Prix Caylus MS, 9r.

15. Quatremère, Prix Caylus MS, 16r–17v.

16. Quatremère's sarcasm was due to the increasing awareness of what seemed, by the eighteenth century, to be a strongly superstitious and illogical vein in the traditional attitudes toward Egypt. In addition to discussing the physical characteristics of stone, Quatremère provides a second explanation for the size of blocks used in remote antiquity, namely that "dans l'origine des sociétés, l'ame des hommes sortant en quelque sorte des mains de la nature, et incapable d'eprouver de petites sensations, communique sa force à tous les arts, et à tous les moyens qu'on y employe." Quatremère, Prix Caylus MS, 17v–18r.

17. Quatremère's assertion that Egypt lacked machines is derived from Diodorus Siculus, *Historical Library*, book 2, ch. 2.

18. ". . . une infinté d'invention aussi ingénieuses et aussi simples." Quatremère, Prix Caylus MS, 18r. Quatremère was no doubt referring to Domenico Fontana's *Della trasportazione dell'obelisco vaticano* (1590).

19. The seven wonders of the world include the following Alexandrian-era tourist attractions: the pyramids of Egypt, the Gardens of Semiramis at Babylon, the statue of Zeus at Olympia, the temple of Artemis at Epheseus, the Mausoleum of Halicarnassus, the Colossus of Rhodes, and the Lighthouse of Alexandria. The list was compiled for the first time by Antipater of Sidon during the second century B.C. When speaking of the pyramids, Diodorus Siculus refers to this tradition. The list was repeated by a Byzantine rhetorician and recorded in the works of Philo of Byzantium. During the modern period, the tradition is repeated again by J. B. Fischer von Erlach in *Entwurf einer historischen Architektur* (1721).

20. He singled out for particular refutation the proposals of both Pliny and de Maillet. See Quatremère, Prix Caylus MS, 40r–40v.

21. He wrote, "le même esprit de simplicité de grandeur et de

solidité règne également dans la construction des autres Edifices de l'Egypt." Quatremère, Prix Caylus MS, 22v.

22. ". . . diminuer le merveilleux de ces monstrueux Edifices." Quatremère, Prix Caylus MS, 19r. Herodotus provides elaborate explanations for the technique of constructing pyramics in *The Histories*, book 2, chapter 125, a passage Quatremère refers to in the Prix Caylus MS, 20r, n. 1.

23. Section three is subdivided into two parts, the first concerning the disposition of temples, dimensions, plans and elevations, the second concerning columns, pilasters, bases, capitals, abaci, entablatures, ceilings, doors, stairs, and the form and function of pyramids.

24. ". . . les Egyptiens étalerent toute la pompe de leur architecture, et c'est d'après les ruines de ces monumens qu'on peut se former quelqu'idée de leur habilité et de leur goût dans cet art." Quatremère, Prix Caylus MS, 26v.

25. He wrote that they were an assemblage "de Portiques, de cours, de vestibules, de Galleries, de salles jointes les unes aux autres et environnées de murs, chacune de ces parties ordinairement indépendante du tout." Quatremère, Prix Caylus MS, 27v.

26. Quatremère, Prix Caylus MS, 29v.

27. Of Egyptian plans he wrote "comme un autel rond donna, selon Winkelman, la naissance aux Temples circulaires, un morceau de pierre aux Pyramide, une Cabanne couverte aux Edifices les plus pompeux de l'architecture Grecque, il paroitroit que l'enceinte d'un Bercail auroit été l'origine des plans Egyptiens," and that "climat, usages, materiaux, tout généralement concourût chez eux à rendre leurs plans aussi faciles que simples et grands," Quatremère, Prix Caylus MS, 29v and 31r.

28. "L'élevation dont le plan fait ordinairement la base et qui en porte toujours le caractère et l'esprit, nous présente dans les Edifices Egyptiens, la même simplicté et la même uniformité, les mêmes formes s'y trouvent répetées jusqu'à la monotonie, on n'y remarque d'autre caractère que celui de la solidité poussée jusqu'à l'excès." Quatremère, Prix Caylus MS, 31v.

29. Quatremère makes an interesting remark about a room in a temple that did have small apertures. He wrote that they were "percées

dans l'epaisseur du mur en forme conique, à peu près comme nos fenêtres de prison qui s'evasent dans l'interieur de manière seulement à admettre le jour, sans que du dehors on puisse voirs dans l'interieur." Quatremère, Prix Caylus MS, 39v.

30. "Cette colonne porte avec soi l'histoire de son origine d'une manière trop claire pour qu'on puisse la méconnoitre, et sert à prouver qu'on ne doit pas rapporter à une cause unique l'Architecture Egyptienne: Il est évident que la forme de cette colonne vient des premiers constructions en bois ou la petitesse des arbres engager les constructeurs a en reunir plusieurs petits ensembles, pour suppléer au défaut des grosses poutres, il fallait assûrer cette réunion et en faire un corps solide, les lier ou avec des cordes, ou avec des cercles de fer, et ces different formes furent transportés dans les colonnes de pierre que l'Architecture substitue à ces supports imparfait." Quatremère, Prix Caylus MS, 32r–32v.

31. Quatremère, Prix Caylus MS, 4v.

32. See the entries "barrière" and "bizarrerie" in the *Encyclopédie méthodique*, where he uses Ledoux's *barrières* as notable examples of this architectural impiety.

33. "Nous distinguerons dans l'Architecture Egyptienne deux espèces de Décoration, celle qui provient des divers objets d'embélissements étrangers à la forme des batimens, tels que les statües et autres choses semblables, . . . et celle qui est adherente aux formes elles mêmes de l'Architecture, qui en fait en quelque sorte partie, comme l'ornement, le bas relief, la peinture etc. Cette distinction très sensible fera la division naturelle de cette section." Quatremère, Prix Caylus MS, 41r.

34. On Quatremère's understanding of the origins of Egyptian sculpture, see Quatremère, Prix Caylus MS, 50r.

35. "Mais on a trop voulou rechercher l'origine de l'ornement dans la nature. Inutilement prétend t'on que les herbages crus fortuitment autour les Edifices, ou que les plantes dont la semence peut avoir été portée par le vent sur les diverses parties des cabanes, ayant donné naissance à ce genre d'embelissment. Ce que l'on peut dire de plus raisonable sur ce sujet, c'est que l'on décora dans des jours de fêtes, les Edifices sacrés des fleurs, des fruits et des plantes qu'on offroit à la Divinité, ainsi que des têtes de victimes, des instrumens de Sacrifice et autres choses

semblables, et que la sculpture, pour perpétuer ces ornemens passagers, réalisa en pierre tous ces différens objects." Quatremère, Prix Caylus MS, 44r–44v.

36. "Mais par une ingratitude commune à tous les Nations dont la vanité fait le principal caractère, ces mêmes Grecs redevables de leurs lumières à l'Egypte, firent tout ce qu'ils pûrent pour nier la dette immense que leur reconnaissance ne vouloit plus payer, ils ne viserent plus qu'à se faire passer auprès des autres nations pour les inventeurs des arts qu'ils perfectionnerent, et des Sciences, où ils n'égalèrent jamais leurs Maîtres." Quatremère, Prix Caylus MS, 54r.

37. "Pendant très longtems les arts de la Grèce eurent avec ceux de l'Egypte la plus grande analogie." Quatremère, Prix Caylus MS, 55r. The fifth section of Quatremère's essay is entitled "De l'imitation des Grecs," "imitation" referring to Egyptian forms usurped by the Greeks. Only in the version of the essay published in 1803 does Quatremère use the word *imitation* to refer to *mimesis*. The significance of this change in meaning will be discussed in chapter 3.

38. Quatremère, Prix Caylus MS, 60r.

39. ". . . de se mûrir plus lentement, de faire plus d'essai et de ne réaliser que tard en des matières plus durables les ébauches que les Egyptiens se préstèrent trop de fixer et d'arrêter dans leurs Edifices." Quatremère, Prix Caylus MS, 56r.

40. ". . . échanger les demeures de la nature contre celle de l'art." Quatremère, Prix Caylus MS, 4v.

41. "D'après cet exposé il est évident que les causes premières de l'Architecture Grecque étant, en certains points, différentes, cet art dût y prendre un caractère généralement original que cette Nation lui imprima et dont elle sût couvrir et cacher encore les larcins faites à l'Egypte, à tous égards l'Architecture Egyptienne ne doit être regardée que comme l'ébauche de la Grecque; les Grecs, par la supériorité qu'ils acquirent dans les autres arts d'imitation, parvinrent à un systême raisonné de proportions par les quelles ils ont fixé les règles de cet art, et la justesse de leur goût, qui sût saisir ce point milieu entre toutes les qualités opposées, nous a donné les vrais modèles du beau en nous laissant le désespoir de les égaler jamais. *Si donc les Egyptiens furent dans le fait les inventeurs de l'Architecture, les Grecs le furent de la belle Architecture;* . . . les

Egyptiens conçurent les premières idées, mais ils ne les soumirent pas à la réflexion et à la critique et ne les réduisirent pas en principes, par conséquent les Grecs sont excusable de s'etre crû les Maitres en ce genre, et cette Nation qui dans la carrière des arts a toujours vaincu ses rivaux doit encore ici remporter la Couronne." Quatremère, Prix Caylus MS, 64r–64v, my emphasis.

42. ". . . dotati dalla natura di un gusto piu delicato." Del Rosso, Prix Caylus MS, part II, 13.

43. ". . . i Greci confesavano d'aver ricercati, e copiati tutti i Generi di fabbriche che dallo spirito intraprendente degl'Egiziani venivono prodotte. . . . Ma tutta la particolarità non abbastanza lodabile degl'Architetti Greci é consistita nel intelligenza e buon gusto con la quale hanno condotte le Fabbriche loro, e particolarmente in ciò che concerne le proporzioni, gli Ornati, la leggiedria delle masse, e dei contorni, e quella grazia, e sveltezza di cui son ripiene la loro felici produzioni." Del Rosso, Prix Caylus MS, part II, 71–72.

44. Caylus, "De l'architecture ancienne" (1756, read January 7, 1749), 297.

45. See Caylus, "De l'architecture ancienne," 302ff.

46. "Ce ne sont point les commencemens de cet art qui m'étonnent; de quelque façon que ce soit, ils sont faciles à concevoir: ce sont ses progrès, sur-tout quand je considère l'état dans lequel les Grecs l'ont reçû, & celui dans lequel il est sorti de leurs mains." Caylus, "De l'architecture ancienne," 286–287.

47. ". . . non celle qui frappe par une agréable harmonie, & qui annonce dès le premier coup d'oeil la nature de la chose qu'elle décore; mais la bâtisse solide & majestueuse, où l'on voit le germe de tout ce que les Grecs ont sçu y découvrir." Caylus, *Recueil d'antiquités*, 1:3.

48. "Revenons à ces Grecs auxquels il faut attribuer toutes les finesses & les proportions que nous admirons dans leurs ouvrages d'Architecture, & qu'ils ont tirées du sentiment juste & délicat qu'ils ont porté dans tous les arts & dans toutes les sciences. . . . Cet arrangement me paroît d'autant plus juste, que ces deux arts que nous avons vûs traités d'une façon plus brute, mais toûjours grande, par les Egyptiens, ont successivement acquis, & en portion égale, entre les mains des Grecs: ils

les onts conduits l'un & l'autre au dernier degré du sublime par le goût, la délicatesse, le sentiment & la légèrté qu'ils y ont ajoûtés." Caylus, "De l'architecture ancienne," 300.

49. "Les Egyptiens ont esquissé l'Architecture pesamment, les Grecs l'ont dessiné avec beaucoup de grace . . . Les premiers ont étonné par la grandeur des masses, et leurs formes ont été sans agrément. Les seconds ont brillé par la pureté des contours et ont inventé les plus belles formes." Laugier, *Observations sur l'architecture* (1765), v–vi.

50. "L'unité dans l'ordonnance d'un bâtiment est une des principales beautés de l'architecture; les Grecs ont excellé dans cette partie; ils devoient à la verité beaucoup aux Egyptiens; mais ces derniers n'avoient pour ainsi dire qu'ébauché l'art . . . Il faut l'avouer, les Grecs, doués d'un heureux génie, avoient saisi, avec justesse, les traits essentiels qui la caractérisent; ils ne tardèrent pas à comprendre qu'il ne suffisoit pas d'imiter, mais qu'il falloit encore choisir. Jusqu'à eux, les ouvrages de l'Art n'avoient guère été recommandables que par l'énormité des masses et par l'immensité des entreprises; mais ces Peuples plus éclairés, crurent qu'il valoit mieux plaire à l'esprit que d'étonner les yeux, et jugèrent que l'unité et les proportions devoient être la base de tous les ouvrages de l'Art." Blondel, *Cours d'architecture*, 1:396, 453–454. On Blondel, see Middleton, "Jacques François Blondel and the 'Cours d'Architecture,'" and Harrington, *Changing Ideas on Architecture in the "Encyclopédie."*

51. "Quand on considère que les Egyptiens avoient déjà exécuté une grande partie des Monuments dont nous avons parlé ci-dessus, lorsque quelques-uns de leurs Héros passerent dans la Grece, & y apprirent aux habitants, qui étoient encore des especes de sauvages, leurs loix & le culte de leurs divinités, on est tenté de croire, que les Grecs leurs doivent la plus grand partie des découvertes qu'ils se sont attribuées dans l'Architecture. Mais si d'un autre côté on examine par combien de degrés les Grecs ont passé, de la disposition simple des cabannes, que la nécessité leur fit construire, *avant qu'ils connussent les Egyptiens*, aux temples les plus magnifiques; Si l'on observe encore qu'ils ont formé un systême régulier sur les Ordres, au lieu qu'il ne paroît pas que les Egyptiens en aient suivi aucun; on est forcé en quelque sorte de reconnoître les Grecs pour un peuple qui a inventé, à quelques idées près qu'il peut avoir pris des Egyptiens, l'art de se construire des Edifices. Ainsi, si nous accordons aux Egyptiens la gloire de s'être signalés les premiers par la grandeur &

l'immensité des Monuments qu'ils ont élevés, nous ne pouvons refuser aux Grecs l'honneur d'avoir imaginé l'Architecture qui porte leur nom." Le Roy, *Les ruines*, 2d ed., xiii, my emphasis. The second edition considers the relationship between Greek and Egyptian architecture in greater detail than the first, which will be discussed further below.

52. In the "Discours sur l'histoire de l'Architecture civile," p. iv of the first edition of *Les ruines*, Le Roy wrote of man's first architectural efforts, "c'est en vain qu'on cherchoit à découvrir dans l'obscurité des premiers âges du monde quels étoient précisément ces essais, et combien de siecles s'écoulerent avant que les différentes sorte de cabannes, imaginés par les hommes, eussent acquis quelque degré de perfection. Loin de pouvoir pénétrer dans ces temps si reculés, nous n'appercevons pas même, par le secours seul d'Histoire, la chaîne qui a conduit un peuple très-célebre à des idées plus relevées."

53. On Paestum see Serra, ed., *La Fortuna di Paestum*, and Mustilli, "Prime memorie delle rovine di Paestum."

54. "Les premiers pas que les Grecs firent dans l'Architecture furent si heureux, qu'ils ne s'en sont jamais écartés . . . Ils disposerent leurs cabannes avec tant de sagesse, qu'ils en ont toujours conservé la forme, même dans leurs Temples les plus magnifiques." Le Roy, *Les ruines*, 2d ed., xiii. In the first edition he had described the beginning of architecture thus: "les découvertes que les premiers hommes ont fait dans l'Architecture, ne devoient pas être fort au-dessus de ce que l'instinct enseigne aux animaux pour se garantir des injures de l'air, et elles étoient sans doute variées" (p. iv).

55. The standard biography of Winckelmann is Justi, *Winckelmann und seine Zeitgenossen*. On Winckelmann in relation to French thought, see Fontius, "Winckelmann und die französische Aufklärung."

56. "L'arte del disegno ne' suoi principi é stata la stessa appo più popoli disparati l'uno dall'altro, non per communicazione della maniera d'operare e de' fini che si avevano in operando, ma per natura, la quale a tutti nell'insegnare incomincia dal semplice e dal più facile." Winckelmann, *Monumenti antichi inediti* (1767), xii.

57. Winckelmann, *Histoire de l'art chez les anciens* (1766, first published as *Geschichte der Kunst des Alterthums* in 1764).

58. "Mr Le Roy paroit s'être trompé lorsqu'il a voulu pretendre que une cabane rustique ait servi de modele aux Egyptiens pour leurs plus grands edifices: Prejugé qu'il a peut être puisé dans Vitruve qui en dit autant des Grecs. Il semble raisonnable de conjecturer que les premiers Egyptiens avant de s'etre reunis en corps de nation, vivoyent comme les Troglodytes, dans des cavernes, des Rochers d'Etiopie; et cela etant, ce seroit une caverne qui auroit servi de modele à leurs primiers essais d'architecture, et non pas une Cabanne . . . Il paroit donc que Mr Le Roy n'ait imaginé que les Cabannes ayent été le modele de l'architecture, parce qu'il n'a point entrevû qu'à celles ci avoit servi de modele une Caverne, qui a été la premiere retraite artificelle du genre humain." Del Rosso, Prix Caylus MS, part I, 2–5.

59. Del Rosso in fact devoted at least part of his essay to a chronological account of the development of Egyptian architecture not because he had any new data to offer but because it offered a mass of evidence supporting the idea that Greek architecture was derivative and hence no different from Roman. He claims, for example, that the Egyptians had "civilized" the Greeks and that the latter's borrowings were so extensive and profound that the Doric order should rightly be called the Egyptian order. He concluded by contrasting the degree to which the Greeks had obfuscated their borrowings with the degree to which the Romans had at least had, according to Del Rosso, the good manners to acknowledge their masters. See also Del Rosso's *Richerche sul'architettura egiziana*, 158 and 200. Belgrado's *Dell'architettura egiziana* is even more radical in its pro-Italic campaign. Belgrado went so far as to use the cave to suggest a direct link between Egyptian and Etruscan architecture, attempting thereby to suggest that Roman architecture was derived more from Italic than from Greek tradition.

60. ". . . renverser d'une manière triomphant cette cabane de bois qu'on nous a toujours proposé comme la source de l'architecture chez tous les peuples." Quatremère, Prix Caylus MS, 5r.

61. It might be noted that despite the conceptual importance Quatremère gave to primitive architecture, he never found visual reconstructions of primitive architectural types relevant, publishing such images neither in *De l'architectue égyptienne* nor in any of his subsequent books on architecture.

62. Del Rosso, for example, describes the Greeks as "dotati della

natura" in terms of their ability to attain aesthetic perfection, and Blondel refers to them as "doués d'un heureux génie." On the history of this concept as expressed by the word *goût* in the context of architecture, see Szambien, *Symétrie, goût, caractère.*

63. As mentioned above, Quatremère held the fact that primitive Egyptians had never "*appris* à échanger les demeures de la nature contre celle de l'art" responsible for the little progress made by Egyptian architecture as a whole. See his Prix Caylus MS, 4v, my emphasis.

64. ". . . les institutions morales . . . les causes politiques et Religieuses qui ont influées sur la forme et l'Ordonnance des Batimens." Quatremère, Prix Caylus MS, 8r.

65. The delay has been credited to indifference and to the need for archaeological revisions, neither of which was the case as will be demonstrated below. See E. Quatremère, "Notice," 666, and Rowlands, "Quatremère de Quincy," 19.

66. The Academy's permission was not needed simply to publish an essay written under its aegis, but was required to publish with the Academy's privilege. As this stamp of approval was the most tangible benefit for the laureate, it seems unlikely that Quatremère would have neglected this procedure. In the minutes of the Académie des Inscriptions et Belles-Lettres for the years 1786–1789, there are records of at least three different authors of competition essays seeking either permission to publish a *mémoire*, permission to publish with academic privilege, or simply seeking a copy of the original manuscript for corrections. There is no record of any such attempt on Quatremère's part.

67. On the *Description de l'Egypte*, see Munier, *Tables de la Description de l'Egypte*; Thiry, *Bonaparte en Egypte*; Laurens, *Les origines intellectuelles de l'expédition d'Egypte*; and the recent edition of the *Description, Monuments of Egypt: The Napoleonic Edition*, ed. Gillispie and Dewachter.

68. Quatremère refers to the new materials both in the letter cited below and in the entry on Egypt in the second volume of the *Encyclopédie méthodique*, published in 1801. Specifically, he refers to a series of articles collectively entitled "Description abrégée des principaux monumens de la Haute-Egypte," published in the *Moniteur universel*, nos.

300, 301, 306, 307, 308, 314, 315, and 316, in 1800 and written by Ripault, one of the scholars sent to Egypt as part of Napoleon's expedition.

69. Denon's *Voyage* was published in 1802. Quatremère's biographers claim Denon wrote letters of introduction on Quatremère's behalf while a member of the French Embassy in Naples. My extensive search through the archives of the Ministère des Affaires Etrangères in Paris yielded no trace of these letters. On the relationship between Denon's work and the *Description*, see Nowinski, *Baron Dominique Vivant Denon*.

70. A list of works not predominantly political in nature published by Quatremère during the Revolution reveals the extent of his activities at that time, but also comes to a sudden halt at the time of his exile: *Considérations sur les art du dessin en France suivie d'un plan d'académie, ou d'école publique, et d'un systême d'encouragemens* (1791); *Encyclopédie méthodique*, vols. 1 and first half of 2 (1788 and 1801); *Discours prononcé à l'Assemblée des Représentens de la Commune, le Vendredi 2 avril 1790, sur la liberté des theatres et le rapport des commissaires* (n.d.); *Dissertation sur les opéras bouffons italiens* (1789); *Lettres sur la préjudice qu'occasionneroient aux arts et à la science, le déplacement des monumens de l'art de l'Italie* (1796); *Rapport approuvé par le Comité d'Instruction Publique de l'Assemblée legislative, sur les réclamations des directeurs de théatres, et la proprieté des auteurs dramatiques* (1792); *Rapport et projet de decret présentés a l'Assemblée Nationale, par M. Quatremère, au nom du Comité de l'Instruction Publique, le 14 novembre 1791, sur les réclamations des artistes qui ont exposé au salon du Louvres* (1791); *Rapport fait par Quatremère, au nom d'une commission spéciale, sur l'exemption du droit de patente en faveur des peintres, sculpteurs, graveurs & architects* (1797).

71. Quatremère could not even hope for an academic position until after the amnesty of 18 Brumaire enabled him to return from Germany. By then the Institut was controlled by Napoleon, to whom Quatremère was still suspect because of his letters against the spoilage of works of art during the Napoleonic campaign in Italy (see chapter 4 below). Before attempting to seek election to the Institut, it was undoubtedly necessary for Quatremère to wait until some of the outcry that had been caused by his letters had died down. Moreover, the royal academies, suppressed during the Revolution, had been resurrected and transformed into the Institut National des Sciences et des Arts in 1795. Further reor-

ganization by Napoleon revived in substance the old Académie des Inscriptions et Belles-Lettres, under the new name of "classe nouvelle d'histoire et de littérature ancienne." This took place in 1803, the year Quatremère began his campaign to become a member.

72. The Academy was not the only recipient of Quatremère's new book: he also sent a copy to Canova on March 30, 1803.

73. "La societé Savante qui revit en vous et que le Gouvernement vient de rendre a ses anciens travaux a daigné jadis accueillir l'ouvrage que j'ai l'honneur de vous adresser. En proposant des recherches sur l'Architecture Egyptienne, et en apellant l'attention de l'Europe Savante sur cet objet, l'Academie des belles lettres avoit dès lors autant qu'il etoit en elle preludé a la conquête litteraire de l'Egypte. Les decouvertes [du] a la memorable expedition qui a eu lieu depuis, aux travaux des savants et a la munificence du gouvernement qui les encourage, repandront sans doute sur tous les arts de cette contrée des lumieres nouvelles qui eclaireront un grand nombre de questions. On trouvera peut etre que ces circonstances ne sont pas favorable a la publication d'un ouvrage ecrit il y a vingt ans sur un des principaux arts de l'Egypte. Mais . . . j'ai été enhardi par la garantie meme de la societé celebre qui avoit jugé que les renseignements acquis jusqu'a lors pouvoient suffire au programme qu'elle avoit donné. . . . Le presenter aujourdhuy de nouveau en vous rappellant qu'il obtint autrefois vos suffrages c'est le replacer sous une protection aussi utile qu'honorable. Sera-t-il permis a l'auteur de mettre a profit cette occasion de solliciter encore pour lui cette meme bienveillance qui encouragea ses premiers efforts et qu'il envisagera toujours comme la plus precieuse recompense de ses travaux." Archives de l'Académie des Inscriptions et Belles-Lettres, MS E305.

74. Guigniaut, "Notice," 386.

75. "Cet écrit accueilli dans le tems par l'Académie n'avoit pas encore été imprimé . . . J'ai pensé que dans un moment où tous les esprits étoient portés vers la connoissance de l'antique Egypte, de ses arts, de son génie et de son goût, il pourroit n'être pas hors de propos de publier, ce qu'on avoit pu acquérir de lumières d'après les anciens renseignemens, ne fut-ce que pour mieux faire sentir tout ce qu'on devra aux nouveaux. J'ai cru qu'un parallèle entre ce qu'on savoit, et ce qu'on va savoir, établiroit encore mieux l'état des connoissances nouvellement acquises. J'ai imaginé même que tout ce qui seroit capable de faire naître la con-

troverse sur un sujet aussi curieux que celui-ci, ne pouvoit qu'être utile aux arts." Quatremère, *De l'architecture égyptienne*, x–xi.

76. "Peut-être trouvera-t-on qu'il paroît trop tard ou trop tôt. Je ne répondrai ni à l'une, ni à l'autre objection." Quatremère, *De l'architecture égyptienne*, x.

77. ". . . conçu dans des [vus] et dans un systeme de recherche et de critique independante en grande partie des observations positives dont le public attend le resultat." Letter to the Academy cited above, Archives de l'Académie des Inscriptions et Belles-Lettres, MS E305.

78. "Je répète que ne donnant aucune description de monumens, je n'ai dû m'engager dans aucune discussion de détails à cet égard. Je n'ai prétendu que me former, et donner une idée de l'origine, des principes et du goût de l'Architecture égyptienne, et la comparer sous les mêmes rapports à l'Architecture grecque." Quatremère, *De l'architecture égyptienne*, xi.

79. The mistaken assumption that the 1785 and 1803 texts are identical is probably based on the subtitle of the later version, *Dissertation qui a remporté, en 1785, le prix proposé par l'Académie des Inscriptions et Belles-Lettres*. This assumption is repeated even in recent literature on Quatremère. Morales, "The Origins of Modern Eclecticism," notes the delay in publication but is not aware of the differences between the two versions. A substantial portion of the content of these changes was complete by at least 1801, when his article on Egyptian architecture appeared in the second volume of his *Encyclopédie méthodique*.

80. Quatremère incorporated some of the archaeological data Ripault had published in the *Moniteur universel* for his article on Egypt in the *Encyclopédie méthodique*. In *De l'architecture égyptienne*, however, he referred to Ripault not in order to cite his data but only to contest Ripault's insistence on the fact that Greek architecture derived from Egyptian. See the *Encyclopédie méthodique*, 2:294, and *De l'architecture égyptienne*, 225–226. Otherwise, no new scientific data is included. Quatremère was interested in historical information but came increasingly to see it as a form of knowledge independent of theoretical concerns. This development is suggested by the fact that although he would ultimately exclude the Napoleonic findings from *De l'architecture égyptienne*, his 1785 dissertation described the need for the kind of expedition Napoleon

was to produce: "le voyage de l'Egypte a toujours été trop dispendieux pour que de simples particuliers ayent pû le faire fructueusement et les révolutions perpétuelles de ce Pays le rendent de jour en jour plus périlleux et plus inaccessible à le curiosité des voyageurs. Cependant, l'interêt des arts, la connaissance de l'antiquité aujourd'huy très avancée et plus repandüe que jamais, les progrès de l'histoire naturelle, tout sollicite ce voyage, tout concourt à le rendre indispensable, mais il ne faudroit pas qu'il fût abandonné aux ressources bornées de quelques personnes et aux spéculations intéressées qui ne dirigent que trop souvent l'esprit des voyageurs dans de semblables projets. La protection d'un Roi qui fait chérir son nom dans son Royaume autant qu'il le fait respecter au dehors, pourroit seule enlever à la Nation rivale de la France la gloire d'une enterprise dont les arts et les sciences attendent les plus grands avantages." Prix Caylus MS, 65r.

81. "La première contiendra la recherche de quelques-unes des causes qui ont influé sur l'état des arts en Egypte, et spécialement sur son Architecture. La seconde, sera l'analyse et le développement de l'Architecture égyptienne, sous le triple rapport de la construction, de la disposition et de la décoration. La troisième partie offrira le résumé des principes, du caractère et du goût de cette Architecture, les différences essentielles qui la séparent de l'Architecture grecque, et les rapprochemens qu'on aperçoit entr'elles." Quatremère, *De l'architecture égyptienne*, 9–10.

82. Part two of *De l'architecture égyptienne*, entitled "Analyse de l'architecture égyptienne," contains sections 2, 3, and 4 of the manuscript, respectively "De la construction des édifices," "De la forme des édifices," "De la décoration des édifices." For a detailed comparison of the contents of the two versions, see Appendix B.

83. For additional comments on the implications of these titles and on the relationship between Quatremère and the Napoleonic expedition, see my "In the Names of History."

84. "Je ne crois point que ce soit dans les souterrains creusés par les premiers habitans de l'Egypte qu'il faille chercher uniquement et exclusivement les principes de son architecture . . . Je pense que chez certains peuples l'architecture peut avoir eu une double origine, et les Egyptiens me paroissent être dans ce cas. Je ne rejette pas chez eux l'origine de la cabanne . . . voilà la raison pour laquelle on trouve dans

leurs Edifices un mélange de ces deux principes." Quatremère, Prix Caylus MS, 5r.

85. "L'une et l'autre Architecture devront se considérer comme étant sans rapport générique entr'elles, comme deux espèces distinctes dans leur conformation essentielle. L'antériorité de l'une sur l'autre, quand elle seroit aussi démontrée qu'il est difficile de le faire, seroit un argument de peu de valeur dans cette maitère. Peu importe, en effet, la date de leur naissance, si chacune nâquit d'un germe différent." Quatremère, *De l'architecture égyptienne*, 19.

86. This distinction is further revealed by a comparison of the title of section 1 in the 1785 *mémoire*, "De l'architecture et de son origine en Egypte," and the publication title of 1803, *De l'architecture égyptienne considérée dans son origine, ses principes et son gôut, et comparée sous les mêmes rapports à l'architecture grecque.* While the former refers to architecture and its origin (singular) in Egypt, the latter refers to the origin of architecture in Egypt in comparison to a potentially different origin in Greece.

87. "Si le langage appartient à l'humanité, les langues qui sont les modifications locales d'une faculté générale appartiennent à des sociétés partielles ou à des nations? . . . Dans cette recherche on se méprendroit gravement, si confondant les principes généraux de la grammaire universelle qui appartient au langage, avec les règles de la Syntaxe propre à chaque langue, on prétendoit établir entre deux langues une filiation fondée uniquement sur ce qu'elles auroient l'une et l'autre des déclinaisons et des conjugaisons. Personne que je sache n'est tombé sur cette matière dans une semblable méprise. On pourroit dire, au contraire, que presque personne n'a échappé à celle du même genre en fait d'Architecture. On a presque toujours confondu les maximes générales de l'art de bâtir qui sont communes à toutes les architectures, avec les principes particuliers et les données originaires de chaque Architecture, en sorte qu'on a imaginé des filiations et des rapports de parenté entre les espèces les plus étrangères." Quatremère, *De l'architecture égyptienne*, 12–13.

88. On universal grammar, see Aarsleff, *From Locke to Saussure* and "The Tradition of Condillac." On Cartesian linguistics and the notion of language as a reflection of man's mental capacity, as well as other eighteenth-century concepts of language and of language study, see chapter 3 below.

89. "Inférer des rapprochemens généraux qu'on trouve entre deux Architectures que l'une est le produit de l'autre, est . . . un abus aussi insoutenable, que le seroit la prétention de faire dériver une langue d'une autre, parce qu'il se trouveroit entr'elles la similitude de certains points qui appartiennent à la grammaire universelle." Quatremère, *De l'architecture égyptienne*, 226–227.

90. "Combien d'auteurs ne prétendent-ils pas qu'on trouve en Egypte l'origine de l'Architecture grecque, parce qu'avant les Grecs, les Egyptiens avoient employé dans leurs édifices des colonnes, des chapiteaux, des corniches, etc. . . . Il ne faut, ni des notions très-approfondies, ni une grande force de raisonnement pour apercevoir que plusieurs des conformités qu'on rencontre entre les architectures des différens peuples n'indiquent, ni une communauté d'origine, ni une communication de goût." Quatremère, *De l'architecture égyptienne*, 13.

91. "On trouve assez généralement établie chez tous les écrivains qui ont parlé de l'Architecture, une opinion que personne, ce me semble, n'a encore entrepris de discuter, et qui tend à placer chez une nation primitive l'origine de cet art, à faire honneur de sa découverte à un premier peuple *inventeur* qui l'auroit transmise à ses voisins, et de proche en proche au rest des nations. L'Egypte étant, à beaucoup d'égards, le premier peuple qui nous soit historiquement connu, et ayant été réellement en plus d'un genre l'école des peuples que les documens historiques font paroître après lui sur la scène du monde, on l'a regardé naturellement comme l'inventeur de beaucoup d'arts et de sciences: on y a placé aussi le berceau de l'Architecture, on lui en a attribué l'invention." Quatremère, *De l'architecture égyptienne*, 11. As noted above, the notion of Egypt as the cradle of civilization was already commonplace in Diderot's *Encyclopédie*.

92. "L'invention de l'Architecture doit se mettre sur la même ligne que celle du langage, c'est-à-dire, que l'une et l'autre invention ne peuvent s'attribuer à aucun homme, mais sont les attributs de l'homme." Quatremère, *De l'architecture égyptienne*, 12.

93. Quatremère, *De l'architecture égyptienne*, 110. Quatremère had made substantially the same point in 1785, but not in association with language theory.

94. Vitruvius, *Ten Books on Architecture*, Book II, chapter 1.

95. "Parmi les causes qui ont dû déterminer d'une manière très-active les formes caractéristiques des diverses Architectures, on ne sauroit nier que le genre de vie des sociétés naissantes ne doive se mettre au premier rang: et il faut avouer que cette cause est une des plus faciles à apercevoir. On la trouve écrite dans l'histoire des peuples, et on la trouve empreinte sur leurs monumens." Quatremère, *De l'architecture égyptienne*, 15.

96. "Je crois donc entrer pleinement dans les vues du programme de l'Académie, si je démontre en quoi les deux Architectures dont il s'agit, n'ont pu et ne peuvent ni se rapprocher, ni dériver l'une de l'autre." Quatremère, *De l'architecture égyptienne*, 227. Quatremère's isolation of the substructures of Greek and Egyptian architecture did not negate the possibility that there were overlaps in their superstructures. He posited the Corinthian capital, the disposition of large temples, the labyrinth, the pyramidal form, caryatids, and the sphinx as elements of Greek architecture that had derived from Egypt. See Quatremère, *De l'architecture égyptienne,* section titled "Ce Qu'il paroît que les Grecs ont emprunté à l'Architecture égyptienne," 246–266.

II
Architectural Etymology

1. On the persistence and universality of this search for the first hut, see Rykwert, *On Adam's House in Paradise.* See also Rykwert's *The First Moderns.*

2. See Stafford, *Voyage into Substance*, and Adams, *Travelers and Travel Liars.*

3. See Manuel, *The Eighteenth Century Confronts the Gods;* Frey, *The Eclipse of Biblical Narrative;* Rossi, *The Dark Abyss of Time;* and Pastine, "Storia sacra e scrittura sacra."

4. Bossuet, *Discours sur l'historie universelle* (1700), and Boulanger, *L'antiquité dévoilée par ses usages* (1768). See also Rousseau, *Essay on the Origin of Languages,* in *The First and Second Discourses,* ed. and trans. Gourevitch, 267–268 (first published posthumously in 1782 as *Essai sur l'origine des langues*), and in the same edition, the *Discourse on the Origin and the Foundations of Inequality among Men,* 174. Natural occurrences were also stressed by Buffon in *Histoire naturelle* (1749–

1804). On Bossuet and French historiography see Trenard, "L'historiographie française d'après les manuels scolaires." On Boulanger see Manuel, *The Eighteenth Century Confronts the Gods*, 210–228; Hampton, *N. A. Boulanger et la science de son temps*; Venturi, *L'antichità svelata e l'idea di progresso in N. Boulanger*; Gennep, "Contributions à l'histoire de la méthode ethnographique"; and Cherpack, "Warburton and Some Aspects of the Search for the Primitive," 226–227.

5. Condillac's speculations on the origin of language depended on this notion, as will be discussed below. On the Bible and French historiography see Moser, "Pour et contre la Bible," and De Certeau, "L'idée de traduction de la Bible au XVIIe siècle."

6. The problem had in fact already begun to be confronted during the seventeenth century. On Leibniz, for example, and religious orthodoxy in the context of changes in attitudes toward history, see Rossi, *The Dark Abyss of Time*. On eighteenth-century anthropology in general, see Duchet, *Anthropologie et histoire au siècle des lumières*; Gliozzi, *Adamo e il Nuovo Mondo*; and Hogden, *Early Anthropology in the Sixteenth and Seventeenth Centuries*.

7. On the importance of comparative method, see Hubert, *Les sciences sociales dans l'Encyclopédie*, 84ff.

8. This endeavor was begun by Athanasius Kircher. Other notable examples of the interest in China during the eighteenth century are Grosier's *Histoire générale de la Chine* (1777–1785) and Voltaire's *Lettres chinoises, indiennes et tartares* (1776). On China in the eighteenth century, see Dawson, *The Chinese Chameleon*; Etiemble, *Les Jésuites et la Chine*; Guy, "The French Image of China before and after Voltaire"; Zoli, "Il mito settecentesco della Cina in Europa"; Van Kley, "Europe's Discovery of China"; Pinot, *La Chine et la formation de l'esprit philosophique en France*; Lach, "China and the Era of Enlightenment"; Lach, "Leibniz and China"; Lach, *Asia in the Making of Europe*; and Maury, *L'ancienne Académie des Inscriptions et Belles-Lettres*, 261–263.

9. For example, Le Roy wrote, "Ce rapport, tout éloigné qu'il est de l'Architecture Chinoise avec l'Architecture Egyptienne, paroîtroit favorable à l'opinion que M. de Guignes, de l'Académie des Inscriptions, travaille à établir, que les Chinois ne sont qu'une colonie des Egyptiens" (*Les ruines*, 1758, iv, note a), and wrote again in 1770, "Ce rapport de

l'Architecture Chinoise avec l'Architecture Egyptienne, semble prouver, comme M. de guignes l'a avancé, que les Chinois ne sont qu'une colonie des Egyptiens" (*Les ruines*, 1770, vol. 2, xviii, note a). De Guignes's theories were condemned, on the other hand, by Voltaire. In his *Lettres chinoises*, 70–77, Voltaire describes the attempt to relate the Chinese and the Egyptians as a fantasy, a passage cited in turn by Quatremère.

10. See also de Pauw's *Recherches sur les Grecs* (1788). On de Pauw, see Church, "Corneille de Pauw." Several extensive refutations of de Pauw were published in *Mémoires concernant l'histoire, les sciences, les arts, les moeurs, les usages, etc des chinois; par les missionaires de Pekin* (1776–1814, 17 vols.).

11. De Pauw, *Philosophical Dissertations*, trans. J. Thomas (London, 1795), 2:320.

12. Quatremère also owned copies of de Pauw's *Recherches philosophiques sur les Chinois et les Egyptiens* and *Recherches sur les Grecs*. Once Quatremère was a member of the Academy, however, his allegiance seems to have shifted. His 1805 essay "Sur de Paw et son opinion sur la beauté des femmes" accords de Pauw a few important insights but chiefly and rather scathingly condemns him as a novelty-seeking lover of paradox.

13. While the sale catalogue for Quatremère's library (*Bibliothèque de M. Quatremère de Quincy*, 1850) provides a rich account of his readings and sources, it is not a reliable indication of what he might have read before and during the Revolution. Quatremère's possessions—including his library—were confiscated during the Revolution and never returned in full. The one document that might have shed light on the books he owned during the early and formative period of his life, the inventory of his sequestered goods, is missing from the Archives Nationales. While a dossier under his name is included in the liasse T1662, papiers séquestrés, dépôt 3706, the inventories themselves have been missing since 1986. The Arsenal, MS 6498, tome XII, and the Bibliothèque de l'Institut de France, MS 2555, pièce 65, contain documents pertaining to Quatremère's attempts to recover his library. They unfortunately do not contain an inventory of the library itself.

14. All citations are taken from *Customs of the American Indians Compared with the Customs of Primitive Times*, ed. and trans. William N. Fenton and Elizabeth L. Moore. On Lafitau, see Duchet, "Discours

ethnologique et discours historique"; Lemay, "Histoire de l'antiquité et découverte du nouveau monde"; De Certeau, "Writing vs. Time"; Vidal-Naquet, "Les jeunes"; and Vidler, *The Writing of the Walls*, 8–12.

15. Lafitau, *Customs of the American Indians*, 27.

16. Lafitau, *Customs of the American Indians*, 36.

17. See De Certeau, "Writing vs. Time," 57.

18. This work was reprinted several times and was translated into English in 1775 and into Italian in 1761. On the relationship between Lafitau and Goguet, see Gennep, "Contributions." See also Gusdorf, *Histoire de la science à l'histoire de la pensée*.

19. Goguet draws parallels with modern Persia. See Lemay, "Histoire de l'antiquité."

20. Neither Goguet nor Patte had been to Egypt. The plates in *De l'origine des loix* are reengravings from standard sources, such as Norden's *Voyage d'Egypte et de Nubie*, as are the plates in Quatremère's *De l'architecture égyptienne*.

21. "D'un caractère si cruel & si féroce, qu'ils n'ont entre eux ni société ni commerce . . . peu différens des bêtes brutes, ils n'ont pour retraite que les antres & les cavernes . . . privés enfin des notions les plus simples & les plus ordinaires ces peuples n'ont de l'homme que la figure." Goguet, *De l'origine des loix*, 1:4.

22. Goguet, *De l'origine des loix*, 1:127.

23. "Les premiers monumens de l'architecture proprement dite, ont dû être assez grossiers et assez informes." Goguet, *De l'origine des loix*, 1:131.

24. Goguet's main source on Egyptian architecture is Maillet's *Description de l'Egypte*.

25. "Tous les peuples policés ont êu sur cette partie des Arts des lumieres à peu près égales." Goguet, *De l'origine des loix*, 2:203. When Goguet credits Greek architecture with the best, "soit pour la majesté, la beauté & la délicatesse, soit pour la solidité," he is quoting Roland Fréart de Chambray's *Parallèle de l'architecture antique et de la moderne* (1650).

26. "Les Grecs ne sont point les inventeurs de l'Architecture, si par ce mot on entend simplement l'Art de lier différens matériaux & d'en composer d'édifices pour la commodité & les divers usages de la vie . . .

Mais l'Architecture ne consiste pas uniquement dans la main d'oeuvre & dans un simple travail méchanique . . . C'est des Grecs que l'Architecture a reçu cette regularité, cette ordonnance, cet ensemble, qui sont en possession de charmer nos yeux . . . Dans ce sens, on peut dire que les Grecs ont inventé l'Architecture. Ils n'ont rien emprunté à cet égard des autres nations. C'est un art qu'ils ont créé entierement." Goguet, *De l'origine des loix*, 2:202–203.

27. On the term *invention*, see Kemp, "From *Mimesis* to *Fantasia*."

28. Even in more detailed aspects of the analysis of Egyptian architecture, Goguet and Quatremère adhere to the same traditions. Both, for example, characterize Egyptian architecture as solid, immense, without proportion or principle, and able to produce only an effect of "étonnement."

29. The *Law Tracts* were translated as *Essais historiques sur les loix*. On Home, see McGuinness, *Henry Home, Lord Kames*.

30. Home, *Sketches*, 1:39 and vi.

31. Home, *Sketches*, 1:49.

32. Rousseau, in his *Essay on the Origin of Languages*, 266, also refers to "the three states of man considered in relation to society. The savage is a hunter, the barbarian a herdsman, civil man a tiller of the ground."

33. Home, *Sketches*, 1:55, 87.

34. De Pauw, *Philosophical Dissertations*, 1:1.

35. De Pauw, *Philosophical Dissertations*, 1:185.

36. "Considérations sur l'état de l'architecture chez les Egyptiens et les Chinois." Despite this similarity in method, de Pauw disagreed with many particular aspects of Goguet's interpretation of Egyptian architecture.

37. De Pauw, *Philosophical Dissertations*, 2:10, 36. Like Quatremère, and unlike Del Rosso, de Pauw does not suggest that the cave served universally as a model for huts, but argues that the two were independent first forms of architecture.

38. De Pauw, *Philosophical Dissertations*, 2:10.

39. De Pauw, *Philosophical Dissertations*, 2:1–2. De Pauw is not entirely clear with respect to the isolated nature of the origins of Greek architecture. As noted above, he unequivocally asserts different origins for Egyptian and Greek architecture, namely the cave and the hut. Elsewhere, however, he seems to suggest that certain elements of Greek architecture had in fact been taken from Egypt. For example, he wrote that "the many errors, so generally adopted with regard to the progress of the arts, seem to have proceeded from a passage in Varro, who says positively that in Greece they were all invented in the course of one thousand years. . . . Never did he advance any thing more evidently false; because the Greeks cannot be said by any means to have invented the arts. Either they went in search of them, or had them transmitted by others." *Philosophical Dissertations*, 1:22. Similarly, with respect to the Corinthian order, de Pauw wrote: "The adventure of the basket, found by Callimachus, supported by leaves of acanthus, is nothing more than a childish fable, invented by the Greeks, who wished to conceal their having borrowed anything from the Egyptians, while the contrary is manifestly evident. They pretended likewise that the triglyphs of the Doric order represented the ends of the beams resting on the architrave. But they were invented by the Egyptian architects, or sculptors, who never employed wood." *Philosophical Dissertations*, 2:59. Lafitau also distinguished between tents and huts in the context of primitive architecture, associating the former with nomads and the latter with agriculturalists.

40. De Pauw, *Philosophical Dissertations*, 2:36–37.

41. De Pauw, *Philosophical Dissertations*, 2:1–2.

42. "Le besoin de faire des systèmes sur l'origine des peuples & de leurs arts, a toujours porté les hommes à chercher un point de départ fixe, d'où toutes les connoissances se son répandues. On veut (& cela est assez dans la nature de l'analogie) que les peuples se soient succédés comme des générations, & de même qu'on pose un premier homme, on veut aussi poser un peuple primitif, où l'on puisse remonter pour y trouver l'origine de tous les autres, & la source de toutes les inventions. Longtemps on a fait des Egyptiens ce peuple primitif, & c'étoit en Egypte qu'on plaçoit la tige de toutes les connoissances, de toutes les croyances, de toutes les opinions qui ont régné dans le monde. On alloit jusqu'à imaginer des rapports entre l'Egypte & la Chine." "Architecture Indienne," *Ency-*

clopédie méthodique, 2:549. The last sentence and its somewhat sarcastic reference to those who envision relations between Egypt and China clearly refers to the controversy between de Guignes and de Pauw and even more clearly sides with the latter.

43. I am not here referring to the concept of originality in terms of creative genius but in terms of first models. On the former, see Mortier, *L'originalité*.

44. For the classic study of primitivism, see Lovejoy and Boas, *A Documentary History of Primitivism and Related Ideas*.

45. Lafitau, for example, devoted an entire chapter to the analysis of language, and, as mentioned above, de Pauw's work was instigated by an essentially linguistic question. See Formigari, *Linguistica e antropologia nel secondo Settecento*, and Albertan-Coppola, "La question des langues dans les *Moeurs des sauvages américains* de Lafitau."

46. Humbert, "L'évolutionisme et la linguistique."

47. See Mallory, *In Search of the Indo-Europeans*; Aarsleff, *The Study of Language in England*; and Knight, *The Geometric Spirit*, 145ff.

48. It has been suggested, for example, that Condillac's particular approach to the analysis of language actually led him to the problem of origins, including those of art. See Knight, *The Geometric Spirit*, 145ff. See also Harnois, "Les théories du langage en France de 1660 à 1821," 44ff.

49. Port-Royal was the center for the Jansenist religious community. For general introductions to language studies in eighteenth-century France, see Juliard, *Philosophies of Language in Eighteenth-Century France*; Kuehner, *Theories on the Origin and Formation of Language*; and Harnois, "Les théories du langage en France." Less introductory but still wide in scope is Viertel's "Concepts of Language Underlying the 18th-Century Controversy about the Origin of Language." For bibliography on the Port-Royal Grammar and on the history of language studies in general, see Porset, "Grammatista Philosophans." On Port-Royal in particular, see Lakoff, "La Grammaire générale et raissonnée."

50. Harnois, "Les théories du langage en France," 17. See also Taska, "Grammar and Linguistics in the *Encyclopédie*."

51. See Juliard, *Philosophies of Language*, 13–20, and Kuehner, *Theories on the Origin and Formation of Language*, 13–16.

52. The historiography of eighteenth-century language theory divides the field into the following categories: the traditional or orthodox theory, based on scripture, the rational or conventional theory introduced by Port-Royal, and the sensationalist or organic theory most intimately associated with Condillac. For overviews of this categorization, see Kuehner, *Theories on the Origin and Formation of Language*, and Berry, "Adam Smith's *Considerations on Language*."

53. See Berry, "Adam Smith's *Considerations on Language*," esp. 131, and Kuehner, *Theories on the Origin and Formation of Language*, 20ff.

54. Knight, *The Geometric Spirit*, 147.

55. See Acton, "The Philosophy of Language in Revolutionary France."

56. An obvious example, as noted above, is Vitruvius. Knight, *The Geometric Spirit*, 147, n. 5, also points to this coincidence in the work of Lucretius and Horace. See also Kaye, "Mandeville on the Origin of Language," and Jespersen, *Language: Its Nature, Development and Origin*, 19ff.

57. This search often went so far as to include practical applications of language theory, as in the teaching of deaf-mutes. See, for example, Diderot, "Lettre sur les sourds et muets" (1751). On this letter, see Knowlson, "The Idea of Gesture as a Universal Language." A related application was the development of various universal languages, discussed below.

58. See Cordemoy, *Discours physique de la parole* (2nd ed., 1677), 23ff.

59. Rousseau, *Discourse on the Origin and the Foundations of Inequality Among Men*, 154.

60. Rousseau, *Essay on the Origin of Languages*, 244 and 240. On this essay, see Claparède, "Rousseau et l'origine du langage"; Derrida, "La linguistique de Rousseau"; and Starobinski, "Rousseau et l'origine des langues."

61. Rousseau, *Discourse on the Origin and the Foundations of Inequality Among Men*, 157–158.

62. See Harnois, "Les théories du langage en France," 69ff. Rousseau's *Social Contract* was first published as *Du contract social ou principes du droit politique* (Amsterdam, 1762).

63. "Les effets de la Parole sont inappréciables; *elle est la base de la société* & la source des douceurs qu'on y éprouve; par elle, nous manifestons nos besoins, nos craintes, nos plaisirs, nos lumieres, & nous recevons de la part des autres les secours, les conseils, les avis, les connoissances qui nous sont nécessaires: . . . c'est par ce moyen de communication que l'espèce humaine parvient au dégré de perfecionnement dont elle est susceptible: . . . sans cette émulation, l'Homme, isolé, plongé dans une langeur stupide, n'auroit presqu'aucune supériorité sur les animaux." Court de Gébelin, *Histoire naturelle de la parole* (1776), 3–4, my emphasis. The complete 9-volume work, *Le monde primitif considéré, analysé et comparé avec le monde moderne*, was first published in Paris, 1771–1782. Court de Gébelin was not the only writer to distinguish between speech and language during the eighteenth century. Diderot wrote, "Nos écrits n'opèrent sur une certaine classe de citoyens, nos discours sur toutes" (cited in Habermas, *The Structural Transformation of the Public Sphere*, 257, n. 15). The distinction between "langue" and "parole," however, was not made with great theoretical rigor until Saussure and will not play a significant role in my discussion. On Court de Gébelin, see Lefèvre, "La génétique du language selon Antoine Court de Gébelin," and Cherpack, "Warburton and Some Aspects of the Search for the Primitive."

64. This view was codified by D'Alembert in the *Encyclopédie* when he wrote that languages were "born along with societies." See D'Alembert, *Preliminary Discourse to the Encyclopedia of Diderot*, 32. The importance of the relationship between language and society in the *Encyclopédie* is stressed by Hubert, *Les sciences sociales dans l'Encyclopédie*. See also Rykwert, *Adam's House*, 140.

65. On this point see Harnois, "Les théories du langage en France," 69–71, and Kuehner, *Theories on the Origin and Formation of Language*, 31. While Rousseau discussed the development of language in terms of the nuclear family, Condillac avoided heresy by considering how language might have developed if a male and female child had been

isolated from civilization after the flood. See Knight, *The Geometric Spirit*, 154.

66. See, for example, Cordemoy, *Discours physique de la parole*.

67. Turgot used language in written form to distinguish between prehistorical and historical ages. For example, he wrote "les temps historiques ne peuvent remonter plus haut que l'invention de l'écriture," in his *Plan de deux discours sur l'histoire universelle*, 1751, cited in Duchet, "Discours ethnologique," 615.

68. For interesting comments on the history of etymology in this context, see Mooney, *Vico in the Tradition of Rhetoric*, 194.

69. Court de Gébelin provides the following explication of his frontispice, entitled "Mercure conduit par l'Amour, ou Invention du langage et de l'écriture": "Mercure conduit par l'Amour, vient enseigner aux hommes l'art d'exprimer leurs idées par la Parole, et celui de les peindre par l'Ecriture: telle fut la source des Arts et de la Société, selon les Anciens. Jusques alors les hommes avoient été réduits à une vie errante et vagabonde, ou à chasser; et c'est le genre de vie dont on les voit occupés dans le lointain du Tableau.

"Osiris combla d'honneurs Mercure, nous dit Diodore de Sicile, parce qu'il vit en lui des talens extraordinaires pour tout ce qui peut être avantageux à la Société humaine. C'est Mercure qui le premier forma une langue exacte et réguliere, au lieu des sons grossiers et informes dont on se servoit; il inventa les premiers caractères, et régla jusqu'à l'harmonie des mots et des phrases.

"Cette allégorie prouve le cas infini que les Anciens faisoient de la Parole et de l'Ecriture; que seroient en effet les hommes sans ces deux véhicules de la pensée? Mais qu'est-ce qui leur inspira l'usage et l'exercise, si ce n'est l'amour sociale et le désir de se rendre mutuellement heureux? Ce n'est que ce désir du bonheur commun qui peut enflammer le génie, et lui faire produire ces Arts merveilleux qui sont la gloire de l'esprit humain, la base de la société, les aîles sur lesquelles l'homme s'éléve jusques aux Cieux et agrandit sans cesse l'empire de son intelligence.

"Les Gaulois ne faisoient pas moins de cas de Mercure; ils l'adoroient, nous dit Jules César, comme l'inventeur des Arts; ils le peignoient avec une chaîne d'or qui sortoit de sa bouche, et avec laquelle il conduisoit tout le monde par les oreilles." *Histoire naturelle de la parole,* 382–383.

70. "Les hommes s'entendent par le même principe que ceux d'entre les animaux qui s'avertissent par des cris, de leurs besoins, de leurs sensations, de leurs désirs. . . . On a confondu le moment où, pour la premiere fois, on fit usage des mots, avec les tems postérieurs où l'on employa ces mots déjà connus; l'homme commençant une société, & l'homme survenant dans une société déjà formée, déjà en possession d'une Langue à laquelle il est obligé de se conformer. Il est certain que dans ces derniers cas, on ne remonte jamais à un modéle pris dans la Nature; qu'on ne le voit nulle part; qu'on n'apperçoit qu'un usage; & que cet usage éprouvant des variations continuelles, paroît n'avoir absolument rien que d'arbitraire. Mais on se trompera, toutes les fois qu'on conclura que ce modéle n'existe pas, & que les mots sont arbitraires." Court de Gébelin, *Histoire naturelle de la parole,* 19–20.

71. See Elledge, "The Naked Science of Language." This understanding culminated in theories of signs and in the study of language as conducted by the Idéologues and especially by Destutt de Tracy; see his *Elémens d'idéologie* (3d ed., 1817).

72. On Condillac's view of the relationship between language and ideas, see Van Duzer, *The Contribution of the Ideologues to French Revolutionary Thought,* 23ff.

73. See Knight, *The Geometric Spirit,* and Kuehner, *Theories on the Origin and Formation of Language.* Aarsleff, in *The Study of Language in England,* 17, notes that, although he never wrote about it directly, etymology was of great importance to Condillac.

74. See Harnois, "Les théories du langage en France," 31ff. Juliard, *Philosophies of Language,* stresses the relationship between language and the notion of progress. On progress and the arts more generally, see Gombrich, *Ideas of Progress and Their Impact on Art.*

75. On the variability of this time scale see Berry, "Adam Smith's *Considerations on Language,*" and Formigari, "Language and Society in the Late Eighteenth Century."

76. See Hubert, *Les sciences sociales dans l'Encyclopédie,* 336ff.; Stromberg, "History in the Eighteenth Century"; and Dubois, *Mythe et*

langage au seizième siècle. On language as revelatory of culture with respect to Court de Gébelin, see Juliard, *Philosophies of Language.* Although there is no evidence to suggest Quatremère knew his work, Vico was an important source and instigator of this phenomenon generally. See Clark, "Herder, Cesarotti and Vico"; Pons, "Vico and French Thought"; and Rossi, "Vico e il mito dell'Egitto."

77. "D'après la langue d'une peuple, en un mot, on peut peindre d'une manière plus exacte que d'après ses monumens historiques: on y suit sans peine les progrès des sciences et des arts, et la route qu'ils one tenue." Court de Gébelin, *Histoire naturelle de la parole,* 82–83.

78. "L'histoire des colonies et leurs parcours sur la surface de la terre, tient fort près à l'histoire des langages. Le meilleur moyen de découvrir l'origine d'une nation est de suivre, en remontant, les traces de sa langue comparée à celles des peuples avec qui la tradition des faits nous apprend que ce peuple a eu quelque rapport." De Brosse, *Traité de la formation méchanique des langues,* l:xlviii. See Juliard, *Philsophies of Language,* 62, and Aarsleff, *The Study of Language in England,* 34.

79. See Knight, *The Geometric Spirit,* 191ff.

80. *Essai sur l'origine des connaissances humaines,* quoted in Knight, *The Geometric Spirit,* 189.

81. This development was encouraged by the introduction of new cultures to Europe, and has been related both to language studies and to early forms of comparative anthropology. See Aarsleff, *From Locke to Saussure,* esp. 161. On the importance of travel literature during this period see Stafford, *Voyage into Substance,* Adams, *Travelers and Travel Liars,* and the volume *L'europa cristiana nel rapporto con le altre culture nel secolo XVII.*

82. On the status of architecture during the eighteenth century, see Harrington, *Changing Ideas on Architecture.*

83. Although systems and theories are not identical, Quatremère interrelates them in the passage cited: ". . . nous dirons qu'on use [le mot système] ordinairement pour désigner la théorie du principe originaire d'où cet art est né . . . l'idée de système est applicable à plus d'une sorte d'architecture, et que chacune peut avoir le sien." Quatremère, *Encyclopédie méthodique,* 3:424. Winckelmann had previously made reference

to the system of art: "Je prends la mot *Histoire*, dans la signification la plus étendue qu'il a dans la langue Grecque, et mon dessein est de donner un essai d'un système de l'Art." *Histoire de l'art*, i.

84. The use of the word *type* in reference to categories of building programs and functions, as codified by Pevsner's *A History of Building Types*, is often traced to Durand's *Recueil et parallel des édifices en tout genre anciens et modernes* (1800). This lineage is incontrovertible but also incomplete since the word *type* itself—which carried specific meanings in the eighteenth century that were fundamental to the development of architectural typology in general—does not appear in Durand. The *Recueil et parallel* is often translated as *Survey and Comparison of Buildings of All Types*, although Durand used only the terms *genre* or *espèce*. The full history of type in architecture has yet to be written. Some additional remarks on the subject will be offered in the conclusion. On Durand, see Szambien, *Jean-Nicolas-Louis Durand*, and Villari, *J. N. L. Durand*. On the relationship between the notion of type in Durand and Quatremère, see Vidler, "The Idea of Type"; Oechslin, "Per una ripresa della discussione tipologica"; and Mead, "'Buildings of All Types.'"

85. "L'erreur qu'on se propose de combattre en ce genre repose sur l'opinion qu'il existe une Architecture commune à tous les peuples, laquelle auroit une origine locale, et dont il ne s'agiroit que de démêler la généalogie." *De l'architecture égyptienne*, 226.

86. Greek and Egyptian architecture, according to Quatremère, were "sans rapport générique entr'elles, comme deux espèces distinctes dans leur conformation essentielle. L'anteriorité de l'une sur l'autre . . . seroit un arguement de peu de valeur . . . Peu importe, en effet, la date de leur naissance, si chacune nâquit d'un germe différent." *De l'architecture égyptienne*, 19.

87. On the use of the word *germ* in language theory and especially in De Brosse, see Juliard, *Philosophies of Language*, 31.

88. "L'on se rappelle qu'au commencement de cet écrit, on a fait mention des trois principaux types d'où sont émanées les différentes Architectures que nous connoissons; ces trois principaux types sont la tente, les souterrains, la cabane ou la charpente." *De l'architecture égyptienne*, 239.

89. "Trois genres de vie se sont nécessairement partagé le premier

âge des sociétés. La nature, selon la diversité des contrées où elles se trouvèrent placées, leur présenta un de ces trois états qui distinguent encore aujourd'hui les différentes régions de la terre. Les hommes furent, en raison de leurs positions variés, ou chasseurs, ou pasteurs, ou agriculteurs . . . Les peuples chasseurs ou ictiophages n'auront dû, pendant longtems, se construire aucune habitation. [Ils] trouvent plus commodes de se creuser des demeures en terre, ou de profiter des excavations toutes préparées par la nature . . . Le peuple pasteur, sans cesse en mouvement . . . ne peut user de ces demeures creusées par la main de la nature. Une habitation fixe ne sauroit le retenir; il lui en faut de mobiles et qui puissent le suivre: delà, de tout tems, l'usage des tentes. L'agriculture, au contraire, exige une vie tout à-la-fois active et sédentaire. Elle dût suggérer aux hommes de se bâtir des demeures plus solides et plus fixes. L'agriculteur, d'ailleurs, vivant sur son champ et de ce qu'il produit, a des provisions à serrer; il lui faut une habitation sûre, commode, saine et étendue. La cabanne de bois, avec son toit, dût bientôt s'élever." *De l'architecture égyptienne,* 15–16.

90. ". . . [les] trois principaux types d'où sont émanées les différentes Architectures que nous connoissons." *De l'architecture égyptienne,* 239.

91. "Les types essentiels de la charpente, avec toutes ses parties constitutives, se trouvent empreints dans l'ensemble et dans tous les détails de l'Architecture grecque . . . le caractère propre et spécial de son Architecture [Egypte] ne retrace aucune des formes et des combinaisons de la charpente; qu'enfin, elle se modela sur un type tout différent de celui des Grecs, et ce type fut celui des souterrains." *De l'architecture égyptienne,* 26–27.

92. See the entry on Chinese architecture in Quatremère's *Encyclopédie méthodique,* 1:653–671, esp. 670.

93. The terms in French are "première origine," "première form," and "premiers modèles." Quatremère, Prix Caylus MS, 4v, 3r, and 7v.

94. Quatremère, Prix Caylus MS, 1v. The same can be said of his use of the word *germ,* cited above, although in that case the reference is more to the developing science of natural history than to the tradition of architectural anthropomorphism.

95. "Il est . . . vraisemblable de rechercher dans les Caisses des Momies le premier type de figures Egyptiennes. Le désir de conserver et de perpétuer l'image de l'homme après sa mort, inspira l'idée d'assimiler l'enveloppe du corps à la forme qu'elle renfermoit." Quatremère, *Prix Caylus MS*, 50r.

96. On type in relation to the Renaissance concept of *idea*, see Lee, "*Ut Pictura Poesis*," 209, and Panofksy, *Idea*.

97. For a translation of Quatremère's article, see Vidler, "The Idea of Type." For additional interpretations of Quatremère's architectural typology, see Schneider, *L'Esthétique classique chez Quatremère de Quincy*, 43ff; Vidler, "The Hut and the Body"; Oechslin, "Per una ripresa della discussione tipologica"; Morales, "The Origins of Modern Eclecticism"; and Rykwert, *On Adam's House*, 44ff.

98. Although Quatremère's use of the word *type* is most systematic in his architectural texts, it also appears in his writings on the other fine arts. In the latter context, however, *type* sheds light especially on Quatremère's theory of imitation and will be discussed in chapter 3.

I have been able to locate only a single original source that clarifies, if only slightly, the publication history of the *Encyclopédie méthodique*. Some time after all three volumes had been published, Quatremère had not received what he felt was payment in full for his work. In seeking to rectify this situation, he had a letter written that suggests each volume was written during the years just preceeding publication. The document, contained in the Archives of the History of Art, The Getty Center for the History of Art and the Humanities, is reprinted in full in Appendix C. In the absence of the original contract or other corroborative evidence, however (many contracts between author and publisher are located in the Kenneth Spencer Research Library, University of Kansas, Lawrence, Kansas, MS 99 but those for Quatremère and the architectural dictionary are not among them), the implications of the Getty document cannot be accepted as established fact. The general process of preparing the *Encyclopédie méthodique*, fully described in Darnton's *The Business of Enlightenment*, often began with a collection of the relevant tear sheets from Diderot's original *Encyclopédie*. Thus it would be hazardous to assume categorically that articles on subjects that appear early in the alphabet and that were thus the first to be published were actually the first to be written. Nevertheless both this new document and references

Quatremère made in the *Encyclopédie méthodique* text to other publications do suggest a rough correlation between date of publication and date of authorship. The document also corroborates Darnton's description of how certain dictionaries, including the one on architecture, were afterthoughts, and how the publication process was constantly and precipitously interrupted by political events and changing business fortunes. These conditions had a strong impact on the *Encyclopédie méthodique*, particularly with respect to its size and its inclusion of illustrations. For example, in the first volume Quatremère indicates that a choice of illustrations had been made, although the images themselves had not been executed. Ultimately, in part because the *Encyclopédie méthodique* had grown to an unmanageable and unsellable size, they were never published. It should also be pointed out that in the Getty document Quatremère claims to have received no assistance from the two men who were hired to ease the burden of preparing the third volume of the dictionary in particular. Although Quatremère may have received less assistance than expected, he did receive some. Several articles in the third volume were written by Jean-Nicolas Huyot (1780–1840) and Antoine Laurent Castellan (1772–1838). For further information on the *Encyclopédie méthodique*, see Harrington, *Changing Ideas on Architecture*, and Watts, "The *Encyclopédie méthodique*."

99. "Les contradictions étranges qui se rencontrent dans tous les ouvrages où l'on a recherché la naissance de l'architecture proviennent nécessairement de ce qu'on n'a pas apperçu distinctement cette triple origine . . . On se tromperoit encore, si l'on vouloit dans chaque pays ne rapporter qu'à un principe unique les résultats de cet art; puisqu'il est possible que chez certains peuples l'architecture ait eu un double principe, comme nous le ferons voir de l'architecture Egyptienne." *Encyclopédie méthodique*, 1:111. On the other hand, Quatremère came to think that Egyptian architecture had had a single origin in the cave before he published *De l'architecture égyptienne*. In the article on Egypt published in the *Encyclopédie méthodique* in 1801, Quatremère wrote, "Le caractère spécial & propre de son architecture ne retrace aucune des formes de la charpente; on peut donc assurer que cette architecture se modela sur un type différent de celui des Grecs, & ce type fut celui des souterrains." *Encyclopédie méthodique*, 2:286.

100. "L'arbre est le type primitif de la colonne, non pas l'arbre

tel qu'il existe dans les bois, mais bien l'arbre déjà taillé et façonné par la charpente." *Encyclopédie méthodique*, 1:83.

101. Laugier uses the word *model* in both the 1753 and 1755 editions of his *Essai sur l'architecture*. In translating Laugier, Rykwert (*On Adam's House*, 44) uses "type" for the original "modèle." On Laugier, see also Herrmann, *Laugier and Eighteenth Century French Theory*.

102. ". . . les différens genres de construction furent les types premiers de l'architecture." *Encyclopédie méthodique*, 1:251. Rondelet wrote all of the articles on construction in the first two volumes of the *Encyclopédie méthodique*.

103. The relationship between Viel de Saint-Maux and Quatremère is complex. Viel came closer to Quatremère's interest in the relationship between language and architecture than perhaps any other French figure of the late eighteenth century. In his *Lettres sur l'architecture* (1787), Viel frequently discussed the origins of art in language, particularly with reference to the hieroglyph, and structured his polemic around the difference between artificial and natural forms of expression. Moreover, in note 4 of his seventh letter, Viel refers to one of his own publications, entitled *Considérations sur l'origine de la peinture et du langage*. I have not been able to locate this text, but Viel's reference includes pagination and thereby indicates that he had indeed published the work and was not merely intending to do so. Despite this proximity of interest, Viel and Quatremère differed profoundly in how they conceived of both language and architecture and of their relationship. While Quatremère emphasized the rational abstraction of classicism, Viel stressed the symbolic nature of its forms and ascribed its origins to religious and agricultural ritual. These differences are clearest in Quatremère's article on allegory in the *Encyclopédie méthodique* where he implicitly refers to and explicitly criticizes Viel's attempt to reduce "toute l'architecture en Allégorie." For example, he ridicules Viel's interpretation of the pediment as "un triangle mystérieux, emblême de la divinité." However, Quatremère's own understanding of the pediment is not without a metaphorical component since he defines it as either the roof itself or as "la réprésentation du toît." Quatremère's notion of allegory will be further discussed below.

104. "Ma finalmente in qual parte di mondo trovansi le case

fabbricate di mano della Natura, che gli architetti debbano pigliare come archetipo?" Algarotti, *Saggio sopra l'architettura* (1784), 20.

105. ". . . un symbole, un signe ou une figure d'une chose à venir . . . Les types ne sont pas de simples conformités ou analogies que la nature fait naître entre deux choses d'ailleurs différentes, ni des images arbitraires, qui n'on d'autres fondement que la ressemblance casuelle d'une chose à une autre. Il faut outre cela que Dieu ait eu une intention particulière de faire un type, & qu'il ait déclaré expressément que ce type en est un." *Encyclopédie ou Dictionnaire raisonné des sciences, des arts et des métiers*, s.v. "type."

106. These examples are taken from the *Encyclopédie:* "le sacrifice d'Abraham, l'agneau paschal, etc. étoient les types ou figures de notre rédemption. Le serpent d'airain étoit le type de la croix, etc."

107. On typology and biblical exegesis see Lampe and Woollcombe, *Essays on Typology*, and Daniélou, "*Sacramentum Futuri.*"

108. For parallel examples in literature, see Korshin, "The Development of Abstract Typology in England, 1650–1820."

109. See Littré, *Dictionnaire de la lange française* (1881), s.v. "type." Littré quotes Destutt de Tracy writing of the "croyance qui a fait prendre les produits de notre raison pour une espèce de type inné," a perspicacious remark summing up the transformation that the concept had undergone. On the relationship between this aspect of type and character, see chapter 3 below.

110. See Iversen, *The Myth of Egypt;* Iversen, "Hieroglyphic Studies of the Renaissance"; Giehlow, "Die Hieroglyphenkunde des Humanismus in der Allegorie der Renaissance"; and Dieckmann, *Hieroglyphs,* esp. 161ff. Dieckmann's discussion of Louis-Claude de Saint-Martin's *Le tableau naturel des rapports qui existent entre Dieu, l'homme et l'univers* clearly traces the relationship of Saint-Martin's use of type in his theory of divine emanations and universal concordance to the hieroglyph.

111. This aspect of Kircher's work is carefully analyzed in Rivosecchi, *Esotismo in Roma barocca,* 49–75.

112. See David, *Le débat sur les écritures et l'hiéroglyphe.* On

Vico and the modern, antimystical interpretation of hieroglyphs, see Rossi, *The Dark Abyss of Time.*

113. Already in 1803, Quatremère gave the following analysis of hieroglyphs: "On est d'accord qu'il faut dans ce qu'on appelle hiéro- glyphes distinguer trois espèces de signes, ceux qui font voir les choses par la figure entière de ces choses, ceux qui indiquent l'idée de la chose par des portions de figures, et ceux qui représentent les mots ou les sons qui les forment par des signes abrégés et conventionnels semblables aux lettres alphabétiques et qui étoient une écriture cursive. Ces deux der- nières espèces d'hiéroglyphes ne peuvent donc se considérer que comme de véritables inscriptions. Ce seroit un abus de prêter à ces signes une valeur décorative dont ils ne sont pas susceptibles." *De l'architecture égyptienne,* 162. This analysis derives from Warburton's *The Divine Lega- tion of Moses Demonstrated in Nine Books* (1737). In the second volume of the *Encyclopédie méthodique,* 458, Quatremère quotes Warburton directly in order to refute his suggestion that Gothic architecture origi- nated as an imitation of forests. Sections of Warburton's *Divine Legation of Moses* were translated by Léonard de Malpeines as *Essai sur les hiéro- glyphes des Egyptiens* (1744). Quatremère would also have felt the influence of Warburton indirectly, in both Condillac and the *Encyclopédie.* On Warburton, see Cherpack, "Warburton and Some Aspects of the Search for the Primitive."

114. Etienne Quatremère's *Recherches critiques et historiques sur la langue et la littérature de l'Egypte* (1808) helped establish that Coptic and hieroglyphs were related.

115. "Destinés à recevoir sur toutes leurs surfaces des inscriptions en caractères symboliques, il faut les regarder comme de grands livres toujours ouverts à l'instruction publique . . . Tous les monumens étoient des espèces de bibliothèques publiques, leurs ornemens étoient des lé- gendes . . . des monumens qui étoient sans aucune métaphore des dépos- itaires des rites, des dogmes, des exploits, de la gloire; enfin de l'histoire philosphique ou politique de la nation." *De l'architecture égyptienne,* 59.

116. On the book of nature, see Dieckmann, *Hieroglyphics;* Cur- tius, *European Literature and the Latin Middle Ages,* esp. 319ff.; Staf- ford, *Voyage into Substance;* and Moser, "Pour et contre la Bible," 1524.

117. Warburton, *The Divine Legation of Moses,* vol. 3, book iv, esp. 89.

118. Compare Boullée's completely different (and much more traditional) use of the book metaphor in the context of architectural character and its source in nature: "O nature, qu'il est bien vrai de dire que tu es le livre des livres, la science universelle." See Boullée's *Architecture*, ed. Pérouse de Montclos, 75.

119. Warburton, *The Divine Legation of Moses*, vol. 3, book iv, 132.

120. Warburton, *The Divine Legation of Moses*, vol. 3, book iv, 95 and 75ff.

121. "C'est sur les murs des grands temples de l'Egypte qu'on voit sculptés de ces hiéroglyphes en figures colossales, qui représentent assez l'idée de ce qu'on entend par bas-reliefs, comme ornemens de l'architecture." *Encyclopédie méthodique*, 2:519. On the relationship between hieroglyphs and art, see Todorov, "Esthetique et semiotique au XVIIIe siècle"; Stafford, *Voyage into Substance* and *Symbols and Myth*; and, especially with respect to Diderot, Simowitz, *Theory of Art in the Encyclopédie*.

122. "Il faut dire que les arts du dessin doivent et ont dû véritablement leur origine aux besoins de l'écriture." Quatremère, *Considérations sur les arts du dessin*, 29–30. Imitation was central to the relationship Quatremère perceived between hieroglyphs and art. For him the hieroglyph represented an infantile form of imitation based on simple copies of nature, and it was not until the development of abstract alphabets that writing became parallel to idealized imitation. Although Quatremère did divide hieroglyphs into three categories based on their relative abstraction of nature, the true abstraction of hieroglyphs was not understood until after their decipherment. See chapter 3 for his theory of imitation.

123. Hieroglyphs are described as "speaking pictures" in Perry's *A View of the Levant*. Quatremère cites the English edition of this work. For other aspects of the notion of "speaking pictures," see chapter 3 below.

124. See *De l'architecture égyptienne*, 13, and above.

125. See *Encyclopédie méthodique*, 2:458, and Quatremère's *Lettres sur la préjudice*, 69.

126. *De l'architecture égyptienne*, 226.

127. ". . . colonnes, des traverses, des chapiteaux et d'autres parties qui sont les élémens naturels de l'art de batir, et ne sont par conséquent à toutes les architectures du monde, que ce que sont aux diverses langues les élémens de la grammaire universelle." *Encyclopédie méthodique*, 2:373.

128. See the *Encyclopédie méthodique*, 2:215 and 3:50.

129. Quatremère defined the metaphysic of architecture as that "qui fait particulièrement connaître l'essence de l'art," while he defined the theory of architecture as that which guides "l'artiste dans ses ouvrages, & le public dans le jugement qu'il en porte." *Encyclopédie méthodique*, 1:v.

130. Although many examples might be selected to illustrate Quatremère's point, he himself said of Gondoin's building, "Un seul mot fera l'éloge de ce monument. Il est l'ouvrage le plus classique du dix-huitième siècle." *Histoire de la vie et des ouvrages des plus célèbres architectes*, 2:332.

131. For a quite different understanding of Quatremère's relationship to history, see Potts, "Political Attitudes."

132. "Quelque estimable que soit son *Histoire de l'art*, elle ressemble toujours plus à une chronologie qu'à une histoire." Quatremère, *Lettres sur l'enlèvement des ouvrages de l'art antique* (1836), 206. For additional comments on Winckelmann, see Quatremère's "Eloge de M. Visconti" in his *Recueil de notices historiques* (1834), 146–176. On Winckelmann's view of history, see Potts, "Winckelmann's History of Ancient Art" and "Winckelmann's Construction of History"; Lepenies, "L'altro fanatico"; Pommier, "Winckelmann et la vision de l'Antiquité classique."

133. ". . . à la fois chronologique, historique, théorique et didactique, l'ouvrage qui puisse devenir le traité universel de cet art." *Encyclopédie méthodique*, 3:313. Having already claimed that his own architectural dictionary encompassed "la partie historique & descriptive, la partie métaphysique, la partie théorique, la partie élémentaire ou didactique, & la partie pratique" of architecture, this plea may have been somewhat ironic.

134. See Middleton, "The Abbé de Cordemoy and the Graeco-Gothic Ideal."

135. "Il ne s'ensuit pas, que tout . . . soit également beau, et qu'il n'y en ait de préférable." *Encyclopédie méthodique,* 3:424.

III
The Language of Imitation

1. Quatremère's best-known work on mimetic theory is the *Essai sur la nature, le but et les moyens de l'imitation dans les beaux-arts* (1823), also published in English, translated by J. C. Kent, as *An Essay on the Nature, the End, and the Means of Imitation in the Fine Arts* (1837). The original French edition has recently been reprinted as *De l'imitation* with introductions by Leon Krier and Demetri Porphyrios. However, because *De l'imitation* is both a late work and a general discussion of the subject, my exploration of Quatremère's theory of imitation will focus on texts that deal primarily with architecture.

2. The section is entitled "De l'imitation des Grecs" and describes evidence of "les parties d'imitation positive." Quatremère, Prix Caylus MS, 64r. Quatremère underscores in this section the way in which the Greeks had known how to "couvrir et cacher encore les larcins faites à l'Egypte."

3. Following the publication of many works devoted to Greek architecture, notably Le Roy's *Les ruines des plus beaux monuments de la Grèce* of 1758, French architects began to reject Roman architecture as a model for contemporary practice with increasing frequency. See *Age of Neo-Classicism;* Drexler, ed., *The Architecture of the Beaux-Arts;* Braham, *The Architecture of the French Enlightenment;* Harris, "Le Geay, Piranesi and International Neo-classicism in Rome"; Middleton and Watkin, *Neo-classical and Nineteenth Century Architecture;* and Rosenblum, *Transformations in Late Eighteenth Century Art.*

4. Quatremère said of the Greeks that "la justesse de leur goût . . . nous a donné les vrais modèles du beau en nous laissant le désespoir de les égaler jamais." Prix Caylus MS, 64r.

5. The following discussion is based on the two-part article "Sur la manière d'imiter la bonne architecture grecque." I have included the full text of this article in Appendix D. On this article see Lipstadt, "Early Architectural Periodicals." Quatremère's criticism is explicitly directed against Victor Louis's work at the Château de la Trompette in Bordeaux.

He has similar comments to make about Ledoux's Parisian *barrières*. See the articles "barrière," "bossage," and "entrée" in the *Encyclopédie méthodique* and his comments in Legrand and Landon's *Description de Paris et de ses édifices*, vol. 1, part ii, 7.

6. In the article on "autorité" in the *Encyclopédie méthodique*, 1:176, Quatremère cites Chambray saying "Les Grecs, plus voisins de la nature, apperçurent bien plus nettement les choses que nous n'entrevoyons qu'avec peine, après une longue étude de l'architecture antique." Quatremère then adds: "aussi leurs ouvrages sont-ils devenues, pour nous, l'équivalent de la nature même."

7. This claim may be compared with one by Winckelmann, "there is but one way for the moderns to become great, and perhaps unequalled; I mean, by imitating the ancients." Winckelman, "On the Imitation of the Painting and Sculpture of the Greeks," trans. Henry Fuseli, 1.

8. With respect to stylistic imitation, Quatremère also distinguished between "adoption," which includes taking over the entire system of a foreign architecture as the Romans did, and "emprunter," which includes only transporting specific elements from a foreign architecture as the Greeks did. See *De l'architecture égyptienne*, 246.

9. There is no complete history of architectural imitation. For a few specialized discussions, see Summers, "Michelangelo on Architecture"; Tafuri, *L'architettura del manierismo nel cinquecento europeo*; Bialostocki, "The Renaissance Concept of Nature and Antiquity"; and Wittkower, *Architectural Principles in the Age of Humanism*. On imitation, architecture, and *natura naturata/naturans*, see also I. Lavin, *Bernini and the Unity of the Visual Arts*, 6–13. For a discussion of imitation in a context more directly relevant to Quatremère's theory of architecture, see Stafford, *Voyage into Substance*, 8ff. On the relation among the arts generally, see also Hagstrum, *The Sister Arts*; Praz, *Mnemosyne*; and Barkan, *Nature's Work of Art*.

10. "La Sculpture et la Peinture atteignirent plutôt un certain degré de perfection que l'Architecture. La raison est que celle-ci a beaucoup plus d'idéal que lex deux autres. Elle n'a point un objet déterminé dans la Nature qu'elle doivent imiter: elle est fondée sur les regles générales & les loix de la proportion. La Sculpture et la Peinture, ayant

commencé par la simple imitation, trouverent toutes leurs regles dans la contemplation de l'homme. Ce model les renfermoit toutes, et elles n'avoient pour-ainsi-dire qu'à voir et exécuter. L'Architecture étoit obligée de chercher les siennes dans la combinaison de plusieurs proportions: une infinité d'opérations étoient nécessaires pour les découvrir." Winckelmann, *Histoire de l'art chez les anciens*, 1:236–237.

11. For a discussion of and bibliography on the "idéal," see Panofsky, *Idea*.

12. ". . . de [sic] levarsi in alto coll'intelletto, e derivare un sistema d'imitazione dalle idee delle cose più universali, e più lontane dalla vista dell'uomo. E quasi che con giusta ragione dir si potrebbo, che tra le arti ella tiene quel luogo, che tiene tra le scienze la Metafisica." Algarotti, *Saggio sopra l'architettura*, 21.

13. In the *Système figuré des conoissances humaines* Diderot prepared for the *Prospectus* of the *Encyclopédie* in 1750, architecture was excluded from the category of imagination, the branch of knowledge under which painting and sculpture were grouped. Architecture was however united with the other arts in the revised version of the *Système figuré* published following the *Discours préliminaire* in the first volume of the *Encyclopédie*. See Harrington, *Changing Ideas on Architecture*. On the history of the categorization of the arts, see Kristeller, "The Modern System of the Arts." Distinguishing architectural imitation in a positive light goes back at least as far as Thomas Aquinas, who, according to David Summers "preferred the example of architecture as a metaphor for artistic making precisely because its clearly artificial or functional forms circumvented the problem of the relationship of the artist's conception to the forms of the visible world and therefore to the ideas in the Divine Mind." See Summers, "Michelangelo on Architecture," 156, and Panofksky, *Idea*.

14. "Cet art, en apparence, plus asservi à la matière que les deux autres, est dans le fait plus idéal, plus intellectual, plus métaphysique qu'eux." Quatremère, *Encyclopédie méthodique*, 1:120.

15. "L'architecture . . . n'imite la nature qu'en transposant dans ses ouvrages les qualités de son modèle. Cet art n'imite aucune forme, mais bien l'esprit de celles qui l'environment." Quatremère, *Encyclopédie méthodique*, 1:495.

16. "Cette théorie, je le sais, est tout à fait neuve." Quatremère, *Encyclopédie méthodique*, 1:495.

17. "Nous avons vu à la verité que les primitives habitations, suggérées par le besoin, sont devenues partout une espèce de modèle offert à l'imitation de l'art." Quatremère, *De l'architecture égyptienne*, 41.

18. "Mais ce modèle n'est point la nature . . . et l'on ne sauroit appeler art d'imitation, que celui qui imite la nature." Quatremère, *De l'architecture égyptienne*, 41.

19. "Creusées par la main de la nature." Quatremère, *De l'architecture égyptienne*, 16.

20. "Les souterrains doivent présenter à l'art un modèle d'une espèce si finie, si complète que l'imitation n'a rien à y ajouter et ne peut rien entreprendre au-delà . . . Les souterrains n'offrent, partout et en tout sens, que des superficies froides et lisses. Rien . . . n'y présente la réalité ni l'idée de parties, de rapports, de divisions, de proportions. Les objets mêmes, que l'art imagina pour en corriger la monotonie, étant étrangers au fond du principe qui les créa, rien dans la décoration de cette Architecture ne se trouva nécessaire ou fondé en raison." Quatremère, *De l'architecture égyptienne*, 239–241.

21. ". . . trop de petites choses à imiter." Quatremère, *De l'architecture égyptienne*, 239.

22. ". . . l'une sensible et l'autre abstraite, l'une qui repose sur les premiers modèles des habitations originaires dans chacque pays, l'autre qui a sa base dans la connoissance des lois de la nature et des impressions que notre âme reçoit de la vue des rapports des objets." Quatremère, *De l'architecture égyptienne*, 205.

23. Quatremère also argued that if and when new materials such as brick, stone, and marble were introduced to Chinese architecture, they resulted in too great a disparity between model and copy. Nevertheless he greatly admired the "légèrté" and "gaeté" of Chinese architecture. See his article on Chinese architecture in the first volume of the *Encyclopédie méthodique*, esp. 670. On this point, see also Szambien, *Symétrie, goût, caractère*, 147ff.

24. ". . . lentement par une suite d'essais insensibles et de répétitions." Quatremère, *De l'architecture égyptienne*, 229.

25. "Avant que la cabane pût devenir le type de l'Architecture grecque, il fallût qu'elle-même eut reçu sa perfection . . . La cabane sans perdre la simplicité de sa forme permière aura vu ses supports, ses combles, ses porches, ses plafonds, ses proportions se combiner, se modifier, s'embellir successivement et se disposer avec plus de recherche et d'élégance. . . . Un tel modèle acquit relativement à l'art imitateur la force et l'autorité de la nature." Quatremère, *De l'architecture égyptienne*, 229–230.

26. On Laugier, see Herrmann, *Laugier*, esp. 43ff., and Middleton, "The Abbé de Cordemoy and the Graeco-Gothic Ideal." See also Laugier's *Observations sur l'architecture* (1765).

27. "La petite cabane rustique . . . est le modele sur lequel on a imaginé les magnificences de l'Architecture. C'est en se raprochant dans l'exécution de la simplicité de ce premier modele, que l'on évite les défauts essentiels, que l'on saisit les perfections véritables . . . Ne perdons point de vûe notre petite cabane rustique." Laugier, *Essai sur l'architecture*, 10. The translation is from Laugier's *An Essay on Architecture*, trans. Wolfgang and Anni Herrmann, 12.

28. "Dans tout ordre d'Architecture, il n'y a que la colonne, l'entablement & le fronton qui puissent entrer essentiellement dans sa composition." Laugier, *Essai sur l'architecture*, 10 (translation, *An Essay on Architecture*, 12–13). With respect to convention, Laugier maintained "qu'il y avoit dans l'Architecture des beautés essentielles, indépendantes de l'habitude des sens, ou de la convention des hommes." *Essai sur l'architecture*, xi. Cf. Claude Perrault's notion of positive and arbitrary beauty in *Ordonnance des cinq espèces de colonnes selon la méthode des anciens* (1683). On Perrault, see Herrmann, *The Theory of Claude Perrault*.

29. "Ce modèle, réel ou fictif, quel qu'il fût, étoit déjà lui-même un ouvrage de l'art." Quatremère, *Encyclopédie méthodique*, 1:454. Marmontel also refuted Laugier's notion of the primitive hut in the article "art" he contributed to the *Encyclopédie*'s *Supplément*. See Harrington, *Changing Ideas on Architecture*, 113.

30. "Ne considérèrent cette imitation de la charpente que comme la squelette de l'art, propre à être revetu des formes raisonnées que les proportions pouvoient lui donner . . . la charpente enfin étoit plutôt

l'ébauche que la modéle de l'art. . . . . Ils comprirent que le plaisir, ennemi de la servitude, secoueroit les chaînes qu'une imitation trop rigoureuse des formes nécessaires pourroit lui imposer; & de-là est née cette métamorphose ingénieuse, qui dans ce systême imitatif déguise l'objet imité sous le voile de l'invention, la vérité sous l'apparence de la fiction." Quatremère, *Encyclopédie méthodique,* 1:467.

31. ". . . trompé sans être induit en erreur." Quatremère, *De l'architecture égyptienne,* 243. Quatremère's paradoxical notion of truthful fiction in imitation has been studied in relation to his theories of the figurative arts. See Gombrich, *Art and Illusion,* 278–279; Lebensztejn, "De l'imitation dans les beaux-arts"; Shiff, "Representation, Copying, and the Technique of Originality," esp. 337 and 348.

32. "En général le vrai but de l'imitation n'est pas de se substituer tellement à son modèle que la ressemblance produise une identité capable de décevoir et de faire prendre le change. Au contraire, pour que nous en jouissions, il faut que nous apercevions que l'objet imitant n'est que l'image de l'objet imité. Là, en effet, ou par un excès d'illusion factice ou de rapprochement naturel, on croit voir la chose même imitée, dans son imitation, ce n'est plus l'image de cette chose elle-même, et là où l'on ne croit pas voir l'image d'une chose, on ne croit pas voir d'imitation. On n'en voit point." Quatremère, *De l'architecture égyptienne,* 206.

33. Lodoli never published anything on architecture, but his ideas were recorded by Memmo in *Elementi dell'architettura lodoliana* (1786) and by Algarotti in his *Saggio sopra l'architettura.* Significant differences in these two accounts led to difficulties in distinguishing between Lodoli's ideas and those ascribed to him by his chroniclers. Quatremère seems to have assumed, correctly according to Edgar Kaufmann's sorting out of these discrepancies, that Memmo's publication constituted a fair account of Lodoli's ideas while Algarotti's was a critique of Lodoli and an exposition of an essentially independent theory of architecture. Quatremère's criticism of Lodoli and sympathy for Algarotti is consistent with this view. See Kaufmann, "Memmo's Lodoli."

34. See Rykwert, "Lodoli on Function and Representation."

35. "Cependant il se trouve bien des personnes qui blâment l'architecture de s'être réduite à imiter les premières constructions de bois: ils trouvent mauvais que la pierre soit représentative d'une autre matière:

ils plaignent en quelque sorte les marbres d'être ainsi dégradés par un rôle subalterne, assujettis qu'ils sont à nous rendre les formes pauvres & misérables des premières cabanes. Il voudroient que chaque matière puisât en elle-même & dans sa nature, sa forme & ses diversités de goût. Nous avons déja fait voir que la pierre, en se copiant elle-même, ou pour mieux dire en ne copiant rien, n'eut offert aucune forme à l'art, aucune variété à l'oeil, aucune rapport à l'esprit. Cela se prouve par l'architecture Egyptienne, & la nature de ses élévations froides, monotones & insipides." Quatremère, *Encyclopédie méthodique*, 1:114. An almost identical passage is contained in *De l'architecture égyptienne*, 242, where Quatremère mentions Lodoli by name.

36. "L'homme craint autant la vérité que le mensonge: il veut être séduit mais non trompé. C'est sur cette connoissance de son âme, que les arts, ces menteurs aimables et véridiques, fondent tout leur empire." *Encyclopédie méthodique*, 1:115.

37. ". . . un art raisonné." Quatremère, *De l'architecture égyptienne*, 241.

38. The saying is attributed to Simonides by Plutarch, *De gloria Atheniensium*, III, 346F–3476c.

39. See Lee, *"Ut Pictura Poesis."* See also Praz, *Mnemosyne*.

40. A similarly analogous form of imitation influenced calligraphy in the form of anthropomorphic alphabets, some of which made reference to the human figure only through proportional schemes. Building on this typographical tradition, architectural alphabets were developed that were mimetic not only by analogy to the proportions of the human body but also by analogy to the anthropomorphic conventions of this graphic medium. A well-known example is Johann David Steingruber's *Architectonisches Alphabeth* published in Schwabach in 1773. Other Steingruber publications include *Architectura Civilis* and *Practica Burgerlicher Baukunst*. See Mariano, "L'Alfabeto architettonico di J. D. Steingruber."

41. Since *ut pictura poesis* had in effect already become *ut poesis pictura*, a more correct formulation might be *ut poesis architettura*. On *ut pictura poesis* and architecture, see Szambien, *Symétrie, goût, caractère*, 174ff., and Palme, "Ut architectura poesis."

42. ". . . vivacité d'une poésie ou d'une musique oculaire." Quatremère, *De l'architecture égyptienne*, 42.

43. On rhetoric and art theory see Summers, "Contrapposto," esp. 344ff., and Montagu, "Charles Le Brun's 'Conference sur l'Expression Générale et Particulière.'" See also Kennedy, *Classical Rhetoric and Its Christian and Secular Tradition.*

44. Lamy, *Rhétorique ou l'art de parler* (1675), xvi: "fondements d'un édifice," "ornements de l'éloquence."

45. The relationship between rhetorical and architectural theory has been examined by Coulet in "La métaphore de l'architecture dans la critique littéraire au XVIIe siècle," and by Guiheux and Rouillard in "Echanges entre les mots et l'architecture."

46. "La varietà e la sorgente del piacere: nei discorsi come nel Architettura, ella serve a divertire lo Spirito, e la vista." Del Rosso, Prix Caylus MS, 139.

47. "Les formes, les types, les détails de l'architecture grecque . . . ne sont autre chose, que ce que les mots, si l'on peut dire, sont à l'art d'écrire." Quatremère, *Encyclopédie méthodique*, 3:457. See also Quatremère's "De l'emploi des sujets d'histoire moderne dans la poésie, et de leur abus dans la peinture" and "Dissertation sur la diversité du génie et des moyens poétiques des différens arts."

48. "Vitruve, cet excellent et judicieux architecte qui vivait sous Auguste, remarque que dans la structure des temples, on suivait l'ordre qui exprime le caractère de la divinité à qui le temple était dédié. . . . Il en est de même des discours; les fleurs et les gentillesses de l'éloquence ne sont pas propres pour un sujet grave et plein de majesté." Lamy, *Rhétorique*, 336.

49. "Un'analisi minuta e giusta . . . dei rudimenti primi della Grammatica, dirò così, dell'Architettura potrà forse sciogliere gli argomenti della più sottile Filosofia." Algarotti, *Saggio sopra l'architettura*, 24–25.

50. ". . . le language libre de la prose et le language poétique." Quatremère, *De l'architecture égyptienne*, 134. Rhetoric was a basic component of general education during the eighteenth century and Quatremère must already as a young student not yet seriously interested in architecture have come upon the association of rhetoric and architecture in works such as Lamy's.

51. "Arts ou Langages dont les productions sont transitoires ou instantannées: Art de la Pantomime Langage d'action; Art de la Parole Langage des sons articulés; Art de la Musique Langage des sons modulés. Arts ou Langages dont les productions sont fixes et durables: Art de la Sculpture Langage par l'imitation des formes de tous les objets visibles et palpables; Art de l'Architecture Langage par le moyen des dispositions ingénieuses et significatives dont les constructions sont susceptibles; Art de la Peinture Langage par le moyen des couleurs, disposées et appliquées avec intelligence et intention sur des surfaces unies." *Dictionnaire des Beaux-Arts*, 1:iii.

52. An interest in this aspect of language appears, for example, in Hancarville, *Recherches sur l'origine, l'esprit et les progrès des arts de la Grèce* (1785); Hancarville, *Antiquitées étrusques, grecques et romaines*, (1785–1788); and Du Bos, *Réflexions critiques sur la poësie et sur la peinture* (1770). See also Saisselin's "Architecture and Language" and "*Ut Pictura Poesis*," as well as Stafford, *Symbols and Myth*. Stafford also discusses the fact that Quatremère's *De l'architecture égyptienne* was known to Humbert de Superville (*Symbols and Myth*, 118 and 130 note 25).

53. See Rudowski, "The Theory of Signs in the Eighteenth Century," as well as Colish, *The Mirror of Language*. See also above, chapter 1.

54. See Aarsleff, *The Study of Language in England*, 15.

55. "Il y a dans la nature . . . un modèle commun à tous les arts, et dès-lors il doit y avoir des règles d'imitation qui leur sont communes. C'est ainsi qu'il y a une grammaire universelle qui comprend les lois du langage, autant que le langage, propriété de l'espèce humaine, se fonde sur quelque principes dérivant des lois de l'intelligence et des sensations; et il y a la grammaire particulière à chaque langue ou à chaque idiôme, et qui comprend les variétés et les modifications que les causes locales ou particulières impriment en chaque pays, à l'art de manifester les pensées par des sons ou par des signes." Quatremère, *Encyclopédie méthodique*, 2:543.

56. "En examinant attentivement les principes d'imitation de chaque art, on s'aperçoit qu'il se fait entre l'art imitateur & la nature imitée, & entre l'art & le spéctateur, certains pactes ou contrats, qu'on appelle conventions. C'est au moyen de ces conventions que l'art produit

les plaisirs qu'on est en droit d'attendre de lui. L'art de l'architecture, abstraction faite de l'imitation intellectuelle ou métaphysique de la nature, sous le rapport de laquelle elle peut établir un système de principes & de règles capables de soumettre la raison, n'est véritablement dans son imitation positive qu'un composé de conventions." Quatremère, *Encyclopédie méthodique*, 2:69–70. On convention in imitation, see also Quatremère's *De l'imitation*, troisième partie, paragraphs 2 and 3.

57. See, for example, Cordemoy, *Discours*, 23ff.

58. On this point, see Formigari, "Language and Society," 282.

59. See "Language and the Idea of Progress," chapter 4 of Juliard's *Philosphies of Language*.

60. "Tous les objets se trouverent ainsi nommés par imitation ou par comparaison. Cependant presque tous les noms paroissent arbitraires par le fait, et ils varient sans cesse d'une langue à l'autre: mais ceci n'anéantit point les vérités que nous venons de développer. La plûpart des noms, imitatifs dans l'origine, se sont altérés insensiblement, en sorte qu'on ne peut appercevoir sans une extrême attention leurs rapport avec les objets qu'ils désignent." Court de Gébelin, *Histoire naturelle de la parole*, 14.

61. Rousseau, *Essay on the Origin of Languages*, 244.

62. See Knight, *The Geometric Spirit*, 170.

63. "Dans l'enfance des sociétés, les idées sont simples, comme la langage et l'écriture, qui n'en sont que la peinture . . . A mesure que ceux-ci se compliquent, les idées, si simples qu'elles étoien [sic], deviennent composées; le language par figures et l'écriture par signes cessent d'être de mise, parce qu'il n'y a plus ni assez de figures entières, ni assez de signes complets pour exprimer toutes les combinaisons de la pensée. Vient alors le règne des abstractions avec les subtilités de la métaphysique." Quatremère, *Rapport fait au Directoire du Département de Paris, sur les travaux entrepris, continués ou achevés au Panthéon*, 73–74. The precise context of this passage involves the need to respect the conventions of the language of allegory. Quatremère's views on allegory and on the transgressions of artistic convention will be discussed below.

64. ". . . en caractères si lisibles, que rien au monde ne peut ni

ôter, ni ajouter à son évidence morale." Quatremère, *De l'architecture égyptienne*, 237.

65. "Dans son pays natural, on ne sauroit dire qu'il ait eu une signification particulière. Jamais le langage intellectuel de l'Architecture ne fut connu des Egyptiens. Comment supposer que des hommes qui dans le même édifice employoient indistinctement et avec promiscuité toutes les sortes de chapiteaux, ayent ou l'intention de faire exprimer telle ou telle qualité, à telle ou telle forme, à tel ou tel ornement; ayent enfin conçu l'idée d'un ordre, c'est-à-dire, d'un assemblage de parties en rapport entr'elles, et dans une telle harmonie, que leur aspect éveille nécessairement dans l'âme du spectateur une sensation analogue et correspondante." Quatremère, *De l'architecture égyptienne*, 251–252.

66. For discussions by Quatremère of the primarily emotional impact of Egyptian architecture, see *De l'architecture égyptienne*, 22 and 55, and *Encyclopédie méthodique*, 2:317. On the other hand, it was precisely this aspect of Egyptian architecture that appealed to sensationalists like Boullée and Le Camus de Mézières.

67. For a slightly different view of Quatremère's relationship to this idea, see Will, *Intelligible Beauty in Aesthetic Thought from Winckelmann to Victor Cousin.*

68. In general, universal languages were manifestations of dissatisfaction with the quality of linguistic precision, particularly in philosophical discourse. On universal language, see Dieckmann, *Hieroglyphics*, 103–104; Knight, *The Geometric Spirit*, 168ff.; Stafford, *Symbols and Myth*; Knowlson, *Universal Language Schemes in England and France*; and Marrone, "Lingua universale e scrittura segrete nell'opera di Kircher." See also the following passage from Condorcet's *Esquisse*, quoted in Van Duzer, *The Contribution of the Ideologues*, 98: "une langue universelle est celle qui exprime par les signes, soit des objets réels, soit ces collections bien déterminées qui, composées d'idées simples et générales, se trouvent les mêmes, ou peuvent se former également dans l'entendement de tous les hommes; . . . la langue universelle s'y apprendroit avec la science même comme celle de l'algèbre; on connoîtroit le signe en même temps que l'objet, l'idée, l'opération qu'il désigne." One of the better-known examples of a universal language is John Wilkins's *An Essay towards a Real Character, and a Philosophical Language* (1668).

69. ". . . cette sorte de langage et d'écriture universelle." Quatre-mère, *Essai sur l'idéal dans ses applications pratiques* (1837), 321.

70. "L'architecture a pu être, dans l'origine, un art purement imitatif: deux arbres qui formoient un berceau ont donné au sauvage l'idée d'une cabane, et cette idée a fait naître celle d'une maison. Les grottes construites par la nature, nous ont fourni le premier plan des voûtes construites par l'art. De beaux arbres placés les uns à côté des autres, ont peut-être suggéré l'idée de nos belles colonnades. Mais bientôt l'architecture s'agrandissant avec nos besoins et avec nos institutions a bien plus appartenu à la société qu'à la nature elle-même." Portalis, *De l'usage et de l'abus de l'esprit philosophique* (2d ed., 1827), 1:258. Although the first edition of this work was published only in 1820, Qua-tremère had probably been made familiar with its content by Portalis himself. They had met while both were exiled in Germany, a meeting Portalis made note of, and while Portalis was writing *De l'usage et de l'abus de l'esprit philosophique*. He dictated the work to his son in 1798. On their relationship, see Schneider, *Quatremère de Quincy*, 12, and Schneider, *L'esthétique classique*, 81.

71. Quatremère disagrees specifically on the origin of vaults in caves. Egyptian architecture, although derived from the cave, never in fact developed arcuated building technology. While Quatremère is ada-mant on this point, basing his argument on evidence supplied by Pockocke and Pliny, his disagreement with Portalis is minor and implicit. Rather, his criticism is aimed at de Pauw who Quatremère felt had only suggested that Egyptians constructed vaults in order to emphasize the difference between Egyptian and Chinese architecture. Had de Pauw read Macart-ney's *Voyage dans l'intérieur de la Chine et en Tartarie*, according to Quatremère, he would have known that it was the Chinese rather than the Egyptians who built vaults and thus would have been able to maintain their dissimilarity without factual error. See Quatremère, Prix Caylus MS, 25r, *De l'architecture égyptienne*, 102–104, and *Encyclopédie méthodique*, 2:300.

72. Quatremère, *De l'architecture égyptienne*, 38–59, 200, 205.

73. "Telle est, en effet, la puissance irrésistible de ce principe conservateur de la société, du principe de l'immuabilité, lorsqu'il est né et s'est fortifié avec les élémens même de cette société." Quatremère, *De l'architecture égyptienne*, 45.

74. Quatremère ultimately devoted entire texts to considerations of both the ideal and imitation. See his "Sur l'idéal dans les arts du dessin" (1805), *De l'imitation* (1823), and *Essai sur l'idéal dans ses applications pratiques aux oeuvres de l'imitation propre des arts du dessin* (1837).

75. "On voit donc comment, sans parler même de telle ou telle croyance religieuse, dont l'esprit peut quelquefois s'opposer au perfectionnement des signes qu'elle admet, ces signes reçoivent de la sainteté même de leur emploi, une autorité capable d'empêcher toute espèce de modification dans leurs formes. . . . La force de l'usage et la sanction du respect public, y attachent des sensations, des souvenirs, des rapports d'une nature telle, que l'altération du signe en produiroit une dans la chose signifiée." Quatremère, *De l'architecture égyptienne*, 47.

76. "Ces caractères eussent cessé d'être lisibles dès eussent commencé à devenir imitatifs." Quatremère, *De l'architecture égyptienne*, 43 and 162.

77. ". . . à l'émancipation de la faculté imitative dans l'homme civilisé." Quatremère, *De l'architecture égyptienne*, 43.

78. "Lorsque le type d'une société repose sur un respect constant et inviolable pour tout ce qui a déjà été, lorsque toutes les institutions tendantes à la conservation de l'ordre social établi avec toute l'énergie dont elles sont capables, mettent en honneur le soin de perpétuer toutes les pratiques et en discrédit l'esprit d'innovation; lorsque le germe d'un tel système s'est développé avec une nation, ou que, pour mieux dire, une nation s'est développée dans un tel système, la durée de sa manière d'être semble devoir être éternelle.

"Chez un peuple dont les habitudes sont ainsi constituées, les ouvrages des arts éprouvent une sorte de perfectionnement fort différent de la perfection qu'y produisent ailleurs le goût et la facilité du changement. Ce qu'on remarque, c'est que l'usage de suivre les formes de prédécesseurs acquiert autant de force dans les choses de peu d'importance, que dans celles qui paroissent en avoir le plus. C'est pour cela que les objets qui servirent de signe primitive aux divers langages de la société, restent constamment les mêmes, subsistent sans altération, et se transmettent d'âge en âge aussi fidèlement que les lois, les moeurs, les institutions." Quatremère, *De l'architecture égyptienne*, 44.

79. The parallel is not only methodological but also thematic.

Although no longer imposed by the requirements of the Prix Caylus essay competition, Quatremère's *Considérations* contain an elaborate comparison between Egyptian and Greek art.

80. Quatremère's use of "counterrevolution" in reference to social liberty and emancipation, in the Revolutionary year of 1791, is surely significant. Although his political vocabulary fluctuated in keeping with the different times in which his texts were written and with the different audiences and functions they were to have, the general thrust of his ideas remained constant: he equated the potential for intellection and artistic imitation with political freedom, civil equality, and contractual as opposed to imposed social interaction.

81. "Dépositaires de la gloire des peuples, ils en divinrent les historiens; ils servirent enfin la société sous tous les rapports attachés au language le plus éloquent et le plus énergique qui fut jamais." Quatremère, *Considérations sur les arts du dessin*, 30.

82. ". . . mêlés à tous les actes civils, politiques et religieux, ils [les arts du dessin] s'incorporerent avec tous les besions de l'ordre social." Quatremère, *Considérations sur les arts du dessin*, 31.

83. "La co-relation des arts du dessin avec les besoins essentiels de la société, voilà la première et la plus forte des causes morale productrices des arts. Lorsque ces arts favorisent aussi puissement la société, la société n'a pas besoin de les protéger." Quatremère, *Considérations sur les arts du dessin*, 31.

84. "Je ne veux point parler ici de l'action moral du gouvernement sur le génie des hommes, action incontestable et visible à tous, et qu'on peut mettre au rang des causes premières qui influent sur les arts. Le gouvernement qui donne à toutes les facultés de l'homme le plus grand ressort, est celui qui repose sur les vrais principes de la liberté. Mais un gouvernement libre peut se développer sous des formes plus ou moins favorables aux arts du dessin. La plus propice à leur succès sera sans contredit la forme populaire ou démocratique." Quatremère, *Considérations sur les arts du dessin*, 33.

85. ". . . liaison intime des arts du dessin avec tous les besoins de la société, de la religion et de la politique"; "je m'apperçois que, sans y penser, j'ai presque tracé l'image de la Grèce." Quatremère, *Considérations sur les arts du dessin*, 37 and 35–36.

86. The history of the relationship between architectural and social theory of the eighteenth century has not received adequate attention. Most studies have focused on city planning, and follow the development of the ideal city from Filarete's Sforzinda to the social reformers of the nineteenth century and finally to the International Style. The development of social theories of architecture, however, was not entirely dependent on an interest in the urban environment. The idea that architecture itself was a socially expressive medium was prerequisite to the notion that architecture could be used as a vehicle for social change. The work of Quatremère and many of his contemporaries certainly constitutes an important contribution to this development. For more on this point, see Chapter 4 below, and Leith, *The Idea of Art as Propaganda*.

87. See, for example, Rosenblum, *Transformations in Late Eighteenth Century Art*, 68.

88. ". . . dans leurs parties de grandeur et de solidité, et la séparation d'un si grand nombre de Républiques et de petits Etats ne leur permettant pas d'exécuter d'aussi grandes entreprises, ils se renfermèrent sagement dans leurs moyens; et c'est à cette nécessité que j'attribuerois la différence de leurs opérations. Avec d'opulence, je crois qu'ils auroient fait comme les Perses, c'est-à-dire, qu'ils auroient imité leurs modèles sans aucune restriction; car une grande masse de bâtiment imprine toûjours; elle est comme une figure colossale de laquelle on n'exige point de finesses, et que le dépense ou la multiplication des forces suffisent pour rendre recommandable aux yeux des hommes. . . . Les bâtiment des premiers Grecs étant proportionnés à leur opulence, leur petitesse exigea des recherches qui, dans la suite, devinrent un moyen de perfection, d'autant mieux que tout se réunit en eux pour y parvenir; la religion, les exercices, le genre de spectacles et, qui plus est, l'honneur de chaque ville qui se piquoit et n'étoit occupée que des moyens de l'emporter sur les autres villes de la Grèce, en excitant ses citoyens à se distinguer par quelque partie des arts, ou par quelque vertu: car l'un et l'autre marchoit d'un pas assez égal dans l'esprit de ce peuple." Caylus, "De l'architecture ancienne," 303–304.

89. ". . . cherchèrent la beauté dans leurs édifices plus que l'immensité, et cette grandeur morale qui vient de l'art et tient aux proportions, plus que celle qui n'est que linéaire, qui dispense de goût et résulte de la masse." Quatremère, *De l'architecture égyptienne*, 33.

90. On Perrault, see Herrmann, *The Theory of Claude Perrault*.

91. "La constitution et le gouvernement de la Grèce furent très favorables à l'Art; il s'éleva et se perfectionna à l'ombre de la liberté qui a toujours fleuri dans la Grèce." Winckelmann, *Histoire d l'art chez les anciens*, 222.

92. Winckelmann, *Monumenti Antichi inediti*, xv–xvi.

93. For interpretations of Piranesi in this light, see Wittkower, "Piranesi's 'Parere su l'architettura,'" and Junod, "Tradition et innovation dans l'esthétique de Piranèse." For additional bibliography, see Middleton's "Giovanni Battista Piranesi, Review of Recent Literature."

94. In order to illustrate the imaginative scope of Roman design, Quatremère planned to use plates from Piranesi's *Della magnificenza ed architettura de' Romani* in his volumes for the *Encyclopédie méthodique*. Neither these nor the other plates Quatremère intended to include were executed. See Quatremère, *Encyclopédie méthodique*, 1:614 and 2:31.

95. See Calvesi, *Carceri, Mole Adriana, Vedute di Roma/Castel Sant'Angelo*, one of five catalogues published separately but part of the exhibition *Piranesi nei luoghi di Piranesi* (Rome, 1979); McDonald, *Piranesi's Carceri*; Praz, *Giovanni Battista Piranesi*; and Junod, "Tradition et innovation."

96. Belgrado, *Dell'architettura egiziana*, 129. Piranesi's attempt to prove the antiquity and integrity of Italic traditions by suggesting that Roman architecture derived from Etruscan, which in turn derived from Egyptian, brought with it not only a more positive view of Egyptian architecture than that held by the French but a more positive view of Egyptian government as well.

97. "Parmi les anciens Peuples, tout étoit lié par des rapports inséperables: le culte, la culture, la législation, le commerce, les sciences et les arts, les objets que présente la Nature, toutes ces causes . . . venoient se ranger et se correspondre sur les Monumens." Viel de Saint-Maux, *Lettres sur l'architecture*, seventh letter, 7.

98. "Le sol de la Grèce étoit le terrain le plus convenable à la semence de l'Art, et ce ciel Grec celui dont l'influence étoit la plus propre à la faire germer." Winckelmann, *Histoire de l'art chez les anciens*, 219.

99. "On conçoit aisément que le climat peut influer beaucoup sur le tempérament et la constitution organique des hommes. Il n'est pas plus difficile de comprendre comment il influe sur leur façon de penser toujours modifiée par les circonstances extérieures surtout par l'éducation, la constitution et le gouvernement, particuliers à chaque peuple." Winckelmann, *Histoire de l'art chez les anciens*, 39–40.

100. Winckelmann, *Histoire de l'art chez les anciens*, 50.

101. On Sulzer's contributions to the *Encyclopédie* and their relationship to contemporary architectural theory, see Harrington, *Changing Ideas on Architecture*, 150ff. Quatremère also owned the second edition of Sulzer's *Allgemeine Theorie der schönen Künste*, published in Leipzig in 1792. See *Bibliothèque de M. Quatremère de Quincy*, 48.

102. In the preamble to his *De l'imitation*, Quatremère used Kant and Sulzer as foils in his defense of the universality of his own theory of the fine arts. Metaphysicians like Kant, he wrote, "pour embrasser la théorie entière de l'imitation dans les beaux-arts, ont tenté d'en ramener toutes les notions à un principe général, mais si élevé, mais placé dans une région si peu accessible à la compréhension du plus grand nombre, que ceux même qui croient y atteindre, n'y saisissent qu'une sorte de point de concentration, où le tout absorbe ses parties." Others, such as Sulzer, Quatremère continued, "se traînant en théoriciens sur les routes multipliées de l'analyse, se sont flattés de détailler, partie par partie, l'ensemble d'une doctrine générale, applicable dans chaque objet à chacun des beaux-arts: mais, en visant à l'universalité, ils ont manqué l'unité: ils ont eu trop de pièces à réunir, pour en faire un corps; et dans l'incohérence de leur ouvrage, les parties n'ont pu produire un tout." See Quatremère, *De l'imitation*, vi.

103. "L'origine de l'architecture remonte donc aux temps les plus reculés, et ne doit pas être cherchée en un seul pays. Il seroit également agréable et instructif de pouvoir mettre sous les yeux les principaux genres de goût en fait d'architecture, en rassemblant les dessins d'édifices considérables chez les diverses nations qui ont cultivé cet art, sans avoir de communication entr'elles. On en pourroit bien tirer des éclaircissemens sur le caractère national de ces peuples. On retrouveroit par-tout les mêmes principes sans doute, mais la maniere de les appliquer seroit bien différente." *Supplément à l'Encyclopédie*, s.v. "architecture." This pas-

sage by Sulzer contains many of the same ideas found in the exerpt from Quatremère's competition essay cited in chapter 1, note 6.

104. "Qu'y a-t-il, par exemple, de plus essentiel que les liens de la société pour conduire l'homme au bonheur et au principal objet de sa destination? Or ces liens tiennent aux agrémens mutuels que les hommes se procurent. . . . C'est donc aux beaux-arts à revétir d'agrémens divers nos habitations, . . . et sur-tout notre langage, la principale de nos inventions, et non seulement, comme tant de personnes se l'imaginent à tort, pour que nous ayons la simple jouissance de quelques agrémens de plus, mais principalement afin que les douces impressions de ce qui est beau, harmonieux et convenable, donnent une tournure plus noble, un caractère plus relevé à notre esprit et à notre coeur." *Supplément à l'Encyclopédie*, s.v. "Beaux-Arts."

105. "Mais ce qui mérite une attention plus distinguée de la part de ceux aux sons de qui le bonheur des citoyens est confié, c'est la langue, cet instrument le plus important et le plus universel dans nos principes opérations. Rien ne préjudicie plus à toute une nation qu'un langage barbare, dur, incapable de bien rendre la délicatesse des sentimens, et la finesse des pensées. La raison et le goût se forment et s'étendent dans la même proportion dans laquelle la langue se perfectionne, puisqu'au fond le langage n'est autre chose que la raison et le goût transformés en signes sensibles." *Supplément à l'Encyclopédie*, s.v. "Beaux-Arts." Sulzer also suggests, for example, that while the Greeks may have originally imported the arts as one did exotic plants, "les beaux-arts sont des plantes indigenes, qui sans exiger aucune culture pénible, croissent dans tous les lieux où la raison a acquis quelque développement."

106. ". . . puisque les beaux-arts doivent, selon leur essence et leur nature, servir de moyens pour accroître et assurer le bonheur des hommes, il est . . . nécessaire qu'ils pénétrent jusqu'à l'humble cabane du moindre des citoyens; il faut que le soin d'en diriger l'usage et d'en déterminer l'emploi entre dans le système politique, et soit un des objets essentiels de l'administration de l'état." *Supplément à l'Encyclopédie*, s.v. "Beaux-Arts."

107. ". . . certaines maximes fondamentals, certaines notions directrices qui soient comme la base du caractère national." *Supplément à l'Encyclopédie*, s.v. "Beaux-Arts."

108. For recent studies of character in French eighteenth-century architectural theory, see Szambien, *Symétrie, goût, caractère;* Hernandez, *Grundzüge einer Ideengeschichte der Französischen Architekturtheorie;* Guiheux and Rouillard, "Echanges entre les mots et l'architecture"; and Tanis Hinchcliffe's introductory remarks to translated extracts from the *Encyclopédie méthodique* in *9H*, no. 7 (1985), 25ff. More generally, see also Archer, "Character in English Architectural Design," and Rowe, "Character and Composition."

109. Because of its length and intricate structure, an outline of this article is included in Appendix E.

110. "Il [caractère] signifie dans le langage figuré ce qui constitue la nature des êtres d'une manière distinctive et propre à chacun." *Encyclopédie méthodique,* 1:477.

111. See Watelet, *Essai sur les jardins* (1774). On Watelet and the picturesque, particularly in relation to garden theory, see Wiebenson, *The Picturesque Garden in France.*

112. The influence of Watelet's conception of picturesque landscape on architecture was immediate and widespread. Charles Louis Clérisseau, for example, in his *Antiquitées de la France* of 1778, maintained that insofar as architecture imitates nature, it too gives pleasure and an impression "pareille à celle que nous éprouvons à l'aspect d'un paysage riche et varié ou d'une chaîne de montagnes majestueuses" (viii).

113. ". . . quel que soit la langage des différens arts, qu'il se compose de paroles ou de sons, de couleurs ou de formes." *Encyclopédie méthodique,* 1:488. Many elements in Quatremère's article on character, notably the distinction he makes between society in general and particular societies, are derived from the article on character in the original *Encyclopédie.*

114. "Quelles que puissent être les causes subalternes et incidentes qui peuvent concourir à la formation du caractère général de chaque architecture, je ne saurois en donner d'autre définition que celle qui en rapporte la cause à l'action primordiale de la nature, en y ajoutant toutefois une action indirecte de cette même nature et une action directe de la société, quoique toujours subordonnée à la première, et je dirai que le caractère d'architecture des différens peuples consiste *dans une manière d'être, dans une conformation nécessitée par les besoins physiques*

*et les habitudes morales, et dans laquelle se peignent les climats, les
idées, les moeurs, les goûts, les plaisirs et le caractère même de chaque
peuple.*" *Encyclopédie méthodique*, 1:492, his emphasis.

115. "Pourroit-on se refuser au même genre d'intérêt, en jettant
un coup-d'oeil sur cette multiplicité de formes imaginées par les différents
familles d'hommes qui peuplent ce globe, pour la construction ou l'em-
bellissement de leurs demeures." *Encyclopédie méthodique*, 1:491.

116. Quatremère did not apply each of his six types of character
to every subject he analyzed. When discussing architecture "proprement
dite," however, he returned to a systematic distinction between distinctive,
essential, and relative character. On the other hand, he did not continue
rigidly to distinguish between physical and moral character in architecture. Instead, he described the latter part of his essay as primarily an
exploration of the impact of human moral character on architects and
architecture. Moreover, he inverted the sequence in which he had initially
presented the three types of character in order to be able to discuss
distinctive character first, essential second, and relative character, the
most important to architecture, last.

117. "L'art de caractériser, c'est à dire, de rendre sensibles, par
les formes matérielles, les qualités intellectuelles et les idées morales qui
peuvent s'exprimer dans les édifices, ou de faire connaître, par l'accord
et la convenance de toutes les parties constitutives d'un bâtiment, sa
nature, sa propriété, son emploi, sa destination." *Encyclopédie méthodique*, 1:502.

118. "Le caractère . . . en tant que signe indicatif de ce qu'un
édifice est ou doit être, se présent à nous sous deux rapports." *Encyclopédie méthodique*, 1:503.

119. "Caractère relatif du genre idéal . . . consiste dans l'expression des qualités ou idées, qui sont du ressort de l'art métaphysiquement
considéré. . . . Mais, comme avant de plaire, l'architecture doit servir,
rarement voit-on dans les édifices, que l'architecte, maître absolu de son
sujet, soit libre d'y imprimer ce caractère idéal, c'est-à-dire, de n'exprimer
que des rapports intellectuels par le moyen des formes architectoniques."
Encyclopédie méthodique, 1:503.

120. "Ainsi l'architecte chargé d'élever un temple à une divinité,
ne devoit avoir d'autre soin, d'autre pensée, que. . . . d'employer les

moyens de fixer, par les formes de l'architecture, ces résultats fugitifs de la pensée." *Encyclopédie méthodique*, 1:504.

121. "Qu'on en juge par la nature du langage dans lequel il peut s'expliquer." *Encyclopédie méthodique*, 1:504.

122. Quatremère wrote that a building based on the principles of a Greek temple "vous fera lire, dans les moindres détails, les signes distinctifs de la toute-puissance que doit respirer son ouvrage." *Encyclopédie méthodique*, 1:504.

123. "S'il n'existe aucune correlation d'intelligence entre lui et le peuple auquel il parle; ce langage mourra bientôt par le défaut d'être entendu." *Encyclopédie méthodique*, 1:505.

124. "[Caractère relative du genre imitatif] consiste . . . dans l'indication vraie, fidelle et aussi variée que cet art le comporte, des usages et de la destination des édifices. . . . Ce genre de caractère [imitatif], qui sans doute, quoique inférieur au premier par la mesure des conceptions qu'il exige, ne doit faire qu'un avec lui, a cependent cette différence, qu'il est appliquable à tous les édifices possible, qu'il peut plus ou moins se recontrer dans tous les pays, et qu'il peut être soumis à des observations uniformes et à des règles constantes. . . . Tout édifice, quel qu'il soit, est destiné à un usage quelconque. C'est l'expression apparente de cet usage qui constitue le caractère relatif." *Encyclopédie méthodique*, 1:503, 505, 506.

125. "Alors ne craignez pas que l'artiste manque de moyens pour caractériser son ouvrage, ni de juges pour l'apprecier et comprendre le langage de son art." *Encyclopédie méthodique*, 1:507.

126. Quatremère gave each of these elements a separate heading: "Gradation de richesse et de grandeur des édifices," "Indication des qualités propre à chaque édifice," "Formes générales et partielles de l'architecture," "Genre de construction," "Réssources de la décoration," and "Attributs."

127. ". . . un langage dont les signes, les expressions, doivent être doués d'une signification précise et capable de rendre des idées. Sans cela, l'on n'y voit plus qu'un jargon inintelligible composé de formules puériles et insignificative, ou de caractères muets pour l'esprit. . . . Ce seroit donc en vain que ce langage présenteroit à l'artiste les moyens les plus éner-

giques de rendre ses idées et de donner à tous les édifices une sorte
d'éloquence visible, et, si l'on peut dire, oculaire, s'il ne parvient à en
acquérir l'intelligence et à en manier habilement les ressorts." *Encyclopédie méthodique,* 1:515. See also Quatremère's article on "abus" and
"convention."

128. While many of Quatremère's ideas on allegory were related
to his study of hieroglyphs, they were also influenced by Winckelmann and
Sulzer. See Winckelmann's "Essai sur l'allégorie" and Sulzer's "Discours
sur l'allégorie," published together in *De l'allégorie, ou traités sur cette
matière; par Winckelmann, Addison, Sulzer, etc.* (Paris, an VII). For
Quatremère's view of the notion of allegory, see his article on the subject
in the *Encyclopédie méthodique*; Schneider, *L'esthétique classique*, 48ff.;
Benoit, *L'art français sous la Révolution*, 26–41; and Rubin, "Allegory
versus Narrative."

129. "Quelle pauvre ressource que celle d'une inscription sans
laquelle j'ignorerois cependant le genre et la destination de l'édifice que
s'offre à ma vue!" *Encyclopédie méthodique*, 1:515–516.

130. Although Quatremère's theory of architecture in general is
related to the notion of allegory, he gives only one example of a pure and
direct architectural allegory, the Roman temple of Virtue and Honor. The
building, as described by Quatremère, is in two parts, one dedicated to
Virtue and the other to Honor. Because the visitor must walk through the
former section in order to arrive at the latter, the building constitutes an
allegory of how one achieves honor through virtue. This same example is
mentioned by Winckelmann in his "Essai sur l'allégorie." The tradition
of interpreting the Roman temple in this way was established by Giacomo
Lauro in his *Antiquae urbis splendor* (1612). On Lauro, see Del Pesco, *Il
Louvre di Bernini*, 145ff.

131. "Le système de l'architecture . . . fait introduire dans la
décoration une progression de richesse ou de simplicité, de variété ou
d'uniformité, qui constitue une sorte de langage très-intelligible, lorsque,
d'une part, l'artiste fait le parler, et que de l'autre le spectateur fait le
comprendre. . . . L'allegorie est un discours figuré, mais elle est l'expression simple et naturelle de ces arts d'imitation que ne parlent que par
signes ou par figures. . . . Au moyen de l'allégoire . . . l'art se fait réellement
historien et narrateur; il nous explique l'objet géneral et particulier qu'il

traite; il nous informe du but moral comme de l'emploi physique de son édifice." *Encyclopédie méthodique*, 2:179.

132. "La décoration allégorique . . . dit plus, elle dit mieux que toutes les légendes dont on peut charger les frontispices et les murs." *Encyclopédie méthodique*, 2:179. ". . . ces menteurs aimables et véridiques." *Encyclopédie méthodique*, 1:115.

133. *Encyclopédie méthodique*, 1:516ff. Quatremère claims to have read this story in the work of Aristarchus, but says several times he doesn't remember exactly where or when he read it and that the details have escaped him. While Quatremère therefore considers the specific text irrelevant, the reference to Aristarchus is crucial, for he was believed to personify absolute critical judgment.

134. On the history of character in literature as well as in the visual arts, see Baldwin, "The Relation of the English 'Character' to Its Greek Prototype"; Woestijne, "Les sources du 'Discours sur Théopraste' de Jean de la Bruyère"; Boyce, *The Theophrastian Character in England to 1642*; Boyce, *The Polemical Character, 1640–1661*; David, *Le débat sur les écritures et l'hiéroglyphe*, 31–42; and Dillon, "Complexity and Change of Character in Neo-Classical Criticism." On Le Brun in particular, see Montagu, "Charles Le Brun's 'Conférence.'"

135. ". . . le caractère qui convient à chaque espèce d'édifice." Boffrand, *Livre d'architecture*, 2.

136. "Tous les agrémens pour être parfaits doivent *paroître* avec un caractère d'utilité." Batteux, *Les beaux-arts reduits à un même principe* (1747), 48.

137. See Blondel, *Cours d'architecture*, 2:229ff.

138. Variety and proportion are "l'origine des différens genres ou caractères qui distinguent les ordres d'Architecture. . . . Comme dans les pièces dramatiques, une seule action remplit le scène, il faut de même dans un édifice observer l'unité de caractère, et que cette vérité fixe d'abord l'imagination, en frappant les yeux." Le Camus, *Le génie d'architecture*, 63.

139. In speaking of how contemporary architecture may use the orders to create a modern temple, Quatremère wrote: "Mais les modes déjà trouvés de l'architecture, se sont-ils pas la base certaine des caractères

que l'architecture peut peindre aux yeux? On en conveint: mais ces modes élémentaires, ou ce qu'on appele les ordres, sont en petit nombre; et s'ils étoient aussi bornés qu'ils le paroissent, l'architecture se trouveroit réduite à la plus grande pauvreté dans son expression. C'est parce que les modes peuvent se modifier d'une manière indéfinie; c'est parce que les proportions son variables dans leur application, que l'artiste, habile à s'emparer de ces ressources va, dans l'ordonnance générale de son édifice, vous donner l'idée de l'immensité de dieu qui l'habite." *Encyclopédie méthodique*, 1:504.

140. "Partout l'idée de Dieu se trouve écrite par l'art de bâtir, en caractères jusqu'à présent ineffaçables." *Encyclopédie méthodique*, 3:449. That both the words *type* and *character* can be defined in relation to the alphabet only confirms this assertion.

141. ". . . les Grecs formèrent l'écriture architecturale, et à l'aide desquels ils furent exprimer un si grand nombre d'idées et de sensations diverses." *Encyclopédie méthodique*, 2:72.

142. "Ce n'est donc pas à faire dans une église, le *fac simile* d'un temple grec, que doit tendre l'imitateur intelligent de l'antique: mais en employant les formes, les types, les détails de l'architecture grecque, qui ne sont autre chose, que ce que les mots, si l'on peut dire, et les formules du discours, sont à l'art d'écrire, il doit s'efforcer non de faire ce qui fut fait par les grands architectes de l'antiquité, mais de fair ce qu'ils auroient fait, si d'autres usages, d'autres convenances, d'autres besoins politiques civils et religieux, leur eussent prescrit d'autres obligations." *Encyclopédie méthodique*, 3:457.

IV
The Republic of the Arts

1. In examining mimetic works of art Quatremère had claimed, as cited above, that "il se fait entre l'art imitateur et la nature imitée, et entre l'art et le spéctateur, certains pactes ou contrats." *Encyclopédie méthodique*, 2:69–70.

2. Some of Quatremère's political pamphlets include *Discours prononcé par le cit. Quatremere-Quincy, au tribunal criminel du départe-ment de la Seine, le 22 thermidor, an quatrieme de la République; Motion d'ordre faite par Quatremere, au nom de la Commission d'Instruction*

publique sur le projet présenté par la commission de l'aliénation des presbytères; Opinion de M. Quatremère, député du département de Paris, sur les dénonciations faites contre M. Duport; Opinion de Quatremère, sur le renouvellement des Bureaux centraux; Opinion de Quatremère, sur le second projet relatif aux réunions politiques; Rapport fait par Quatremère, au nom de la Commission d'Instruction publique, sur le mode et l'organisation des biens affectés aux bourses des ci-devant collèges de Paris; Rapport sur la pétition de M. de Rossel, Fait au nom du Comité d'Instruction publique.

3. To the best of my knowledge a complete history of the notion of the Republic of Letters is unavailable, but in our present context see Chartier, *The Cultural Origins of the French Revolution*; Roche, *Le siècle des Lumières en province*; Pomeau, *L'Europe des Lumières*; Fumaroli, *L'age de l'eloquence*. On Jean Leclerc and his *Nouvelles de la République des Lettres*, see also Pomeau's *L'age classique*, 24–26. No one has studied the use of the phrase "Republic of the Arts" in the eighteenth century, but its use in the nineteenth century, when, for example, a journal entitled *La République des Arts* was established, is discussed by M.-C. Chaudonneret, "1848: 'La République des Arts.'" See also Chaudonneret's *La figure de la République*.

4. Chartier gives the following description of the Republic of Letters: "Founded on the free engagement of the will, on equality among its interlocutors, and on the absolutely disinterested exercise of the intellect, the Republic of Letters (invented not by the Philosophes but by men of learning in the preceding century) provided a model and a support for free public examination of questions regarding religion or legislation." See his *The Cultural Origins of the French Revolution*, 26.

5. The Commune des Arts was established on July 7, 1793, and was then succeeded by the Société Populaire et Républicaine des Arts as well as by the Club Révolutionnaire des Arts. See Benoit, *L'art français*, 178ff., and Pevsner, *Academies of Art*, 199ff.

6. On Miranda, see Parra-Perez, *Miranda et la Révolution française*.

7. This publication was also issued with an additional title page designating the work as *Lettres sur le projet d'enlever les monumens de l'Italie*; the contents are otherwise identical. A second edition, published

in Rome in 1815, has been studied by Antonio Pinelli in his "Storia dell'arte de cultura della tutela." A reprint of the original edition, *Lettres à Miranda sur le déplacement des monuments de l'art de l'Italie*, has recently provided the context for an important introductory essay by Edouard Pommier. On the question of Revolutionary spoliation more generally, see Müntz, "Les annexions de collections d'art"; Saunier, *Les conquêtes artistiques de la Révolution et de l'Empire*; Schneider, *Quatremère de Quincy*, 164–178; and Blumer, "La commission pour la recherche des objets de sciences et arts en Italie."

8. Quatremère claims that the letters to Miranda were first published in the journal *Le redacteur*. A complete search through the journal reveals that although the question of spoliation is frequently debated, Quatremère's letters do not appear. It is difficult to determine what role Quatremère's ideas may have played in this debate. Most of the controversy occurred during that summer, so if Quatremère's letters were unknown before July 31, 1796, the earliest possible publication date of *Lettres sur la préjudice*, his contribution to the debate would have been negligible. For a detailed analysis of the publication history, see Pommier's introduction to *Lettres à Miranda*.

9. Quatremère went to England at Canova's request in order to see the marbles. His observations were recorded in a series of letters to the sculptor published as *Lettres écrites de Londres à Rome, et addressées a M. Canova sur les Marbres d'Elgin* (1818). In 1836, Quatremère published the two sets of letters together as *Lettres sur l'enlèvement des ouvrages de l'art antique a Athènes et a Rome*. See also Quatremère's biography of Canova, *Canova et ses ouvrages*, where additional correspondence is included.

10. The two situations "matériellement semblables, si l'on veut, diffèrent entièrement, sous les points de vue les plus importans. Or ces points de vue, sont ceux des intérêts de la morale avant tout; ceux des circonstances politiques qui ont motivé et autorisé l'enlèvement dont il s'agit; ceux de la science et du goût; enfin ceux de la conservation même de ces ouvrages." *Lettres sur l'enlèvement*, ix. Quatremère argued that three fundamental differences between the contexts surrounding the seizure of the Elgin marbles and the Italian works rendered them incomparable. First was the difference in the physical condition of the objects. While the Italians had cultivated and protected both antiquities and mod-

ern art since the Renaissance, the Parthenon was and would continue to be in disrepair with its sculpture nearing a state of total disintegration. Second was the question of the legality of the seizure of these objects. Napoleon had transgressed every known moral, civil, and military law, whereas Lord Elgin had paid for and received official permission to take the marbles. Third, Quatremère was concerned about the accessibility of these objects. Travel to Italy was relatively simple and inexpensive while Greece was still beyond the means of most Europeans. Despite the objectivity of his stated thesis, the subtext of Quatremère's argument reflects a picturesque enchantment with Italy and an acknowledgment of the importance to the French historical imagination that travel to Italy had played, an enchantment not matched by modern travels to Greece. Moreover, although Quatremère upheld the Greek ideal over the Roman, his was a true idealization, unconcerned in great measure with the contemporary reality of Greece. For additional comments on Quatremère's attitudes toward Italy, see below.

11. See *Le Rédacteur,* no. 153 (29 floréal an IV [May 18, 1796]) and no. 173 (17 prairial an IV [June 5, 1796]).

12. There were those, however, who objected to this politicization of the arts. A notable example was the man who became Napoleon's architect, Pierre-François-Léonard Fontaine. On his first meeting with the Premier Consul in 1799, Fontaine responded to Napoleon's proposal to house the antiquities taken from Italy in the Invalides with the following remarks: "Je trouve cette idée fausse. Que peuvent avoir de commun les chefs-d'oeuvre de l'art venus d'Italie avec l'armée qui en avait fait la conquête? Quel effet produiraient l'Apollon, la Vénus et le Laocoon sous les voûtes et le dôme des Invalides? Si l'on veut élever à l'armée des trophées de reconnaissance dans son palais de retraite, ce sont les drapeaux pris par elle à l'ennemi, qui sont aujourd'hui dans les greniers des Tuileries, qu'il faut suspendre aux voûtes de l'église des Invalides." While David, also present at this meeting, hesitated at Napoleon's suggestion out of concern that the Invalides was not large enough for the purpose, Fontaine objected to the use of art for political gain and to the indiscriminate mixing of military and cultural conquest. Fontaine recorded this event in his *Mia Vita,* recently published in *Pierre-François-Léonard Fontaine, Journal, 1799–1853,* 2:1334. The various ways in which Fontaine described his remarkable first encounter with Napoleon are discussed by Bruno Foucart, in his introductory essay, "P. F. L. Fontaine, Du Journal au

Mémorial," *Journal*, l:xxii. I am indebted to R. Middleton for this reference.

13. This argument and its supporting documentation are thoroughly presented by Pommier in his introduction to *Lettres à Miranda*.

14. "Je croirois . . . injurieux au dix-huitième siècle, de le soupçonner capable de faire revivre ce droit de conquête des Romains, qui rendoit les hommes et les choses la propriété du plus fort. Qui ne sait que ce droit absurde et monstrueux reposoit dans le code public de Rome, sur la même base que l'esclavage? Quand une longue civilization, due à la culture générale des sciences et des arts; quand la vraie théorie des droits sacrés de l'humanité, et des rapports politiques des nations, n'auroient pas, depuis long-temps, bannie du code public de l'Europe jusquaux traces de ce prètendu droit de conquête, l'experience et l'exemple même du peuple Romain, et le mémorable châtiment que l'univers fit éprouver à ce tyran des peuples, suffiroient, je pense, pour désabuser quiconque entreprendroit de rétablir d'aussi odieuses maximes." *Lettres sur la préjudice*, 7–8.

15. "L'esprit de conquête dans une république, est entièrement subversif de l'esprit de liberté." *Lettres sur la préjudice*, 2.

16. "Ainsi, je ne puis bien répondre à votre question, qu'en faisant abstraction de ce faux intérêt partiel, qui est la partage des ignorans ou des fripons: ce sera comme membre de cette république générale des arts et des sciences, et non comme habitant de telle ou telle nation, que je discuterai cet intérêt que toutes les parties ont à la conservation du tout." *Lettres sur la préjudice*, 4.

17. "En effet, vous le savez, les arts et les sciences forment depuis long-temps en Europe une république, dont les membres, liés entre eux par l'amour et la recherche du beau et du vrai qui sont leur pacte social, tendent beaucoup moins à s'isoler de leurs patries respective, qu'à en rapprocher les intérêts, sous le point de vue si précieux d'une fraternité universelle. Cet heureux sentiment, vous le savez encore, ne peut être étouffé même par ces discordes sanglantes qui poussent les nations à s'entredéchirer. Malheur à l'homme insensé autant que cruel, qui voudroit éteindre l'étincelle du feu sacré de l'humanité et de la philanthropie, que la culture des arts et des sciences entretient encore dans le coeur de quelques hommes . . . par une heureuse révolution, les arts et les sciences

appartiennent à toute l'Europe, et ne sont plus la propriété exclusive d'une nation. C'est à maintenir, à favoriser et à augmenter cette communauté, que doivent tendre toutes les pensées, tous les efforts de la saine politique et de la philosophie." *Lettres sur la préjudice*, 2–4.

18. "La philosophie, l'historie, la science des langues, l'intelligence des poètes, la chronologie du mond, l'astronomie scientifique, la critique, sont autant de parties séparées de ce qu'on appelle la république des arts, et intéressées à son integralité." *Lettres sur la préjudice*, 16–17.

19. "Le véritable museum de Rome, celui dont je parle, se compose, il est vrai, de statues, de colosses, de temples, d'obélisques, de colonnes triomphales, de thermes, de cirques, d'amphithéâtres, d'arcs de triomphe, de tombeaux, de stucs, de fresques, de bas-reliefs, d'inscriptions, de fragmens d'ornemens, de matériaux de construction, de meubles, d'utensiles, etc. etc.; mais il ne se compose pas moins des lieux, des sites, des montagnes, des carrières, des routes antiques, des positions respectives des villes ruinées, des rapports géographiques, des relations de tous les objets entre eux, des souvenirs, des traditions locales, des usages encore existans, des parallèles et des rapprochemens qui ne peuvent se faire que dans le pays même." *Lettres sur la préjudice*, 22.

20. "Combien d'artistes ne quittent qu'à Rome ces préjugés locaux . . . qui, comme autant d'accens défectueux, ne se perdent que dans la capitale de la république des arts." *Lettres sur la préjudice*, 46.

21. Quatremère enumerated many benefits gained by preserving the Italian context: he stressed in particular the didactic value of being able to compare the various Italian schools of painting and the economic value for contemporary Italy of its artistic past.

22. "Ne convenez-vous pas que tout objet déplacé est une pierre enlevée à l'édifice qui est en train de se rebatîr, et par conséquent que tout projet de démembrement du museum de Rome, est un attentat contre la science, un crime de léze-instruction publique?" *Lettres sur la préjudice*, 26.

23. "Qu'est-ce que l'antique à Rome, sinon un grand livre dont le temps a détruit ou dispersé les pages, et dont les recherches modernes remplissent chaque jour les vides, et réparent les lacunes?" *Lettres sur la préjudice*, 20. See above for a discussion of other aspects of the book metaphor. Quatremère made very few changes to his letters to Miranda

for the publication of 1836. The changes he did make, however, were significant. Although a full investigation of these emendations is beyond the scope of this study, it is worth noting that they consist in revisions to his discussion of the science of antiquarianism contained in the third letter. What he considered up-to-date scholarship in 1796 was hopelessly out-of-date by 1836. Thus, citations of Gébelin, Bailli, Rabaud, and Dupuis in the first edition are replaced by references to Lessing and Caylus.

24. "Je parle de cette science qui doit rattacher nos connoissances à celles du passé, qui doit faire revivre une foule de notions perdues, qui doit porter à la philosphie et aux arts des lumières toujours nouvelles." *Lettres sur la préjudice*, 23.

25. He had similar objections to a French museum filled with French art when contrived and artificially displayed. His outspoken views on museums ultimately led to his campaign to shut Lenoir's Musée des Monuments Français. On the latter subject, see Schneider, *Quatremère de Quincy*, 179–197; Schneider, "Un ennemi du Musée des Monuments Français"; Huard, "La salle du XIIIe siècle du Musée des Monuments Français"; Vanuxeum, "Aperçus sur quelques tableaux représentant le Musée des Monuments Français de Lenoir"; Greene, "A. Lenoir and the Musée des Monuments Français during the French Revolution"; Bann, "Historical Text and Historical Object"; Erlande-Brandenburg, *The Cluny Museum;* and Duro, "'Un livre ouvert à l'instruction.'" It is interesting that, despite profound differences in opinion, Lenoir and Quatremère both used the book metaphor in this context.

26. "La découverte, ou, pour mieux dire, le recouvrement de l'antiquité, est une véritable résurrection." *Lettres sur la préjudice*, 25.

27. In addition to the primary *Considérations*, Quatremère also published a *Suite aux Considérations sur les arts du dessin* and a *Second Suite aux Considérations sur les arts du dessin*. The latter publications revise his original proposal in light of contemporary debate and criticism. The *Suite aux Considérations* contains critiques of other related projects presented to the Assemblée Nationale and includes long and interesting digressions on engraving and the notion of genre. The *Seconde Suite aux Considérations* presents refinements and corrections of a more narrowly pedagogic and institutional kind and includes a suggestion to establish a unified center for all the arts and sciences. This suggestion became a model

for what was to become the Institut de France. The history of academic reforms in general and Quatremère's role in particular have been discussed by Luke, "The Politics of Participation," and Rowlands, "Quatremère de Quincy," 80–120.

28. "La France a-t-elle besoin d'entretenir à ses frais une académie ou école publique des arts du Dessin? Et quel seroit le mode le plus avantageux à adopter dans un semblable institution?" Quatremère, *Considérations*, viii.

29. Quatremère wrote that "la liberté de la presse dans un état," is parallel to "la libre exposition publique accordée indistinctement à tous les artistes dans le même lieu." See *Considérations*, 102. Controversy over the salons was of course one of the events that precipitated this aggressive period of academic reform.

30. Despite his hostility toward museums, Quatremère did envision that collections of ancient architectural fragments, plaster casts, and even originals would be available for students to study. Moreover, and still despite his reservations toward removing art from its context, he wrote "je voudrois qu'on formât une galerie de statues antiques originales, parce qu'il y a dans ces monumens originaux, je ne sais quel caractère de beauté, je ne sais quel préjugé de respect, je ne sais quelle authenticité et quelle vivacité de leçons, que jamais l'empreinte en plâtre de ces statues ne communique." *Considérations*, 128ff.

31. That Quatremère considered painting, sculpture, and architecture equal members in the Republic of the Arts is demonstrated by their parallel importance in the *école du dessin*. He thus democratized the once hierarchical relationship between these three arts, but did not extend this equalizing process to all media. (Engraving, for example, was excluded.) Quatremère's understanding of this subject derived primarily from Batteux. To my knowledge, he is the only other writer to have connected the relationship between the arts to the structure of a republic, although he never developed the idea into a coherent theory. In discussing different styles of poetry, Batteux claimed that "les arts forment une espèce de république, où chacun doit figurer selon son état." See his *Les beaux-arts reduits à un même principe*, 169.

32. "Qui croiroit qu'il existe dans Paris deux écoles d'architecture distinctes par le local, le choix des maîtres, le nature des leçons? Que

l'on montre dans l'une l'architecture, comme art de goût, et dans l'autre comme art de besoin; qu'on aille ici pour apprendre à décorer; qu'il y ait une école pour apprendre à faire une temple, et une autre école pour apprendre à faire un pont . . . Ce démembrement d'instruction, en décomposant l'essence de cet art, a porté le coup le plus funeste aux deux parties. Il a habitué les uns à croire que le goût dispense de la solidité et les autres que les calculs peuvent remplacer le génie." *Considérations*, 93–94. Quatremère is referring to the Ecole des Ponts et Chaussées, founded by the engineer Jean-Rodolphe Perronet in 1747. For the history of other changes made in schools of architecture, see the chronology of the Ecole des Beaux-Arts compiled by Annie Jacques and Anthony Vidler in Vidler, ed., *Paris under the Academy: City and Ideology*, 151–157, and Rabreau and Mosser, "L'Académie Royale d'architecture et l'enseignement de l'architecture au XVIIIe siècle." Quatremère's emphasis on the need for particular intimacy between engineering and design was later reiterated by Charles Viel in his *De l'impuissance des mathématiques pour assurer la solidité des batimens et recherches sur la construction des ponts* (1805). In arguing that "tout principe de construction, quel que soit l'édifice et son module, dépend uniquement de la connexité qui existe dans toutes les parties de l'architecture," Viel cites Quatremère's *De l'architecture égyptienne*. See *De l'impuissance des mathématiques*, 6 and 65.

33. "On ne cesse de s'étonner que des peintres ou des sculpteurs, obligés à tout instant de faire entrer l'architecture dans leurs ouvrages, ignorent jusqu'aux caractères disinctifs des ordres: qu'un architecte soit obligé d'emprunter une main étrangère pour dessiner les figures dont il orne ses projets. C'est-là sans doute un inconvénient que tout le monde peut saisir. Mais le plus grand et que l'on apperçoit moins, est l'appauvrissement réel de chaque art, qui, privé de l'analogie des autres, voit de plus en plus décroître son patrimonie, ses idées se resserrer, et dessécher le germe de ses conceptions." *Suite aux considérations*, 10–11.

34. "C'est division qui, au lieu d'une république dont tous les artistes seroient les concitoyens, a fait de tous les arts des empires réellement séparés par le régime de leur institution, par les barrières des préjugés, de l'habitude et de la rivalité." *Suite aux considérations*, 10. See also the article on "accord" in the *Encyclopédie méthodique*, 1:7, where Quatremère describes the specialization of schools of art thus: "depuis les Arts, se faisant des écoles et des règles à part, ont rompu la parenté qui les unissoit jadis, et ne forment plus, si l'on peut dire, une espèce de

république fédérative, on a vu chaque Artist concentré dans l'art qu'il professe, ignorer jusqu'aux plus simples élémens des autres Arts."

35. "Il n'y a point de république des arts . . . un peuple d'artistes est un chimère." *Seconde Suite aux Considérations,* 18.

36. ". . . en dehors de la circonscription des pouvoirs politiques." *Seconde Suite aux Considérations,* 12. Quatremère went so far as to describe calculating "les élémens d'une école sur ceux d'une république" as the "comble de la déraison." See his *Considérations,* 89.

37. "Le droit de citoyen dans cette république imaginaire ne pourroit appartenir qu'au plus habiles et aux savans." *Seconde Suite aux Considérations,* 20.

38. "Le principe moral de toute élection est qu'elle doit être faite par ceux qui peuvent le mieux la faire, et qui ont le plus grand intérêt à ce qu'elle soit bien faite. D'aprés celà la nature des choses veut que le peuple choisisse par lui-même ses magistrats, parce qu'étant toujours intéressé à bien choisir, on suppose toujours qu'il trouve dans son intérêt les lumières nécessaires pour discerner ceux qui méritent sa confiance. . . . Je ne crois pas qu'il y ait d'autres principes pour l'élection de ceux qui doivent professer les arts; mais il y a cette différence, que, dans l'ordre politique, nous partons d'une base certaine, qui est le peuple, et que cette base nous manque dans l'ordre de choses en question . . . Il est donc évident que le principe politique des élections, ou celui qui repose sur le droit naturel, ne sauroit s'appliquer à une corporation d'artistes, parce qu'elle n'est point une république; il est évident que le principe moral des élections ou celui que tend à leur perfection, dans la supposition fantastique d'une république d'artists, lui prescriroit encore d'ôter à la multitude ignorante le pouvoir des élections, à moins qu'on ne suppose une république d'artiste également habile." *Considérations,* 108–112. Quatremère also defined the asymmetry as follows: "Les êtres dont se compose une société, sont et doivent être égaux, par le droit de nature, quand ils ne le seroient pas par la loi, puisqu'ils sont tous des hommes. Les êtres dont se compose une école, sont et doivent être inégaux, par la nature des choses, quand ils ne le seroient pas par celle de l'institution, puisque les uns qui apprennent, sont ignorans, et que les autres qui enseignent, sont savans." *Considérations,* 89–90.

39. "Dans l'institution du nouveau gouvernement qui doit faire

le bonheur de la France, rien n'a plus fortement frappé le législateur et le peuple que le vice des anciennes élections, qui émanoient toutes d'un pouvoir arbitraire." *Considérations*, 107. The relationship Quatremère established between elections, *concours*, and the Republic of the Arts seems to have set the parameters for the reappearance of the issue during the nineteenth century. See Chaudonneret, "1848."

40. ". . . nous devons nous en tenir plutôt au principe moral qui vise à la perfection de l'élection, qu'au principe politique qui assure les droits des électeurs." *Considérations*, 108–109.

41. "Je sens bien que ce défaut apparent de conformité est le point le plus difficile à faire approuver de ceux qui, sensibles à une régularité symmétrique dans toutes les institutions publiques, les veulent apprécier plutôt d'aprés la rigueur des principes que par la bonté des effets." *Seconde Suite aux Considérations*, 19.

42. ". . . soumis lui-même, par la nature des institutions nouvelles, à tous les parallèles de l'égalité, à toutes les censures de la liberté, à tous les chocs des combats publics." *Seconde Suite aux Considérations*, 17.

43. ". . . on a faussement accusé d'avoir voulu bannir les arts de sa république. . . . En vain s'appuyeroit-on de l'exemple de Sparte, qu'on croit avoir été en partie le modèle de la république imaginaire de Platon." *Considérations*, 55, 57.

44. ". . . Platon vouloit seulement, tant par le choix des sujets qu'ils traiteroient que par la perfection de leur exécution . . . faire servir [les arts] à former le coeur et à cultiver l'entendement du peuple." *Considérations*, 56.

45. "La rigeur inconsidérée de quelques moralistes modernes, confondant les effets avec les causes, a, je le sais, accusé les arts de corrompre les moeurs, lorsque d'autres accusent les moeurs de corrompre les arts. Tous ont raison. La solution de ce cercle vicieux, consiste dans la réciprocité d'action entre les moeurs et les arts." *Considérations*, 53.

46. "Oui, ce texte prouve, ce que démontre la lecture entière de la République de Platon, savoir: qu'au lieu d'être un ouvrage sur la politique, elle est un ouvrage de morale, dans lequel un système métaphorique de gouvernement, devient le point de parallèle abstrait, d'un

traité non moins abstrait, sur la justice et la vertu, portées l'une et l'autre à un point fort au-dessus des forces ordinaires de l'homme." Quatremère, *Essai sur l'idéal* (1837), 23.

47. In the quickly growing bibliography on the Pantheon the most recent additions relevant to the present discussion are: Ozouf, *La fête révolutionnaire*; Chevallier and Rabreau, *Le Panthéon*; Bonnet, "Naissance du Panthéon"; Biver, *Le Panthéon à l'époque révolutionnaire*; Ozouf, "Le Panthéon: L'ecole normale des morts"; the volume *Soufflot et l'architecture des Lumiéres,* particularly Etlin's essay, "Grandeur et décadence d'un modéle"; Luke, "The Politics of Participation"; Rowlands, "Quatremère de Quincy," 303–600; the exhibition catalogue *Le Panthéon*; and Grammaccini, "Jean-Guillaume Moitte" and "J.-G. Moitte et la Révolution française."

48. The three reports are: *Rapport sur l'édifice dit de Sainte-Geneviève, fait au Directoire du département de Paris* (1791); *Rapport fait au Directoire du Département de Paris, le 13 Novembre 1792, l'an premier de la République Français, sur l'état actuel du Panthéon fran-çais;* and *Rapport fait au Directoire du Département de Paris, sur les travaux entrepris, continués ou achevés au Panthéon Français depuis le dernier compte, rendu le 17 Novembre 1792, et sur l'état actuel du monument;* hereafter cited as *Rapport* 1, *Rapport* 2, and *Rapport* 3. For a more detailed analysis of their chronology, see Lacroix's compilation of the *Actes de la Commune de Paris pendant la Révolution,* 4:290ff. Parts of *Rapport* 1 were also published as *Extrait du premier rapport présenté au Directiore dans le mois de mai 1791, sur les mesures propre à trans-former l'église dite Sainte-Geneviève en Panthéon Français.*

49. On the administrative aspect of Quatremère's contribution to the Pantheon, see Rowlands, "Quatremère de Quincy," 526–608, and Deming, "Le Panthéon révolutionnaire," esp. 113–115.

50. "S'imagine t-on, de bonne foi, qu'il sera jamais possible d'é-tablir un grand système d'idées et de décoration dans un monument, tant que les artistes se croiront en droit de s'en diviser par portions égals tous les sujets, et de s'en répartir l'éxecution comme d'un bien commun? . . . Un monument parfait seroit celui qui pourroit recevoir l'existence de la main seule de l'homme qui en a enfanté le projet . . . cette possibilité n'est qu'une chimère . . . c'est en proportion du plus ou du moins d'action immédiate d'un architecte sur ses coopérateurs, et du plus ou du moins

d'influence directe de l'auteur sur l'exécution de toutes les parties, qu'un édifice acquiert la perfection qui lui est propre . . . Comment donc peut-on prétendre assujettir l'inventeur d'un projet à recevoir d'un concours dont il ne seroit pas le juge, les collaborateurs de son inventions, les traducteurs de ses pensées, ou pour mieux dire, ses co-inventeurs?" *Rapport* 3, 76–77.

51. Quatremère claimed that the artistic quality of his efforts would be judged "au tribunal du goût et de l'opinion publique," and told the Directoire du Département with respect to his administrative efforts that "je le remercieraie de m'avoir fait jouir de la seule récompense que j'ambitionne, son estime appuyée du suffrage de la République." *Rapport*, 2, 4–6. On the concept of public opinion in the eighteenth century see Chartier, *The Cultural Origins of the French Revolution*, and Habermas, *The Structural Transformation of the Public Sphere*.

52. "Cet état de choses sera l'effet inévitable du système absurde établi entre les ouvriers qui, par une parodie absurde du gouvernement, regardent leurs travaux comme leur propriété, le bâtiment comme un république dont ils sont les concitoyens, et croyent en conséquence qu'il leur appartient de se nommer leurs chefs, leurs inspecteurs, et de se distribuer arbitrairement les travaux. L'on juge bien que dans une telle hiérarchie tout contrôle seroit dangereux, que toute inspection n'est qu'une vaine formalité, et qu'il doit se former une coalition de complaisance réciproque entre tous les agens, destructive de toute espéce de subordination." *Rapport* 1, 20.

53. "Tout ce qu'on pouvoit faire de mieux a été pratiqué au Panthéon, pour la distribution des travaux." *Rapport* 3, 79.

54. Quatremère also intended to introduce other programmatic changes and clarifications, particularly the separation of church and state and a greater respect for the distinction between burial and commemoration. On this subject, see Etlin, *The Architecture of Death*.

55. The blocking of the windows, the most permanent as well as most criticized of Quatremère's interventions, has traditionally been part of another controversy that surrounded the Pantheon from the time of its construction, namely the building's structural stability. Quatremère tangentially used the argument of strengthening the dome to justify his decision to close the windows, but they are unrelated issues, as has been well

demonstrated by Jacques Guillerme in his essay "Le Panthéon: une matière à controverse," in the exhibition catalogue *Le Panthéon*, 151–174.

56. Quatremère wrote that suppressing the windows "étoit le moyen le plus active propre à redonner à sa masse le caractère de gravité qu'indiquoit la destination." *Rapport* 3, 15.

57. "J'ai voulu," he wrote, "que la figure de la République ou de la Patrie, substituée à l'ancienne patrone . . . parût être, comme elle le doit, la Divinité du temple." *Rapport* 2, 27.

58. Years later in his article "Mémoire sur la manière dont étoient éclairés les temples des Grecs et des Romains" (1818), Quatremère suggested that most Greek temples were hypaethral. The link between this archaeological thesis and his design for the Pantheon was first established by Schneider, *Quatremère de Quincy*, 214. The history of the persistence of Gothic tradition in French architecture was definitively examined by Middleton in "The Abbé de Cordemoy and the Graeco-Gothic Ideal."

59. *Rapport* 1, 29 and 23.

60. ". . . une sorte de mérite révolutionnaire." *Rapport* 3, 53. Years later Quatremère no longer used political vocabulary to describe Soufflot's design. Instead he stated simply that "le monument de Soufflot fut véritablement celui qui remit en honneur le style de l'antiquité." *Histoire de la vie et des ouvrages des architectes*, 2:344.

61. "Mon premier soin . . . fut donc de faire disparoître tout ce qui pouvoit rappeler le caractère d'une église. L'édifice destiné à être une église en retraceroi toujours l'idée par sa forme et ses détails." *Rapport* 2, 8 and 11. The passage in which Quatremère notes Ste.-Geneviève's ineradicably ecclesiastical form is actually a paraphrase of objections others had made to using Ste.-Geneviève as the framework for the Pantheon. Many alternative proposals were made to eliminate fully the ecclesiastical *parti* of Ste.-Geneviève. Charles Norry, for example, suggested encasing the entire building such that it would have the form of a rotonda. (See his *Hommage à la Convention nationale d'un projet d'achèvement du Panthéon français*.) Quatremère's scheme was dependent on his view that "trente années d'habitude rendent difficile un changement" (*Rapport* 3, 11).

62. Quatremère most often discussed the design of Ste.-Gene-

viève using the general terms of church architecture. For example, he complained of its "trop grande similitude avec les vitraux des église" (*Rapport* 2, 12). On the other hand, he did describe its vaults as belonging "au système des Gothiques" (*Rapport* 3, 63). Moreover, the "légèrté" he emphasized as characteristic of Ste.-Geneviève is a term he used almost as a synonym for Gothic in other architectural texts. See, for example, both his articles on Gothic and lightness in the *Encyclopédie* and the entry on Soufflot in his *Histoire de la vie et des ouvrages des architectes*. On the concept of "légèrté" in French architectural theory of this period, see Szambien, *Symétrie, goût, caractère*.

63. "Chaque génération a semblé vouloir s'y inscrire, pour prendre acte des variations de son style et de son opinion." *Rapport* 3, 72. In his judgment, for example, architects had created of the Louvre nothing more than a "monument Historique" and done nothing less than alter "l'histoire et mentir à la posterité." *Rapport* 3, 49, 48, and 51. Quatremère's historicization and contextualization of his intervention at Ste.-Geneviève is most readily apparent from his division of *Rapport* 1 into three historically discrete sections: "De l'état de l'édifice de Sainte-Geneviève, jusqu'à l'époque de l'administration municipale," "De l'état actuel de l'édifice de Sainte-Geneviève sous l'administration municipale," and "De l'état futur de l'édifice dit de Sainte-Geneviève." While he used this organization to great rhetorical effect, it suggests a conceptual approach to historicism parallel to that evinced by the design of the Pantheon itself.

64. "Ce monument, quoiqu'il soit l'ouvrage de la Révolution, ne lui a pas été spécialement consacré." *Rapport* 3, 73.

65. "Mais les ressources de la sculpture lui rendent ce qui lui manque: elles expliquent ce qui étoit indécis; elles développent ce qui étoit caché." *Rapport* 3, 72.

66. The whole was to be crowned by two colossi, one of La Patrie which he hoped to design himself for the interior, and one of La Renomée for the summit of the cupola. He replaced the crucifix and angels, source of religious salvation, with La Patrie, source of the abolition of untruths and of the banishment of the aristocracy. Similarly, charity, the keys to heaven, and eternal grace were replaced by education, jurisprudence, and civic virtue.

67. See *Rapport* 1, 6ff.

68. Quatremère was strongly opposed to proposals that had been made for transforming Soufflot's iconography into the theme of religious tolerance by applying to the as yet undecorated pendentives attributes of additional cults. He wrote "flattés de l'espoir de consacrer, par les hiéroglyphes de l'art, le systême philosophique de la tolérance universelle, déjà quelques artistes avoient conçu le projet de graver sur le reste de l'édifice les symboles des autres cultes . . . Vous jugerez, Messieurs, ce qu de tels rapprochemens pourroient offrir de choquant pour la raison, de ridicule aux yeux de l'opinion, de dangereux par rapport au préjugé, et d'incompatible avec le culte moral que vous devez instituer dans cet édifice civique. Nous vous proposons d'adopter de préférence, dans la décoration de votre panthéon philosophique, les attributs et les emblèmes de cette religion vraiment universelle, à laquelle tous les peuples doivent se rallier. Cette religion est la morale." *Rapport* 1, 28–29.

69. Quatremère describes Soufflot's unrealized plan in *Rapport* 1, 4.

70. "On verroit d'une part ce que la patrie fait pour l'homme et de l'autre, ce que l'homme doit à la patrie." *Rapport* 1, 26.

71. Quatremère altered his design for the Pantheon's entry by the time of the final report. The Declaration of the Rights of Man is given center stage, with "instruction publique" and "jurisprudence" to its right and patriotic "dévouement" and the "Loi" to its left. While this change perhaps softened the impact of the original idea, the idea remained the same. He continued to view society in structural terms, and wrote, for example, "comme toute bonne société doit établir l'instruction et la justice pour tous, tous doivent en retour à la société l'obéissance aux loix et le sacrifice de leur personne à la chose publique." *Rapport* 3, 10.

72. "J'ai pensé que le code de nos lois contenu d'une part dans une déclaration des droits, et de l'autre dans une constitution, seroit bien placé sous le portique de ce Panthéon philosophique. Cette idée m'a conduit . . . à y exprimer par analogie, moins les traits de la Révolution que ses bienfaits, et moins son histoire que sa morale." *Rapport* 2, 26.

73. "Quant au faits, ils devoient se prendre parmi ceux de l'histoire ancienne, ou de l'histoire des Français, qui ne pouvoit daté que de la Révolution. J'ai cru que, dans ce premier monument national, on devoit enfin renoncer à se voir tributaire des anciens; qu'il falloit enfin s'appar-

tenir à soi-même, et que les effigies des Grecs et des Romains devoient cesser de figurer, là où commenceroient à briller celles des Français devenus libres. Il devenoit par trop hasardeux aussi de confier si-tôt à la sculpture plusieurs des faits de la Révolution, que l'histoire n'a pas encore dégagés des personnages qui en furent les instrumens, pour les donner tout entiers au peuple qui en fut le moteur. Les traits d'histoire copiés de si près, ressemblent aux objets qu'on voit à la louppe; il eût fallu sacrifier des vérités locales et accidentelles à la vérité générale; il eût fallu effacer des figures, ou se résoudre à les voir effacer par le temps . . . L'histoire de celle-ci [la Révolution] devra trouver place dans les temples que la liberté va voir s'élever de toutes parts; il falloit ici chanter ses effets plus que ses actions, et célébrer son règne plutôt que sa conquête." *Rapport* 3, 72–73.

74. This argument is exactly parallel to one Quatremère made with respect to the use of ancient dress in contemporary art in his *Essai sur l'idéal*, analyzed by Schneider, *L'esthétique classique*, 44ff.

75. Quatremère asserted that "le langage par figures et l'écriture par signes" characterized expression during "l'enfance des sociétés." *Rapport* 3, 73–74.

76. Quatremère maintained that because during early stages of social development "idées sont simples, comme le langage et l'écriture," he had determined to use simple allegorical motifs that were "clairs et à la portée de tous; j'ai voulu qu'ils expliquâssent le monument et n'eûssent pas besoin d'être expliqués par lui." *Rapport* 3, 75. He was hoping preemptively to respond to criticism that allegory was a dead language. He acknowledged that "dans les sphères de l'abstraction et dans les régions de la métphysique, l'on est toujours sûr d'être sublime; mais on court le risque de ne l'être que pour soi." He therefore maintained that "après avoir appris aux uns à parler ce langage, il faudroit apprendre aux autres à le comprendre." Teaching the French public to speak the language of allegory constituted an important aspect of the Pantheon's didactic function. See the *Rapport* 3, 74ff.

77. *Rapport* 1, 3 and 34. Quatremère had in mind activities such as civic ceremonies to be held on the grounds surrounding the building. On the urban aspects of Quatremère's design, see Etlin, "Grandeur et décadence," and Deming, "Le Panthéon révolutionnaire."

78. Quatremère returned to the notion of the arts' moral public function in his *Considérations morales sur la destination des ouvrages de l'art* (1815). In addition to considering the building a national monument and a "panthéon philosophique," Quatremère also referred to it as an "édifice civique" (*Rapport* 1, 29).

79. The notion of a civic temple bears further exploration, for while the use of pediments on secular and domestic buildings was legitimized already by Palladio, the sanctification of civic architecture was conceptually impossible without what might be called a modern understanding of the state. Quatremère provides interesting remarks on the relationship between the civic and the sacred in his article on the temple, which he defines as a building consecrated to the cult and adoration of the divinity, in the *Encyclopédie méthodique*, 3:448: "L'idée d'un Etre suprême, créateur et conservateur de tous les êtres, s'est toujours trouvée partout, la premiére dans l'ordre des idées, qui ont fondé les sociétés. . . . De là l'érection des édifices sacrés, lieux de réunion ou des croyances et des cérémonies communes, devenant le lieu des esprits, produisent cet accord moral qui d'hommes incohérens et isolés, forme un corps politique, sous le nom de *cité*, de *peuple* ou de *nation*" (his emphasis).

Conclusion

1. Most literature on Soane emphasizes his indebtedness to Laugier, inferred from the 11 copies of the *Essai sur l'architecture* Soane owned, and, to a lesser degree, to Cordemoy and Le Camus de Mézières. The essential sources on Soane are Stroud, *Sir John Soane, Architect*; du Prey, *John Soane*; du Prey, *John Soane's Architectural Education*; Stroud, *The Architecture of Sir John Soane*; and Summerson, *Sir John Soane*.

2. The catalogue of his library kept in the Sir John Soane Museum shows that he also owned Quatremère's *Considérations sur les arts du dessin*, *Le Jupiter Olympien*, *Restitution des deux frontons du temple de Minerve à Athenes*, *Monuments et ouvrages d'art antiques*, *Histoire de la vie et des ouvrages des plus célèbre architectes*, and two copies of the *Encyclopédie méthodique*. The fact that Soane owned several copies of a book does not necessarily indicate a particular concern for that author. Soane was deeply involved in teaching, and owning several copies of a publication would have enabled him to lend them to students.

I hope to consider the complex chronology of Soane's lectures at the Royal Academy in a separate study. References will thus be made either directly to dated archival sources, or to the version of the lectures published as *Lectures on Architecture*, ed. Arthur T. Bolton.

3. Soane seems to have read *De l'architecture égyptienne* first on August 27, 1806, and again on September 25, 1806. In a separate notebook he began a translation on July 7, 1807. Other journals contain additional notes on the book, indicating that Soane read from it in 1819, extensively in 1820, and finally in 1821. The references to Quatremère are recorded in the following MS documents at the Sir John Soane Museum: "Architecture—Extracts, Crude Hints, suggest[s] from reading different works & from occasional reflexions thereon," 1818, vol. 3, Soane Case E Right (this notebook also contains some loose notes on Quatremère, including sketches from plates of *De l'architecture égyptienne*); "Extracts, Crude Hints & etc., relating to Architecture," 1819, #1, Soane Case E Right; "Quatre mer de Quincy [sic] on the Egyptian architecture," 1807, Soane Case E Right (Soane's translation of *De l'architecture égyptienne*). I am grateful to R. Middleton for suggesting that I look into the connection between Soane and Quatremère.

4. Soane did not, however, use the word *type*. See his *Lectures on Architecture*, 15–25. Ironically, the one element that Quatremère conceded the Greeks had indeed borrowed from the Egyptians, the Corinthian capital, is a concession disputed by Soane (*Lectures on Architecture*, 35).

5. *Lectures on Architecture*, 16.

6. MS, "Architecture—Extracts, Crude Hints," 1818, vol. 3, 71.

7. MS, "Architecture—Extracts, Crude Hints," 1818, vol. 3, 72–75. This passage is from Soane's rough notes on *De l'architecture égyptienne* and not from the proper translation of the book he began but left unfinished. While both versions are quite exact with respect to the original French, I hope to analyze the translation itself as well as the other sources of Soane's lectures in another context.

8. "Peut-être encore, parmie les hommes de l'art, se rencontrera-t-il [Quatremère] des esprits sévères qui, ne pouvant se contenter que d'observations et de conséquences positives, trouveront que l'auteur s'est quelquefois trop livré aux conjectures, aux hypothéses et que, caressant

avec trop de complaisance ces enfans de son imagination, il a cherché et vu, dans ces circonstances, moins ce qui était réellement que ce qui avait pu ou avait dû être; mais tous s'accorderont pour rendre justice au double talent de l'auteur qui les fait jouir d'un ouvrage aussi bien composé que bien écrit; rempli d'aperçus fins, ingénieux, savans; développé avec clarté, dicté par une logique suivie, par une dialectique abondante en conséquences le plus souvent justes, et toujours déduites avec adresse, alors qu'on serait tenté de les croire plus spécieuses que solides." Laya, review of *De l'architecture égyptienne*. See also my "In the Names of History."

9. "Cet auteur est, en effet, un des écrivains les plus ingénieux qui se soient occupés d'architecture; mais les doctrines philosophiques de M. Quatremère rappellent fidèlement les tendances du siècle qui l'a vu naître, et ses théories d'art se deduisent très logiquement de ses idées philosophiques. Ni les unes ni les autres ne sont donc complètes. Elles pèchent par insuffisance, quelquefois par ignorance; elles seules ne sauraient répondre aux besoins de ce temps-ci: nous sommes au beau milieu du 19ème siècle, et les travaux de Quatremère ont la plupart de leurs racines dans le 18ème. Autre temps, autres doctrines." Daly, *Revue générale d'architecture*, 7 (1847–1848): 435–436. Daly was referring specifically to Guillaume-Abel Blouet, appointed Professeur· de Théorie de l'Architecture at the Ecole des Beaux-Arts in 1846. On Daly, see Van Zanten, "César Daly and the Revue Générale de l'Architecture"; Van Zanten, "Form and Society"; Lipstadt and Mendelsohn, eds., *Architectes et ingénieurs dans la presse*; and Becherer, *Science Plus Sentiment*.

10. In connection with Daly's critique an observation might be made regarding the debate on how Quatremère managed the transition from the *ancien régime* to the nineteenth century. Quatremère has been associated with the Idéologues, who have traditionally been thought of as mere codifiers of the eighteenth-century contributions of the Philosophes. More recently, however, the Idéologues have come to be seen as instrumental in transforming the political philosophy of the Philosophes into politics—in large measure by means of language theory—thus linking eighteenth-century social theorists such as Rousseau to nineteenth-century social reformers such as Comte. These new historiographical insights suggest that a comparison of Quatremère's *De l'architecture égyptienne* with an important document of Idéologue philosophy, Volney's *Voyage en Syrie et en Egypte*, would be fruitful. On a superficial level, both publications explore the same subject, and coincidentally contain plates by the

same engraver, Antoine Joseph Gaitte, better known as Ledoux's engraver. More substantively, however, they both used Egypt from the points of view of their respective fields as a creative bridge from what had previously been theoretical ideas about society to society itself. On the Idéologues, see Garnham, "Who were the *Idéologues?*"; Van Duzer, *The Contribution of the Ideologues to French Revolutionary Thought*; Moravia, "Les Idéologues et l'âge des Lumières"; Busset and Trabant, eds., *Les idéologues*; Staum, "The Class of Moral and Political Sciences, 1795–1803"; Chevalier, Desirat, and Horde, "Les idéologues"; Kennedy, *A Philosophe in the Age of Revolution*; and Picavet, *Les Idéologues*. On Volney in particular, see Gaulmier, *L'Idéologue Volney*.

11. "Je ne nie pas la valeur de cette théorie . . . Mais les origines sont toujours si obscures, qu'il vaut mieux ne pas les sonder; et tout en trouvant cette explication fort ingénieuses, je ne m'y arrête pas; je la prends pour ce qu'elle est, sans y attacher beaucoup d'importance. L'architecture égyptienne est là, qui pose devant nous; et je trouve qu'il vaut mieux l'étudier dans ce que nous voyons, que d'essayer de savoir, au milieu des ténèbres, quelles conceptions ont présidé à sa naissance." Barthélemy Saint-Hilaire, *Lettres sur l'Égypte*, 312. Barthélemy's letters on Egypt, all except the tenth, precisely that on Egyptian architecture, were previously published, most in the *Journal des Débats*, by Sylvestre de Sacy. Barthélemy, being both an academician and an orientalist, wrote the notice on Etienne Quatremère published in the *Journal des savants* in 1857. On Barthélemy, see Carré, *Voyageurs et écrivains*, 2:205ff.

12. Barthélemy, *Lettres sur l'Égypte*, 335, 313, 314.

13. "Quand nous parcourions ces ruines colossales et que nous admirions ces portails, ces colonnades, ces obélisques, ces palais, ces colonnades et ces temples, une réflexion assez pénible nous revenait sans cesse. Voilà bien la demeure des prêtres et des rois. Mais les peuples, où logeaient-ils? Voilà les splendides abris de la richesse et de la puissance. Mais la foule, où sont ses asiles et ses maisons?" Barthélemy, *Lettres sur l'Égypte*, 307–308.

14. "Son mémoire, qui a 71 ans de date à l'heure qu'il est, n'a point été surpassé; et je doute fort qu'il le soit jamais. Les hiéroglyphes, mieux compris et plus étudiés, nous apprendront bien des détails essentiels sur l'histoire des potentats qui ont dressé ces édifices gigantesques. Ils ne nous apprendront rien sur la valeur de l'art égyptien. C'est là

simplement une question d'esthétique, que l'arachéologie n'a pas même
à regarder . . . Il est vrai qu'on peut être bien inférieur aux Grecs et être
encore bien grand. L'étude de M. Quatremère de Quincy le prouve, quoiqu'aboutissant à une critique; et je crois que, tout en mettant l'architecture égyptienne fort au-dessous de sa rivale, il aura contribué plus que
personne à la placer encore bien haut. Pour ma part, c'est lui qui m'a
appris à en tenir tant de compte en me faisant pénétrer quelque peu dans
ses mystères, dont elle-même d'ailleurs n'a peut-être pas eu conscience."
Barthélemy, *Lettres sur l'Égypte*, 307, 336–337.

15. Gottfried Semper, for example, refuted many particulars of
Quatremère's theories of polychromy and imitation in architecture but
was nevertheless deeply indebted to Quatremère's work on these subjects.
For Quatremère's influence on Semper, see Malgrave, introduction to *Gottfried Semper*.

16. For the meaning and use of type in modern architectural
theory see, McLeod, review of Rossi's *The Architecture of the City*;
Colquhoun, "The Type and Its Transformations"; Rossi, *The Architecture
of the City*; Moneo, "On Typology"; Vidler, "The Third Typology"; Argan,
"On the Typology of Architecture."

17. "On the Analogy between Language and Architecture,"
Annals of the Fine Arts, 1820. This anonymous article was first noted by
Stafford in *Symbols and Myth*.

18. On Labrouste's library and its connection to the work of
Victor Hugo see the definitive studies by Neil Levine, "The Book and the
Building," "The Romantic Idea of Architectural Legibility," and "Architectural Reasoning in the Age of Positivism." Levine suggests a possible
point of connection between Quatremère's description of Egyptian buildings as libraries and the design of Labrouste's library in "The Book and
the Building," 264, n. 95. On Labrouste, see also Van Zanten, *Designing
Paris*.

19. "Il est bien important, et je ne cesserai de le dire, pour que
le langage de l'architecture ait de la valeur, pour que ses signes soient
compris et fassent l'effet qu'on peut en attendre . . . il faut, pour qu'ils
disent quelque chose, qu'on veuille bien ne pas les employer à rien dire."
Quatremère, *Encyclopédie méthodique*, 1:508.

BIBLIOGRAPHY

Aarsleff, Hans. *From Locke to Saussure: Essays on the Study of Language and Intellectual History.* Minneapolis, 1982.

Aarsleff, Hans. *The Study of Language in England, 1780–1860.* Princeton, 1967.

Aarsleff, Hans. "The Tradition of Condillac: The Problem of the Origin of Language in the Eighteenth Century and the Debate in the Berlin Academy before Herder." In *Studies in the History of Linguistics, Traditions and Paradigms,* ed. D. Hymes. Bloomington, Ind., 1974, 93–156.

Académie des Inscriptions et Belles-Lettres. *Comptes Rendus.*

Acton, H. B. "The Philosophy of Language in Revolutionary France." In *Studies in Philosophy,* ed. J. N. Findlay. London, 1966, 143–168.

Adams, Percy G. *Travelers and Travel Liars 1660–1800.* New York, 1980.

Adler, Jacob G. C. *Museum Cuficum Borgianum Velitris.* Rome, 1782.

Age of Neo-Classicism. Exhibition catalogue, The Arts Council of Great Britain, London, 1972.

Albertan-Coppola, Sylvaine. "La question des langues dans les *Moeurs des sauvages américains* de Lafitau." *Dixhuitième siècle,* 22 (1990), 125–138.

Algarotti, Francesco. *Saggio sopra l'architettura.* Venice, 1784.

Anderson, Robert, and Ibrahim Fawzy, eds. *Egypt Revealed: Scenes from Napoleon's 'Description de l'Egypte.'* Cairo, 1987.

Archer, John. "Character in English Architectural Design." *Eighteenth-Century Studies,* 12 (Spring 1979), 339–371.

Argan, Giulio Carlo. "On the Typology of Architecture." *Architectural Design*, 33 (1963), 564–565.

Arnauld, [Antoine], and [Claude] Lancelot. *Grammaire générale et raisonnée contenant les fondemens de l'art de parler; expliqué d'une manière claire et naturelle; les raisons de ce qui est commun à toutes les langues, et les principales différences qui s'y rencontrent; et plusieurs remarques nouvelles sur la langue françoise.* Paris, 1660.

Baker, Keith Michael. *Inventing the French Revolution: Essays on French Political Culture in the Eighteenth Century.* Cambridge, 1990.

Baldwin, E. C. "The Relation of the English 'Character' to Its Greek Prototype." *Modern Language Association Publications*, 18 (1903), 412–423.

Bann, S. "Historical Text and Historical Object: Poetics of the Musée Cluny." *Lotus*, 35 (1982), 36–43.

Barkan, L. *Nature's Work of Art: The Human Body as Image of the World.* New Haven and London, 1975.

Barthélemy Saint-Hilaire, J. *Lettres sur l'Egypte.* Paris, 1857.

Batteux, Charles. *Les beaux-arts reduits à un même principe.* Paris, 1747.

Becherer, Richard. *Science Plus Sentiment: César Daly's Formula for Modern Architecture.* Ann Arbor, 1984.

Belgrado, Jacopo. *Dell'architettura egiziana. Dissertazione d'un corrispondente dell'Accademia delle Scienze di Parigi.* Parma, 1786.

Belgrado, Jacopo. *Delle sensazioni del calore, e del freddo.* Parma, 1764.

Belgrado, Jacopo. *Dell'esistenza di Dio da' teoremi geometrici dimostrata.* Udine, 1777.

Benoit, François. *L'art français sous la Révolution et l'Empire. Les doctrines, les idées, les genres.* Paris, 1897.

Bernal, Martin. *Black Athena: The Afroasiatic Roots of Classical Civilization*, vol. 1, *The Fabrication of Ancient Greece 1785–1985.* New Brunswick, 1987.

Berry, C. "Adam Smith's *Considerations on Language.*" *Journal of the History of Ideas,* 35 (January–March 1974), 130–138.

Bialostocki, J. "The Renaissance Concept of Nature and Antiquity." In *Acts of the Twentieth International Congress of the History of Art.* 4 vols. Princeton, 1963, 2:19–30.

Bibliothèque de M. Quatremère de Quincy, Collection d'ouvrages relatifs aux Beaux-Arts et a l'archéologie; dont la vente aura lieu le lundi 27 Mai 1850. Paris, 1850.

Biver, Marie-Louise. *Le Panthéon à l'époque révolutionnaire.* Paris, 1982.

Blondel, Jacques-François. *Cours d'architecture, ou traité de la décoration, distribution & construction des bâtiments; contenant les leçons donnés en 1750, et les années suivante,* . . . 6 vols. Paris, 1771–1777.

Blumer, M.-L. "La commission pour la recherche des objets de sciences et arts en Italie (1796–1797)." *La Révolution française,* 87 (1934), 62–88, 124–150, and 222–259.

Boffrand, Germain. *Livre d'architecture.* Paris, 1745.

Bonnet, Jean-Claude. "Naissance du Panthéon." *Poétique,* 33 (1978), 46–65.

Boschot, Adolphe. "Le centenaire d'un esthéticien, Quatremère de Quincy." In *Institut de France, Publications Diverses de l'année 1940,* 17–30.

Boschot, Adolphe. *Maîtres d'hier et de jadis.* Paris, 1944.

Bossuet, Jacques Benigne, Evêque de Meaux. *Discours sur l'histoire universelle.* Paris, 1700.

Boulanger, Nicolas-Antoine. *L'antiquitée dévoilée par ses usages ou Examen critique des principales opinions, cérémonies et institutions religieuses et politiques des différents peuples de la terre.* Amsterdam, 1768.

Boullée, Etienne-Louis. *Architecture, Essai sur l'art.* Ed. Jean-Marie Pérouse de Montclos. Paris, 1968.

Boyce, B. *The Polemical Character, 1640–1661: A Chapter in English Literary History.* Lincoln, Neb., 1955.

Boyce, B. *The Theophrastian Character in England to 1642.* Cambridge, Mass., 1947.

Braham, Allan. *The Architecture of the French Enlightenment.* Berkeley and Los Angeles, 1980.

Bruce, James. *Voyage aux sources du Nil, en Nubie et en Abyssinie, pendant les années 1768, 1769, 1770, 1771, & 1772.* 6 vols. Paris, 1790–1792.

Buffon, Georges Louis Leclerc, Comte de. *Histoire naturelle, générale et particulière.* Paris, 1749–1804.

Busset, W., and J. Trabant, eds. *Les Idéologues. Sémiotique, théories et politiques linguistiques pendant la Révolution française. Foundations of Semiotics,* vol. 12. Amsterdam and Philadelphia, 1986.

Calvesi, Maurizio. *Carceri, Mole Adriana, Vedute di Roma/Castel Sant'Angelo.* Exhibition catalogue for *Piranesi nei luoghi di Piranesi.* Rome, 1979.

Carré, Jean-Marie. *Voyageurs et écrivains français en Égypte.* 2 vols. Cairo, 1932.

Carrott, Richard G. *The Egyptian Revival, Its Sources, Monuments, and Meaning, 1808–1858.* Berkeley, Los Angeles, London, 1978.

Cassirer, Ernst. *The Philosophy of the Enlightenment.* Trans. Fritz C. A. Koelln and James P. Pettegrove. Princeton, 1951.

Catalogue d'objets d'arts, antiquités égyptiennes, grecques et romaines, vases grecs, terres cuites, figurines en bronze, sculptures en marbre, dont deux bustes de Canova, médailles, miniatures, dessins et belles estampes anciennes et modernes, composant le cabinet de feu de M. Quatremère de Quincy. Paris, 1850.

Caylus, Anne Claude Philippe de Tubières, Comte de. "De l'architecture ancienne." *Histoire de l'Académie Royale des Inscriptions et Belles-Lettres,* 23 (1756), 286–320 (read January 7, 1749).

Caylus, Anne Claude Philippe de Tubières, Comte de. *Recueil d'anti-*

quités égyptiennes, étrusques, grecques et romaines. Paris, 1752–
1767.

Chartier, Roger. *The Cultural Origins of the French Revolution*. Trans.
L. G. Cochrane. Durham and London, 1991.

Chaudonneret, M.-C. "1848: 'La République des Arts.'" *The Oxford Art
Journal*, 10, no. 1 (1987), 58–70.

Chaudonneret, M.-C. *La figure de la République. Le Concours de 1848*.
Notes et documents des musées de France, 13. Paris, 1987.

Cherpack, Clifton. "Warburton and Some Aspects of the Search for the
Primitive in Eighteenth-Century France." *Philological Quar-
terly*, 36 (April 1957), 221–233.

Chevalier, Jean-Claude, Claude Desirat, and Tristan Horde. "Les Idéologues: le sujet de l'histoire et l'étude des langues." *Dialectiques*,
12 (1976), 33–40.

Chevallier, Pierre, and Daniel Rabreau. *Le Panthéon*. Paris, 1977.

Church, H. W. "Corneille de Pauw and the Controversy over His
Recherches philosophiques sur les Américains." *PMLA*, 51
(March 1936), 178–206.

Claparède, E. "Rousseau et l'origine du langage." *Annales de la Société
J. J. Rousseau*, 14 (1935), 95–120.

Clark, Robert T., Jr. "Herder, Cesarotti and Vico." *Studies in Philology*,
44 (October 1947), 645–671.

Clayton, Peter A. *The Rediscovery of Ancient Egypt: Artists and Travel-
lers in the 19th Century*. London, 1982.

Clérisseau, Charles Louis. *Antiquitées de la France*. Paris, 1778.

Colish, Marcia L. *The Mirror of Language: A Study in the Medieval
Theory of Knowledge*. New Haven and London, 1968.

Collins, Peter. *Changing Ideals in Modern Architecture, 1750–1950*. Mon-
treal, 1965.

Colquhoun, Alan. "The Type and Its Transformations." Chapter 2 of
*Essays in Architectural Criticism: Modern Architecture and His-
torical Change*, Cambridge, Mass., and London, 1981.

Cordemoy, Géraud de. *Discours physique de la parole.* 2d ed. Paris, 1677.

Coulet, H. "La métaphore de l'architecture dans la critique littéraire au XVIIe siècle." In *Critique et création littéraires en France au XVIIe siècle,* ed. M. Fumaroli. Colloques internationaux du Centre National de la Recherche Scientifique, 557. Paris, 1977, 291–309.

Court de Gébelin, Antoine. *Histoire naturelle de la parole, ou précis de l'origine du langage et de la grammaire universelle. Extraite du Monde primitif.* Paris, 1776.

Curl, James Steven. *The Egyptian Revival.* London, 1982.

Curtius, Ernst Robert. *European Literature and the Latin Middle Ages.* New York, 1963.

D'Alembert, Jean le Rond. *Preliminary Discourse to the Encyclopedia of Diderot.* Trans. Richard N. Schwab. Indianapolis and New York, 1963.

Daly, César. *Revue générale d'architecture,* vol. 7. Paris, 1847–1848.

Daniélou, J. *"Sacramentum Futuri." Etudes sur les origines de la typologie biblique.* Paris, 1950.

Darnton, Robert. *The Business of Enlightenment: A Publishing History of the Encyclopédie 1775–1800.* Cambridge, Mass., and London, 1979.

David, M. V. *Le débat sur les écritures et l'hiéroglyphe aux XVIIe et XVIIIe siècles et l'application de la notion de déchiffrement aux écritures mortes.* Paris, 1965.

Dawson, R. *The Chinese Chameleon: An Analysis of European Conceptions of Chinese Civilisation.* London and New York, 1967.

De Brosse, Charles. *Traité de la formation mécanique des langues et des principes physiques de l'étymologie.* 2 vols. Paris, 1801.

De Certeau, Michel. "L'idée de traduction de la Bible au XVIIe siècle." *Recherches de science religieuse,* 66 (1978), 73–92.

De Certeau, Michel. "Writing vs. Time: History and Anthropology in the Works of Lafitau." *Yale French Studies,* 59 (1980), 37–65.

Del Pesco, Daniela. *Il Louvre di Bernini nella Francia di Luigi XIV*. Naples, 1984.

Del Rosso, Giuseppe. *Richerche sul'architettura egiziana*. Florence, 1787.

Del Rosso, Giuseppe. *Richerche sul'architettura egiziana*. 2d ed., Siena, 1800.

Deming, M. K. "Le Panthéon révolutionnaire." In *Le Panthéon, symbole des révolutions: De L'Eglise de la Nation au Temple des grands hommes*. Exhibition catalogue, Centre Canadien d'Architecture and Caisse Nationale des Monuments Historiques et des Sites, Paris, 1989, 97–150.

Denon, Dominique Vivant. *Voyage dans la Basse et la Haute Egypte*. London, 1802.

Derrida, Jacques. "La linguistique de Rousseau." *Revue Internationale de Philosophie*, 21 (1967), 443–462.

Description de l'Egypte ou Recueil des observations et des recherches qui ont été faites en Egypte pendant l'expédition de l'armée française, publié par les ordres de Sa majesté l'empereur Napoléon le Grand. Paris, 1809.

Destutt Comte de Tracy, M. *Elémens d'idéologie*. 3d ed. Paris, 1817.

Dictionnaire des Beaux-Arts. 2 vols. Paris, 1788–1805. Part of *Encyclopédie méthodique, ou par ordre de matières*, ed. C.-J. Panckoucke, Paris, 1788–1825.

Diderot, Denis. "Lettre sur les sourds et muets." In *Oeuvres complètes*, ed. J. Assézat. Paris, 1875.

Dieckmann, Liselotte. *Hieroglyphics: The History of a Literary Symbol*. St. Louis, 1970.

Dillon, George L. "Complexity and Change of Character in Neo-Classical Criticism." *Journal of the History of Ideas*, 35 (January–March 1974), 51–63.

D'Origny, Pierre-Adam. *Dissertations ou on examine quelques questions appartenantes à l'histoire des anciens Egyptiens*. s.l., 1752.

D'Origny, Pierre-Adam. *L'Egypte ancienne ou Mémoires historiques et artistiques sur les objets les plus importans de l'histoire du grand empire des Egyptiens.* Paris, 1762.

Drexler, Arthur, ed. *The Architecture of the Ecole des Beaux-Arts.* Exhibition catalogue, The Museum of Modern Art, New York, 1977.

Dubois, Claude-Gilbert. *Mythe et langage au seizième siècle.* Bordeaux, 1970.

Du Bos, Abbé. *Réflexions critiques sur la poësie et sur la peinture.* Paris, 1770.

Duchet, Michèle. *Anthropologie et histoire au siècle des lumières.* Paris, 1971.

Duchet, Michèle. "Discours ethnologique et discours historique: le texte de Lafitau." *Studies on Voltaire and the Eighteenth Century,* 152 (1976), 607–623.

Du Prey, Pierre de la Ruffinière. *John Soane's Architectural Education, 1753–80.* New York, 1977.

Du Prey, Pierre de la Ruffinière. *John Soane: The Making of an Architect.* Chicago, 1982.

Durand, Jean-Nicholas-Louis. *Recueil et parallel des édifices en tout genre anciens et modernes.* Paris, 1800.

Duro, P. "'Un livre ouvert à l'instruction': Study Museums in Paris in the Nineteenth Century." *The Oxford Art Journal,* 10, no. 1 (1987), 44–57.

Dussaud, René. *La nouvelle Académie des Inscriptions et Belles-Lettres (1795–1914).* Paris, 1946.

Eco, Umberto. "A Componential Analysis of the Architectural Sign/Columns." In Geoffrey Broadbent et al., *Signs, Symbols, and Architecture.* New York, 1980, 213–232.

Elledge, Scott. "The Naked Science of Language, 1747–1786." In *Studies in Criticism and Aesthetics, 1660–1800, Essays in Honor of Samuel Holt Monk,* ed. H. Anderson and J. S. Shea. Minneapolis, 1967, 266–295.

Encyclopédie ou Dictionnaire raisonné des sciences, des arts et des métiers. Facsimile of the first edition of 1751–1780. Stuttgart–Bad Cannstatt, 1966–1967.

Erlande-Brandenburg, A. *The Cluny Museum.* Paris, 1983.

"L'état civile des citoyens nobles de Paris en 1789." In *Mémoires de la société de l'histoire de Paris et de l'Ile-de-France,* 26 (1899).

Etiemble, R. *Les Jésuites et la Chine, la querelle des rites (1552–1773).* Paris, 1966.

Etlin, R. A. *The Architecture of Death.* Cambridge, Mass., 1984.

Etlin, R. A. "Grandeur et décadence d'un modèle: L'église Sainte-Geneviève et les changements de valeur esthétique au XVIIIe siècle." In *Soufflot et l'architecture des Lumières.* Paris, 1982, 26–37.

Etrennes à la vérité ou almanach des aristocrates. Paris, 1790.

L'europa cristiana nel rapporto con le altre culture nel secolo XVII. Atti del Convegno di studio di Santa Margherita Ligure (19–21 May 1977). Florence, 1978.

Fagan, Brian M. *The Rape of the Nile: Tomb Robbers, Tourists, and Archaeologists in Egypt.* New York, 1975.

Fischer von Erlach, J. B. *Entwurf einer historischen Architektur.* Vienna, 1721.

Fontaine, Pierre-François-Léonard. *Journal, 1799–1853.* 2 vols. Paris, 1987.

Fontana, Domenico. *Della trasportazione dell'obelisco vaticano.* 2d ed., Naples, 1604.

Fontius, M. "Winckelmann und die französische Aufklärung." In *Sitzungbericht der Deutschen Akademie der Wissenschaften zu Berlin, Klasse für Sprachen, Literatur und Kunst.* Berlin, 1968.

Formigari, Lia. "Language and Society in the Late Eighteenth Century." *Journal of the History of Ideas,* 35 (April–June 1974), 275–292.

Formigari, Lia. *Linguistica e antropologia nel secondo Settecento.* Messina, 1972.

Fréart de Chambray, Roland. *Parallèle de l'architecture antique et de la moderne.* Paris, 1650.

Frey, H. W. *The Eclipse of Biblical Narrative: A Study in Eighteenth and Nineteenth Century Hermeneutics.* New Haven, 1974.

Fumaroli, Marc. *L'age de l'eloquence. Rhétorique et "res literaria" de la Renaissance au seuil de l'époque classique.* Hautes Études Médiévales et Modernes, 43. Geneva, 1980.

Garnham, B. G. "Who Were the *Idéologues?*" In *Studies in the French Eighteenth Century Presented to John Lough by Colleagues, Pupils and Friends,* ed. D. J. Mossop, G. E. Rodmell, and D. B. Wilson. Durham, 1978, 66–81.

Gaulmier, Jean. *L'Idéologue Volney 1757–1820, Contribution à l'histoire de l'orientalisme en France.* Geneva and Paris, 1980; first published Beirut, 1951.

Gennep, A. van. "Contributions à l'histoire de la méthode ethnographique." *Revue de l'histoire des religions,* 67 (1913), 320–338; 68 (1913), 32–61.

Giehlow, Karl. "Die Hieroglyphenkunde des Humanismus in der Allegorie der Renaissance." *Jahrbuch der kunsthistorischen Sammlungen des allerhöchsten Kaiserhauses.* 32, no. 1. Vienna, 1915.

Gillispie, C. C., and M. Dewachter, eds. *Monuments of Egypt: The Napoleonic Edition.* 2 vols. Princeton, 1987.

Gliozzi, G. *Adamo e il Nuovo Mondo: La nascita dell'antropologia come ideologia coloniale dalle genealogie bibliche alle teorie razziali: 1500–1700.* Florence, 1977.

Goguet, Antoine-Yves. *De l'origine des loix, des arts, et des sciences; et de leurs progrès chez les anciens peuples.* 3 vols. Paris, 1758.

Gombrich, E. H. *Art and Illusion: A Study in the Psychology of Pictorial Representation.* Princeton, 1956.

Gombrich, E. H. *Ideas of Progress and Their Impact on Art.* New York, 1971.

Grammaccini, Gisela. "Jean-Guillaume Moitte (1746–1810). Leben und Werk." Ph.D. diss., University of Hamburg, 1988.

Grammaccini, Gisela. "J.-G. Moitte et la Révolution française." *Revue de l'art*, 83 (1989), 61–70.

Greene, Christopher M. "A. Lenoir and the Musée des Monuments Français during the French Revolution." *French Historical Studies*. 12 (1981), 200–223.

Greener, Leslie. *The Discovery of Egypt*. London, 1966.

Greenhalgh, Michael. "Quatremère de Quincy as a Popular Archaeologist." *Gazette des Beaux-Arts* (1968), 249–256.

Grimsley, Ronald. *Sur l'origine du langage*. Geneva, 1971.

Grosier, Abbé Jean-Baptiste Gabriel Alex. *Histoire générale de la Chine*. Ed. P. J.-A.-M. Moyriac de Mailla. 13 vols. Paris 1777–1785.

Guignes, Joseph de. *Mémoire dans lequel on prouve que les Chinois sont une colonie égyptienne*. Paris 1759.

Guigniaut, Joseph Daniel. "Notice sur la vie et les travaux de M. Quatremère de Quincy." *Mémoires de l'Institut National de France, Académie des Inscriptions et Belles-Lettres*, 25 (1877), 361–412.

Guigniaut, Joseph Daniel. *Notice sur la vie et les travaux de M. Quatremère de Quincy*. Paris, 1866.

Guiheux, Alain, and Dominique Rouillard. "Echanges entre les mots et l'architecture dans la seconde moitié du XVIIe siècle à travers les traités de l'art de parler." *Les cahiers de la recherche architecturale*, 18, no. 4 (1985), 18–27.

Guillerme, Jacques. "The Idea of Architectural Language: A Critical Inquiry." *Oppositions* (Fall 1977), 21–26.

Gusdorf, Georges. *Histoire de la science à l'histoire de la pensée*. Paris, 1966.

Guy, B. "The French Image of China before and after Voltaire." *Studies on Voltaire and the 18th Century*, 21 (1963), 123–131.

Habermas, Jürgen. *The Structural Transformation of the Public Sphere: An Inquiry into a Category of Bourgeois Society*. Trans. T. Burger and F. Lawrence. Cambridge, Mass., 1989.

Hagstrum, Jean H. *The Sister Arts: The Tradition of Literary Pictorialism and English Poetry from Dryden to Gray.* Chicago and London, 1968.

Hampton, J. N. *A. Boulanger et la science de son temps.* Geneva, 1955.

Hancarville, P. F. Hugues d', *Antiquitées étrusques, grecques et romaines.* 5 vols. Paris, 1785–1788.

Hancarville, P. F. Hugues d', *Recherches sur l'origine, l'esprit et les progrès des arts de la Grèce; sur leurs connections avec les arts et la religion des plus anciens peuples connus; sur les monumens antiques de l'Inde, de la Perse, de reste de l'Asie, de l'Europe et de l'Egypte.* 3 vols. London, 1785.

Harnois, Guy. "Les théories du langage en France de 1660 à 1821." Paris, Société d'Edition "Les Belles Lettres," n.d.

Harrington, Kevin. *Changing Ideas on Architecture in the "Encyclopédie." 1750–1776.* Ann Arbor, 1985.

Harris, John. "Le Geay, Piranesi and International Neo-classicism in Rome, 1740–1750." In *Essays in the History of Architecture Presented to Rudolf Wittkower,* ed. D. Fraser. H. Hibbard and M. Lewine. London, 1967, 189–196.

Hautecoeur, Louis. "L'expédition du premier Empire." *Napoléon, revue des études napoléoniennes,* 14 (January–February 1925), 81–87.

Hautecoeur, Louis. *Histoire de l'architecture classique en France,* vols. 4 and 5. Paris, 1952 and 1953.

Hernandez, Antonio. *Gundzüge einer Ideengeschichte der französischen Architekturtheorie von 1560–1800.* Basel, 1972.

Herrmann, Wolfgang. *Laugier and Eighteenth Century French Theory.* London, 1962.

Herrmann, Wolfgang. "The Problem of Chronology in Claude-Nicholas Ledoux's Engraved Work." *Art Bulletin,* 26 (1960), 191–210.

Herrmann, Wolfgang. *The Theory of Claude Perrault.* London, 1973.

Histoire de l'Académie Royale des Inscriptions et Belles-Lettres, vol. 40. Paris, 1780.

Hogden, M. T. *Early Anthropology in the Sixteenth and Seventeenth Centuries.* Philadelphia, 1964.

Home, Henry (Lord Kames). *Elements of Criticism.* Edinburgh, 1762.

Home, Henry (Lord Kames). *Essais historiques sur les loix.* Paris, 1766.

Home, Henry (Lord Kames). *Sketches of the History of Man.* 2 vols. Edinburgh, 1774.

Howard, S. "The Antiquarian Market in Rome and the Rise of Neo-classicism: A Basis for Canova's New Classics." *Studies on Voltaire and the Eighteenth Century,* 153 (1976), 1057–1068.

Huard, G. "La salle du XIIIe siècle du Musée des Monuments Français à l'École des Beaux-Arts." *Revue de l'art ancien et moderne,* 47, (1925), 113–126.

Hubert, René. *Les sciences sociales dans l'Encyclopédie. La philosophie de l'histoire et le problème des origines sociales.* Paris, 1923.

Humbert, A. "L'évolutionisme et la linguistique." *Revue de philosophie,* 19 (1911), 316–360.

Hunt, Lynn. *Politics, Culture, and Class in the French Revolution.* Berkeley and Los Angeles, 1984.

Iverson, Erik. "Hieroglyphic Studies of the Renaissance." *The Burlington Magazine,* 100 (1958), 15–21.

Iverson, Erik. *The Myth of Egypt and Its Hieroglyphics in European Tradition.* Copenhagen, 1961.

Jespersen, Otto. *Language: Its Nature, Development and Origin.* London, 1922.

Jouin, Henry. *A.-C. Quatremère de Quincy, deuxiéme secrétaire perpétuel de l'Académie des Beaux-Arts.* Paris, 1892.

Juliard, Pierre. *Philosophies of Language in Eighteenth-Century France.* The Hague and Paris, 1970.

Junod, Philippe. "Tradition et innovation dans l'esthétique de Piranèse." *Étude de Lettres* (July–September 1982), 3–24.

Justi, Carl. *Winckelmann und seine Zeitgenossen.* Leipzig, 1866–1872.

Kaufmann, Edgar, Jr. "Memmo's Lodoli." *Art Bulletin*, 46 (1964), 159–175.

Kaye, F. B. "Mandeville on the Origin of Language." *Modern Language Notes*, 39 (1924) 136–142.

Kemp, Martin. "From *Mimesis* to *Fantasia*: The Quattrocento Vocabulary of Creation, Inspiration and Genius in the Visual Arts." *Viator*, 8 (1977), 347–399.

Kennedy, Emmet. *A Philosophe in the Age of Revolution: Destutt de Tracy and the Origins of Ideology*. Philadelphia, 1978.

Kennedy, George A. *Classical Rhetoric and Its Christian and Secular Tradition from Ancient to Modern Times*. Chapel Hill, 1980.

Kircher, Athanasius. *Oedipus aegyptiacus, hoc est universalis hieroglyphicae veterum doctrinae temporum iniuria abolitae instauratio . . .* Rome, 1652.

Knight, Isabel F. *The Geometric Spirit: The Abbé de Condillac and the French Enlightenment*. New Haven and London, 1968.

Knowlson, J. R. "The Idea of Gesture as a Universal Language in the Seventeenth and Eighteenth Centuries." *Journal of the History of Ideas* (1965), 495–508.

Knowlson, J. R. *Universal Language Schemes in England and France*. Toronto, 1975.

Körner, Hans, and Friedrich Piel. "'A mon ami Antoine Quatremère de Quincy,' Ein unbekanntes Werk Jacques-Louis Davids aus dem Jahre 1779." *Pantheon*, 43 (1985), 89–96.

Korshin, Paul J. "The Development of Abstract Typology in England, 1650–1820." In *Literary Uses of Typology from the Late Middle Ages to the Present*, ed. E. Miner. Princeton, 1977, 147–204.

Kristeller, Paul Oskar. "The Modern System of the Arts." In *Renaissance Thought II, Papers on Humanism and the Arts*. 2 vols. New York, 1965, 2:163–227.

Krufft, Hanno-Walter. *Geschichte der Architekturtheorie von der Antike bis zur Gegenwart*. Munich, 1985.

Kuehner, Paul. *Theories on the Origin and Formation of Language in the Eighteenth Century in France.* Philadelphia, 1944.

Labrouste, Henri. "Restauration de Paestum." In *Monuments antiques.* Paris, 1877.

Lach, D. F. *Asia in the Making of Europe.* Chicago, 1965.

Lach, D. F. "China and the Era of Enlightenment." *Journal of Modern History,* 14 (1941), 209–223.

Lach, D. F. "Leibniz and China." *Journal of the History of Ideas,* 6 (1945), 436–455.

Lacroix, Sigismond, ed. *Actes de la Commune de Paris pendant la Révolution.* 7 vols. Paris, 1895–1920.

Lafitau, Joseph François. *Customs of the American Indians Compared with the Customs of Primitive Times* (Paris, 1724). Trans. and ed. William N. Fenton and Elizabeth L. Moore. Toronto, 1974.

Lafitau, Joseph François. *Moeurs des sauvages ameriquains, comparées aux moeurs des premiers temps.* Paris, 1724.

Lakoff, Robin. "La Grammaire générale et raisonnée ou la Grammaire de Port-Royal." In *History of Linguistic Thought and Contemporary Linguistics,* ed. Herman Parret. Berlin and New York, 1976, 348–374.

Lampe, G. W. H., and K. J. Woollcombe. *Essays on Typology.* London, 1957.

Lamy, Bernard. *Rhétorique ou l'art de parler.* Paris, 1675.

Landes, Joan. *Women and the Public Sphere in the Age of the French Revolution.* Ithaca, 1988.

Lapauze, Henry. *Procès-verbaux de la commune Générale des Arts, de peinture, sculpture, architecture et gravure (18 juillet 1793–tridi de la première décade du deuxième mois de l'an II) et de la Société Populaire et Républicaine des Arts (3 nivôse an II–28 Floréal an III.)* Paris, 1903.

Laugier, Marc-Antoine. *Essai sur l'architecture.* Paris, 1755.

Laugier, Marc-Antoine. *An Essay on Architecture.* Trans. Wolfgang and Anni Herrmann. Los Angeles, 1977.

Laugier, Marc-Antoine. *Observations sur l'architecture.* Paris, 1765.

Laurens, Henri. *Les origines intellectuelles de l'expédition d'Egypte, 1689–1798.* Istanbul and Paris, 1987.

Lauro, Giacomo. *Antiquae urbis splendor . . .* Rome, 1612.

Lavin, Irving. *Bernini and the Unity of the Visual Arts.* New York and London, 1980.

Lavin, Sylvia. "In the Names of History: Quatremère de Quincy and the Literature of Egyptian Architecture." *Journal of Architectural Education* (May 1991), 131–137.

Laya, [Jean-Michel]. Review of *De l'architecture égyptienne.* In *Le moniteur universel,* 24 thermidor an 11 de la République (12 Aug. 1803), no. 324, 1437–1439.

Lebensztejn, Jean-Claude. "De l'imitation dans les beaux-arts." Review of A. C. Quatremère de Quincy, *De l'imitation* (Brussels, 1980). In *Critique: Revue générale des publications françaises et étrangères,* 38, no. 416 (January 1982), 3–21.

Le Bihan, Alain. *Francs-Maçons Parisiens du Grand Orient de France.* Paris, 1966.

Le Bruyn, Corneille. *Voyage au Levant.* Paris, 1725.

Le Camus de Mézières, Nicolas. *Le génie d'architecture ou l'analogie de cet art avec nos sensations.* Paris, 1780.

Lee, Renssalaer W. "*Ut Pictura Poesis:* The Humanistic Theory of Painting." *Art Bulletin,* 22 (1940), 197–269. Also published separately in book form, New York and London, 1967.

Lefèvre, Marc. "La génétique du langage selon Antoine Court de Gébelin." *Mémoires et publications de la société des Sciences, des Arts et des Lettres du Hainaut,* 83, (1970), 39–59.

Legrand, J. G., and C. P. Landon. *Description de Paris et de ses édifices, avec un précis historique et des observations sur le caractère de leur architecture, et sur les principaux objets d'art et de curiosité qu'ils renferment.* Paris, 1808.

Leith, James A. *The Idea of Art as Propaganda in France 1750–1799: A Study in the History of Ideas.* Toronto, 1965.

Lemay, Edna. "Histoire de l'antiquité et découverte du nouveau monde chez deux auteurs du XVIIIe siècle." *Studies on Voltaire and the Eighteenth Century*, 153 (1976), 1313–1328.

Lepenies, Wolf. "L'altro fanatico. Scienza e storia nella concezione estetica di Winckelmann." *Intersezioni*, 3, no. 2 (August 1983), 303–316.

Le Roy, Julien-David. *Observations sur les edifices des anciens peuples, précédées de réflexions préliminaires sur la critique des ruines de la Grèce, publiée dans un ouvrage anglois, intitulé "Les antiquités d'Athènes", et suivies de recherches sur les mesures anciennes.* Amsterdam, 1767.

Le Roy, Julien-David. *Les ruines des plus beaux monuments de la Grèce, considérées du côté de l'histoire et du côté de l'architecture.* Paris, 1758; 2d ed. 1770.

Levine, Neil. "Architectural Reasoning in the Age of Positivism: The Neo-Grec Idea of Henri Labrouste's Bibliothèque Saint-Geneviève." Ph.D. diss., Yale University, 1975.

Levine, Neil. "The Book and the Building: Hugo's Theory of Architecture and Labrouste's Bibliothèque Ste-Geneviève." In *The Beaux-Arts and Nineteenth-Century French Architecture*, ed. Robin Middleton. Cambridge, Mass., 1982, 138–174.

Levine, Neil. "The Romantic Idea of Architectural Legibility: Henri Labrouste and the Neo-Grec." In *The Architecture of the Ecole des Beaux-Arts*, ed. Arthur Drexler. Exhibition catalogue, The Museum of Modern Art, New York, 1977.

Lipstadt, H., and H. Mendelsohn, eds. *Architectes et ingénieurs dans la presse: polémique, debat, conflit.* Paris, 1980.

Lipstadt, Hélène. "Early Architectural Periodicals." In *The Beaux-Arts and Nineteenth-Century French Architecture*, ed. Robin Middleton. Cambridge, Mass., 1982, 50–58.

Littré, E. *Dictionnaire de la langue française*. Paris, 1881.

Lovejoy, A. O., and G. Boas. *A Documentary History of Primitivism and Related Ideas*. Baltimore, 1935.

Lucas, Paul. *Troisième voyage du Sieur Paul Lucas fait en MDCCXIV etc. par ordre de Louis XIV, dans la Turquie, l'Asie, la Sourie, la Palestine, la Haute et la Basse Egypte, etc*. Rouen, 1719.

Luke, Yvonne. "The Politics of Participation: Quatremère de Quincy and the Theory and Practice of 'Concours publiques' in Revolutionary France 1791–95." *The Oxford Art Journal*, 10, no. 1 (1987), 15–43.

Macartney, G. *Voyage dans l'intérieur de la Chine et en Tartarie*. Paris 1798.

McDonald, William. *Piranesi's Carceri: Sources of Invention*. Northampton, 1979.

McGuinness, A. E. *Henry Home, Lord Kames*. New York, 1970.

McLeod, Mary. Review of Aldo Rossi's *The Architecture of the City*. In *Design Book Review* (Winter 1984), 49–55.

Maillet, Benoit de. *Description de l'Egypte . . . composé sur les Mémoires de M. de Maillet, ancien consul de France au Caire, par M. l'Abbé le Mascrier*. Paris, 1735.

Malgrave, Harry. Introduction to *Gottfried Semper: The Four Elements of Architecture and Other Writings*. Cambridge, 1989.

Mallet du Pan. *Correspondance inédite de Mallet du Pan avec la cour de Vienne (1794–1798)*. Ed. André Michel. Paris, 1884.

Mallory, J. P. *In Search of the Indo-Europeans: Language, Archaeology and Myth*. London, 1989.

Malpeines, Léonard de. *Essai sur les hiéroglyphes des Egyptiens*. 2 vols. Paris, 1744.

Manuel, Frank E. *The Eighteenth Century Confronts the Gods*. Cambridge, Mass., 1959.

Mariano, Fabio. "L'alfabeto architettonico di J. D. Steingruber." *Eupalino*, 4 (April 1985), 48–54.

Marrone, Caterina. "Lingua universale e scrittura segrete nell'opera di Kircher." In *Enciclopedismo in Roma Barocca*. Venice, 1986, 78–87.

Mauro, Tullio de. "Giambattista Vico: From Rhetoric to Linguistic Historicism." In *Giambattista Vico, an International Symposium*, ed. G. Tagliacozzo. Baltimore, 1969, 279–295.

Maury, Alfred L. F. *L'ancienne Académie des Inscriptions et Belles-Lettres*. 2d ed. Vol. 2 of *Les académies d'autrefois*. Paris, 1864.

Maury, Alfred L. F. "Quatremère de Quincy." In *Biographie universelle ancienne et moderne, nouvelle édition*, ed. L. G. Michaud. Paris, 1811–1847, 34:608–614.

Mead, Christopher. "'Buildings of All Types,' Jean-Nicholas-Louis Durand." *Design Book Review* (Summer 1983), 12–15.

Memmo, Andrea. *Elementi dell'architettura lodoliana o sia l'arte del fabbricare con solidità scientifica e con eleganza non capricciosa*. Rome, 1786.

Mémoires concernant l'histoire, les sciences, les arts, les moeurs, les usages, etc des chinois; par les missionaires de Pekin. 17 vols. Paris, 1776–1814.

Messina, Maria Grazia. "L'arte di Canova nella critica di Quatremère de Quincy." In *Studi canoviana*. Rome, 1973, 119–151.

Middleton, Robin. "The Abbé de Cordemoy and the Graeco-Gothic Ideal: A Prelude to Romantic Classicism." *Journal of the Warburg and Courtauld Institutes*, 25 (1962), 278–320; 26 (1963), 189–196.

Middleton, Robin. "Giovanni Battista Piranesi, Review of Recent Literature." *Journal of the Society of Architectural Historians*, 41 (1982), 333–344.

Middleton, Robin. "Hittorff's Polychrome Campaign." In *The Beaux-Arts and Nineteenth-Century French Architecture*, ed. Robin Middleton. Cambridge, Mass., 1982, 174–196.

Middleton, Robin. "Jacques François Blondel and the 'Cours d'Architecture.'" *Journal of the Society of Architectural Historians*, 18 (December 1959), 140–148.

Middleton, Robin, and David Watkin. *Neo-Classical and Nineteenth Century Architecture*. New York, 1980.

Momigliano, Arnaldo. "Ancient History and the Antiquarian." *Journal of the Warburg and Courtauld Institutes*, 13 (1950), 285–315.

Moneo, Rafael. "On Typology." *Oppositions*, 13 (1978), 23–45.

Montagu, Jennifer. "Charles Le Brun's 'Conférence sur l'Expression Générale et Particulière.'" Ph.D. diss., University of London, 1959.

Montesquieu, Charles-Louis. *De l'Esprit des Lois, avec les réponses de l'auteur, ses notes, les observations d'Helvétius, Voltaire et Condorcet, et les objections des autres critiques*. 2 vols. Paris, 1824.

Montesquieu, Charles-Louis. "Essai sur le goût dans les choses de la nature." In *Oeuvres de Monsieur de Montesquieu*. London, 1772, 3:557–580.

Montfaucon, Bernard de. *L'antiquité expliquée et représentée en figures*. Paris, 1719–1722.

Mooney, Michael. *Vico in the Tradition of Rhetoric*. Princeton, 1985.

Morales, Ignasi de Solà. "From Memory to Abstraction: Architectonic Imitation in the Beaux-Arts Tradition." *Lotus International*, 33 (1981), 112–120.

Morales, Ignasi de Solà. "The Origins of Modern Eclecticism: The Theories of Architecture in Early Nineteenth Century France." *Perspecta*, 23 (1987), 120–133.

Moravia, Sergio. "Les Idéologues et l'âge des lumières." *Studies on Voltaire and the Eighteenth Century*, 154 (1976), 1465–1486.

Mortier, Roland. *L'originalité, une nouvelle catégorie esthétique au siècle des lumières*. Geneva, 1982.

Moser, Walter. "Pour et contre la Bible: croire et savoir au XVIIIe siècle." *Studies on Voltaire and the Eighteenth Century*, 154 (1976), 1509–1528.

Munier, Henri. *Tables de la Description de l'Egypte, suivies d'une bibliographie sur l'expédition française de Bonaparte*. Cairo, 1936.

Müntz, E. "Les annexions de collections d'art de bibliothèques et leur rôle dans les relations internationales, principalement pendant la Révolution française." *Revue d'histoire diplomatique* (1895), 375–393.

Mustilli, Domenico. "Prime memorie delle rovine di Paestum." *Studi in onore di Riccardo Filangieri*. Naples, 1959, 3:105–121.

Niebuhr, Carsten. *Description de l'Arabie d'après les observations et recherches faites dans le pays même.* 2 vols. Paris, 1779.

Norden, F. L. *Travels in Egypt and Nubia.* 2 vols. in 1. London, 1757.

Norden, F. L. *Voyage d'Egypte et de Nubie, par Mr. Frederic Louïs Norden, capitaine des vaisseaux du Roi.* 2 vols. in 1. Copenhagen, 1755.

Norry, [Charles]. [*Hommage à la Convention nationale d'un projet d'achèvement du Panthéon français.*] Paris, an I [1793].

Nowinski, Judith. *Baron Dominique Vivant Denon (1747–1825): Hedonist and Scholar in a Period of Transition.* Rutherford, Madison, and Teaneck, 1970.

Oechslin, Werner. "Per una ripresa della discussione tipologica." *Casabella*, 49 (January–February 1985), 66–75.

Oechslin, Werner. "Pyramide et sphère. Notes sur l'architecture révolutionnaire du XVIIIe siècle et ses sources italiennes." *Gazette des Beaux-Arts*, 77 (1971), 201–238.

"On the Analogy between Language and Architecture." *Annals of the Fine Arts*, 5 (1820), 242–283.

Ozouf, Mona. *La fête révolutionnaire, 1789–1799.* Paris, 1976.

Ozouf, Mona. "Le Panthéon: L'école normale des morts." In *Les lieux de mémoire: la République*, ed. Pierre Nora. Paris, 1984, 139–166.

Palme, Per. "Ut architectura poesis: Idea and Form, Studies in the History of Art." *Figura*, 1 (1959), 95–107.

Panofsky, Erwin. *Idea: A Concept in Art Theory.* Columbia, South Carolina, 1968.

Le Panthéon, symbole des révolutions: De l'Eglise de la Nation au Temple des grands hommes. Exhibition catalogue, Centre Canadien d'Architecture and Caisse Nationale des Monuments Historiques et des Sites, Paris, 1989.

Paroy, Marquis de. *Opinions religieuses, royalistes et politiques de M. Antoine Quatremère de Quincy, imprimées dans deux rapports fait au Département de Paris, publiées par M. le M [arquis] de P [aroy].* Paris, 1816.

Parra-Perez, C. *Miranda et la Révolution française.* Paris, 1925.

Pastine, Dino. "Storia sacra e scrittura sacra." In *Enciclopedismo in Roma barocca.* Venice, 1986, 27–39.

Pauw, Cornelius de. *Philosophical Dissertations on the Egyptians and Chinese.* trans. Capt. J. Thomson. London, 1795.

Pauw, Cornelius de. *Recherches Philosophiques sur les Américains ou Mémoires intéressants pour servir à l'histoire de l'espèce humaine.* Berlin, 1768–1769.

Pauw, Cornelius de. *Recherches philosophiques sur les Egyptiens et les Chinois.* Berlin 1773.

Pauw, Cornelius de. *Recherches sur les Grecs.* Berlin, 1788.

Pérouse de Montclos, Jean-Marie. *Etienne-Louis Boullée, 1728–1799, Theoretician of Revolutionary Architecture.* New York, 1974.

Perrault, Claude. *Ordonnance des cinq espèces de colonnes selon la méthode des anciens.* Paris, 1683.

Perry, Charles. *A View of the Levant: Particularly of Constantinople, Syria, Egypt & Greece, in which Their Antiquities, Government, Politics, Maxims, Manners, and Customes, (with Many Other Circumstances & Contingencies) Are Attempted to Be Described and Treated On.* London, 1743.

Pevsner, Nikolaus. *Academies of Art.* New York, 1973.

Pevsner, Nikolaus. "The Egyptian Revival." In *Studies in Art, Architecture and Design.* London and New York, 1968, 1:212–235.

Pevsner, Nikolaus. *A History of Building Types.* Princeton, 1976.

Picavet, F. *Les Idéologues. Essai sur l'histoire des idées et des théories*

scientifiques, philosophiques, religieuses, etc. en France depuis
1789. Paris, 1891.

Pinelli, Antonio. "Storia dell'arte e cultura della tutela, Les 'Lettres à
Miranda' di Quatremère de Quincy." *Ricerche de storia
dell'arte: Storia dell'arte e politica della tutela, scavi, editti,
musei, processi, mercanti, ispettori, inventari, restauri,* 8 (1978–
1979), 43–62.

Pinot, V. *La Chine et la formation de l'esprit philosophique en France:
1640–1740.* Paris, 1932.

Pococke, Richard. *A Description of the East, and Some Other Countries,*
vol. 1, *Observations on Egypt.* London, 1743.

Pococke, Richard. *Voyages de Richard Pococke . . . en Orient, dans
l'Egypte, l'Arabie, la Palestine, la Syrie, la Grèce, la Thrace,
etc., traduite de l'Anglois sur la seconde edition, par une société
de gens de lettres.* 7 vols. Paris, 1772.

Pomeau, René. *L'age classique, 1680–1720.* Paris, 1968–1971.

Pomeau, René. *L'Europe des Lumières. Cosmopolitisme et unité euro-
péene au XVIIIe siècle.* Paris, 1966.

Pommier, Edouard. "Winckelmann et la vision de l'antiquité classique
dans la France des Lumières et de la Révolution." *Revue de
l'art,* 83 (1989), 9–20.

Pons, Alain. "Vico and French Thought." In *Giambattista Vico, an International Symposium,* ed. G. Tagliacozzo. Baltimore, 1969, 165–
186.

Porset, Charles. "Grammatista philosophans, les sciences du langage de
Port-Royal aux ideologues, (1660–1818), bibliographie." In *La
Grammaire Generale des modistes aux ideologues,* ed. A. Joly
and J. Stefani eds., Lille, 1977.

Portalis, J. E. M. *De l'usage et de l'abus de l'esprit philosophique durant
le dix-huitième siècle.* 2d ed. Paris, 1827.

Potts, A. D. "Political Attitudes and the Rise of Historicism in Art Theory." *Art History,* 1 (June 1978), 191–213.

Potts, A. D. "Winckelmann's Construction of History." *Art History*, 5 (December 1982), 377–407.

Potts, A. "Winckelmann's History of Ancient Art in Its Eighteenth Century Context." Ph.D. diss., Warburg Institute, University of London, 1978.

Praz, Mario. *Giovanni Battista Piranesi, Le Carceri*. Milan, 1979.

Praz, Mario. *Mnemosyne: The Parallel between Literature and the Visual Arts*. Princeton, 1970.

Prevost, M., and R. d'Amat, eds. *Dictionnaire de biographie française*. Paris, 1956.

Quatremère, Etienne. "Notice historique sur la vie de M. Quatremère de Quincy. Premier article." *Journal des Savants* (1853), 657–669.

Quatremère, Etienne Marc. *Recherches critiques et historiques sur la langue et la littérature de l'Egypte*. Paris, 1808.

Quatremère de Quincy, A. C. "Aux auteurs du Journal." *Journal de Paris*, no. 42 (February 11, 1787), 181–183.

Quatremère de Quincy, A. C. *Canova et ses ouvrages ou mémoires historiques sur la vie et les travaux de ce célèbre artiste*. Paris, 1834.

Quatremère de Quincy, A. C. *Collection des lettres de Nicolas Poussin*. Paris, 1824.

Quatremère de Quincy, A. C. *Considérations morales sur la destination des ouvrages de l'art*. Paris, 1815.

Quatremère de Quincy, A. C. *Considérations sur les arts du dessin en France suivie d'un plan d'académie, ou d'école publique, et d'un système d'encouragemens*. Paris, 1791.

Quatremère de Quincy, A. C. *De l'architecture égyptienne considérée dans son origine, ses principes et son goût, et comparée sous les mêmes rapports à l'architecture grecque. Dissertation qui a remporté, en 1785, le prix proposé par l'Académie des Inscription et Belles-Lettres*. Paris, 1803.

Quatremère de Quincy, A. C. "De l'emploi des sujets d'histoire moderne dans la poésie, et de leur abus dans la peinture." *Recueil des discours prononcés dans la séance publique annuelle de l'Institut Royal de France, le dimanche 24 avril, 1825*, 5, no. 2 55–65. Paris, 1825.

Quatremère de Quincy, A. C. *De l'imitation.* Reprint of *Essai sur la nature, le but et les moyens de l'imitation dans les beaux-arts*, with introductions by Leon Krier and Demetri Porphyrios. Brussels, 1980.

Quatremère de Quincy, A. C. *Dictionnaire d'architecture.* 3 vols. Part of *Encyclopédie méthodique, ou par ordre de matières*, ed. C.-J. Panckoucke, Paris, 1788–1825.

Quatremère de Quincy, A. C. *Dictionnaire historique d'architecture, comprenant dans son plan les notions historiques, descriptives, archaeologiques, biographiques, théoriques, didactiques et practiques de cet art.* 2 vols. Paris, 1832.

Quatremère de Quincy, A. C. *Discours prononcé à l'Assemblée des Représentens de la Commune, le vendredi 2 avril 1790, sur la liberté des theatres et le rapport des commissaires*, n.d.

Quatremère de Quincy, A. C. *Discours prononcé par le cit. Quatremère-Quincy (sic), au tribunal criminel du département de la Seine, le 22 thermidor, an quatrieme de la République.*

Quatremère de Quincy, A. C. "Dissertation sur la diversité du génie et des moyens poétiques des différens arts, extraite d'un essai de théorie sur le systême imitatif des arts et le génie poétique de chacun d'eux." Lue à la séance publique de l'Institut, le 7 vendémiare an XIII, 29 Sept. 1804. *Mémoires de l'Institut, Supplément*, 31, no. 17.

Quatremère de Quincy, A. C. *Dissertation sur les opéras bouffons italiens.* Paris, 1789.

Quatremère de Quincy, A. C. *Dizionario storico di architettura.* Ed. V. Farinati and G. Teyssot. Venice, 1985.

Quatremère de Quincy, A. C. *Essai sur la nature, le but et les moyens de l'imitation dans les beaux-arts.* Paris, 1823. See also Quatremère de Quincy, *De l'imitation.*

Quatremère de Quincy, A. C. *Essai sur l'idéal dans ses applications pratiques aux oeuvres de l'imitation propre des arts du dessin.* Paris, 1837.

Quatremère de Quincy, A. C. *An Essay on the Nature, the End, and the Means of Imitation in the Fine Arts.* Trans. J. C. Kent. London, 1837.

Quatremère de Quincy, A. C. "Extracts from the Encyclopédie Méthodique d'Architecture." Introduction by Tanis Hinchcliffe. *9H*, 7 (1984), 25–40.

Quatremère de Quincy, A. C. "Extrait d'un ensemble de recherches historiques et philosophiques sur la cause principale du développement et de la perfection des beaux-arts chez toutes les nations." *Mémoires de l'Institut National des sciences et des arts, Supplément*, Piéces détachées, publiées séparément par l'Institut ou par ses Membres. 65, no. 44, 1826.

Quatremère de Quincy, A. C. *Extrait du premier rapport présenté au Directiore dans le mois de mai 1791, sur les mesures propre à transformer l'église dite Sainte-Geneviève en Panthéon français.* Paris, 1792.

Quatremère de Quincy, A. C. *Histoire de la vie et des ouvrages de Raphaël, ornée d'un portrait.* Paris, 1824.

Quatremère de Quincy, A. C. *Histoire de la vie et des ouvrages des plus célèbres architectes du XIe siècle jusqu'à la fin du XVIIIe, accompagnée de la vue du plus remarquable de chacun d'eux.* 2 vols. Paris, 1830.

Quatremère de Quincy, A. C. *Le Jupiter Olympien ou l'Art de la sculpture antique considéré sous un nouveau point de vue . . .* Paris, 1814.

Quatremère de Quincy, A. C. *Lettres à Miranda sur le déplacement des monuments de l'art de l'Italie.* Edition of *Lettres sur la préjudice*, with introduction by Edouard Pommier. Paris, 1989.

Quatremère de Quincy, A. C. *Lettres écrites de Londres à Rome, et adressées a. M. Canova sur les Marbres d'Elgin, ou les sculptures du temple de Minerve à Athènes.* Rome, 1818.

Quatremère de Quincy, A. C. *Lettres sur la préjudice qu'occasionneroient aux arts et à la science, le déplacement des monumens de l'art de l'Italie, le démembrement de ses écoles et la spoliation de ses collections, galeries, musées, etc.* Paris, an IV [1796].

Quatremère de Quincy, A. C. *Lettres sur la préjudice qu'occasionneroient aux arts et à la science, le déplacement des monumens de l'art de l'Italie, le démembrement de ses écoles et la spoliation de ses collections, galeries, musées, etc.* Rome, 1815.

Quatremère de Quincy, A. C. *Lettres sur l'enlèvement des ouvrages de l'art antique a Athènes et a Rome écrites les unes au célèbre Canova les autres au général Miranda.* Paris, 1836.

Quatremère de Quincy, A. C. "Mémoire sur la manière dont êtoient éclairés les temples des Grecs et des Romains." *Histoire et mémoires de l'Institut de France, Classe d'Histoire et de Littérature Ancienne,* 3 (1818), 166–284.

Quatremère de Quincy, A. C. "Mémoire sur la restitution du Temple de Jupiter Olympien à Agrigent, d'après la description de Diodore de Sicile, et les fragmens qui en subsistent encore." *Histoire et mémoires de l'Institut Royal de France, Classe d'Histoire et de Littérature Ancienne,* 2 (1815), 270–306.

Quatremère de Quincy, A. C. *Monumens et ouvrages d'art antiques restitués d'après les descriptions des écrivains grecs et latins et accompagnés de dissertations archaeologiques.* Paris, 1829.

Quatremère de Quincy, A. C. *Motion d'ordre faite par Quatremère, au nom de la Commission d'Instruction Publique sur le projet présenté par la commission de l'aliénation des presbytères.* Séance du 11 Thermidor, an V, Corps Législatif, Conseil des Cinq-Cents, Paris. [Paris, 1797].

Quatremère de Quincy, A. C. *Notice historique sur la vie et les ouvrages de M. Dufourny.* Paris, 1834.

Quatremère de Quincy, A. C. *Opinion de M. Quatremère, député du Département de Paris, sur les dénonciations faites contre M. Duport, ci-devant ministre de la justice. Prononcée le 2 juin 1792.* Paris, [1792].

Quatremère de Quincy, A. C. *Opinion de Quatremère, sur le renouvelle-*

ment des Bureaux centraux. Séance du 19 Messidor an V, Corps Législatif, Conseil des Cinq-Cents, Paris. [Paris, 1797].

Quatremère de Quincy, A. C. *Opinion de Quatremère, sur le second projet relatif aux réunions politiques.* Paris, n.d.

Quatremère de Quincy, A. C. *Projet de décret présenté a l'Assemblée Nationale, au nom du Comité d'Instruction Publique, relatif au paiement des appointemens dus aux professeurs de l'école publique de chant & de déclamation.* Paris, n.d.

Quatremère de Quincy, A. C. *Rapport approuvé par le Comité d'Instruction Publique de l'Assemblée legislative, sur les réclamations des directeurs de théatres, et la proprieté des auteurs dramatiques.* [Paris], 1792.

Quatremère de Quincy, A. C. *Rapport et projet decret présentés a l'Assemblée Nationale, par M. Quatremère, au nom du Comité de l'Instruction Publique, le 14 novembre 1791, sur les réclamations des artistes qui ont exposé au salon du Louvres.* Paris, 1791.

Quatremère de Quincy, A. C. *Rapport fait au Directoire du Département de Paris, le 13 Novembre 1792, l'an premier de la République Française, sur l'état actuel du Panthéon français; sur les changemens qui s'y sont opérés, sur les travaux qui restent à entreprendre, ainsi que sur l'ordre administratif établi pour leur direction et la comptabilité.* Paris, 1793.

Quatremère de Quincy, A. C. *Rapport fait au Directoire du Département de Paris, sur les travaux entrepris, continués ou achevés au Panthéon français depuis le dernier compte, rendu le 17 Novembre 1792, et sur l'état actuel du monument, de deuxième jour du second mois de l'an 2eme de la République Française, une et indivisible.* [Paris, 1793.]

Quatremère de Quincy, A. C. *Rapport fait par Quatremère, au nom de la Commission d'Instruction Publique, sur le mode et l'organisation des biens affectés aux bourses des ci-devant collèges de Paris.* Séance du 9 Fructidor, an 5, Corps Législatif, Conseil des Cinq-Cents, Paris. [Paris, 1797.]

Quatremère de Quincy, A. C. *Rapport fait par Quatremère, au nom d'une commission spéciale, sur l'exemption du droit de patente en*

faveur des peintres, sculpteurs, graveurs & architectes. Séance
du 13 messidor, an V, Corps Législatif, Conseil des Cinq-Cents,
Paris. [Paris, 1797.]

Quatremère de Quincy, A. C. *Rapport sur la pétition de M. de Rossel,
fait au nom du Comité d'Instruction Publique.* Paris, 1792.

Quatremère de Quincy, A. C. *Rapport sur l'édifice dit de Sainte-Geneviève, fait au Directoire du Département de Paris.* Paris, 1791.

Quatremère de Quincy, A. C. *Recueil de dissertations archéologiques.*
Paris, 1836.

Quatremère de Quincy, A. C. *Recueil de notices historiques lues dans les
séances publiques de l'Académie Royale des Beaux-Arts à l'Institut.* Paris, 1834.

Quatremère de Quincy, A. C. *Restitution des deux frontons du temple de
Minerve à Athenes.* Paris, 1825.

Quatremère de Quincy, A. C. *Seconde Suite aux Considérations sur les
arts du dessin; ou Projet de réglemens pour l'école publique des
arts du dessin; et de l'emplacement convenable à l'Institut
National des Sciences, Belles-Lettres et Arts.* Paris, 1791.

Quatremère de Quincy, A. C. *Suite aux Considérations sur les arts du
dessin, ou Réflexions critiques sur le projet de status et réglemens
de la majorité de l'Académie de Peinture et Sculpture.* Paris,
1791.

Quatremère de Quincy, A. C. *Suite du Recueil de notices historiques lues
dans les séances publiques de l'Académie Royale des Beaux-Arts
à l'Institut.* Paris, 1837.

Quatremère de Quincy, A. C. "Sur de Paw et son opinion sur la beauté
des femmes." *Le Moniteur,* an XIII [1804/5], 421.

Quatremère de Quincy, A. C. "Sur la manière d'imiter la bonne architecture grecque." *Journal des batimens civils,* no. 29 (6 nivose, an
9 [December 27, 1800]) 3–7, and no. 30 (9 nivose, an 9 [December
30, 1800]), 3–5.

Quatremère de Quincy, A. C. *Sur la statue antique de Vénus découverte
dans l'île de Milo en 1820, transportée à Paris, par M. Le Mar-*

quis de Rivière, ambassadeur de France à la cour Ottomane. Notice lue a l'Académie Royale des Beaux-Arts, le 21 Avril 1821. Paris, 1821.

Quatremère de Quincy, A. C. "Sur l'idéal dans les arts du dessin." *Archives littéraires de l'Europe,* 6 and 7 (1805).

Rabreau, D., and M. Mosser. "L'Académie Royale d'Architecture et l'enseignement de l'architecture au XVIIIe siècle." *Archives de l'Architecture Moderne,* 25 (1983), 47–67.

"Le retour d'Egypte." *Connaissance des arts,* 33 (1954), 62–67.

Rivosecchi, Valerio. *Esotismo in Roma barocca, studi sul Padre Kircher.* Rome, 1982.

Roche, Denis. *Le siècle des Lumières en province.* Paris, 1978.

Rochette, Désirée-Raoul. *Discours prononcés aux funérailles de Quatremère de Quincy le 30 décembre 1849.* Paris, 1850.

Rosenau, Helen. *Boullée and Visionary Architecture.* London, 1976.

Rosenblum, Robert. *Transformations in Late Eighteenth Century Art.* Princeton, 1967.

Rossi, Aldo. *The Architecture of the City.* Cambridge, Mass., and London, 1982.

Rossi, Paolo. *The Dark Abyss of Time: The History of the Earth and the History of Nations from Hooke to Vico.* Chicago and London, 1984.

Rossi, Paolo. "Vico e il mito dell'Egitto." In *Omaggio a Vico.* Naples, 1968, 24–37.

Rousseau, J. J. *The First and Second Discourses Together with the Replies to Critrics and Essay on the Origin of Languages.* Ed. and trans. Victor Gourevitch. New York, 1986.

Rowe, Colin. "Character and Composition; or Some Vicissitudes of Architectural Vocabulary in the Nineteenth Century." *Oppositions,* no. 2 (January 1974), 41–60.

Rowlands, Thomas F. "Quatremère de Quincy: The Formative Years, 1785–1795." Ph.D. diss., Northwestern University, 1987.

Rubin, James Henry. "Allegory versus Narrative in Quatremère de Quincy." *The Journal of Aesthetics and Art Criticism*, 44 (1986), 383–392.

Rudowski, Victor Anthony. "The Theory of Signs in the Eighteenth Century." *Journal of the History of Ideas*, 35 (1974), 683–690.

Rykwert, Joseph. *The First Moderns: The Architects of the Eighteenth Century*. Cambridge, Mass., and London, 1980.

Rykwert, Joseph. "Lodoli on Function and Representation." In *The Necessity of Artifice*. New York, 1982, 115–122.

Rykwert, Joseph. *On Adam's House in Paradise: The Idea of the Primitive Hut in Architectural History*. 2d ed. Cambridge, Mass., and London, 1984.

Saisselin, Rémy G. "Architecture and Language: The Sensationalism of Le Camus de Mézières." *The British Journal of Aesthetics*, 15 (1975), 239–254.

Saisselin, Rémy G. "*Ut Pictura Poesis:* Du Bos to Diderot." *The Journal of Aesthetics and Art*, 20 (Winter 1966), 145–157.

Sauneron, Serge. *L'égyptologie*. Paris, 1968.

Saunier, C. *Les conquêtes artistiques de la Révolution et de l'Empire*. Paris, 1902.

Schneider, R. *L'esthétique classique chez Quatremère de Quincy*. Thèse présentée a la faculté des lettres de l'université de Paris. Paris, 1910.

Schneider, R. *Quatremère de Quincy et son intervention dans les arts*. Paris, 1910.

Schneider, R. "Un ennemi du Musée des Monuments Français." *Gazettes des Beaux-Arts* (1909), 353–370.

Serra, Joselita Raspa, ed. *La Fortuna di Paestum e la memoria del dorico 1750–1830: concetti essenziali al percorso espositivo*. Exhibition catalogue, Palazzo Braschi, Rome, October 7–November 23, 1986.

Shiff, Richard. "Representation, Copying, and the Technique of Originality." *New Literary History*, 15 (Winter 1984), 333–363.

Simowitz, Amy Cohen. *Theory of Art in the Encyclopédie.* Ann Arbor, 1983.

Soane, Sir John. *Lectures on Architecture.* Ed. Arthur T. Bolton. London, 1929.

Soufflot et l'architecture des Lumières. Actes du colloque. Paris, 1982.

Spon, Jacob, and George Wheler. *Voyage d'Italie, de Dalmatie, de Grèce, et du Levant fait aux années 1675 & 1676 par Jacob Spon et George Wheler.* 2 vols. The Hague, 1724.

Stafford, Barbara Maria. *Symbols and Myth: Humbert de Superville's Essay on Absolute Signs in Art.* Cranbury, N.J., 1979.

Stafford, Barbara Maria. *Voyage into Substance: Art, Science, Nature, and the Illustrated Travel Account, 1760–1840.* Cambridge, Mass., and London, 1984.

Starobinski, Jean. "Rousseau et l'origine des langues." In H. and F. Schalk, eds., *Europäische Aufklärung, H. Dieckmann zum 60 Gebrustag.* Munich and Allach, 1967, 281–300.

Staum, Martin B. "The Class of Moral and Political Sciences, 1795–1803." *French Historical Studies,* 9 (Spring 1980), 371–396.

Steingruber, J. D. *Architectonisches Alphabeth.* Schwabach, 1773.

Steingruber, J. D. *Architectura Civilis.* Augsburg, s.d.

Steingruber, J. D. *Practica Burgerlicher Baukunst.* S.l., 1765.

Stoppini, G. A., ed. *Dalla 'Libreriola' dell'architetto fiorentino, Giuseppe del Rosso.* Florence, Biblioteca Riccardiana, 1983.

Stromberg, R. N. "History in the Eighteenth Century." *Journal of the History of Ideas,* 12 (April 1951), 295–304.

Stroud, Dorothy. *The Architecture of Sir John Soane.* London, 1961.

Stroud, Dorothy. *Sir John Soane, Architect.* London, 1984.

Stuart, James, and Nicholas Revett. *The Antiquities of Athens.* 4 vols. London, 1762–1816.

Sulzer, J. G. *Allgemeine Theorie der schönen Künste.* 2d ed. Leipzig, 1792.

Sulzer, J. G. "Discours sur l'allégorie." In *De l'allégorie, ou traités sur cette matière; par Winckelmann, Addison, Sulzer, etc.* Paris, an VII [1798/9], 2:210–274.

Summers, David. "Contrapposto: Style and Meaning in Renaissance Art." *Art Bulletin*, 59 (September 1977), 336–361.

Summers, David. "Michelangelo on Architecture." *Art Bulletin*, 54 (June 1972), 146–157.

Summerson, John. *The Classical Language of Architecture.* Cambridge, Mass., 1963.

Summerson, John. *Sir John Soane, 1753–1837.* London, 1952.

Szambien, Werner. *Jean-Nicolas-Louis Durand, 1760–1834. De l'imitation à la norme.* Paris, 1984.

Szambien, Werner. *Symétrie, goût, caractère, théorie et terminologie de l'architecture à l'âge classique, 1550–1800.* Paris, 1986.

Tafuri, Manfredo. *L'architettura del manierismo nel cinquecento europeo.* Rome, 1966.

Taska, Betty Keene. "Grammar and Linguistics in the *Encyclopédie*." *The French Review*, 46 (May 1973), 1159–1171.

Teyssot, Georges. "Neo-classic and 'Autonomous' Architecture: The Formalism of Emil Kaufmann." In *On the Methodology of Architectural History, Architectural Design Profile*, ed. Dimitri Porphyrios. London, 1981, 25–30.

Thiry, Jean. *Bonaparte en Egypte.* Paris, 1973.

Todorov, Tzvetan. "Esthetique et semiotique au XVIIIe siècle." *Critique*, 29 (January 1973), 26–39.

Trenard, Louis. "L'historiographie française d'après les manuels scolaires, de Bossuet à Voltaire." *Studies on Voltaire and the Eighteenth Century*, 155 (1976), 2083–2111.

Van Duzer, C. H. *The Contribution of the Ideologues to French Revolutionary Thought.* Baltimore, 1935.

Van Kley, E. J. "Europe's Discovery of China and the Writing of World History." *American Historical Review*, 66 (1971), 358–385.

Vansleb, R. D. *Nouvelle relation en forme de journal d'un voyage fait en Egypte par le P. Vansleb, R.D. en 1672 & 1673.* Paris, 1677.

Vanuxeum, J. "Aperçus sur quelques tableaux représentant le Musée des Monuments Français de Lenoir." *BSHAF*, 1972 (Année 1971), 145–151.

Van Zanten, Ann Lorenz. "César Daly and the Revue Générale de l'Architecture." Ph.D. diss., Harvard University, 1981.

Van Zanten, Ann Lorenz. "Form and Society: César Daly and the Revue Générale de L'Architecture." *Oppositions*, 8 (1977), 137–145.

Van Zanten, David. *The Architectural Polychromy of the 1830s.* New York, 1977.

Van Zanten, David. *Designing Paris: The Architecture of Duban, Labrouste, Duc, and Vaudoyer.* Cambridge, Mass., 1987.

Vaubertrand, F. *L'humanité et la Terreur.* Paris, 1843.

Venturi, F. *L'antichità svelata e l'idea di progresso in N. Boulanger.* Bari, 1947.

Vercoutter, Jean. *A la recherche de l'Egypte oubliée.* Paris, 1986.

Vidal-Naquet, Pierre. "Les jeunes: Le cru, l'enfant grec et le cuit." In *Nouveau objets*, ed. J. Le Goff and P. Nora. Vol. 3 of *Faire de l'historie.* Paris, 1974, 137–168.

Vidler, Anthony, "The Hut and the Body: The 'Nature' of Architecture from Laugier to Quatremère de Quincy." *Lotus International*, 33 (1981), 102–112.

Vidler, Anthony. "The Idea of Type: The Tranformation of the Academic Ideal, 1750–1830." *Oppositions*, 8 (1977), 95–115.

Vidler, Anthony, ed. *Paris under the Academy: City and Ideology.* Special issue of *Oppositions*, 8, 1977.

Vidler, Anthony. "The Third Typology." *Oppositions*, 7 (1976), 1–4.

Vidler, Anthony. *The Writing of the Walls: Architectural Theory in the Late Enlightenment.* Princeton, 1987.

Viel, Charles. *De l'impuissance des mathématiques pour assurer la soli-*

dité des batimens et recherches sur la construction des ponts. Paris, 1805.

Viel de Saint-Maux, J. L. *Lettres sur l'architecture des anciens et des modernes, dans lesquelles se trouve développé le génie symbolique que préside aux monumens de l'antiquité.* Paris, 1787.

Viertel, John. "Concepts of Langauge Underlying the 18th-Century Controversy about the Origin of Language." In *Report of the Seventeenth Annual Round Table Meeting in Linguistics and Language Studies,* ed. Francis P. Dineen. Washington, 1966, 109–132.

Villari, Sergio. *J. N. L. Durand (1760–1834): Art and Science of Architecture.* Trans. Eli Gottlieb. New York, 1990.

Vitruvius Pollio, Marcus. *The Ten Books on Architecture.* Trans. M. H. Morgan. New York, 1960.

Volney, C. F. *Voyage en Egypte et en Syrie.* Reprint of 1799 edition, introduction by Jean Gaulmier. Paris, 1959.

Volney, C. F. *Voyage en Syrie et en Egypte, pendant les années 1783, 1784, & 1785.* 2 vols. Paris, 1787.

Voltaire, François Marie Arouet de. *Lettres chinoises, indiennes et tartares.* Paris, 1776.

Wallon, Henri. "Centenaire de l'élection de Quatremère de Quincy à l'Institut, classe d'histoire et de littérature ancienne, le 16 février 1804. Notice supplémentaire sur sa vie et ses travaux." *Académie des Inscriptions et Belles-Lettres, Comptes Rendus* (1903), 538–580.

Wallon, Henri. *Notice supplémentaire sur la vie et les travaux de Quatremère de Quincy par son successeur immédiate . . . lue en séance publique annuelle du 13 novembre 1903.* Paris, 1903.

Warburton, W. *The Divine Legation of Moses Demonstrated in Nine Books.* 4th ed. London, 1765.

Watelet, Claude Henri. *Essai sur les jardins.* Paris, 1774.

Watts, George B. "The *Encyclopédie Méthodique.*" *Publications of the Modern Language Association of America,* 73 (1958), 348–366.

Wiebenson, Dora. *The Picturesque Garden in France*. Princeton, 1978.

Wilkins, John. *An Essay towards a Real Character, and a Philosophical Language*. London, 1668.

Will, Frederick. *Intelligible Beauty in Aesthetic Thought from Winckelmann to Victor Cousin*. Tübingen, 1958.

Winckelmann, J. J. "Essai sur l'allégorie, principalement a l'usage des artistes." Dédié à la Société royale des sciences de Gottingen. Vol. 1 of *De l'allégorie, ou traités sur cette matière; par Winckelmann, Addison, Sulzer, etc.* Paris, an VII [1799].

Winckelmann, J. J. *Histoire de l'art chez les anciens*. Paris, 1766.

Winckelmann, J. J. *Monumenti antichi inediti*. Rome, 1767.

Winckelmann, J. J. "On the Imitation of the Painting and Sculpture of the Greeks." Trans. Henry Fuseli. In *Winckelmann, Burckhardt, Panofsky, and Others: German Essays on Art History*, ed. Gert Schiff. The German Library, vol. 79. New York, 1988.

Winckelmann, J. J. *Remarques sur l'architecture des anciens*. Paris, 1783.

Wittkower, Rudolf. *Architectural Principles in the Age of Humanism*. New York, 1971.

Wittkower, Rudolf. "Piranesi's 'Parere su l'architettura.'" *Journal of the Warburg and Courtauld Institutes*, 2 (1938), 147–158.

Wittkower, Rudolf. *Selected Lectures of Rudolf Wittkower: The Impact of Non-European Civilizations on the Art of the West*. Ed. D. M. Reynolds. New York, 1989.

Woestijne, P. van de. "Les sources du 'Discours sur Théopraste' de Jean de la Bruyère." *Revue belge de philologie et histoire*, 15 (1936), 839–858.

Wortham, John David. *The Genesis of British Egyptology, 1549–1906*. Norman, Okla., 1971.

Zoega, G. *Numi Aegyptii imperatorii prostantes in Museo Borgiano Velitris, Adjectis praeterea quotquot reliqua hujus classis numismata ex variis museis atque libris colligere obtigit*. Rome, 1787.

Zoli, S. "Il mito settecentesco della Cina in Europa e la moderna storiografia." *Nuova Rivista Storica*, 1974.

INDEX

Printed in Great Britain
by Amazon

32465015R00196